SLAVES TO ROME

Paradigms of Empire in Roman Culture

MYLES LAVAN

CAMBRIDGE
UNIVERSITY PRESS

CAMBRIDGE UNIVERSITY PRESS
Cambridge, New York, Melbourne, Madrid, Cape Town,
Singapore, São Paulo, Delhi, Mexico City

Cambridge University Press
The Edinburgh Building, Cambridge CB2 8RU, UK

Published in the United States of America by Cambridge University Press, New York

www.cambridge.org
Information on this title: www.cambridge.org/9781107026018

First published 2013

Printed and bound in the United Kingdom by the MPG Books Group

A catalogue record for this publication is available from the British Library

Library of Congress Cataloguing in Publication data
Lavan, Myles, 1977–
Slaves to Rome : paradigms of empire in Roman culture / Myles Lavan.
p. cm. – (Cambridge classical studies)
Includes bibliographical references.
ISBN 978-1-107-02601-8 (hardback)
1. Latin literature – History and criticism. 2. Slavery in literature. 3. Imperialism in literature. 4. Slaves – Rome. 5. Elite (Social sciences) – Rome – History. 6. Latin language – Political aspects – Rome. 7. Rhetoric, Ancient. 8. Language and culture – Rome. 9. Rome – Politics and government – 30 BC–AD 476 I. Title.
PA6030.S6L38 2013
878′.0108–dc23
2012029701

ISBN 978-1-107-02601-8 Hardback

IN MEMORY OF MY FATHER
VIVIAN LAVAN
1944–2011

CONTENTS

PREFACE

This book originated as a doctoral dissertation written at St John's College, Cambridge. It was revised and expanded during a Research Fellowship at Sidney Sussex College. The finishing touches were added at the University of St Andrews. I am grateful to all three institutions for their support.

The book owes much to the supervisors of the thesis from which it developed. William Fitzgerald oversaw its early stages before leaving Cambridge for King's College London. The bulk was written under the incisive guidance of Mary Beard. Peter Garnsey stepped in for a term and very generously continued to read and discuss my work as it progressed. My examiners John Patterson and Greg Woolf provided valuable criticism and advice. I also have a special debt to Robin Osborne, who has been very generous with his counsel throughout.

Many others have taken the time to discuss my work as it evolved. I am particularly indebted to those who read this book in whole or in part: Rebecca Flemming, Daniel Jew, Victoria Moul, Marden Nichols, Stephen Oakley, Richard Payne, Andrew Wallace-Hadrill, John Weisweiler and Chris Whitton. I am grateful to the anonymous readers for Cambridge University Press for their valuable suggestions and to Nigel Holmes at the *Thesaurus Linguae Latinae* for sharing bibliography on *socius*. I also thank the team at Cambridge University Press, especially Michael Sharp, Christina Sarigiannidou and copy-editor Ian McAuslan, for their hard work in bringing this book to press.

Thanks too to my other friends in Dublin, Cambridge, St Andrews and elsewhere and to my family – Lavans, McCulloughs and

Delvauxs – for their interest and encouragement. This book was finished too late to thank my father for his warm and unstinting support for all my endeavours, but it is dedicated to his memory.

My greatest debt is to Joke Delvaux. Without her, this project would never have been begun – let alone completed.

ABBREVIATIONS AND OTHER CONVENTIONS

Journal titles are abbreviated in the Bibliography following the conventions of *L'Année philologique*, with a few easily recognised exceptions. The abbreviations used for Latin and Greek works are those of S. Hornblower and A. Spawforth, eds., *The Oxford Classical Dictionary*, 3rd edition (Oxford, 2003) where available and otherwise those of P. G. W. Glare, ed., *Oxford Latin Dictionary* (Oxford, 1996) and H. G. Liddell, R. Scott and H. S. Jones, eds., *A Greek-English Lexicon*, 9th edition (Oxford, 1996) respectively. The only exceptions are Cassius Dio, who is cited as Dio, and Seneca's dialogues, which are cited by name rather than number. Other abbreviations used in the footnotes are listed below. Note that Latin and Greek texts are printed following the different conventions for literary, epigraphic and papyrological texts as appropriate. One important consequence is that square brackets indicate a conjectured restoration for lost or illegible text in an inscription or papyrus, but an editorial deletion in a literary text.

Abbott–Johnson	F. F. Abbott and A. C. Johnson, eds., *Municipal Administration in the Roman Empire* (Princeton, 1926).
AE	*L'Année épigraphique* (Paris, 1888–).
A&R	J. Reynolds, ed., *Aphrodisias and Rome: Documents from the Excavation of the Theatre at Aphrodisias Conducted by Professor Kenan T. Erim, together with Some Related Texts* (London, 1982).

CFA	J. Scheid, ed., *Commentarii fratrum Arvalium qui supersunt: les copies épigraphiques des protocoles annuels de la confrérie arvale (21 av.–304 ap. J. C.)* (Rome, 1998).
CIL	*Corpus inscriptionum Latinarum* (Berlin, 1863–).
Ehrenberg–Jones	V. Ehrenberg and A. H. M. Jones, eds., *Documents Illustrating the Reigns of Augustus and Tiberius* (Oxford, 1955).
FIRA	S. Riccobono, J. Baviera, C. Ferrini, J. Furlani and V. Arangio-Ruiz, eds., *Fontes iuris Romani antejustiniani*, 2nd edn, 3 vols. (Florence, 1968).
IGRR	R. Cagnat, ed., *Inscriptiones Graecae ad res Romanas pertinentes*, 3 vols. (I, III, IV) (Paris, 1906–27).
ILLRP	A. Degrassi, ed., *Inscriptiones Latinae liberae rei publicae* (Florence, 1957–63).
ILS	A. Dessau, ed., *Inscriptiones Latinae selectae*, 3 vols. (Berlin, 1892–1916).
McCrum–Woodhead	M. McCrum and A. G. Woodhead, eds., *Select Documents of the Principates of the Flavian Emperors, Including the Year of Revolution: A.D. 68–96* (Cambridge, 1961).
Oliver	J. H. Oliver, ed., *Greek Constitutions of Early Roman Emperors from Inscriptions and Papyri* (Philadelphia, 1989).
OLD	P. G. W. Glare, ed., *Oxford Latin Dictionary* (Oxford, 1996).
ORF	H. Malcovati, *Oratorum Romanorum fragmenta liberae rei publicae*, 4th edn, 2 vols. (Turin, 1976–9).
P Harr.	*Rendel Harris Papyri* (Cambridge, 1938 and Zutphen, 1985).

P Mich.	*Michigan papyri* (Vations, 1931–).
P Oxy.	*Oxyrhynchus papyri* (London, 1898–).
RDGE	R. K. Sherk, *Roman Documents from the Greek East* (Baltimore, 1969).
RGDA	A. E. Cooley, *Res Gestae divi Augusti: Text, Translation and Commentary* (Cambridge, 2009).
RIB	R. G. Collingwood and R. P. Wright, *The Roman Inscriptions of Britain*. Volume 1. *The Inscriptions on Stone* (Oxford, 1965).
RIT	P. A. Brunt, *Roman Imperial Themes* (Oxford, 1990).
RP	R. Syme, *Roman Papers* (Oxford 1979–91).
RS	M. Crawford, ed., *Roman Statutes* (London, 1996).
SEG	*Supplementum epigraphicum Graecum* (Leiden, 1923–).
*SIG*³	W. Dittenberger, ed., *Sylloge inscriptionum Graecarum*, 3rd edn, 4 vols. (Leipzig, 1915–24).
Smallwood *GCN*	E. M. Smallwood, ed., *Documents Illustrating the Principates of Gaius, Claudius and Nero* (Cambridge, 1967).
Smallwood *NTH*	E. M. Smallwood, ed., *Documents Illustrating the Principates of Nerva, Trajan and Hadrian* (Cambridge, 1966).
TLL	*Thesaurus Linguae Latinae* (Munich, 1900–).
Welles	C. B. Welles, ed., *Royal Correspondence in the Hellenistic Period: A Study in Greek Epigraphy* (New Haven, 1934).

INTRODUCTION

The ambitions and aspirations of imperial powers deserve just as much scrutiny as their actual practice. This book investigates how the elite that governed the Roman empire envisaged their shared imperial project. It does so by exploring how Roman writers draw on the paradigmatic power relations of everyday life – notably those of masters and slaves, patrons and clients, and parents and children – in order to conceptualise and represent the subjection of the provinces. It examines the relative importance of these different models for empire across almost three centuries of Latin literature, from the middle of the first century BCE through to the beginning of the third CE. It draws particular attention to the prominence of the language and imagery of chattel slavery in Roman accounts of empire. These tropes of Roman mastery and provincial slavery epitomise an aspect of Roman imperialism that is insufficiently acknowledged in modern scholarship on this period. This book is simultaneously a study in elite self-definition, highlighting the imperial character of the identity espoused by most Roman writers. These men see themselves as members of a ruling power, elevated above the subject peoples who comprise most of the population of the empire.

Three points deserve to be clarified at the outset. First, this is a book about imperialism, not the principate. By 'imperialism', I mean 'the practice, the theories and the attitudes of a dominating metropolitan centre ruling a distant territory'.[1] If 'empire', like *imperium* in Latin, blurs the distinction between monarchy and the conquest and rule of foreign peoples, it is because the Roman emperors and later monarchs invested so much in the idea that the two are inextricably linked.[2] Rome had an empire long before it

[1] The definition is borrowed from Said 1993 p. 8.

[2] On the process by which the noun *imperium* came to be used both of Rome's territorial empire and of the monarchical power of the emperor, see Richardson 2008 (especially p. 185) and Nicolet 1991 p. 15. On the importance of conquest and empire to the ideology

had an emperor and that empire continued to be seen as distinctly 'Roman' (whatever that might mean) long after the creation of the monarchy. Second, the focus is on Rome's provincial subjects, not the 'barbarians'. The distinction between civilisation and barbarism, between the inhabitants of the empire (or at least its civilised communities) and the barbarians at its margins, obviously played an important role in the ideology and practice of Roman imperialism.[3] But this book aims to draw attention to a different division, one that is imposed squarely upon the population of the empire, by focusing on the peoples whom Roman texts most often label 'the allies' (*socii*) – distinguished from those beyond the reach of Roman power by their incorporation into the empire and dependence on Rome but also marked off from their Roman rulers by some combination of citizen status, geography, ethnicity and culture (an ambiguity I return to below).[4] Third, this is a study of language. It explores how men who saw themselves as members of an imperial people described their power over the peoples they regarded as their subjects. But it assumes that these discursive practices were inextricably bound up with the operations of Roman power in the provinces. The literary texts discussed in this book emerged from, and circulated within, the same social milieu that supplied the governors and other officials who administered the provinces. The contrasting paradigms of masterly, patronal and parental authority embody very different perspectives on the ethics of empire and the proper ends and means of provincial governance. These tropes must have both reflected and guided their conduct as governors, commanders and administrators. Susan Mattern has examined the values that guided this governing elite in its dealings with 'the enemy' – the barbarians

of the principate, see Ando 2000 ch. 8. The interdependence of empire and monarchy was reaffirmed by the early-modern monarchies. See e.g. Wortman 1995–2000 pp. 6–7 and Pagden 1995, especially chs. 1 and 2.

3 On the tropes of barbarism in Roman discourse and visual culture, see especially Dauge 1981 and Ferris 2000 and Schneider 1986 respectively. On the ideological significance of the distinction between civilisation and barbarism for Roman imperialism, see especially Woolf 1998 ch. 3, Woolf 1993b, Veyne 1993 and Alföldi 1952. These focus on barbarians beyond the frontier; for 'internal' barbarians, see especially Shaw 2000.

4 This is not to claim that Romans always regarded the subject peoples as a homogeneous group. Roman texts are replete with particular ethnic stereotypes. See especially Isaac 2004 and Balsdon 1979.

beyond the frontier.[5] This book explores the norms that governed their interactions with 'the allies' – the peoples they regarded as their subjects.

Paradigms of power

Roman texts draw on a wide range of metaphors to describe the imperial project. Representations of the empire as a body or a vast fabric or structure serve to assert its unity and indissolubility.[6] Similar metaphors serve to affirm the primacy of the city of Rome – as the head (*caput*) of the empire or, in Valerius Maximus' formulation, the keystone (*columen*) of the world.[7] Pastoral metaphors describe the condition of the provinces. Tiberius is said to have warned some governors who were over-eager to tax the provinces that a good shepherd should shear his flock, not skin them.[8] Another trope is to represent the provinces as an extension of a metaphorical household. Cicero writes that Cato used to call Sicily the 'larder (*cella penaria*) of the state' and

[5] Mattern 1999.

[6] Suetonius writes that Augustus treated the allied kings 'like limbs and parts of the empire' (*nec aliter uniuersos* [sc. *reges socios*] *quam membra partisque imperii curae habuit*, Suet. *Aug.* 48). The metaphor of organic unity is familiar from domestic political discourse. Perhaps the most famous example is the speech by Menenius Agrippa telling the plebs that their hostility to the senate is as misguided as it would be for the limbs of a body to defy the belly (Livy 2.32.9–12). See further Heubner 1963–82 ad Tac. *Hist.* 1.16.1 and Momigliano 1942 pp. 117–18. On the *corpus imperii*, see especially Kienast 1982 and Béranger 1953 pp. 218–38. For the empire as a fabric or structure, see e.g. Cerialis' warning to rebellious Gauls that the empire is a *compages* that has coalesced over eight hundred years and cannot be torn asunder without bringing destruction on them all (*octingentorum annorum fortuna disciplinaque compages haec coaluit, quae conuelli sine exitio conuellentium non potest*, Tac. *Hist.* 4.74.3). Compare the description of the empire as a fabric (*contextus*) at Sen. *Clem.* 1.4.2.

[7] Rome is variously described as *caput orbis*, *c~ orbis terrarum*, *c~ rerum*, *c~ mundi* and *c~ imperii* (TLL s.v. *caput* 426.29–54). The metaphor of city as *caput* is not specific to Rome, but is regularly used of the chief cities of peoples or regions. See ibid. 425.74–426.29. The same metaphor is enlisted in the justification of monarchy – a healthy body having a single head. See especially Béranger 1953 pp. 218–38. For architectural metaphors, see e.g. Val. Max. 2.8.praef. (*disciplina militaris acriter retenta ... ortumque e paruula Romuli casa totius terrarum orbis fecit columen*) and ibid. 8.14.1 (*totiusque terrarum orbis summum columen arx Capitolina possideret*).

[8] *praesidibus onerandas tributo prouincias suadentibus rescripsit boni pastoris esse tondere pecus, non deglubere* (Suet. *Tib.* 32.2). Aelius Aristides criticises the Persians for not knowing how to rule as shepherds – an art the Romans, he implies, have mastered (*Or.* 26.18).

himself describes the provinces as 'country estates (*praedia*) as it were of the Roman people'.[9] Livy describes Syracuse as the 'granary and treasury (*horreum atque aerarium*) of the Roman people'.[10] Other metaphors are more idiosyncratic. The second-century historian Florus, for example, communicates the relentlessness of Roman expansion by comparing it both to a forest fire (*ignis*) and to a disease (*contagium*) that overwhelms its victims one by one.[11]

The list of figurative representations of empire could easily be extended, but that is not the aim of this book. I focus more narrowly on a set of metaphors, comparisons and analogies with a special paradigmatic importance – those drawn from the world of social relations.[12] To compare Roman power and authority to that of a master, patron or parent or, conversely, to represent provincial subjection and dependency in terms of slavery, clientage or childhood is to conceptualise empire in terms of the concrete and familiar power structures of daily life. These metaphors are particularly revealing because they show how empire is imagined to be like and unlike everyday practices of domination that will have been intimately familiar to the elite, most of whom were themselves masters, patrons and parents (among other roles). The assertion of continuities and discontinuities between different domains of power is an important ideological operation in any society. In Roman culture this is particularly true of attempts to define the proper limits of the masterly mode of domination. This can be

[9] Larder: *itaque ille M. Cato Sapiens cellam penariam rei publicae nostrae, nutricem plebis Romanae Siciliam nominabat* (2*Verr.* 2.5). On the second metaphor in Cato's dictum, the (usually servile) wet nurse, see further p. 113. Estate: *quasi quaedam praedia populi Romani sunt uectigalia nostra atque prouinciae.* (2*Verr.* 2.7). Cf. *Leg. agr.* 2.80 where Capua is the Roman people's finest estate (*fundus*).

[10] *horreum atque aerarium quondam populi Romani* (Livy 26.32.3). Elsewhere in Livy, Capua is Rome's granary (*uberrimus ager marique propinquus ad uarietates annonae horreum populi Romani fore uidebatur*, 7.31.1).

[11] Florus 1.18(2).1.and 1.3.8. See further p. 102.

[12] In my focus on paradigmatic social relationships I obviously owe much to Matthew Roller's study of the metaphors of master and father in representations of the principate (Roller 2001 ch. 4), though I depart from his approach to conceptual metaphor (see n. 59 below). Another inspiration was Foucault 1979, an analysis of the historical significance of the intrusion of the language of the household into political discourse in the sixteenth and seventeenth centuries. Cf. also Purcell 1986, a short but suggestive discussion of the master, the commander and the judge as the three paradigms of governance in Roman culture.

seen, for example, in claims that husbands should not behave like masters to their wives or in the repeated insistence that an emperor should not behave like a master to other Roman citizens (or at least his senatorial peers).[13] The significance of such claims lies precisely in the paradigmatic importance of the master–slave relationship as the extreme example of absolute power exercised without constraint or limit and without any obligation for the welfare of the dependant.

These metaphors are also important because they constitute a structured system of mutually exclusive paradigms which lend themselves to the task of delineating other, more abstract power structures such as empire. Matthew Roller has demonstrated that the contrasting figures of the master and father are central to debate about the powers, duties and legitimacy of the princeps in the Julio-Claudian period.[14] This book shows that social relations play a similarly paradigmatic role in discourse about empire. But they are configured quite differently. Whereas mastery is almost invariably a negative paradigm when applied to the principate, serving to exemplify the behaviour of a tyrannical ruler, it often provides a normative model for Roman rule, with Roman texts insisting that the subject peoples are indeed like slaves. Moreover, the most important alternative to the paradigm of mastery is not parental authority, as it is in discourse about the principate, but the model of patron or benefactor. Paternal (and maternal) metaphors do have a place in the language of empire, but it is not until relatively late – in the changed world of the fourth and fifth centuries CE – that they play a significant role. Gendered language is also noticeably absent. Gender relations do not supply a vocabulary of power and subjection in the same way as slavery and clientage. Their significance for the language of imperialism is both more subtle and less systematic.[15]

Remarkably little attention has been given to these tropes for the relationship between centre and periphery – or indeed to the broader language of empire (as John Richardson has noted in his

[13] For husbands and wives see e.g. Livy 34.7.12–13 and Joshel and Murnaghan 1998; for emperors and subjects, see Roller 2001 ch. 4.

[14] Roller 2001 ch. 4.

[15] See e.g. pp. 173–4 on Plin. *Pan.* 30–2.

recent monograph on the semantics of *imperium* and *prouincia*).[16] This is in striking contrast to the extensive work on the visual tropes used to represent the condition of the subject peoples in Roman art. Images of foreign men, women and children, often portrayed as dejected captives, and female personifications of peoples, lands and provinces are common in the art of the Roman empire.[17] Particularly significant examples are the relief sculptures of the peoples (*ethnē*) and islands of the empire in the Sebasteion at Aphrodisias (possibly based on the representations in the lost Augustan *porticus ad nationes* in Rome), the 'provinces' coin series of Hadrian and Antoninus Pius and the images of peoples that ringed the interior of the temple of the Divine Hadrian (Hadrianeum).[18] The iconography of empire draws on a range of visual tropes to represent the condition of the subject peoples. Images of enslavement – chained and dejected captives – are widespread and persistent, particularly in representations of barbarian figures.[19] The use of female figures to personify foreign peoples and lands implicitly exploits the gender code to subordinate the periphery (particularly when the female personifications are juxtaposed with male Roman figures, as for example in the famous reliefs illustrating the conquest of Britannia by Claudius and Armenia by Nero in the Sebasteion at Aphrodisias).[20] A few images and monuments seem to use images of foreign children to offer a different, more paternalistic, vision of Roman rule.[21]

16 Richardson 2008 p. 5, by no means the last word on 'the language of empire'.

17 See especially Ramsby and Severy-Hoven 2007 and Kuttner 1995 on the Augustan era, Ferris 2000 on representations of barbarians, Parisi Presicce 1999, Kuttner 1995 ch. 3 and Smith 1988 pp. 70–7 on the trope of personification, Cody 2003 and Méthy 1992 on representations of the provinces on the coinage and Östenberg 2009 ch. 4 and Beard 2007 ch. 5 on the iconography of the triumph.

18 Sebasteion: Smith 1988. 'Provinces' series: Toynbee 1934. Hadrianeum: Hughes 2009 and Sapelli 1999.

19 See especially de Souza 2011 and Bradley 2004 for images of captives and cf. Smith 1988 on allusions to this 'captive iconography' in the sculpture groups of the Sebasteion and Hadrianeum.

20 Ramsby and Severy-Hoven 2007, Dillon 2006, Rodgers 2003 and Ferris 2000 (esp. 55–60 and 165–8).

21 See in general Uzzi 2005 chs. 6–9 and also Kleiner and Buxton 2008, Kuttner 1995 pp. 100–7 and Rose 1990 on the two (or three) foreign children in the procession scenes on the precinct wall of the Ara Pacis, Kuttner 1995 on the Boscoreale cups and Currie 1996 on the arch of Trajan at Beneventum.

The categories and tropes that constitute the textual counterpart to this iconography of empire have received far less attention. Franz Christ's 1938 dissertation on representations of world rule remains a useful compendium of relevant passages in Latin literature, but it is descriptive rather than interpretative and does not address the metaphors studied here.[22] More promising is a recent monograph by Joel Allen which argues that the different roles played by foreign hostages at Rome (including guest, trophy, son, student and sexual object) could be seen as epitomising the condition of the foreign peoples from whom they came. But Allen's study is problematic in some respects and, in any case, its real focus is on the peoples on the periphery of the empire, not the provincialised population.[23] The most significant forerunner to my study is the long-running debate about the relevance of patronage to Roman conceptions of empire. This was sparked by Ernst Badian's claim that the forms taken by Roman imperialism in the Middle Republic were shaped by the domestic practice of *clientela*.[24] But this has been a narrow and increasingly misguided discussion. It has obscured the fact that patronage is at best one of several competing

[22] Christ 1938.

[23] Allen 2006. Allen must be right that the presence of hostages and other foreign youths in the city of Rome was an important visible reminder of the dependent status of peoples and kingdoms on the periphery of the empire, and that the position of those hostages might be seen as paradigmatic of the condition of the peoples that sent them. This is particularly relevant for the Republican period, when many allied and subject communities sent hostages to Rome. But Allen's argument becomes much more problematic when it comes to the Principate, as it conflates the case of children who came to Rome from the kingdoms and tribes on the edges of the empire either as hostages or students (a slippage that is already problematic, but potentially productive) with that of young nobles from Britain and Gaul being educated in leading cities in their own provinces (pp. 149–50, 163–4), Germans from beyond the frontier who were held as slaves or hostages in the Gallic provinces (pp. 121, 150), and even senatorial youths who were treated as hostages by emperors to ensure the loyalty of their fathers during their time as governors in the provinces (pp. 46–9). The questions of what peoples the 'hostages' represent, where they are on display, and who they are viewed by become thoroughly confused. I am also unconvinced by Allen's conclusion that there was a shift in Roman attitudes to the periphery between the reigns of Augustus and Trajan, from 'welcoming condescension' to 'stampeding military ambition' (p. 252), a conclusion which depends on a reductive dichotomy between 'coerced' and 'voluntary' hostages (these are really two poles of a spectrum) and which is in any case belied by Augustus' campaigns of conquest and Hadrian's relative restraint.

[24] Dmitriev 2010 pp. 437–44, Eilers 2002 pp. 186–9, Ferrary 1997b pp. 113–7, Rich 1989, Gruen 1984 pp. 172–84, Lintott 1981b pp. 61–2, Harris 1979 p. 135 n. 2, Bleicken 1964 and Badian 1958. See further pp. 177–8.

paradigms for Rome's imperial project. The important question is not whether Romans considered their foreign dependants to be in a condition of clientage, but rather how clientage worked as one of several competing models for submission to Rome.

Scope

This study focuses almost exclusively on texts written in Latin because its goal is to examine how the Roman elite that governed the provinces envisaged their shared imperial project. This elite, centred geographically on the city of Rome and socially on the senatorial and equestrian orders and the imperial household, supplied the provincial governors and their staff, the fiscal officials and the legionary and detachment commanders who wielded Roman power in the provinces. Its members were also the principal consumers, the patrons and often the producers of most surviving Latin literature in my period. Indeed many of the texts discussed in this book were written by men of senatorial or equestrian rank who also held office in Rome or the provinces.

Similar questions could be asked about the paradigms that structure the representation of Roman rule in Greek literature. But most Greek texts emerge from contexts that are politically and culturally quite different from those discussed here, and so necessarily stand in a different relationship to Roman power. When one Hellenised Jew (Philo) praises Augustus for not just loosening but undoing the chains that fettered the world and freeing all cities from slavery, while another (Josephus) seeks to convince his countrymen of the necessity of submitting to Rome on the basis that all the most powerful nations of the world have resigned themselves to enslavement by Rome,[25] when Plutarch urges the leaders of Greek

[25] Philo: οὗτός ἐστιν ὁ τὰ δεσμά, οἷς κατέζευκτο καὶ ἐπεπίεστο ἡ οἰκουμένη, παραλύσας, οὐ μόνον ἀνείς· … οὗτος ὁ τὰς πόλεις ἁπάσας εἰς ἐλευθερίαν ἐξελόμενος (*Leg.* 145–7; εἰς ἐλευθερίαν ἐξελέσθαι is the legal term for freeing a slave who has been wrongly enslaved). In the speech that Josephus attributes to the Jewish king Agrippa II (whose arguments are echoed in a speech in Josephus' own voice at 5.362–419), Agrippa reminds his fellow Jews that the Athenians are slaves to the Romans (δουλεύουσιν Ῥωμαίοις, Joseph. *BJ* 2.358), the Spartans tolerate the same masters (ἀγαπῶσιν τοὺς αὐτοὺς δεσπότας, 359), the Spanish too have been enslaved (καὶ τούτους ἐδουλώσαντο Ῥωμαῖοι, 375), as have the Germans (δουλεύουσιν, 377), the Britons (ἐδουλώσαντο Ῥωμαῖοι, 378) and even Parthia,

cities to be obedient to their Roman rulers, but not so obsequious as to invite chains on their neck besides those already on their feet and force their rulers 'to be masters more than they want',[26] or when one second-century *rhetor* (Dio Chrysostom) dismisses the rivalries between Greek cities as the squabbling of fellow slaves, while another (Aelius Aristides) insists that the Romans are the first imperial power to treat their subjects as free men[27] – in all these cases, empire is being envisaged from the perspective of the subject. The question for these writers is whether or not they are slaves. This book is concerned with those who were in a position to ask themselves whether they were masters. It is true that some Greek writers were members of the empire's equestrian and senatorial elite and held high office. But even they were forced by the very act of writing in Greek to negotiate a more complicated relationship to 'Roman' power and 'Roman' culture. There is much to be said about their representations of empire, but it needs to be set in a different frame, one which pays due attention to their triangulation of their own position in relation to the ruling power and its subjects. In any case, the topic of Greek perspectives on the empire has received considerable attention in recent years.[28] This book focuses on the representation of empire by a self-professed imperial elite.

There are two exceptions to the exclusion of Greek texts. The third-century historian Cassius Dio is included because his status as senator and counsellor of several emperors locates him at the centre of Roman power, because his representation of Roman rule as enslavement marks a significant break from earlier Greek historiography and reflects the influence of the Latin tradition, and because his date makes him an invaluable perspective on conceptions of empire

which endures slavery under the pretext of peace (ἐν εἰρήνης προφάσει δουλεύουσαν, 379). Only the Jews disdain to be Rome's slaves (ἀδοξεῖτε δουλεύειν, 361). See further Lavan 2007.

26 μηδὲ τοῦ σκέλους δεδεμένου προσυποβάλλειν καὶ τὸν τράχηλον ... ἀναγκάζουσιν ἑαυτῶν μᾶλλον ἢ βούλονται δεσπότας εἶναι τοὺς ἡγουμένους (*Plut. Prae. ger. reip.* 814F).

27 Dio Chrysostom: ἔστι γὰρ ὁμοδούλων πρὸς ἀλλήλους ἐριζόντων περὶ δόξης καὶ πρωτείων (*Or.* 34.51). Aelius Aristides: μόνοι γὰρ τῶν πώποτε ἐλευθέρων ἄρχετε (*Or.* 26.36). See further p. 211.

28 Among the most significant works are Yarrow 2006, Goldhill 2001, Whitmarsh 2001, Swain 1996, Nutton 1978, Forte 1972 and Bowie 1970.

at the very end of my period.[29] The second exception is the corpus of letters written by emperors and provincial governors to the cities of the East, which is discussed in Chapter 6. Even these texts reveal that Greek accounts of empire necessarily draw on a different cultural repertoire when it comes to conceptualising and representing relations of power.[30] For example, Greek has no direct equivalent for the Roman idea of *clientela*. The introduction of the loan word πάτρων into Greek civic discourse as Roman patronage relations expanded into the Greek East shows that the Roman *patronus* was seen as something different from the traditional Greek figure of the civic benefactor (εὐεργέτης).[31] Conversely, there is no clear Latin equivalent for the 'saviour and benefactor' (σωτὴρ καὶ εὐεργέτης), a common trope of civic discourse and Hellenistic diplomacy and one that was applied to Rome in the Republican period,[32] or for the tyrant city (πόλις τύραννος), which played an important role in earlier Greek discourse about empire.[33]

Within the domain of Latin literature, the analysis ranges widely. This is a subject that demands a broad, cultural approach. Representations of Rome as a masterly or patronal power are too widespread to be reduced to the conventions of particular genres or – even more narrowly – to intertextual relationships between individual texts.[34] These tropes are drawn from a distinctly Roman

[29] See further pp. 106–7.

[30] See Gotter 2008 for an attempt to articulate some of the differences between Athenian and Republican Roman discourses of power.

[31] On the introduction of πάτρων, πατρωνεία, and πατρωνεύειν into Greek inscriptions and the different connotations of Roman patronage and Greek euergetism, see Eilers 2002 ch. 5, Ferrary 1997a and Ferrary 1997b. On the ideals of euergetism, see further Gauthier 1985.

[32] See e.g. the dedication erected by the city of Laodicea on the Capitol honouring τὸν δῆμον Ῥωμαίων γεγονότα ἑαυτῷ σωτῆρα καὶ εὐεργέτην, rendered *populum Romanum benefici ergo* in Latin (*ILLRP* 177 = *ILS* 33), and numerous civic decrees from e.g. Delphi (*SIG*³ 702, 6–7), Magnetum (*SIG*³ 685, 22), Athens (*SIG*³ 704F, 6 and *SIG*³ 717, 15), Ephesus (*SIG*³ 742, 2) and the Amphyctionic League (*SIG*³ 704H, 27). See further Erskine 1994, Ferrary 1988 pp. 124–32, Mellor 1975 pp. 113–14 and Robert 1969.

[33] Thuc. 1.222.3, 1.124.3, 2.63.2; Ar. *Eq.* 1111–14; Pl. *Resp.* 545c, 576c, *Leg.* 711a; Plut. *Per.* 12.2; Lucian *Par.* 48.6. See Tamiolaki 2010 pp. 107–10, Raaflaub 2004 pp. 324 n. 82 and 141–3, Raaflaub 2003, Tuplin 1985, Raaflaub 1979, Schuller 1978, Hunter 1973/4 and de Romilly 1963.

[34] This is not to deny the existence – or the significance – of such intertextuality. See e.g. p. 92 on Verg. *Aen.* 1.281–5 (Jupiter's promise of Roman mastery) and Hom. *Il.* 6.448–65, p. 110 on Dio's use of δουλοῦν and Thucydides, and p. 201 on Livy 34.58.11

repertoire of paradigms of power. They are part of a shared language of imperialism that transcends genre boundaries. The chapters that follow necessarily draw more heavily on those genres in which Roman rule is most often discussed. Historiography figures prominently, because writing Roman history regularly entails the description of Roman conquest, good and bad governance, and native revolt. But the analysis extends to other genres and contexts wherever Roman rule over the provinces is identified, or contrasted, with the familiar power relations of everyday life.

This broad approach is not without its problems. It necessarily involves a degree of simplification and runs the risk of obscuring the particular agendas of individual texts. Metaphors of provincial enslavement or clientage can be developed for different purposes. Tacitus, for example, makes extensive use of the metaphor of enslavement in describing both the conquest of Britain in the *Agricola* and Boudicca's revolt in *Annals* 14, but to quite different effects. Moreover, Tacitus is arguably more interested in using these accounts of enslavement to illuminate the senate's subjection to the emperor than he is in the condition of the provinces themselves. Tacitus' complex narratives (analysed in Chapter 3) illustrate some of the problems inherent in generalising about the implications and functions of these metaphors. This book strives for a balance between close reading of individual texts and analysis of the wider discourse in which they are embedded. But it remains committed to the value of the latter approach. Much has been written about individual writers' representations of or attitudes to Roman imperialism.[35] But there has been a surprising lack of works of wider scope that attempt for Roman discourse the sort of synoptic study that has been provided for modern imperial cultures by influential critics such as Edward Said and David Spurr.[36] Following their example ought to mean adopting their questions and methods, not merely borrowing their conclusions

(*patrocinium libertatis Graecorum*) and Cic. *Off.* 2.27. But to focus exclusively on the relationships between individual texts would be to ignore the structural role that these tropes play in Roman discourse more broadly.

35 See e.g. Riggsby 2006 and Brunt 1978 on Caesar; Steel 2001, Rose 1995 and Brunt 1978 on Cicero; Fear 2011 and Naas 2011 on Pliny the Elder; and Rutledge 2000, O'Gorman 1993 and Benario 1991 on Tacitus.

36 Said 1993, Spurr 1993 and Said 1978.

(as is all too often done).[37] Only broad studies of the tropes of Roman discourse can provide the context necessary to understand the politics of particular representations of empire.

The chronological scope is also broad, extending from the middle of the first century BCE to the beginning of the third century CE – a period that is relatively well represented in the surviving corpus and reveals marked continuity in the language of imperialism. The earliest texts discussed are Cicero's speeches and Caesar's commentaries, which date from the 70s and the 50s BCE respectively. The last text covered in detail is Cassius Dio's *Roman History*, written early in the third century. The starting point is pragmatic: earlier evidence for the Roman language of imperialism is too limited to allow a similar analysis.[38] The end point is provided by Caracalla's extension of citizenship to most of the free inhabitants of the empire around 212 CE, which finally erased one of the most important potential distinctions between Romans and subjects. Moreover, there is little surviving Latin literature from the rest of the third century, while the wealth of material that survives from the fourth century reveals significant changes in the language of imperialism.[39] It is worth emphasising that this means that my focus is on the literature of the Principate. What has been written about the Roman language of imperialism has tended to focus on the Republic, and primarily the Middle Republic, despite the paucity of surviving texts from that period. This is true both of the debate about the significance of patronage for Roman imperialism and of work on the meaning of the term *socii* ('allies').[40] This book redirects attention to the much better represented discourse of the Principate, a period in which the Roman elite remain committed to the project of conquering and ruling foreign peoples.

[37] See Said 1993 p. 9 and 1978 p. 15 on the historical contingency of the discursive structures analysed in those studies.
[38] Attempts to illuminate the ideology of early Roman imperialism from other perspectives include Richardson 2008, Ferrary 1988, Gruen 1984 and Harris 1979.
[39] By the fourth century the noun *prouinciales* has not just completely displaced *socii*, long the term of choice for the subject population, but become a generic label for all the emperor's subjects (pp. 69–70), while there is a notable proliferation of maternal language and imagery in representations of the city of Rome (pp. 208–10). These shifts reflect a number of changes in the empire, including the extension of the citizenship, the growth of Christianity and the withdrawal of the emperor from Rome.
[40] See pp. 26–7 and 177–8.

The culture of Roman imperialism

This analysis of the tropes of Latin literature is a study in the cultural underpinnings of Roman imperialism. It is guided by Edward Said's insights into the role of the novel and other cultural forms in supporting and even impelling the British, French and American imperial projects.[41] Literature must have played a similarly important role in imbuing the Roman elite with a sense of power and entitlement and continually renewing their commitment to the conquest and rule of distant peoples and territories – at least some of which (notably Judaea, Mauretania and Britain) required a significant ongoing investment of energies, resources and even blood.[42] Literature will also have played a role in shaping conceptions of the proper ends and means of Roman power by articulating and perpetuating shared values, beliefs and ambitions. These will have formed part of the normative framework within which the governing elite approached their duties as governors, generals and administrators in the provinces.

This book will not claim that Roman visions of the imperial project can be reduced to any single metaphor. Too many generalisations about the ideology of Roman imperialism have ascribed a definitive 'attitude to' or 'conception of' empire to particular authors, periods or even Roman culture in general.[43] Such claims inevitably extrapolate widely from a few scattered texts and iron out any inconsistencies and contradictions to produce a monolithic and misleading consensus. I take it as axiomatic that the discourse

[41] Said 1993 (an analysis of the complicity of 'high' culture in imperialism which is in many ways more relevant to the study of surviving Latin literature than Said 1978, which focuses on academic and administrative discourses). See also the essays in Hall 2000 on 'cultures of empire'. Culture has received too little attention in the recent spate of comparative work on ancient empires, e.g. Burbank and Cooper 2010, Morris and Scheidel 2009, Scheidel 2009a and Hurlet 2008 (Mutschler and Mittag 2008 is an exception, but it does not go far enough in exploring the links between culture and practice). Scheidel 2009b is an extreme case in its attempt to identify a universal biological impulse to empire.

[42] Recent work has highlighted the role of the army as a force of occupation even in the interior of the empire. See especially Woolf 1993b and Isaac 1992.

[43] See for example Kousser 2005 on 'the Romans' conception of their imperial project' (186), Fear 1996 pp. 16–23 on the 'general intellectual climate in Rome' (16), Gruen 1984 ch. 8 on 'the Roman concept of empire in the age of expansion' and Brunt 1978 on 'the Roman attitude to their empire' (291).

I am describing is a space of debate, not a consensus. My goal is to explore the shape of that debate by mapping the distinctively Roman constellation of paradigmatic power relationships in relation to which competing visions of empire are articulated.

The contrast between patronage and slavery is sometimes deployed in the service of claims of Roman exceptionalism. In Livy, for example, Roman statesmen dealing with Greek states during the second century BCE repeatedly employ a patronal rhetoric to distinguish Roman motives from those of the Hellenistic kings, who are represented as seeking to enslave their subjects.[44] Elsewhere, however, the contrast is used to articulate a distinction within the empire, with the Romans' more fortunate (or more docile) dependants represented as friends or clients, and the rest as slaves. But the different metaphors are often employed independently, and apparently contradictory metaphors can be found coexisting in a given period, in a particular author and even in a single text. They each serve to emphasise different aspects of Roman power. The language of slavery can emphasise the empire's powers of coercion or the self-abnegating service expected of the subjects; references to Roman benefactions affirm the provinces' moral obligation to their beneficent rulers; the language of *clientela* asserts a reciprocal obligation on the part of the Romans to protect their dependants; maternal imagery (when it appears) goes even further, representing Rome as a nurturing power. All of these metaphors have a place in Roman discourse. Together, they embody the complexity and diversity of Roman visions of empire in all periods.

Nevertheless, this book places special emphasis on the paradigm of slavery. This is partly a function of its prominence in Latin literature: if any metaphor deserves to be seen as dominant in this period, it is slavery, not patronage. More importantly, these representations of provincial subjection as enslavement reveal a voice that has received too little attention in scholarship on Roman imperialism in the period of the Principate. Whereas work on the Republic has for some time emphasised Roman militarism and

[44] See p. 201 on the dangers of using these Livian constructs as a source for the rhetoric of Roman diplomacy in the earlier period.

exclusivism,[45] scholarship on the Principate has tended to credit the Roman elite with more benevolent motives (at least with regard to the provinces, if not the barbarians beyond the frontier) – notably a 'civilising mission' and a willingness to assimilate worthy outsiders.[46] The rhetoric of Roman mastery and provincial enslavement reveals a very different side of Roman imperialism and points to important continuities with the imperial ambitions of the Republic. It suggests widespread acceptance of the ultimately coercive character of Roman power and an expectation of total, self-abnegating submission from the subject peoples. It is particularly important because it comes to the fore in the context of conflict – not just the moment of conquest, but also subsequent resistance or rebellion. Roman texts regularly identify rebels with troublesome slaves who need to be crushed into submission. Here the continuities between discourse and practice are particularly obvious. Rebellious provincials were regularly subjected to harsh penalties normally reserved for slaves, notably crucifixion. The alternative was often enslavement.[47] It is one of the aims of this book to recuperate this masterly style in Roman imperialism.

A second emphasis of this book is the surprising continuity in the language of Roman imperialism in the face of the dramatic cultural, social and political changes in the provinces over the three centuries covered by this book. The end of the reign of Augustus inaugurated a period of imperial consolidation in which the frontiers of the

45 The seminal texts are Harris 1979 and Brunt 1978 (= *RIT* pp. 288–323) (especially p. 185 on contempt for provincials).

46 The idea of a 'civilising mission' or 'civilising ethos' has become a trope of scholarship on Roman imperialism in this period (see e.g. Hingley 2005 pp. 24 and 28 and Isaac 2004 p. 184). Detailed treatments include Fear 2011 (reversing the more persuasive conclusion of Fear 1996 pp. 22–3), Kousser 2005, Woolf 1998 ch. 3, Habinek 1998 ch. 8 and Woolf 1993a pp. 118–25. All draw on the same limited pool of texts. Even the oft-cited study of Rome's civilising ethos in Woolf 1998 acknowledges that Latin literature offers 'few explicit accounts of the civilising power of Rome' (p. 57). In my view, what is striking is how little interest Roman authors show in the processes of cultural change that transformed the Mediterranean in this period and which figure so large in modern scholarship. On the idealisation of Rome's openness to virtuous outsiders in the Principate, see especially Dench 2005 (a balanced reading that recognises that openness and plurality were problematised as well as idealised). The goal of this book is not to prove these claims 'wrong' (though I believe they are exaggerated), but rather to highlight the persistence of other, more exclusivist, visions of the imperial project well into the Principate.

47 See further pp. 90–1.

empire stabilised after centuries of expansion. The century following the accession of Augustus also witnessed dramatic cultural changes in the provinces – notably the extension of urbanisation in Spain, Gaul, Africa, southern Syria and the interior of Asia Minor and the spread of Italian styles in consumption, funerary practice, and cult. The changes were most dramatic in the West, but the Greek East was not unaffected. This was not a uniform or unidirectional process; nor was it the result of a central policy of 'Romanisation'. But it did result in a significant convergence of elite, urban culture throughout the empire.[48] This period also saw the large-scale extension of Roman citizenship – a privilege that had been denied to the Italians as recently as 91 BCE – to individuals and entire communities in the provinces. The legions, the core of the army and the mainstay of empire, were increasingly recruited from the provinces, with Italian representation dropping to around 60% under the first three emperors, 20% under the Flavians and Trajan and less than 1% thereafter.[49] The change extended even to the highest ranks of the imperial elite. On one estimate, the representation of provincials in the equestrian order grew from 4% in the Republic to 32% under the Julio-Claudians and reached 68% by the end of the second century.[50] The same process was at work in the senate itself, albeit at a slower pace. The handful of provincial senators in the last generation of the Republic grew to around 20% under the Flavians and reached almost 60% under Severus.[51] One might have expected these transformations to have been reflected in (or even enabled by) changes in the language

[48] On cultural change across the empire, see especially Keay and Terrenato 2001, Fentress 2000, MacMullen 2000, Woolf 1995 and Ward Perkins 1970. See also Woolf 1998 on Gaul, Fear 1996 pp. 170–226 on Baetica, and Woolf 1993a on the East. Woolf 1998 is a model study of the dynamics of cultural change. For local initiative as the driving force, see Woolf 1998, Cherry 1998 and Fear 1996 (see *contra* Whittaker 1997). On hybrid cultures, see especially Woolf 1995.

[49] Brunt 1974 pp. 99–100 (= *RIT* p. 197), based on Forni 1953. See also Forni 1974 and Mann 1983.

[50] Demougin 1988 p. 522. Demougin's analysis of known *equites* is limited to the Julio-Claudian period. The last figure (68% for 161–211 CE) is derived from the narrower analysis of holders of the equestrian *militiae* in Devijver 1992 pp. 226–8, whose findings for the Julio-Claudian period (30%) are in line with those of Demougin (32%).

[51] The figures are derived from the dated but still useful analysis of Hammond 1957. See also Chastagnol 1992 and Panciera 1982.

of imperialism – not least in a softening of the rhetoric of provincial slavery. Yet there is no sign of discontinuity in this period. The tropes of mastery and slavery are as prominent in Pliny and Tacitus as they are in Cicero and Caesar. As late as the mid second century, the historian Florus still sees the production of docile slaves as the *telos* of Roman expansion. It is not until the fourth century CE that significant change can be seen in the language of empire, notably a proliferation of maternal imagery.[52]

An imperial identity

This book is necessarily also a study in the self-definition of the Roman elite. It highlights the extent to which Roman writers espouse an imperial identity, asserting their superior status within a population divided into rulers and ruled.[53] However, it also stresses the slipperiness of this dichotomy. At the beginning of my period it can perhaps be reduced to the juridical distinction between Roman citizens and their non-citizen subjects, usually styled 'the allies' (*socii*) by Roman writers. But other criteria of distinction become operative by the first century CE at the latest, presumably in response to the dissemination of citizenship in the provinces. There is an increasing emphasis on the distinction between Italians and provincials. This can be seen both in the invention and rapid spread of the noun *prouinciales* as a label for the inhabitants of the provinces and in a gradual slippage in the meaning of *socii* whereby it becomes capable of encompassing all provincials, not just non-citizens (Chapter 1). These linguistic developments imply a new focus on geography, ethnicity and/or culture – all of which are potentially at work in the rhetoric of provinciality – in the self-definition of the Roman elite. But the opposition between Italians and provincials does not neatly displace that between citizens and non-citizens. These and other

[52] See pp. 208–10.

[53] In this respect, my book can be seen as a supplement to the rich and wide-ranging study of Roman discourses of identity in Dench 2005, which rightly notes that suprisingly little work has been done on questions of specifically Roman ethnic and cultural self-definition (p. 26).

dichotomies coexist and are often treated as interchangeable in the literature of the Principate. Roman writers of the first two centuries CE identify with an imperial power configured variously and inconsistently as the Roman people, Italy or, even more narrowly, the city of Rome – or simply an underdetermined *nos* ('we').

These inconsistencies suggest a degree of indifference to the distinctions between these categories, distinctions which must have mattered to many provincial citizens. They were clearly of secondary importance to senatorial writers and others close to the centre of power, presumably because they could take their superiority as given, wherever the line between rulers and ruled was drawn. The inconsistencies also reflect the complex political geography of the empire in this period. Power and privilege were distributed across a matrix created by the interaction of several different criteria of distinction, including citizen status (citizens, Latins, non-citizens), geography (Italians and provincials), rank (*honestiores* and *humiliores*) and a hierarchy of status among communities (from *coloniae*, *municipia* and *liberae ciuitates* through regular *ciuitates peregrinae* to communities that had no civic identity at all). The resulting distribution of power and privilege was far too complex to be reduced to any simple dichotomy between rulers and subjects.[54] If, as this book shows, Roman writers insist on imposing such a dichotomy on the empire, this must be recognised as a Roman fiction and part of the self-image of this Roman elite.

This book stresses the continuity in this sense of an imperial identity through the first two and a half centuries of the Principate, despite the diffusion of citizenship and other privileged statuses in the provinces and despite the political disempowerment of the citizen body, whose legislative and electoral powers were appropriated by the senate and the emperor. Several Greek writers of the imperial period question whether the distinction between Romans and subjects can have any significance in a world where all are equally subject to the emperor. Early in the second century the Stoic philosopher Epictetus reminds a prominent Roman senator that he too acknowledges the emperor as master and is thus no less

[54] See further pp. 27–32.

a slave then Epictetus' townsmen in Nicopolis.[55] Aelius Aristides claims that the emperor's supreme power makes everyone equal – even Roman governors and their provincial subjects.[56] Cassius Dio suggests that the non-Romans who fought in the civil war between Caesar and Pompey took particular pleasure in the struggle because the impending enslavement of the Roman people to the victor would reduce the Romans to the same level as their erstwhile slaves.[57] These texts represent the emperor as a great leveller. They insist that creation of the principate collapsed the gap that had existed between the Roman people and their subject population. This book shows that most Latin literature denies this levelling effect. Throughout the first and second centuries CE Latin literature remains an *imperial* literature and Roman writers continue to present themselves as members of an *imperial* people (however vaguely delimited), elevated above the rest of the population of the empire.

The social imaginary

As well as being a study of imperial ideology and elite identity, this book is also an exploration of the Roman social imaginary.[58] There is much to be learned about the ideologies that underlie the Roman practices of slavery and patronage by examining how they are employed as paradigms for empire.[59] For example, the pervasive

55 ἀλλὰ τίς με δύναται ἀναγκάσαι, εἰ μὴ ὁ πάντων κύριος Καῖσαρ; – Οὐκοῦν ἕνα μὲν δεσπότην σαυτοῦ καὶ σὺ αὐτὸς ὡμολόγησας. ὅτι δὲ πάντων, ὡς λέγεις, κοινός ἐστιν, μηδέν σε τοῦτο παραμυθείσθω, ἀλλὰ γίγνωσκε, ὅτι ἐκ μεγάλης οἰκίας δοῦλος εἶ (Epict. *Diss.* 4.1.12–13).

56 οἱ δὲ ἄρχοντες οἱ πεμπόμενοι ἐπὶ τὰς πόλεις τε καὶ τὰ ἔθνη τῶν μὲν ὑφ' ἑαυτοῖς ἕκαστοι ἄρχοντές εἰσι, τὰ δὲ πρὸς αὑτούς τε καὶ πρὸς ἀλλήλους ὁμοίως ἅπαντες ἀρχόμενοι … τοσοῦτος ἅπασιν ἐνέστακται φόβος τοῦ μεγάλου ἄρχοντος καὶ τὰ πάντα πρυτανεύοντος (Aristid. *Or.* 26.31).

57 τὸ δὲ ὑπήκοον καὶ προθύμως καὶ ἀφειδῶς ἐμάχετο, πολλὴν σπουδήν, ὥσπερ ποτὲ ὑπὲρ τῆς σφετέρας ἐλευθερίας, οὕτω τότε κατὰ τῆς τῶν Ῥωμαίων δουλείας ποιούμενοι, ἐπιθυμίᾳ, ἅτε ἐν πᾶσιν αὐτῶν ἐλαττούμενοι, ὁμοδούλους σφᾶς ἔχειν (Dio 41.59.4).

58 I use the term 'social imaginary' to emphasise the social function of representations – their role in constituting social reality itself (cf. Ricoeur 1986, Baczko 1984 and Castoriadis 1987 and, for an application in early modern history, Maza 2003).

59 This is an opportunity missed by Roller 2001's otherwise excellent analysis of the metaphors that structure debate about the principate. His approach – borrowing on the model of conceptual metaphor developed by Lakoff and Turner 1980 – is overly schematic. He draws an untenable distinction between conceptual metaphors, in which

rhetoric of Roman mastery reveals slavery's importance as a normative paradigm of subjection. It is all too easy for our own conviction that slavery is unjust to blind us to the master's ethic that underlies Roman discourse. This book will show that Roman texts regularly turn to slavery for a model of *legitimate* authority – even while acknowledging its fundamentally coercive character. The sheer variety of the metaphors of provincial enslavement also illustrates some of the complexities and contradictions of the Roman vision of slavery.[60] Slavery is regularly invoked as an oppressive and hateful condition, providing a paradigmatic example of degradation, coerced obedience and powerlessness. But it can also be viewed more positively as a paradigm of self-effacement and utter devotion to the welfare of another. Finally, the more elaborate and sustained of these metaphors are important documents of the ideology of slavery in their own right. For example, Tacitus' representation of provincial enslavement in the *Agricola* develops a coherent psychology of slavery in order to explain the dynamics of domination at home and abroad. It implies a vicious circle in which the experience of domination engenders slavishness in the subject and this slavishness perpetuates the state of subjection. This construction of slavishness as a result of enslavement illustrates that slavery can be naturalised without recourse to a genetic theory – that slaves can be made, as well as born.[61]

The language of empire can also illuminate the surprisingly elusive concept of *clientela*. In the wake of Richard Saller's work

a parent domain 'systematically structures' ('is projected en bloc onto') a derived domain, and other metaphors, in which 'no associations significant for the context are imported' (p. 218 n. 9). He also insists that the parent domain is always reduced to a stereotype. See his presentation of 'the stereotypical characteristics and consequent affective overtones of the father-son relationship' (pp. 236–7) and his discussion of stereotypes of slavery (p. 226). Because he takes slavery and the father–son relationship as stereotypes, he treats all metaphors derived from these domains as interchangeable. This book will illustrate the diverse visions of slavery that can be found within metaphors of enslavement.

60 Several recent studies have enriched our understanding of Roman discourses of slavery through similarly oblique approaches, considering how slavery functions as the source of symbol and metaphor. See Martin 1990 on slavery metaphors in early Christian discourse, McCarthy 2000 on slavery in Plautine comedy, Fitzgerald 2000 on slavery in the Roman literary imagination more generally and Edwards 2009 on metaphors of slavery in Seneca.

61 See further pp. 132–5.

on structures of patronage in Roman society, it has become increasingly common for the Roman concept of *clientela* to be explained in terms of asymmetrical exchange and the ethic of reciprocity. But the Roman concept is not so easily pinned down. It is both narrower and broader than Saller's heuristic definition of patronage – narrower because it excludes many relations of asymmetrical exchange that might be classed as patronal, broader because it also encompasses a range of other forms of dependence, notably the legally enforceable dependence of the freedman.[62] The language of *clientela* unites an otherwise heterogeneous cluster of relations and distinguishes them from other relations of dependence. If they have any coherence it is to be found in the social imaginary. Metaphor therefore provides a valuable glimpse of what it is that unites these relationships in the Roman imagination.

Summary

Chapter 1 explores the categories available to Roman writers to refer to the subject population, specifically 'the allies' (*socii*), 'the provinces' (*prouinciae*), 'the provincials' (*prouinciales*), 'the peoples' (*gentes*) and 'the foreigners' (*peregrini*). This list might at first appear to conflate legal, geographic and ethnic categories, but the chapter will show that these terms perform very similar functions within Roman discourse and that they are often treated as interchangeable. It traces some key developments in this vocabulary and relates them to the broader history of imperial ideology. Perhaps most important is the relatively late emergence of *prouinciales* as a term for the inhabitants of the provinces and the gradual slippage in the meaning of *socii* by which it comes to be used of all provincials rather than non-citizens alone. These shifts reveal a new focus on Italian origins or residence at the expense of citizenship in the self-presentation of the imperial elite. The chapter also highlights the prominence and longevity of the label *socii* in the lexicon of empire. Born in the context of Rome's relations with its Italian allies, the term is still being used of Rome's provincial subjects well into the

[62] Saller 1982. See further pp. 179–86.

second century CE. With its connotations of association rather than integration, it testifies to the persistent exclusivism of Roman political rhetoric, which continues to mark many of the inhabitants of the empire as external to the Roman community.

Chapter 2 aims to establish the centrality of the tropes of slavery and mastery to the language of Roman imperialism. Far from being limited to the rhetoric of Rome's enemies as is often assumed, the metaphor of provincial enslavement is widespread in Roman descriptions of the condition of the provinces. It is particularly common in descriptions of conquest and revolt, but is certainly not limited to those contexts. It extends across a wide range of genres and can be traced from the first century BCE to the third CE, becoming if anything more common in the later period. The chapter argues that the ubiquity of such metaphors is particularly significant given the care with which the language of slavery is used – and more often avoided – in domestic political rhetoric. It is indicative of the gulf separating Romans and subjects in Roman political culture.

Where Chapter 2 provides a broad survey, Chapter 3 adopts a narrower focus in order to illustrate the potential diversity within the wider rhetoric of Roman mastery and provincial slavery. It concentrates on Tacitus, one author particularly interested in the parallels between empire and slavery, and examines his representations of Roman rule as enslavement in three successive accounts of provincial resistance: the British narrative in the *Agricola*, the Batavian revolt in *Histories* 4–5 and Boudicca's revolt in *Annals* 14. It shows that these narratives develop the idea of provincial slavery in quite different directions. The *Agricola* draws on a particular model of the psychology of slavery, one which emphasises the slave's complicity in his own subjection, in order to illuminate the morally degrading effects of Roman domination. The Boudicca narrative focuses instead on the fragility of the line dividing freedom from slavery in both the provinces and Neronian Rome. The chapter also shows that all three narratives of resistance to Rome are at least as concerned with the senate's subjection to the emperor as they are with provincial subjection to Rome. The recognition that texts have their own agendas for describing Roman rule is an important caveat for any attempt to use them to write a history of Roman imperial ideology.

Chapters 4 and 5 consider alternatives to the paradigm of slavery. Chapter 4 explores representations of the Romans as benefactors bestowing favours (*beneficia*) on grateful dependants. It shows that this rhetoric of favours draws on the ideology of exchange that played an important role in constructing and affirming relations of dependence between nominally free citizens. These claims of Roman beneficence are always also assertions of Roman power and provincial dependency. The chapter also shows that the symbolic importance attributed to giving and receiving in Roman culture could make Rome's dependency on provincial resources, particularly grain, a potential problem for its self-image as an imperial power.

Chapter 5 focuses more narrowly on the language of *clientela*. It argues that this language has a special force that distinguishes it from the broader rhetoric of favours. The chapter shows that both Cicero and Livy make extensive and systematic use of patronal metaphors in their descriptions of Roman rule, and that these tropes are relatively rare elsewhere in Roman discourse. It explores why the two authors are so distinctive in this respect. The chapter also considers the more limited use of familial imagery to represent the imperial relationship before concluding with an analysis of how the representations of Rome as benefactor or patron explored in Chapters 4 and 5 relate to the rhetoric of mastery discussed in Chapters 2 and 3.

Whereas Chapters 1 to 5 examine the representation of empire in texts that were largely written for an imperial elite, Chapter 6 expands the focus to look at the rhetoric of Roman officials addressing provincial audiences. It asks to what extent the masterly style that is so prominent in Roman literature is visible in the official pronouncements of the Roman state by examining the substantial surviving corpus of edicts and letters issued to provincial communities by emperors and governors. It shows that the language of these texts is very different from that of Latin literature. They focus on the emperor to the almost total exclusion of the Roman people, and espouse an ecumenical rhetoric that obscures any distinctions among the inhabitants of the empire. It argues that these features of official discourse reflect the influence of the conventions of Hellenistic diplomacy and the culture of loyalism in Roman politics. But it also shows that traces of the idea of a two-tier empire and the rhetoric of Roman mastery can be found even here and may indeed be under-represented due to survival bias in the epigraphic corpus.

I

ROMANS AND ALLIES

graues ignominias cladesque duas omnino nec alibi quam in Germania accepit, Lollianam et Varianam, sed Lollianam maioris infamiae quam detrimenti, Varianam paene exitiabilem, tribus legionibus cum duce legatisque et auxiliis omnibus caesis. hac nuntiata excubias per urbem indixit, ne quis tumultus existeret, et praesidibus prouinciarum propagauit imperium, ut a peritis et assuetis socii continerentur.

[Augustus] suffered only two humiliating disasters, and both those in Germany, the defeats of Lollius and Varus. The former was more an embarrassment than a real loss but the latter was almost fatal, costing the lives of three legions with their commander, legates and all auxiliaries. When news reached Augustus, he announced a watch throughout the city to prevent any disturbance. He also extended the terms of the current provincial governors so that the allies could be kept under control by tried and experienced men.

(Suet. *Aug.* 23.1)

The Varian disaster of 9 BCE, in which the recently conquered Germans revolted and overwhelmed their garrison, was long remembered as a moment when Rome's empire tottered on the brink. Suetonius here describes the extraordinary measures Augustus took in its aftermath to maintain order in the city of Rome and to restrain 'the allies'. The latter remark deserves some thought. The provincial governors' subjects – at least those who needed to be kept under control (*contineri*) – are called the *socii*. This is a term more obviously fitted to the looser modes of control that characterised Rome's early expansion than to the provincialised empire of the second century CE. What does it mean that Rome's provincial subjects are still being described as 'allies' in the time of Suetonius?[1] How do the other connotations of the word colour Roman discourse about empire?

[1] The *Lives* were written in the 110s or 120s. See Wallace-Hadrill 1983 p. 1 n. 1.

This chapter investigates the categories available to Roman writers to refer to the subjects of empire. It shows that *socii* is probably the most important such term; it is certainly the longest-lasting. Its closest rival is *prouinciae* ('the provinces'), with its cognate *prouinciales* ('the provincials'). In comparison, the familiar *peregrini* ('foreigners' or 'aliens'), so frequent in modern scholarship, is surprisingly rare. One might object that these terms perform different functions in Roman discourse, in so far as *socii* and *peregrini* are normally legal categories (denoting non-citizens, as opposed to Roman citizens) whereas *prouinciae* and *prouinciales* are geographic categories (denoting provincials, as opposed to Italians). But it would be unwise to insist too much on the distinction. These terms are not always used with such precision and the line between them is often blurred. *Socii* is particularly slippery. Its relationship to other categories and to the legal structure of the empire is far from straightforward. Moreover, all these terms perform very similar functions in Roman discourse in that they articulate a binary division within the population of the empire. This chapter will demonstrate the value of studying them together. They have a history which can illuminate key continuities and changes in the culture of Roman imperialism and in how Roman writers conceive of their place within the imperial order.

The terminology of Roman imperialism is hardly a new subject. But surprisingly little attention has been given to the semantics of *socii*, *prouinciales* and *peregrini*.[2] The one significant exception is the long and heated debate about the meaning of *socii* in Roman foreign relations in the third and second centuries BCE, largely concerned with establishing a taxonomy of Rome's relationships

[2] Mommsen 1887–8 III pp. 652–63 and 723–5 is the most substantial previous analysis of the terms used to refer to Rome's subjects. It is legalistic in its focus – interested in establishing 'proper' rather than 'abusive' terminology – and does not discuss either *prouinciales* or *peregrini*. Note also the brief survey of Latin terms for foreigner at Noy 2000 pp. 1–2 (omitting *socii*) and the survey of the language of *altérité* in Dauge 1981 pp. 396–402 (omitting both *socii* and *prouinciales*). Little or nothing has been written about *peregrini* and *prouinciales*, with the exception of the recent *TLL* articles by Schwind 1995 on *peregrini* and Schrickx 2006 on *prouinciales*, neither of which considers how these terms relate to each other or to *socii*. Mathisen 2006 pp. 1016–17 and 1020–1 and 2009 pp. 149–50 discusses the use of *peregrini* and *prouinciales* in the fourth century.

with foreign communities in that period.[3] The narrow focus has excluded other, equally important questions. The precise legal sense of the term (if it has one) has been privileged over its meanings in other contexts and the usage of later authors such as Cicero and Livy has been valued only in so far as it can be used to reconstruct earlier usage. This chapter treats the discourse of the Late Republic and the Principate as a subject in its own right. It also shows that most surviving texts do not use the label *socii* as precisely as a jurist might – but that we can still draw important conclusions about how and why it is used.

Power and privilege in the Roman empire

First a word on the political structures that underlie this lexicon. This book will show that Roman texts regularly represent the population of the empire as being divided into subject peoples and their Roman rulers. It is important to be clear from the outset that any such dichotomy is an ideological construction imposed on the significantly more complex political geography of the empire. Most obviously, any simple dichotomy obscures the distinction between Roman citizens and the inhabitants of Italy, two overlapping but not identical categories which enjoyed certain advantages over non-citizens and provincials respectively. The citizen body already extended beyond the borders of Italy at the beginning of my period, thanks to Italian emigration and proliferating grants of citizenship to foreigners.[4] The number of provincial citizens became ever more significant with the intensive settlement of Italians abroad by Caesar and Augustus and the progressive enfranchisement of individuals and communities in the provinces over the

[3] The most important interventions are Sherwin-White 1984 ch. 3, Gruen 1984 chs. 1–2, Dahlheim 1968 ch. 4 and Matthaei 1907. See further pp. 37–8 below.

[4] The number of Italians outside Italy in the Late Republic is evident in the numbers claimed to have been massacred by Mithridates in 88 BCE and the legions raised by the Pompeians in Spain, Africa and the East. See Purcell 2006, Brunt 1971 Part II, Wilson 1966 and Hatzfeld 1919. On the enfranchisement of foreigners in the Republican period, see especially Cic. *Balb.* 24 and 36–51 and the evidence collected in Badian 1958 Appendix II with the analysis in Sherwin-White 1973 pp. 291–311.

first two centuries CE, culminating in Caracalla's general grant.[5] A short – and necessarily superficial – overview of the ways in which Roman rule impinged on the lives of the inhabitants of the empire will suffice to show that these and other distinctions worked separately to create a complex map of power and privilege which defies reduction to a simple dichotomy of privileged beneficiaries and exploited subjects of empire.

Taxation was probably the most widely felt imposition of Roman rule.[6] Although the tax burden probably varied from province to province, the system as a whole favoured Italians over provincials, both citizens and non-citizens. The inhabitants of Italy enjoyed immunity from the property tax (*tributum soli*) and poll tax (*tributum capitis*) that were levied on the provinces. Roman citizens in the provinces were fully liable for the property tax (and possibly also the poll tax) unless they were fortunate enough to live in one of the colonies that had received a grant of 'Italian status' (*ius Italicum*), which brought exemption from tribute.[7] The very term *ius Italicum* highlights the fact that this privilege was associated with Italy, not citizenship *per se*. To complicate the picture, it is worth noting that the fiscal immunity enjoyed by Italians was neither complete nor exclusive. Italians did pay the so-called 'indirect taxes' – notably the inheritance tax, sales tax and the taxes on the sale and manumission of slaves – and irregular levies such as the *aurum coronarium*.[8] Conversely, the fiscal privileges of Italians were shared with several provincial communities – not just those colonies that had the *ius Italicum* but also the minority of free cities that enjoyed immunity from

[5] For the overseas colonies founded by Caesar, the triumvirs and Augustus, see Brunt 1971 pp. 255–9, Salmon 1969 ch. 8, Vittinghoff 1952 and Kornemann 1900. Sherwin-White 1973 Part II traces the progressive extension of the citizenship.

[6] On taxation in the Roman empire, see especially Corbier 1991, Corbier 1988, Brunt 1981 (= *RIT* pp. 324–46) with Brunt 1990 pp. 531–40, Neesen 1980 and Jones 1974.

[7] *Ius Italicum*: Jacques and Scheid 1990 pp. 243–5. It is often asserted that Roman citizens were exempt from *tributum capitis* (e.g. Neesen 1980 pp. 117 and 121). They certainly enjoyed this privilege in Egypt (Wallace 1938 p. 407 n. 24). But the fact that Vespasian is recorded as having granted the colony of Caesarea immunity from *tributum capitis* (*Dig.* 50.15.8.7) suggests that Roman citizens were not automatically exempt in all provinces.

[8] Taxation in Italy: Eck 1979. Hadrian's exceptional decision to relieve the Italian cities of the crown tax (*aurum coronarium*, on which see Ando 2000 pp. 175–90) on his accession (SHA *Hadr.* 6.5) suggests that they were normally liable for that extraordinary exaction.

tribute and also a few individuals who enjoyed personal fiscal immunity.[9] Some of the beneficiaries of these grants (notably the inhabitants of free and immune cities) were not even citizens. It is also important to recognise that the economic impositions of Roman rule were not limited to taxation. To judge from provincial complaints, the irregular requisitioning of transport, supplies and lodging for official travellers and armies on the march was if anything more oppressive.[10] Here too Italians probably bore a significantly lighter burden. Yet the evidence of repeated attempts to relieve Italy from these exactions would suggest they remained an issue even there.[11] A privileged few provincials enjoyed formal immunity from such exactions.[12] Again, those who did were not always citizens. Lastly, it is worth observing that Italians, though they enjoyed considerable protection from taxation, did not benefit directly from the extraction of provincial resources. The majority of Rome's revenues were expended maintaining the army. The surplus was consumed by a privileged few: the emperor and his court, the senatorial and equestrian officers who drew large public salaries, and the population of Rome as a whole, whose corn supply, games and public building programmes were financed by provincial tribute.[13] Italians benefited only to the extent that Italy enjoyed more imperial euergetism than did the cities of the provinces.[14]

The Roman state could be brutal to its subjects.[15] One of the distinctively Roman symbols of government was the *fasces*, the bundle of rods and an axe which represented the magistrate's coercive and punitive powers. It was in the face of state violence that the privileges of citizenship came to the fore. The *ius prouocationis*, guaranteed by the *lex Iulia de ui*, protected citizens from

[9] Neesen 1980 pp. 207–8. [10] See especially Kolb 2001 and Mitchell 1976.

[11] Cf. Nerva's boast, *VEHICVLATIONE ITALIAE REMISSA* (Smallwood *NTH* 30). See further Millar 1986 pp. 382–3.

[12] Mitchell 1976 p. 128 n. 145.

[13] See Rathbone 1996, Duncan-Jones 1994 pp. 33–4, Hopkins 1980 pp. 116–20 and Frank 1933–40 v chs. 1–3 on imperial expenditure.

[14] The evidence for a special relationship between the emperors and Italy is discussed by Patterson 2002, Purcell 2000, Brunt 1990 pp. 515–17, Millar 1986 and Eck 1979.

[15] Like many premodern societies, the Roman state relied on brutal and spectacular punishments to protect the community from criminals and outsiders. The savagery of Roman penalties is well evoked by MacMullen 1986.

summary corporal punishment, making it a capital offence for a governor or other magistrate to flog or kill a Roman citizen if he asserted his rights (with some exceptions).[16] Non-citizens enjoyed no such protection against extra-judicial violence by the Roman authorities (unless it was motivated by personal profit, in which case the Roman official could be charged under the extortion laws).[17] Even after conviction, Roman citizens might hope to be punished more leniently than non-citizens.[18] However, citizenship was not the only privilege recognised in the administration of justice. The *honestiores* – senators, equestrians, decurions (not all of whom were Roman citizens) and veterans – also enjoyed some protections against the punitive and coercive powers of the magistrates. By the early second century, their privileges exceeded those enjoyed by citizens.[19]

Conscription was another oppressive aspect of Roman rule. The Roman army probably always depended to some extent on levies to maintain its numbers.[20] With a requirement of twenty-five years of service, usually far from home (although local service became increasingly common after Hadrian), the levy must have been a heavy burden on the communities afflicted.[21] But it was not shared equally. Given the size of the army, conscription can have affected only a minority of the empire's population. The evidence shows that some provinces suffered more than others.[22] An effort seems to have been made to protect Italy from conscription, and the proportion of Italians serving in the legions certainly fell over the first two centuries CE. But it was not always successful: periodic conscription is attested even for Italy.[23] Formal immunity from military

16 *Dig.* 48.6.7, Paulus, *Sent.* 5.26.1 with Cloud 1989, Cloud 1988 and Garnsey 1966.
17 See Brunt 1980 p. 259 for aggravated offences under the *de repetundis* laws.
18 Cf. e.g. Dio 57.15.8 and Plin. *Ep.* 10.96.4, with Garnsey 1970 pp. 261–2 and 268–9.
19 Garnsey 1970. 20 Brunt 1974.
21 See Brunt 1974 pp. 103–7 (= *RIT* pp. 202–6) on conditions of service. The burden of conscription features prominently in the grievances of rebellious provincials as they are imagined in the Roman historians (e.g. Tac. *Hist.* 2.16.2, 4.14.1 and *Ann.* 4.46.1).
22 Estimates for the size of the army at various periods range from 300,000 (Mitchell 1983) to somewhat over 400,000 (Birley 1981). On the unequal burden of conscription, see Brunt 1974 p. 103 (= *RIT.* pp. 200–1) for a list of provinces where *dilectūs* are attested.
23 The declining proportion of Italian legionaries is shown by Webster 1998 p. 108, Mann 1983, Forni 1974 and Forni 1953. See Brunt 1974 pp. 97–9 (= *RIT* pp. 195–7) for evidence of intermittent conscription in Italy up to and including the second century CE.

service was limited to a few privileged individuals – from municipal priests and *apparitores* to philosophers, sophists and *grammatici* – who might be Italians or provincials, citizens or non-citizens.[24]

For the most part, local communities were left to govern themselves. However, Roman authorities did seek to ensure social and political stability by buttressing the power and privileges of local elites throughout the empire.[25] Moreover, certain issues of particular importance were removed from the cities' control. The governor generally assumed jurisdiction over capital crimes and major civil trials; his licence was required for major building projects; the emperor's permission was necessary for cities to raise local taxes.[26] On these issues, there was no great difference in the autonomy enjoyed by Italian and provincial, or citizen and non-citizen communities (and any that did exist were gradually eroded over the course of the first centuries CE).[27] Even Italian cities required imperial permission to raise taxes and were probably subject to the civil and criminal jurisdiction of higher authorities (the praetors and the praetorian prefects respectively).[28] Much more significant was the gap between all these cities and those communities which lacked city status – including rural communities 'attributed' (i.e. subjected) to a neighbouring municipality, tribes administered by military officers, and *coloni* on imperial and private estates.[29]

This brief survey should have revealed the inadequacy of any binary opposition when it comes to tracing the contours of power and privilege in the Roman empire. The distinction between

[24] *Vacatio militiae* is discussed by Brunt 1974 pp. 92–3 (= *RIT* pp. 190–1). For municipal priests and *apparitores* see the *lex coloniae Genetiuae* (*RS* 25) LXII 22–32 and LXVI 37–43; for philosophers, sophists and *grammatici* see *Dig.* 27.1.6.8.

[25] On Roman support for local elites, see especially Brunt 1976 pp. 163–6 and 172–3 (= *RIT* pp. 260–3 and 280–1) and de Ste Croix 1981 pp. 307–17. Cf. Woolf 1998 for the example of Gaul.

[26] Jurisdiction: Galsterer 1996. Building projects: Plin. *Ep.* 10.24 and *Dig.* 50.10.3 and 6 with Jones 1940 pp. 135–6. Raising taxes: *ILS* 6092 and Plin. *Ep.* 10.24 with Jones 1940 p. 135.

[27] See Eck 2000 pp. 278–81, Jacques 1984, Jones 1940 pp. 136–8 and Abbott and Johnson 1926 pp. 90–3 for the trend towards increasing intervention in the second century.

[28] Raising taxes in Italy: *ILS* 2666a with Brunt 1981 p. 161. Jurisdiction in Italy: Galsterer 1996 pp. 410–11.

[29] *Attributi*: Sherwin-White 1973 pp. 356–7. Prefectures: Jacques and Scheid 1990 pp. 188–9. Estates: Jacques and Scheid 1990 pp. 187–8 and Abbott and Johnson 1926 pp. 15–20.

citizens and non-citizens was important (though it is already complicated by the existence of an intermediate category, Latin status, which entailed some of the privileges of citizenship), but so too were those between Italians and provincials, between *honestiores* and *humiliores* and between more and less privileged communities, whatever the status of their residents. If Roman texts insist on dividing the inhabitants of the empire into rulers and subjects, this should be recognised as a Roman fiction – part of the self-image of the Roman elite.

peregrini

In modern scholarship, the non-citizen inhabitants of the empire are usually styled *peregrini* ('foreigners' or 'aliens').[30] This is certainly the technical term for a non-citizen in Roman law.[31] But it is not used anywhere near as widely – or precisely – outside legal discourse. General references to the *peregrini* are surprisingly rare in Latin literature, compared to the many references to 'the allies' (*socii*) and 'the provinces' (*prouinciae*). Seneca jokes that Claudius had to die before he could grant Roman citizenship to the whole world, because some *peregrini* had to be left for seed (*Apocol.* 3). Pliny apologises to Trajan for having requested the enfranchisement of an Egyptian doctor without realising that Egyptians, unlike other *peregrini*, were not eligible for Roman citizenship (*Ep.* 10.6.2). Suetonius records that the emperor Augustus expelled the *peregrini* from the city of Rome during a famine (*Aug.* 42.3). But these examples are few and far between, and largely limited to specifically legal contexts. As we will see, *socii* ('the allies') is by far the more common label for the non-citizen population of the empire.[32]

[30] Schwind 1995 is the only other survey of the use of *peregrinus* known to me. For the *princeps*, *subprinceps* and *optio peregrinorum* (first attested in the Trajanic period) – the officers of the *castra peregrina*, the base for seconded legionaries on the Caelian – see Baillie Reynolds 1923 with Mann 1988. For the Christian trope that believers were *peregrini* – a people whose city is not of this world – see Clark 2004 and Claussen 1991.

[31] See Gai. *Inst. passim*. That *peregrini* appear only twice in the *Digest* reflects the minimal importance of the category following Caracalla's general grant of citizenship. On *peregrini* as a legal term, see further Berger 1953 and Kübler 1937 with Mathisen 2006 esp. pp. 1020–1 for the fourth century CE.

[32] On the use of *externi* ('foreigners') to refer to non-citizens, see p. 234.

It is also important to note that *peregrinus* is not used exclusively as a term for those who lack Roman citizenship. Many of the *peregrini* who figure in the literature and epigraphy of the empire are potentially, and in some cases certainly, Roman citizens. First, the term is used in its legal sense of non-citizen in the context of local citizenship as often as it is of Roman citizenship. In the imperial period, it became the norm to hold Roman citizenship jointly with citizenship of one's city of origin.[33] Municipal epigraphy uses *peregrinus* of those who are not local citizens, regardless of whether they are Roman citizens.[34] The *collegia peregrinorum* (associations of *peregrini*) that are known from cities in Britain, Spain and Germany were not associations of men who lacked Roman citizenship, but rather of those who lacked the local citizenship of the communities in which they lived or traded.[35] Similarly, the point of the *peregrini negotiatiores* who appear in the idealised world of the declamations is not that they are not Roman citizens, but that they are not citizens of the towns in question.[36]

Second, and more important, *peregrinus* always retains the more general meaning of 'foreigner' in addition to its legal sense of 'non-citizen'. It can be a marker of ethnicity, culture or origin, as well as legal status.[37] When L. Manlius Torquatus accused Cicero of being the third 'foreign king' of Rome (*peregrinus rex*) after Tarquin and Numa, this was an ethnic slur against the son of Arpinum, not a challenge to his legal status as a Roman citizen.[38] The Gallic nobles whom Julius Caesar recruited to the senate are called *peregrini* by Suetonius (*Iul.* 80.2). His point is that they were foreigners, not that they lacked citizenship (which they almost certainly held already).[39]

[33] On the development of dual citizenship, see Sherwin-White 1973 esp. pp. 295–306 and 382.

[34] See e.g. *CIL* v 376 and *AE* 2002 1115.

[35] See *RIB* 69, 70 and 71, *ILS* 3905 and 7066, *CIL* XIII 6451 and 6453 and *AE* 1928 181, with Frere and Fulford 2002. See *ILS* 3905 and 7066 for examples of members of *collegia peregrinorum* who have Roman names.

[36] Sen. *Controv.* 2.7, Quint. *Decl. min.* 363.

[37] It is unfortunate that Schwind 1995 conflates these functions (p. 1309.46–74).

[38] See Cic. *Sull.* 22–5.

[39] As Syme has shown, these Gallic senators were probably a mix of citizen colonists from Gallia Cisalpina and Narbo and native dynasts from Gallia Narbonensis whose families had received Roman citizenship one or two generations earlier. See Syme 1937 pp. 130–1 (= *RP* I 33–5), Syme 1939 pp. 79–80 and Syme 1938 p. 15 (= *RP* I 102–3).

When Tacitus writes of the enthusiasm for literature shown by the *peregrini* who come to Rome from the municipalities and colonies, the reference to *municipia* and *coloniae* is clear proof that they are Roman citizens (*Dial.* 7.4). These *peregrini* are marginalised by their origin, ethnicity or culture – not their legal status.

Another ethnic category in the Roman imperial lexicon is *gentes* ('the peoples').[40] From Cicero to Florus, the Roman people is styled the 'conqueror' (*uictor*), 'master' (*dominus*) or 'ruler' (*princeps*, *imperator*, etc.) 'of the peoples' (*gentium*) or 'of all peoples' (*omnium gentium*).[41] These and similar references to the *gentes* represent the empire as a composite of different peoples, united in their subjection to the *populus Romanus* or *gens Romana*.[42]

The use of ethnic categories such as *gentes* and (in some cases) *peregrini* well into the second century CE deserves emphasis, given the tendency in modern scholarship to play down the significance of any ethnic component in Roman self-fashioning.[43] There must have been an ethnic dimension to debates about what it was to be 'Roman' in the first and second centuries CE. Some

[40] Sherwin-White 1973 pp. 437–46 discusses the use of the Latin *omnes gentes* and the Greek τα ἔθνη to refer to the empire as a whole. He notes that *gentes* is not quite synonymous with *prouinciae*, but does not go into the different criteria of division it implies. Nor does he consider how it implicitly delineates the ruling power as a *gens* or *populus*.

[41] *uos omnium gentium domini* (Cic. *Leg. agr.* 2.22), *populus dominus regum, uictor atque imperator omnium gentium* (Cic. *Dom.* 90), *princeps populus et omnium gentium dominus atque uictor* (Cic. *Planc.* 11), *populus Romanus omnium gentium uictor* (Cic. *De or.* 2.76), *nos principes orbis terrarum gentiumque omnium* (Cic. *Phil.* 3.35), *populus Romanus uictor dominusque omnium gentium* (ibid. 6.12), *populus Romanus imperatores omnium gentium* (Sall. *Iug.* 31.20), *populus Romanus gentium moderator* (Sall. *Hist.* 1.55.11), *uictor omnium gentium populus* (Sen. *Controv* 2.1.5), *ciuitas domina gentium* (Vell. Pat. 2.29.4), *ille uictor pacatorque gentium populus* (Sen. *Ben.* 5.15.6), *populus gentium uictor* (Plin. *HN* praef. 16), *dominus gentium populus* (Suet. *Calig.* 35.3), *uictor gentium populus* (Flor. 1.44.3), *populus gentium uictor orbisque possessor* (ibid. 2.1.2), *regum et gentium arbiter populus* (ibid. 2.6.7), *Romani gentium domini* (ibid. 2.26.14).

[42] *gens Romana*: Varro's *De gente populi Romani*, Verg. *Aen.* 1.33 (*tantae molis erat Romanam condere gentem*, a ringing line in a seminal text; cf Quint. *Inst.* 8.5.11) and 6.788–9, Livy 43.11 and 9.3.12, Sen. *Controv.* 10.4.3, Val. Max. 2.4.2 and 5.1.1a, Manilius 3.23, Ov. *Fast.* 2.687, Luc. 9.1014, Suet. *Claud.* 25.3, Fronto *De bello Parthico* 1.

[43] The role of ethnicity in Roman discourses of identity, too often ignored amid claims that being 'Roman' was a political or juridical identity, has recently been re-emphasised by Farney 2007 and Dench 2005 (esp. ch. 4).

provincial citizens, notably the inhabitants of settler *coloniae* and the descendants of other Italian emigrants, could and did claim to be more 'Roman' or 'Italian' than others. Natives of the Spanish provinces who claimed descent from Italian settlers seem to have called themselves *Hispanienses*, to distinguish themselves from the indigenous population, who were called *Hispani*.[44] In the civil wars of 69–70 CE, a long-running conflict between the Gallic cities of Lugdunum and Vienna broke out into open warfare. Lugdunum was a settler colony, established in 43 BCE. Vienna was also a *colonia* of Roman citizens, but its status was an honorary grant; it was originally a native settlement, the tribal capital of the Allobroges. In Tacitus' version of events, the inhabitants of Lugdunum appealed to the legions to support them against the 'foreign' (*externa*) city of Vienna (Tac. *Hist.* 1.65.2). Ethnicity evidently played an important role in at least some constructions of the Roman community.

socii

Socius is a word whose semantic range overlaps with the English 'companion', 'partner', 'ally'.[45] Besides its use in the context of personal relationships and legal partnerships, it also has an important place in the Roman lexicon of empire. It is a very flexible term, whose scope of reference can vary widely depending on the context (more on this later). In a military context, it often serves to denote the non-citizen troops in Rome's armies – the *auxilia* as opposed to

[44] *Hispanienses* vs *Hispani*: Charisius, *Gramm. Lat.* I 106 Keil and e.g. Vell. Pat. 2.51.3 and Mart. 12.*praef*, with Arnold 1889. Cf the Spanish-born Seneca's contempt for *Hispani* at *Apocol.* 3.3.

[45] Wegner 1969 is the fullest discussion of the semantics of *socius*. The most significant analyses of its function in the context of Rome's empire are those of Mommsen 1887–8 III pp. 659–63 and 724–5 and Wegner 1969 ch. 4 (a very limited analysis, which ends with Cicero – and does not even give an adequate account of the complexity of his usage). More cursory treatments include Gruen 1984 ch.1 esp. p. 25 n. 66, Paul 1984 pp. 33–4, Sherwin-White 1984 ch. 3, Harris 1979 pp. 135–6, Sherwin-White 1973 p. 186, Dahlheim 1968 pp. 163–6, Badian 1958 p. 114, Accame 1946 p. 54 n. 2, Heuss 1933 pp. 26 n. 1 and 58 n. 1, Horn 1930 pp. 9–12, Matthaei 1907 and Marquardt 1881–5 I p. 72 (almost all of whom focus exclusively on the Republican period, especially the second century BCE).

the legions.[46] But by far its most common function is to refer to the non-citizen population of the empire. Indeed it is the most common term for the non-citizen subjects of the empire outside the jurists. *Socius*, not *peregrinus*, is the usual antonym of *ciuis* (citizen) throughout surviving Latin literature.[47] The two nouns are often paired in the plural to form a dyad – 'citizens and allies' (*ciues et socii*) – which encompasses the entire population of the empire. A few examples from the early second century will illustrate this widespread usage. Pliny commends Trajan for providing for the welfare of both citizens and allies (*satis factum qua ciuium qua sociorum utilitatibus*, *Pan.* 33.1). In Tacitus, Augustus is praised for treating citizens justly and allies with restraint (*ius apud ciuis, modestiam apud socios*, *Ann.* 1.9.5) and Tiberius consoles himself for the loss of his son by devoting himself to the rights of citizens and the requests of allies (*ius ciuium, preces sociorum tractabat*, *Ann.* 4.13.1). This usage is not limited to literature. It can also be found, for example, in a first-century CE building inscription from Corsica which commemorates harbour works for the benefit of 'citizens and allies'.[48] Used with general reference (i.e. referring to 'the allies' as a class), *socii* embraces all Rome's dependants. It is a term of the widest application, capable of including allied kingdoms and nominally free peoples as well as the inhabitants of the provinces proper. It can extend to everyone who is neither a citizen nor an enemy (*hostis*).[49] By the second century CE, we will see, it could even encompass provincial citizens. That *socii* evolved from a label for a particular kind of dependent community into a generic term capable of encompassing all non-citizens has long been noted, but the process has never been properly analysed.[50] This section

[46] See the examples at Saddington 1970 pp. 90, 94–5 and 107.

[47] See further *TLL* s.v. *ciuis* 1229.9–15. In Cicero, for example, the *ciuis~socius* dyad occurs twenty-six times; *ciuis~peregrinus* only six times. In Tacitus, the former appears ten times; the latter only once.

[48] *Ciuibus sociis* (*AE* 1982 441). The inscription is dated by the editor on stylistic grounds.

[49] *Socii* are regularly contrasted with *hostes*. See *TLL* s.v. *hostis* 3061.33–5. Horn 1930 pp. 9–12 famously concluded that, in Cicero, a *socius* is anyone who is not a *civis* or a *hostis* (p. 11). As we will see, this is an over-simplification.

[50] Note Marquardt 1881–5 I p. 72 and Mommsen 1887–8 III pp. 660 and 725.

will explore how the label 'allies' acquired so wide an application in the provincial empire of the Late Republic and Principate.

The Republican background

Before the enfranchisement of all Italians in the years following 90 BCE, *socii* was the *mot propre* for the non-Latin Italian allies. It is often paired with the 'Latin Name' in phrases such as *socii ac nomen Latinum* ('the allies and the Latin Name') and *socii nominis Latini* (literally, 'the allies of the Latin Name') to refer to the Italians as a whole.[51] The label was certainly also applied to some non-Italian peoples, though its precise scope is a matter of controversy. There has been a long debate about the meaning of the terms *socius* and *amicus et socius* ('friend and ally') in the language(s) of Roman public law and diplomacy in the third and second centuries BCE. It is generally accepted that the use of these terms in Livy and other historians is hopelessly confused.[52] But some scholars have argued that it is wrong to expect legal precision from these later writers, and claimed that it is possible to reconstruct an underlying framework. The term *socii* has been held to be the preserve of peoples who had a formal treaty with Rome or, alternatively, peoples obliged to provide military support to Rome.[53] The major divergences between the various models

[51] See e.g. the *senatus consultum de Bacchanalibus* of 186 BCE which stipulates: 'Let no man who is a Roman citizen or one of the Latin name or the allies wish to attend a meeting of Bacchants' (*Bacas uir nequis adiese uelet ceiuis Romanus neue nominus Latini neue socium quisquam, ILLRP* 511, 7–8). The expression *socii nominis Latini* clearly encompasses the non-Latin Italians as well as the Italians (Briscoe 2008 pp. 216–17). It probably originated as an asyndeton with the genitive undeclined (cf. *socii ac nominis Latini* at Livy 41.8.9 and 41.9.9), though surviving texts treat it as if the genitive were dependent on *socii*. See further Mommsen 1887–8 III.1 pp. 660–3 and Wegner 1969 pp. 95–104. On the structure of Rome's relationship with the Italian *socii*, see Rich 2008 and Sherwin-White 1973 ch. 4.

[52] The inconsistency of the historians is well demonstrated by Dahlheim 1968 pp. 163–4 and Matthaei 1907 pp. 186–7.

[53] Many scholars have concluded that the title *socius* was originally and/or properly reserved for communities that had a formal treaty with Rome. See e.g. Dmitriev 2010 p. 185, Reynolds 1982 p. 77 and Mommsen 1887–8 III.1 pp. 659–60. Matthaei 1907 argued that it was properly used of an even narrower category – those peoples who were treaty-bound to give military support to Rome – and that all other peoples who had amicable relations with Rome but were bound to nothing more than neutrality in the case of war were designated *amici* or *amici et socii*, regardless of whether they had a formal treaty with Rome. Dahlheim 1968 p. 164 n. 1 agrees that the term properly implies some

(especially as regards the term *amicus et socius*) hardly inspires confidence. Others have rejected any such framework, concluding that both *socius* and *amicus et socius* were honorific titles used widely and inconsistently of a range of different autonomous peoples, to denote an amicable relationship.[54]

Setting aside the testimony of later writers, the contemporary evidence is maddeningly limited. We know that the Roman state kept an official list of 'friends' or 'allies' (or both), which included communities and individuals, but we do not know how exclusive these statuses were.[55] Letters and *senatus consulta* sent to Greek cities in the second and first centuries BCE show that Rome bestowed the title 'friend and ally' widely in its diplomatic relations with those cities.[56] However the meagre evidence for the use of *socii* as a category in Roman public law suggests that it may have had a more restricted application there. The term appears in the two second-century laws preserved on the *tabula Bembina* from Urbino. In the extortion law (probably 123 or 122 BCE), the list of statuses in the fragmentary first line (almost certainly an enumeration of the classes of persons entitled to bring a prosecution under the law) reserves the term *socii* for the non-Latin communities of Italy and possibly also non-Italian communities that possessed a treaty with Rome. It clearly excludes other peoples who are 'in the control, dominion and power (*in arbitratu dicione potestate*) or in the friendship (*in amicitia)* [of the Roman

form of military cooperation. Sherwin-White 1984 pp. 58–70 argues that the position of *socius*, more properly *amicus et socius*, was a regulated status 'reserved for free states that had done something to earn it' (66), most of whom will have had formal treaties with Rome (69), and that these were distinct from the *amici*, a group which included cities and individuals of inferior status (66).

54 So Gruen 1984 ch. 1 and esp. p. 25 n. 66 and p. 47.

55 The *SC de Asclepiade* (78 BCE) provides for the enrolment of the Greek naval captains in a 'Schedule of Friends' (*formula amicorum*) (*RDGE* 22, 12). The *SC de Aphrodisiensibus* (8 BCE) resolves that the Aphrodisians are to be exempt from tribute and enrolled 'in the number of the allies' ([εἰς τὸν συ]μμάχων ἀριθμὸν καταταγῆναι, *A&R* 8, 32). Livy also records the addition of Lampsacus and a Macedonian noble to a 'Schedule of Allies' (*formula sociorum*) in 170 and 169 BCE respectively (43.6.10 and 44.16.7). These Livian passages may (i) be imprecise references to the *formula amicorum*, (ii) testify to the existence of a separate *formula sociorum* or (iii) indicate that there was a single list whose proper title was the *formula sociorum et amicorum*. See further Bowman 1990, who concludes that what was originally a *formula sociorum* was expanded to a *formula amicorum et sociorum* in the first century. Both Bowman and Marshall 1968 think these statuses primarily concerned diplomatic reception at Rome.

56 See Eckstein 1999 pp. 407–8, Kallet-Marx 1996 p. 185 and Dahlheim 1965 pp. 165–6.

people]'.[57] In the later agrarian law (111 BCE), a reference to 'any Roman citizen or ally (*socius*) or member of the Latin name' is clearly limited to Italians, since the latter two categories are glossed as 'those from whom [they are accustomed to demand troops in the land of Italy] according to the *formula togatorum*'.[58] However, the term may have been used with a much wider scope in the *lex de provinciis praetoriis* of 100 BCE, which had the declared goal of ensuring that 'the Roman citizens and the allies of the Latin name and likewise of the [foreign] peoples who are in the friendship of the Roman people be able to sail in safety'. Here the familiar phrase 'allies of the Latin name' seems to have been extended by the addition of 'and of [foreign] peoples' to encompass a much wider group of dependants, perhaps including Rome's provincial subjects. But we are dependent here on two Greek translations, which are inconsistent in their phrasing and confused in their syntax, and it is possible that the term was applied only to the Italians.[59] It is

[57] *[– quoi socium no]minisue Latini exterarumue nationum, quoiue in arbitratu dicione potestate amicitiau[e populi Romani –] / ...* '[any of the allies] or of the Latin Name or of the foreign peoples or anyone in the control, dominion and power or the friendship [of the Roman people] ...' (*RS* 1,1). *Socium* is a conjecture here, but some form of *socii* is certain before the reference to the *nomen Latinum*. The natural way to construe the first three elements (*socium nominisue Latini exterarumue nationum*) is as three coordinate genitives linked by the two *–ue*'s (as translated above). In this case the *socii* are the non-Latin Italians (so Venturini 1979 pp. 52–81 and Sherwin-White 1982 pp. 19–20). But it is just conceivable, given the tortured syntax to which the asyndeton *socii Latini nominis* sometimes give rise, that *nominis Latini* and *exterarum nationum* are both dependent on *socium* (i.e. 'the allies of the Latin name or of the foreign peoples') in which case the term would extend to some non-Italian peoples, presumably those with a formal treaty, but would still exclude those denoted by the second *quoi* clause (so Lintott 1992 pp. 110–11 and Crawford 1996 p. 95).

[58] *quei in eo agro loc[o ceiuis] Romanus sociumue nominisue Latini, quibus ex formula togatorum [milites in terra Italia inperare solent, agrum lo]cum publicum populi Romanei de sua possesione uetus possesor proue uetere posseso[re dedit]* (*RS* 2, 21). The clause concerns entitlement to land granted in compensation for land used in the establishment of a colony. For the *formula togatorum*, which recorded the military obligations of the Latin and Italian allies, see Brunt 1971 pp. 545–8.

[59] οἵ τε πολῖται Ῥωμαίων οἵ τε σύμμαχοι ὀνόματος Λατίνου ὁμοίως τε τῶν ἐθνῶν, οἵτινες ἐν φιλίαι τοῦ δήμου Ῥωμαίων εἰσίν, ὅπως μετ' ἀ[σ]φ[α]λείας πλοΐζεσθαι δύνωνται (*RS* 12 Cnidos II 6–11). Crawford 1996 p. 253 suggests the original Latin was: *ciues Romani socii nominis Latini itemque nationum quae in amicitia populi Romani sunt.* The phrase recurs with slight variation in the provision for the consuls to write to foreign peoples, though it is rendered differently in the two Greek translations: ὥστε τοὺς πολίτας Ῥωμαίων καὶ τοὺς συμμάχους Λατίνους τε τῶν τε ἐκτὸς ἐθνῶν, οἵτινες ἐν τῆι φιλίαι τοῦ δήμου Ῥωμαίων εἰσίν, μετ' ἀσφαλείας πλοΐζεσθαι δύνωνται (Cnidos III 31–5, shifting abruptly from consecutive to final construction) and ὅπως πολῖται Ῥωμαίων σύ[μμαχοί]

also significant that the sweeping reference occurs in the preamble to the law and not its specific provisions, where more precise usage might have been necessary. By the end of the first century BCE, however, *socii* has certainly acquired a much wider reference in Roman law. The *senatus consultum Caluisianum* of 4 BCE, which established an alternative procedure for extortion trials, provides that the new procedure can be used if 'any of the allies' (τινες τῶν συμμάχων in the Greek translation) apply in person to one of the magistrates empowered to convene the senate.[60] Here the term 'allies' evidently extends to any non-citizen who might be expropriated by a Roman governor.

In short it is possible that *socii* remained a term with very specific application in Roman public law into the first century BCE (perhaps limited to the non-Latin Italians and certainly excluding the population of the provinces), but the evidence is limited and it had clearly acquired a wider reference by the end of that century. In any case, my concern extends beyond the technical discourse of the law, and it is certain that *socii* was from an early period used

τε ἐκ τῆς Ἰταλίας Λατῖνοι τά τẹ [ἐκτὸς ἔθνη], [οἵτινες ἐν τῆι φιλίαι τοῦ δήμου τοῦ Ῥωμαίων εἰσίν, κατὰ θ]άλασσαν ἀσφαλῶς πλεῖν δύνω[νται] (Delphi B 6–7). Crawford 1996 p. 254 suggests as the original Latin text: *ciues Romani socii nominis Latini exterarumque nationum quae in amicitia populi Romani sunt*. As always, the references to 'the allies of the Latin name' and 'the Latin allies' encompass both Latins and other Italians (n. 51 above). The most natural way to construe the references to the foreign peoples in the genitive both in the first two Greek texts and in the posited Latin originals is as dependent on σύμμαχοι / συμμάχους / *socii* and coordinate with ὀνόματος Λατίνου / Λατίνους / *nominis Latini* respectively, translating along the lines of 'the citizens of Rome and the allies both of the Latin name and of the foreign peoples who are in the friendship of the Roman people' (as Lintott 1992 p. 111 seems to suggest). The English translation in Crawford 1996, however, construes the foreign peoples as coordinate with the citizens and allies, rendering the first formula as 'the Roman citizens and the allies of the Latin name and likewise those of the [foreign] peoples who are in the friendship of the Roman people' and the second as 'the citizens of Rome and the allies and the Latins and those of the foreign nations who are …'. This is a forced translation of the Greek (and the posited Latin). To dissociate the foreign peoples from the allies, a third nominative (an accusative in the second text) would be required. However, the third Greek text (Delphi B 6–7) does render τά τε ἐκτὸς ἔθνη in the nominative so it is just possible that the Latin original read *itemque nationes exterae* and *nationesque exterae* – and that the term *socii* was reserved for the Italians.

60 Oliver 12, 97–101. The law survives in a Greek translation, prefaced by an edict of the emperor Augustus, on a stele from Cyrene. The term is used in the same wide sense in the preamble, which declares that the *senatus consultum* concerns the welfare of 'the allies of the Roman people' (τὴν τῶν συμμάχων τοῦ δήμου τοῦ Ῥωμαίων ἀσφάλειαν, 88–9) and notes that the first extortion laws had been established to make it easier for 'the allies' (οἱ σύμμαχοι) to seek redress (91–2).

with a much wider reference in other contexts. Mommsen thought that it was the enfranchisement of the Italians after the Social War that spurred what he regarded as the misuse of the term to refer to subject peoples.[61] The disappearance of Italian *socii* must indeed have led to a significant shift in the function of the term in Roman discourse. But it is already being applied to thc inhabitants of the provinces in some of the earliest surviving Latin prose, well before the Italian enfranchisement. In a speech in which he boasts of his good conduct as provincial governor, the Elder Cato insists: 'never did I impose prefects on the towns of your allies to plunder their property and children'.[62] Valerius Maximus records the *seueritas* of the second-century consular T. Manlius Torquatus who, when his son was accused of extortion during his term as governor of Macedonia in 141 BCE, took it upon himself to sit in judgement and found him guilty. Valerius quotes his pronouncement that he was satisfied that his son 'took moneys from the allies' (*pecunias a sociis accepisse*).[63] Later in the second century, Q. Caecilius Metellus (later Numidicus) prosecuted a Valerius Messalla for extortion, probably in his capacity as governor of Asia *c.* 120 BCE. A fragment of his speech refers to 'allies' coming to the senate to complain of massive sums of money having been exacted from them.[64] Similar language is used by an unidentified second- or first-century orator quoted in the *Rhetorica ad Herennium* (a rhetorical treatise probably dating from the 80s BCE) who makes exemplary use of *praeteritio* to implicate an opponent in extortion: 'I do not mention that you have taken moneys from the allies (*ab sociis pecunias accepisse*)'.[65] These texts demonstrate that *socii* was

[61] Mommsen 1887–8 III.1 p. 660, though he recognises elsewhere that the use of *socii* to refer to subjects was as old as subjection itself (p. 725).

[62] *numquam <ego> praefectos per sociorum uestrorum oppida imposiui, qui eorum bona liberos diriperent* (*ORF* 8.203 = Sblendorio Cugusi 1982 no. 168). This is from a speech on the *sponsio* he made with Marcus Cornelius which he quotes in his *De sumptu suo* of 164 BCE which is in turn quoted by Fronto. For the original context see Sblendorio Cugusi 1982 ad loc. and Astin 1978 p. 108 n. 13. Cato was governor of Sardinia in 198 BCE and Spain in 195 BCE. For the imposition of *praefecti* on provincial cities, cf. Livy 43.2.12.

[63] Val. Max. 5.8.3.

[64] *socios ad senatum questum flentes uenisse sese pecunias maximas exactos esse* (*ORF* 58.8). The sentence fragment is cited by Gellius (*NA* 15.14.2). For the historical context see Brennan 2000 II pp. 903–4 n. 166 and Syme 1955 pp. 70–1 (= *RP* I pp. 290–1).

[65] *Rhet. Her.* 4.37.

used of provincials well before the Italian enfranchisement – at least when it came to accusations of misconduct by Roman governors (a context I will return to below). In the same period, however, the term could also be used with a much narrower reference to denote the Italians alone. When, for example, the author of the *Rhetorica ad Herennium* writes that the senate considered whether to grant citizenship to 'the allies' during the Social War, he is obviously referring to the Italians alone, not all provincials.[66]

Thus far the evidence is limited and open to divergent interpretations, though it is clear that *socii* was already being used with a varying – and potentially wide – scope of reference. The picture sharpens dramatically with the advent of Cicero, whose extensive corpus finally permits a robust analysis of the term. Cicero's usage clearly illustrates the protean quality of *socii* in the time he was writing (81–43 BCE). When Cicero uses the term with general reference, it often has a narrowly circumscribed extension (i.e. scope of refererence), denoting some subset of Rome's subjects. The *socii* are often contrasted with the *prouinciae* ('the provinces') or the *stipendiarii* ('the tributaries'), in which contexts they must be Rome's nominally autonomous dependants (the 'free peoples' and probably also the allied kingdoms) as opposed to the provincialised population.[67] *Socii* is only one element in a rich lexicon that Cicero uses to describe different modes of association and subjection, often deployed in elaborate lists which disaggregate the components of Rome's empire. The most common formula is the triad *prouinciae*, *liberi populi* (or *liberae ciuitates*), *regna* (or *reges*), in which the three terms presumably denote the provincialised population, the autonomous 'free peoples' and the allied kingdoms respectively (2 *Verr.* 3.207 and 5.168, *Leg. agr.* 1.8 and 2.98, *Balb.* 9). But there

[66] *Rhet. Her.* 3.2. Cf. ibid. 4.22 and *ORF* 43.11.

[67] *Socii* vs *prouinciae*: *Leg. Man.* 71, *Sest.* 98, *Prov. cons.* 13, *Deiot.* 15, *Nat. D.* 3.69, *Off.* 2.27. *Socii* vs *stipendiarii*: *Div. Caec.* 7, 2 *Verr.* 4.134, *Pis.* 98, *Leg.* 3.41, *Balb.* 24. Cf. *Balb.* 27. The *stipendiarii* owe their name to the *stipendium*, the normal term for provincial tribute in the Republic. It is only in the Principate that it is displaced by *tributum*, which was originally the term for the tax periodically levied on citizens until its abolition in 168/7 BCE. See Brunt 1981 p. 161 (= *RIT* p. 325) and Brunt 1966 pp. 2–3 (= *RIT* pp. 349–50). Cicero also uses *socii* to refer to the Italians before the Social War. See especially *Phil.* 12.27 and cf. *socii et nomen Latinum* and similar formulae at *Sest.* 30, *Balb.* 20 and 21, *Brut.* 169, *Rep.* 1.31 and *Fam.* 13.30.1.

are many variations: *socii, amici, stipendiarii* (*Leg.* 3.41), *reges, liberi populi, socii, prouinciae* (*Deiot.* 15) *socii, foederati, liberi populi, stipendiarii* (*Pis.* 98) and *prouinciae, ciuitates liberae, socii, amici, reges* (*Leg. agr.* 1.11).[68] These lists are highly inconsistent in both elements and order. It would be futile to attempt to articulate a single consistent definition for most of thc individual terms. It is probably misguided to expect even the elements of each individual list to be mutually exclusive and collectively exhaustive. The composition of these lists is driven by considerations of structure, rhythm and sound rather than concern for legal precision.[69] *Socii* is particularly slippery, demanding a different interpretation in almost every case. Nevertheless, these lists share a vision of empire which stresses difference rather than similarity among Rome's dependants.[70] They imply the existence of a complex hierarchy of subjection, rather than a simple divide between Romans and subjects.

In all these examples, the *socii* are some privileged group which explicitly excludes Rome's provincial subjects (who are called *prouinciae* or *stipendiarii*). Elsewhere, however, Cicero uses the term with a much broader extension which clearly includes those provincials. Throughout his corpus, the subjects who are abused and (more rarely) safeguarded by Roman governors and their staffs are called *socii*.[71] This is also the term he uses when describing his own activities as governor of Cilicia.[72] In a letter of advice to his

[68] Note also other lists which expressly exclude Rome's tributaries: *socii, reges, ciuitates liberae* (*Sest.* 64), *socii, exterae nationes, reges, tetrarchae* (*Mil.* 76) and *socii, exterae nationes, reges* (*Leg. agr.* 2.47).

[69] See, for example, Vasaly 1993 pp. 222–4 on the variety of such lists in *De lege agraria* 1 and 2 and the rhetorical concerns that drive them.

[70] Richardson 2008 pp. 89–90 and 187, who also notes the significance of these lists, connects them to the fact that *imperium* does not yet have a territorial sense in Cicero. Where later authors could use that word to encompass the whole territory and population ruled by Rome, he argues, Cicero can only fall back on lists such as these. But Cicero *is* capable of using *socii* as a single generic category encompassing all the peoples denoted by these lists.

[71] Corrupt governors are accused of plundering and abusing the 'allies' (*direptio, uexatio sociorum*, etc.): *2 Verr.* 3.88, *Leg. Man.* 57 and 66, *Leg. agr.* 2.32 and 2.72, *Cat.* 1.18, *Sull.* 71, *Pis.* 38, 40 and 48, *Phil.* 10.12, *Parad.* 6.43, *Off.* 2.75 and 3.36, *Fam.* 10.32.2, fr. 9.7 Schoell. The extortion laws were established for the protection of the 'allies': *Div. Caec.* 17–18 and 65, *Verr.* 42, *2 Verr.* 2.15 and 3.127. Good governors show regard for the 'allies': *Planc.* 64, *Leg.* 3.9.

[72] *Fam.* 2.13.3, 15.1.3, 15.3.2 (cf Cato's response at 15.5.1) and 15.4.10.

brother Quintus in his capacity as governor of Asia, Cicero disaggregates the population of that province into citizens (*ciues*) and allies (*socii*).[73] As this passage shows, the *socii* are specifically the non-citizen population of the province. Like later authors, Cicero regularly employs 'citizens and allies' as a dyad to refer to the whole Roman world. Pompey is the commander demanded by everyone, allies and citizens alike (*ab omnibus sociis et ciuibus*, *Leg. Man.* 5); Catiline is accused of murdering citizens and harassing and plundering the allies (*ciuium neces, uexatio direptioque sociorum*, *Cat.* 1.18); a provincial governor is urged to stay by all allies and citizens (*ab omnibus sociis ciuibus*, *Scaur.* 35); a legate's service in Africa impresses citizens and allies alike (*et ciuibus et sociis*, *Lig.* 2).[74] Used in this broad sense, the term embraces all Rome's non-citizen subjects and dependants, eliding any potential distinctions between them.

The rhetoric of the extortion court

It should be clear both that *socii* has a prominent place in Cicero's imperial lexicon and that it is a labile term whose extension can vary widely from context to context. Juxtaposed with other categories such as *prouinciae*, *stipendiarii*, *liberi populi* and *reges* it can serve as a label for some relatively small and usually privileged class of dependants. Elsewhere, it is an umbrella term capable of encompassing all those other categories and working to elide the potential distinctions in the condition of Rome's dependants. Cicero's corpus also offers some insight into what can be at stake in the use of *socii* in one sense rather than another. Particularly significant is the care with which he chooses his terms in his speeches for the *quaestio de repetundis*, the court which allowed provincials to recover moneys extorted by Roman officials.[75] In 70

[73] Note especially *Q Fr.* 1.1.6 on the character of the *socii* and *ciues* of Asia (*constat enim ea prouincia primum ex eo genere sociorum quod est ex hominum omni genere humanissimum, deinde ex eo genere ciuium qui* …). Cf. ibid. 10, 22 and 24.

[74] See also *Leg. Man.* 48, *Red. sen.* 6, *Har. resp.* 58, *Prov. cons.* 12 and 17, *Pis.* 96, *De or.* 2.196, *Rep.* 3.37, *Off.* 2.27, *Fam.* 2.5.1.

[75] On the *quaestio de repetundis* (the standing court for the recovery of assets), see especially Lintott 1992 pp. 10–29 and Lintott 1981a. Cf Brunt 1961 (= *RIT* pp. 53–95) for the Principate.

BCE Cicero undertook the prosecution of Gaius Verres for offences during his term as governor of Sicily, for which he produced seven speeches (only two of which were actually delivered; the others were published after Verres fled Rome). In later years he found himself on the other side of the extortion court, defending Marcus Fonteius' conduct as governor of Gallia Narbonensis (69 BCE), Lucius Valerius Flaccus' conduct in Asia (59 BCE) and Marcus Aemilius Scaurus' conduct in Sardinia (54 BCE).[76] All three of these defence speeches survive, at least in part. It is instructive to observe how Cicero exploits the indeterminacies of the vocabulary of empire to meet the very different rhetorical demands of persuading jurors to convict and to exonerate Romans accused of corruption abroad. These speeches show that the choice of terminology can play a part in a broader strategy of persuasion.[77]

Throughout the *Verrines*, Cicero makes a point of referring to his Sicilian clients as 'allies' (*socii*) and 'friends and allies' (*socii et amici*) of the Roman people.[78] He insists that all Sicilians are *socii*, even though he himself acknowledges that Sicily is comprised of communities with very different statuses – some of which came under Roman control through treaties of alliance, others by conquest.[79] The language of alliance, with the expectations it raises about the Romans' responsibilities to their so-called 'allies', resonates with the benevolent ideals that Cicero espouses throughout the Verrines, notably by representing the Sicilians as Rome's clients (see Chapter 5). The use of *socii* seems to be part of a broader strategy of insisting that Verres' abuse of his office has violated the Romans' collective obligations towards their provincial subjects.

[76] The *Pro Rabirio Postumo* is omitted even though it was delivered in the *de repetundis* court because the case turned on a technical point of law (the liability of those who received money or goods extorted from the provinces).

[77] The use of *socii* is certainly not the only difference between Cicero's prosecution and defence speeches in the *de repetundis* court. For a broader perspective on Cicero's contrasting strategies see Lintott 2008 chs. 7 and 8, Riggsby 1999 pp. 120–50 and Vasaly 1993 pp. 191–218 (none of which addresses the use of *socii*).

[78] Sicilians and other provincials are called *socii* 91 times and *socii et amici* 29 times in the *Verrines*.

[79] For all Sicilians as *socii*, see especially *2Verr.* 5.115 (*cuncti Siculi, fidelissimi atque antiquissimi socii*) and also *Div. Caec.* 12, *2Verr* 2.154 and 3.228. On the different legal statuses of Sicilian cities, see Cic. *2Verr.* 3.13.

This hypothesis about the affective content of the label *socii* is confirmed by its absence from the later speeches for the defence. It is used seven times in the *Pro Fonteio*, but never of the aggrieved provincials. Instead it is applied exclusively to the citizens of the city of Massilia (long-time allies of Rome), who were testifying on Fonteius' behalf.[80] The rest of the inhabitants of the province are explicitly denied the title of *socii* when Cicero insists that *all* the 'allies' are on Fonteius' side:[81]

laudant omnes uestri ciues atque socii, oppugnant idem qui saepissime hanc urbem et hoc imperium oppugnarunt.

All your citizens and allies praise him; those who attack him are the very men who have so often attacked this city and this empire. (Cic. *Font.* 35)

Similarly, the *Pro Flacco* grants the label *socii* not to the aggrieved people of Asia as a whole but to the inhabitants of the one community that supported Flaccus.[82] The same avoidance of the label *socii* can be seen in the *Pro Scauro*, where it is used only once – and then to describe the inhabitants of another province (*Scaur.* 35). Tellingly, Asconius' first-century CE commentary on the speech calls the Sardinians what Cicero would not – *socii*.[83]

The defence speeches propound a polarised view of the Roman world which divides it into Romans and foreign enemies, leaving no room for an intermediate category of dependent peoples. Ethnic labels are ubiquitous, with repeated references to *Galli* in the *Pro Fonteio*; *Graeci*, *Phrygi*, *Lydi* and *Mysi* in the *Pro Flacco*; and *Sardi* and *Afri* (because of the Sardinians' connection to the Carthaginians) in the *Pro Scauro*. The recurring ethnonyms mark the provincials as foreigners and support Cicero's strategy of appealing to ethnic stereotypes in order to disparage the evidence

80 *Font.* 13, 15 (twice), 32 (twice), 34, 35.

81 The contrast between the Massiliote *socii* and the rest of the province recurs at *Font.* 15 and 32.

82 *Flacc.* 71. It is used of other provincials at *Flacc.* 86 and 99, but never specifically of the inhabitants of Asia.

83 Asconius tells us that the prosecution was afraid that Scaurus would use the money he had extorted from the 'allies' (*pecunia quam a sociis abstulisset*) to buy the consulship (Asc. p. 19.11–12 Clark). This is precisely the language we might expect the prosecution to have used.

against his Roman clients.[84] The provincials are not just foreigners, but enemies. The *Pro Fonteio* insists that all the Gauls have recently waged war on Rome (*Font.* 12). The *colonia* of Narbo is a 'watchtower and outpost' set up against them (ibid. 13). Cicero chides the jurors for imagining that the Gauls are anything but congenitally hostile to Rome:

an uero dubitatis, iudices, quin insitas inimicitias istae gentes omnes et habeant et gerant cum populi Romani nomine? sic existimatis eos hic sagatos bracatosque uersari, animo demisso atque humili, ut solent ei qui adfecti iniuriis ad opem iudicum supplices inferioresque confugiunt? nihil uero minus. hi contra uagantur laeti atque erecti passim toto foro cum quibusdam minis et barbaro atque immani terrore verborum … tamen esset vobis magno opere providendum ne, quos ita adflictos a vestris patribus maioribusque accepissetis ut contemnendi essent, eos pertimuisse et eorum minis et terrore commoti esse videremini.

Surely you realise, jurors, that all these peoples have and pursue an innate hostility to the name of the Roman people? Do you think these cloaked and trousered men bear themselves with the subdued and humble demeanour that is customary among those who have suffered injustice and seek refuge as suppliants and inferiors in the assistance of judges? Far from it. No, they are strolling throughout the Forum, in good spirits, heads held high, threatening us and terrifying us with their barbaric and monstrous voices … Even so, you should be taking great pains not to appear to fear and be distressed by the terrifying threats of peoples whom your fathers and ancestors left so crushed as to be despised. (Cic. *Font.* 33–4)

Empire here is an avowedly adversarial relationship. Rome's Gallic subjects will always be her enemies. Their proper state is one of submission and subservience; they ought to be crushed and despised. The climax of the speech represents the prosecution of Fonteius as yet another Gallic invasion of Rome (ibid. 44–6). The *Pro Flacco* too brands the aggrieved provincials enemies as well as foreigners. The Jews, who had complained that Flaccus prevented them from making their customary contributions to the Temple in Jerusalem, are explicitly labelled *Iudaei et hostes* ('Jews and enemies', *Flacc.* 68). As for the Greek inhabitants of the province, Cicero points out that they too were recently enemies and recalls their rebellion during the Mithridatic War (*Flacc.* 58 and 60–1). Even now, he tells the jury, they hate Rome:

[84] Vasaly 1993 pp. 193–205.

in hac igitur urbe se iactant quam oderunt, apud eos quos inuiti uident, in ea re publica ad quam opprimendam non animus eis, sed uires defuerunt.

And so they strut around in this city which they hate; among men whom they detest seeing; in a state which they lacked only the strength, not the will, to destroy. (Cic. *Flacc.* 61)

In short, eschewing the label *socii* is only part of a broader strategy of dismissing his clients' provincial accusers as foreign enemies and representing empire as a hostile, adversarial relationship in which any hint of provincial defiance is to be mercilessly crushed.

The use of *socii* as a label for the inhabitants of the provinces is evidently loaded with implications about the Romans' obligations to their subjects. It is surely no accident that all the second-century examples of *socii* being used in this sense occur in the context of accusations of misconduct by governors. The term lent itself to the needs of those who sought to champion a benevolent style of imperialism or to mobilise outrage at a senatorial rival – whether in the extortion court itself or in the broader arena of personal invective that characterised Roman political discourse throughout the Republic.[85] But there were other perspectives on the proper ends and means of Roman power, and the extortion court was obviously one site in which these different visions of empire were tested against each other. We should not be too quick to dismiss this as a sham. Influence, bribery and factional interests will certainly have played an important role in a court where prominent careers were at stake. Yet at least some of the changing cast of jurors must have wanted to see justice done. And these cases confronted them with an ethical dilemma, bringing the impulse for solidarity with their fellow Romans (and, in Cicero's time, fellow senators) into conflict with more enlightened ideals of governance. Some votes may well have been swayed by the more persuasive attempt to resolve or reframe this ineluctable problem. Case after case, year after year, the extortion court will have constituted an ongoing debate about the nature and ethics of empire. Extortion trials continued in the Principate, though jurisdiction passed from the standing court to the senate (and, for non-senators, the

[85] On the discourse of immorality in Republican politics, see especially Edwards 1993.

emperor), and will have continued to bring the impulse for senatorial solidarity into conflict with concern for the provincial population.[86] Yet most of this rhetoric has been lost. Besides the speeches discussed here, all from the hands of a single author and indeed from a period of only fifteen years, we have only a few fragments of other orators and allusions to extortion trials in the historians and the letters of Pliny. This is a sobering reminder of the limits of any history that we can write about Roman discourse about empire.

The socii *after Cicero*

Cicero uses the label *socii* in two distinct ways which embody very different perspectives on the structure of empire. Used as a label for one of several different classes of subject community, it highlights differences in the condition of Rome's subjects and contributes to a vision of the Roman world as a mosaic of different types of community. Used as an umbrella category for all Rome's non-citizen subjects, it works to elide any distinction other than that between citizens and non-citizens. The two perspectives coexist in Cicero. The latter clearly predominates in later writers. Writers of the first and second centuries CE show little interest in the different statuses of non-citizen communities (though the legal distinctions persisted) and instead almost universally choose to conflate all Rome's subjects under a single generic label, most often *socii*. The elaborate lists and even the differentiating vocabulary which Cicero uses to disaggregate the subject communities all but disappear from Roman discourse.

After Cicero, *socii* is almost exclusively employed as a generic term for all Rome's subjects. Provincials are regularly labelled *socii* and the citizen–ally dyad widely used to encompass the population of the empire as a whole.[87] *Socii* is occasionally used

[86] On changing jurisdiction, see Brunt 1961 pp. 198–201 (= *RIT* pp. 63–6).

[87] Provincials are called *socii* by Caesar's continuators (*B Afr.* 26.3), Sallust (*Cat.* 52.6, 52.12, *Iug.* 31.25, 44.1, *Hist.* 2.47.6, 2.94; cf. Paul 1984 pp. 33–4 on *socii* in Sallust), Livy (e.g. 34.20.3, 39.7.7), Valerius Maximus (4.1.7, 5.8.3, 6.9.7, 6.9.8, 7.6.1c, 8.1.abs.6, 8.7.6), Asconius (p. 19.12 Clark), Quintilian (*Inst.* 4.1.49, 7.4.33, 12.7.2) and Frontinus (*Str.* 4.1.15). For the second century see pp. 61–6. For *ciues~socii* as a dyad, see *B Alex.* 70.7, Sall. *Cat.* 29.3 and 52.20, [Sall.] *Ad Caes. sen.* 1.5.6, Sen. *Clem.* 2.2.1, [Quint.] *Decl. maiores* 3.16 and, for the second century, n. 130 below.

retrospectively to refer to the Italians before their enfranchisement.[88] But it is almost never used to refer to the free peoples or any other special class of dependent community in the empire of the present. A handful of exceptions from the second century CE illustrate the continued plasticity of the term – and also the tendency to archaism in literature of that period.[89] But the overall trend is clear.

The displacement of the narrow sense(s) of *socii* by its generic sense is paralleled by the disappearance of many of the other terms that Cicero uses to denote particular modes of dependency. 'The free peoples' or 'the free states' (*liberi populi* or *liberae ciuitates*) appear as a constituent part of the Roman world some twenty times in Cicero's writings, often in contrast with the provincialised population (*prouinciae* or *stipendiarii*).[90] In all of the first and second

[88] See e.g. Livy *passim*, Val. Max. 6.4.1, 8.6.4, Asc. p. 22.5 and 7 and p. 67.23 Clark and Tac. *Ann.* 1.79.3 (with Furneaux 1896–1907 and Goodyear 1972–81 ad loc.) and 3.27.2.

[89] The one possible exception from the first century is a passage from Asconius' commentary on Cicero's *In Pisonem*, in which he misquotes Cicero's *amicos sociosque* as *socios stipendiariosque*, thus implicitly distinguishing the *socii* from the tribute-paying provincials (Asc. p. 16.21 Clark, ad Cic. *Pis.* 89). But this mistake probably reflects Asconius' knowledge of Cicero's usage elsewhere (cf Cic. *Div. Caec.* 7, 2*Verr.* 4.134, *Balb.* 24), rather than the usage of his own time. In the second century, Pliny twice contrasts the *socii* with the provincialised population (*prouinciae*) in his *Panegyricus* (*Pan.* 7.5 and 17.1). These formulations, reminiscent of Cicero (see n. 67 above), are probably part of the wider strategy of employing a Ciceronian political vocabulary in this speech (see n. 133 below). Tacitus twice uses *socii* to refer to particular sub-groups in the empire. See Tac. *Hist.* 3.55.2 (*foedera sociis, Latium externis dilargiri*), where the *socii* are probably the free peoples and the *externi* provincialised communities (so Mommsen 1887–8 III p. 725), and *Ann.* 15.45.1 (*peruastata Italia prouinciae euersae sociique populi et quae ciuitatium liberae uocantur*). The latter formula has given rise to widely divergent interpretations (contrast Mommsen 1887–8 III p. 725 n. 4, where the *socii* are the provincialised population, with Nipperdey and Andresen 1915 ad loc., where they are the *foederati*), which illustrates the slipperiness of the term. The *socii* are also contrasted with the 'subject peoples' (*nationes sub dicione*) in vows for the safety of the empire and the emperor from the reign of Marcus Aurelius. Though fragmentary, both *CFA* 85 (= *CIL* VI 32383a = 2093) and 87 (= *CIL* VI 32384 = 2094) appear to preserve the formula of the same vow to Jupiter (presumably from the records of two different years), the key part of which has been reconstructed as *si r(es) p.(ublica) p.(opuli) R(omani) Q(uiritium) imperium Romanum exercitus socii nationes quae sub dicione p.(opuli) R(omani) Q(uiritium) sunt incolumes erunt*. The reading is not certain (*socii* here is a conjecture from *s*[– in *CFA* 87 and *nationes* a conjecture from –]*s* in *CFA* 85), but ritual is one context in which we might expect to see such continuity with Republican language.

[90] *Liberi populi* or *liberae ciuitates* contrasted with *prouinciae*/*stipendiarii*: 2*Verr.* 3.207 and 5.168, *Leg. agr.* 1.8, 1.11, 2.15, 2.34 and 2.98, *Balb.* 9, *Pis.* 98, *Deiot.* 15; contrasted

centuries CE, the generalising plural appears only twice outside the jurists.[91] 'The tributaries' (*stipendiarii*) are another class that is important for Cicero. He mentions them five times, usually in contrast with the free peoples (*socii* or *liberi populi*).[92] Yet they are notably absent from later texts. Setting aside Pliny the Elder's geographic survey (a text that is explicitly concerned with legal status and probably drawn from an Augustan source),[93] *stipendiarii* appear only once. Recording Nero's seizure of the property of a former governor who committed suicide before he could be convicted of extortion, Tacitus cynically notes that the emperor had no intention of using it to compensate the aggrieved *stipendiarii* (*Ann.* 4.20.1). It is significant that the term is not used in contrast with *socii* as it is in Cicero but rather to encompass all the inhabitants of the province, emphasising their role as tax-paying subjects. The similar *tributarii* ('tributaries') is used in the same way. A freedman in Petronius' *Satyricon* claims to have become a slave voluntarily because he preferred to be a Roman citizen rather than a *tributarius* (*Sat.* 57; he was evidently confident of his chances of being manumitted). *Tributarius* is his pejorative label for the non-citizen status he has left behind him.[94] When Suetonius records that Augustus once refused to grant citizenship to a Gallic *tributarius* (Suet. *Aug.* 40.3), the contrast is again with citizens rather than other classes of dependant. These passages illustrate the ideological importance of tribute as a symbol of subject status for these Roman writers (this despite the fact that many provincial citizens paid taxes in full).[95] But what matters

with *foederati* (the subset of free peoples that had a formal treaty with Rome): *Balb.* 22, 52, *Pis.* 98; appear alone: 2 *Verr.* 4.68, *Dom.* 23, *Sest.* 64 and 84, *Prov. cons.* 7, *Phil.* 9.4, *Att.* 1.19.9, *Fam.* 15.4.3.

91 Tac. *Ann.* 15.45.1 and Suet. *Vesp.* 8.2. Cf. also Plin. *Ep.* 8.24.2 and 7 on the *liberae ciuitates* of Achaea. Jurists: Proculus apud *Dig.* 49.15.7.1, Aelius Gallus apud Festus, *Gloss. Lat.* p. 244 Lindsay; cf. Servius' note ad Verg. *Aen.* 3.20.

92 *Div. Caec.* 7, 2 *Verr.* 4.134, *Prov. cons.* 10, *Balb.* 24, *Leg.* 3.41.

93 Pliny notes communities of *stipendiarii* twelve times in the geographical survey of Books 3–5 of the *Natural History*. This survey preserves its source's attention to legal status. That source appears to have been Augustan in date (see Shaw 1981 and Teutsch 1962). The *stipendiarii* appear nowhere else in the *HN*.

94 The use of *tributarius* where Cicero would have said *stipendiarius* reflects the displacement of *stipendium* by *tributum* as the term for the direct taxes levied from the provinces. See n. 67 above.

95 These are not the only texts to construct tribute as a mark of subject status, despite the liability to tribute of many provincial citizens (on which see pp. 28–9). Cicero describes provincial *stipendium* as Rome's reward for victory (*quasi uictoriae*

for the purposes of this chapter is, first, that *stipendiarii* and *tributarii* are exceedingly rare in the discourse of the Principate and, second, that when they do appear it is not as one of several categories of dependant, as in Cicero, but rather as alternative labels for provincials or non-citizens in general. They are thus further evidence for the use of a generic rather than differentiating terminology of subjection. This generic terminology displaces the lists of different classes of dependant that are so common in Cicero's descriptions of the Roman empire. No similar list survives from the first century CE, and only four from the second (which may again reflect that period's interest in the language of the past).[96]

All this amounts to a rationalisation of the lexicon of empire. A complex taxonomy of different modes of subjection and dependence gives way to a simple dichotomy between Roman citizens and their subjects. Although there continued to be considerable diversity in legal status among the non-citizen communities of the empire, Roman writers after Cicero show little interest in these distinctions and instead choose to conflate all Rome's non-citizen subjects within a single generic category. This development is part of a broader shift in the language of empire. The same period also saw significant changes in the meaning of both *imperium* and *prouincia*, two other staples of the imperial lexicon.[97] Both terms were originally used in an abstract rather than a territorial sense. A *prouincia* was a magistrate's sphere of responsibility, often ad hoc

praemium et poena belli, Cic. *2 Verr.* 3.12). Statius too connects tribute with conquest. Praising a senator who fulfilled Vespasian's instructions in raising the tax rate in Africa, he labels the tribute a *triumphal* honour won without need of a war (*Libyci quid mira tributi | obsequia et missum media de pace triumphum | laudem?* Stat. *Silv.* 1.4.83–5). At the end of the second century, Tertullian writes that paying tribute was a mark of inferior status and captivity: *sed enim agri tributo onusti uiliores, hominum capita stipendio censa ignobiliora (nam hae sunt notae captiuitatis)* (Tert. *Apol.* 13.6). On the ideological implications of the tribute, see further Mattern 1999 pp. 157–8 and Corbier 1988 pp. 259–60.

96 Pliny, Tacitus and Suetonius each offer a single instance: *exercitus prouincias socios* (Plin. *Pan.* 7.5), *Italia prouinciae ... sociique populi et quae ciuitatium liberae uocantur* (Tac. *Ann.* 15.45.1), *prouinciae ciuitatesque liberae nec non et regna quaedam* (Suet. *Vesp.* 8.2). Another list survives in the fragmentary vows for the safety of the empire and the emperor from the reign of Marcus Aurelius: *imperium Romanum exercitus socii nationes quae sub dicione populi Romani Quiritium sunt* (see n. 89 above).

97 The evolution of these terms has been traced by Richardson 2008, Richardson 2003 and Richardson 1991.

and loosely delimited, not a fixed administrative space. *Imperium* denoted 'power', properly that of a magistrate. References to the *imperium* of the Roman people do not appear until the first century BCE and, when they do, they have the same abstract sense – better translated as 'Roman dominion' or 'supremacy' than 'the Roman empire'.[98] It was a political fact, not a territory. Foreign peoples lived under Roman *imperium*, not within it. It is only in the mid first century BCE that *prouincia* begins to be used to denote territories ruled by Rome and not until the Augustan period that *imperium* is first used in a territorial sense, denoting a bounded space subject to Roman rule.[99] With a delimited territory comes a defined population, and it is probably no accident that Roman usage increasingly represents Rome's subjects as a single, homogeneous category in this period. The *socii* are a class of subjects distinguished both from their Roman rulers and from those outside the reach of Roman power.

These discursive shifts coincide with a change in imperial practice. The period of Roman expansion produced a wide range of different connections between Rome and the communities that came under its sway. This was partly a product of the Roman habit of adopting and adapting existing structures of power, from Hiero's system in Sicily to the institutions of the Hellenistic kingdoms in the East. It also reflected a general preference for ad hoc arrangements tailored to specific circumstances over standardised forms of administration. The Principate saw the gradual rationalisation of administrative practices and the homogenisation of the position of the subject communities. This can be seen, for example, in the progressive encroachment on the privileged status of the 'free cities', nominally immune from the jurisdiction of the provincial governors but increasingly subject to intervention by imperial *curatores*.[100] The evolving usage of *socii* is thus implicated in these broader developments in the administrative structures of empire.

[98] The *imperium populi Romani* is first mentioned at *Rhet. Her.* 4.13. See Richardson 2008 p. 56.

[99] *Prouincia* as territory: Richardson 2008 pp. 81–3. *Imperium* as territory: ibid. ch. 4.

[100] For increasing intervention, see n. 27 above.

prouinciales

In the second century CE, the noun *prouinciales* ('provincials') is widely used – like its cognate *prouinciae* ('the provinces') – to denote the inhabitants of the provinces. This is a relatively late development. The noun appears nowhere in Cicero and is first attested in the *Alexandrian War*, a text written by one of Caesar's continuators in the 40s BCE. The adjectival form is certainly older, occuring twenty-four times in Cicero. But it is almost exclusively used to denote a sphere of activity for Romans, not to refer to people or things native to the provinces.[101] Cicero's use of the adjective reflects the original sense of *prouincia*, denoting the task or responsibility assigned to a magistrate or pro-magistrate. These *prouinciae* were not necessarily geographic (the urban praetor's *prouincia* was the administration of law in the city of Rome), though many were. They were not necessarily carried over from year to year, though again many were. There is no evidence of *prouincia* being used to refer to a territory, in the sense of English 'province', before the first century BCE.[102] Although Cicero does use *prouincia* in such a sense, and even uses it metonymically to denote the population of that territory, the adjective *prouincialis* retains its close connection with Romans and public office.[103] It is often used to specify conduct in an official capacity. When Cicero tells Atticus that his own manner of receiving visitors when governor of Cilicia was not at all 'provincial' (*aditus autem ad me minime prouinciales*, *Att.* 6.2.5), he means that he did not behave like a magistrate in his province – that is, like other provincial governors. *He* did not employ a *cubicularius* ('chamberlain'). Cicero's client Sestius is described as showing unusual *prouincialis abstinentia* ('restraint in office', *Sest.* 7) as a military tribune and *integritas prouincialis* ('honesty in office', *Sest.* 13) as

[101] There are only three exceptions: references to *testes prouinciales* ('witnesses from the province [of Sicily]', *2Verr.* 1.20), *clientelae hospitiaque prouincialia* ('clients and guest-friends in the provinces', *Cat.* 4.23) and *prouincialis dilectus* ('a levy from the provinces', *Fam.* 15.1.5). A similar use can be observed in Caesar who describes a tribe of Gauls as being *prouinciales* – 'part of the province' (*B Gall.* 7.7.4).

[102] On the semantics of *prouincia* in the second century, see Richardson 2008 ch. 2. For non-geographic *prouinciae*, see ibid. p. 79 n. 56.

[103] For Cicero's metonymic use of *prouincia* and *prouinciae* to denote a population, see pp. 42–3 and Richardson 2003 pp. 83–4.

quaestor – very different from the *prouincialis parsimonia* ('provincial thrift') that Tacitus will later ascribe to the city of Marseille (*Agr.* 4.2). Service on the staff of the governor of Africa gave Cicero's client Caelius *prouincialis usus* (probably 'experience in office' rather than 'experience in the provinces'). Explaining to Atticus why he chose to write to the new governor of Macedonia about Atticus' affairs in the province rather than discussing them in a face-to-face meeting, he says he thought they were not *prouincialia*, by which he means that 'they did not concern his province', 'were not official business' (*Att.* 2.1.12). Cicero does also use *prouincialis* to denote a space outside Rome, but it is almost exclusively with reference to the actions and interests of himself and his peers. He writes of *prouincialia negotia* ('activities in the provinces'), *officia prouincialia* ('services rendered in the provinces') and *prouincialia commoda* ('profitable opportunities in the provinces').[104] (It is worth noting that, for Cicero, Italy outside Rome is a 'provincial' space. The antonym to *prouincialis* is *urbanus*, not *Italicus* and Sestius' aforementioned *integritas prouincialis* was displayed in Italy, where he served as a military tribune.[105]) Most significant of all, the *prouinciales homines* and *uiri* ('provincial men' or, better, 'men in the provinces') who appear in Cicero are always Romans abroad, not native inhabitants of the provinces. In his letter of advice to his brother Quintus, he distinguishes between the *prouinciales homines* and the *Graeci* of the province of Asia – i.e. between the Romans resident in the province and its native inhabitants.[106] He even describes himself as a *homo prouincialis* during his time as governor of Cilicia.[107] *Socii*, not *prouinciales*, is the word Cicero uses to refer to the native inhabitants of the provinces.

[104] *Prouincialia negotia*: *Mur.* 43. *officia prouincialia*: *Fam.* 5.19.1 and 16.4.3 (contrasted with *officia urbana*). *prouincialia commoda*: *Att.* 1.17.5 (contrasted with *commoda urbana*). See also *Q Fr.* 1.1.43 (*administratio prouincialis* vs *urbana* of a magistracy held in the provinces rather than the city) and *Fam.* 2.7.4 (*haec prouincialis molestia* of Cicero's unpleasant absence from Rome as governor of Cilicia).

[105] For *prouincialis~urbanus*, see 2*Verr.* 1.20, *Cat.* 4.23, *Att.* 1.17.5, *Fam.* 16.4.3 and *Q Fr.* 1.1.43.

[106] See Cic. *Q Fr.* 1.1.15 (*prouinciales uiri*, contrasted with the *Graeci* at 1.1.16) and 18 (*prouinciales homines* vs *Graeci*). The distinction between *prouinciales* and *Graeci* is essentially identical to that between *ciues* and *socii* which Cicero makes elsewhere in the letter (*Q Fr.* 1.1.6, 10, 22 and 24 with n. 73 above).

[107] Cic. *Fam.* 3.8.1. Cf the similar use of *prouinciales amici* at Cic. *Fam.* 15.20.2.

The evidence for the next century is too exiguous to trace the steps by which *prouincialis* evolved from a label for Romans abroad into a term for all provincials. It is first attested as a noun in the *Alexandrian War* (40s BCE), which records that the rapacity of Cassius Longinus, a praetor in Spain, induced the *prouinciales* to plot his murder.[108] The scope of reference here is unclear. The would-be assassins named later in the text are all men with Roman names from the city of Italica, an Italian settlement founded by Scipio Africanus.[109] It is therefore conceivable that the term is being used with same narrow reference as Cicero's *prouinciales homines* and that we are meant to understand that it was specifically the Roman citizens in the province who were involved in the plot.[110] But the text also says that the whole province (*omnis prouincia*) hated the praetor, which would be consistent with construing the earlier reference to *prouinciales* as encompassing the entire population of the province.[111] In any case, the term has clearly acquired the broader extension when it next appears in the speech of the emperor Claudius advocating the admission of Gauls to the senate (47/8 CE). Although Italians may make better senators than *prouinciales*, says the emperor, *prouinciales* should not be rejected if they can add to the splendour of the senate house.[112] Here the term is employed as the complement of *Italicus*, encompassing all the inhabitants of the provinces. Writing in the 60s CE, Columella similarly contrasts *prouinciales agricolae* (provincial farmers) with Italians.[113] *Prouinciales* also appear in Seneca,

[108] *quibus de causis accidit ut, cum Longinus imperator eadem faceret quae fecerat quaestor, similia rursus de morte eius prouinciales consilia inirent* (*B Alex*. 50.1).

[109] *B Alex*. 52.3–4. See App. *Hisp*. 38 for the foundation of Italica.

[110] Note that the two other instances of *prouincialis* in the text are in reference to Romans or Italians. See *B Alex*. 55.2 where Annius Scapula, another man with an Italian name, is a *prouincialis homo* and 53.5 where a Roman legion long stationed in Spain 'becomes provincial' (*factus prouincialis*).

[111] *nemo enim aut in prouincia natus, ut uernaculae legionis milites, aut diuturnitate iam factus prouincialis, quo in numero erat secunda legio, non cum omni prouincia consenserat in odio Cassii* (*B Alex*. 53.5).

[112] *quid ergo? non Italicus senator prouinciali potior est? ... sed ne prouinciales quidem, si modo ornare curiam poterint, reiciendos puto* (Smallwood *GCN* 369 = *ILS* 212, ii 5–8).

[113] See especially 3.13.1 and also 4.33.6 and 5.4.3. Note that in the last passage, Columella – himself a native of Gades in Spain – identifies himself with a Roman *nos* in contrast to 'the provincial countryman': 'what we achieve by soil preparation, he [the *prouincialis rusticus*] achieves by making a furrow'.

Asconius and the Elder Pliny, though the identity of those so described is indeterminate.[114]

By the end of the first century CE, references to *prouinciales* are widespread and invariably encompass all the inhabitants of the provinces. In the technical language of the law, the term denotes those who are resident in a particular province and thus subject to the governor's jurisdiction. The Younger Pliny writes about a difficult extortion trial in which he represented the province of Baetica. When the governor Caecilius Classicus died before he could be prosecuted, the plaintiffs sought to pursue his accomplices instead. The case turned on the question of whether men who were *prouinciales* (and so subject to the governor) could be punished for assisting him. Pliny succeeded in securing several convictions – apparently to the surprise and chagrin of the defence.[115] According to the third-century jurist Ulpian, the condition of being *prouincialis* was a matter of residence, not birth. In his commentary on the Provincial Edict, he glosses *prouinciales* as referring to 'those who are resident in the province, not those who are born in the province'.[116] The term is used in wider discourse to refer not only to the inhabitants of particular provinces but also the inhabitants of the provinces as a whole. Pliny describes his representation of the inhabitants of Africa and Baetica in extortion trials as 'aiding the *prouinciales*' (*Ep.* 2.11.2). Tacitus, in his version of Claudius' speech on the admission of Gauls to the senate, recalls the extension of the citizenship first to the Transpadani (Italians north of the Po) and then to the best of the *prouinciales* (*Ann.* 11.24.3). Suetonius describes how Vespasian restored the senate's numbers

[114] Seneca praises the virtue of Helvia's sister by observing that during the sixteen years her husband served in Egypt, she never admitted a *prouincialis* into the house (*Helv.* 12.19.6). Asconius, in his commentary on Cicero's speeches, notes that the quaestor Cn. Calpurnius Piso was murdered in Spain by aggrieved *prouinciales* in 64 BCE (Asc. p. 92.23 Clark). The Elder Pliny writes of the filtering of dung for manure by 'some *prouinciales*' (Plin. *HN* 17.53) and of a physician who treated a wealthy *prouincialis* (*HN* 29.22).

[115] Plin. *Ep.* 3.9.15. For the key question, see also 6.29.8 ('at issue was the question of whether *prouinciales* should be punished for being the governor's associates and agents').

[116] *prouinciales eos accipere debemus, qui in prouincia domicilium habent, non eos, qui ex prouincia oriundi sunt* (*Dig.* 50.16.190). It is worth insisting that Ulpian's definition asserts that the term can encompass non-native residents, not that it is limited to them.

by co-opting the best Italians and *prouinciales* (*Vesp.* 9.2). *Prouinciae* is used synonymously, the provinces standing by metonymy for their inhabitants.[117] Both *prouinciales* and *prouinciae* are regularly contrasted with the inhabitants of Italy or – more narrowly – Rome itself.[118] In all these examples, the reference to *prouinciales* clearly encompasses the whole provincial population. There is no basis for the view of some scholars that *prouincialis* refers specifically to men of curial rank or – even more narrowly – members of provincial councils.[119]

The appearance and proliferation of the noun *prouinciales* is further evidence of the growing importance of generic categories in

[117] See the examples catalogued by Richardson 2008 at p. 169 n. 186 and p. 174 n. 237.

[118] *Prouinciae~Italia* or *prouinciales~Italici*: Plin. *Ep.* 9.23.2, Tac. *Hist.* 1.50.2, *Ann.* 3.54.4, 11.22.5, 13.42.4, 15.45.1, Suet. *Iul.* 54.2, *Vesp.* 9.2. *Prouinciae~urbs* or *prouinciales~urbani*: Tac. *Hist.* 1.4.1, *Ann.* 3.34.2, 13.21.4, Suet. *Aug.* 33.3, *Calig.*13.1. They are sometimes contrasted with the armies (*prouiniciales~milites* or *prouinciae~exercitus*) so as to denote the civil population of the provinces. See Tac. *Hist.* 1.4.1, 2.4.2, 4.57.2, 5.1.1, Plin. *Ep.* 10.52.1, 53.1, 100.1, 101.1, 103.1, *Pan.* 59.3, Suet. *Aug.* 64.1, 89.2, *Tib.* 38.1, *Calig.* 13.1, *Ner.* 37.3, 43.1.

[119] Schrickx 2006 p. 2343.42–54 claims that *prouinciales* sometimes refers specifically to the members of provincial councils or local curiae; van den Hout 1999 p. 431 (ad Fronto, *Amic.* 1.18.1) glosses it as 'local magistrates'. There is no first- or second-century evidence for *prouincialis* used with so narrow a reference. The examples that Schrickx cites from Tacitus, Pliny and Fronto show only that the label could be applied to local elites, not that it denoted them exclusively. In the inscription that van den Hout cites as evidence for a narrow sense (*CIL* VIII 587), *Prouincialis* is not a title but the cognomen of the imperial freedman and procurator who dedicated it. Conversely, there is ample evidence that *prouinciales* could encompass all provincials. Besides the examples cited in the text, note also Plin. *Ep.* 9.23.3 (where a stranger asks Tacitus whether he is Italian or *prouincialis*), Tac. *Hist.* 2.80.3 (where the reference to *prouinciales* encompasses the whole non-military population of Syria, coextensive with the metonymic *prouincia* in the preceding sentence) and 2.98.1 (where *prouinciales* denotes the whole population of the province of Africa, coextensive with the reference to *socii* at 97.2). There is, however, some scattered evidence to suggest that *prouinciales* may have acquired a narrower application in the fourth and fifth centuries. When the fourth-century historian Eutropius praises Constantius for his care for the wealth of both *prouinciales* and *priuati* (Eutr. 10.1.2), *prouinciales* seems to be referring to men with public office as opposed to ordinary provincials (*priuati*). It may be used in the same sense in a fifth-century imperial constitution warning provincial governors, their staffs and *prouinciales* that they will be held responsible if they permit violence against Jews or pagans (*Cod. Theod.* 16.10.24.1), particularly since *prouinciales* is replaced by *principales* (a term for local magnates, see Kotula 1982 and *TLL* s.v. *principales* p. 2292, 15–48) in the later copy of the constitution preserved in the *Justinian Code* (*Cod. Iust.* 1.11.6.1), a substitution which suggests that the two could be synonymous. Yet there is also clear evidence that *prouinciales* continued to be used of provincials in general (see pp. 69–70). In any case there is no doubt about the broad scope of the term in the second century.

the Roman language of imperialism. Like *socii*, *prouinciales* is a category that imposes a simple binary divide on the population of the empire. But its emergence also points to a second important development in the discourse and practice of empire. Whereas *socii* usually denotes non-citizens as opposed to citizens, *prouinciales* denotes the inhabitants of the provinces as opposed to those of Italy. The proliferation of references to *prouinciales* over the course of the first century CE reveals a new focus on geography rather than legal status (leaving open the question of whether provincials are defined by residence or birth). In what is an implicit devaluation of the significance of citizenship, it becomes increasingly common for provincial citizens to be bracketed with non-citizens in collective opposition to the inhabitants of Italy. A new distinction between Italians and provincials – that is between centre and periphery – comes to rival, and to some extent displaces, the traditional distinction between citizens and non-citizens in the imaginary geography of empire.

Implicit in this discursive shift is a reconfiguration of the terms in which elite identity is conceptualised and expressed. Those close to the centre of power increasingly distance themselves from provincial citizens by conflating them with the non-citizen population of the provinces. In Pliny and Tacitus it is as often 'the provinces' as 'the allies' who are represented as being the subjects of empire. When Pliny exclaims on the provinces' good fortune in having 'come under our protection and authority' (*quam nunc iuuat prouincias omnes in fidem nostram dicionemque uenisse*, *Pan.* 32.1), his imperial '*nos*' is opposed to 'the provinces', not 'the allies'. One of Tacitus' rebels notes more darkly that 'it is with the provinces' blood that the provinces are conquered' (*prouinciarum sanguine prouincias uinci*, *Hist.* 4.17.2). A Roman general tries to dissuade Gallic tribes from revolt by warning them that the other provinces will remain loyal (*superesse fidas prouincias*, *Hist.* 4.57.2).

This tendency to conflate provincial citizens with non-citizens is probably a response to the ever wider dissemination of Roman citizenship in this period. It is a natural development in the rhetoric of social exclusion, by which the many new citizens in the provinces are implicitly excluded from the locus of power and privilege.

With the label *prouincialis* emerges a derogatory discourse of provinciality in which provincials are derided for their lack of culture.[120] Its practical consequences can be seen in the privileges that elevated the inhabitants of Italy over Roman citizens in the provinces.[121] Like the 'new men' of the Republic, provincial newcomers to the imperial elite could, and did, invert this elite rhetoric of social exclusion with a counter-rhetoric of provincial virtue, which located traditional values in the periphery and decadence in the centre. A famous example is Tacitus' valorisation of his father-in-law Agricola's provincial origins.[122] Tacitus may well have been a provincial himself, from Gallia Narbonensis.[123] Yet a story retold by his friend Pliny hints that even he was leery of the label provincial:

numquam tamen maiorem cepi uoluptatem, quam nuper ex sermone Corneli Taciti. narrabat sedisse secum circensibus proximis equitem Romanum. hunc post uarios eruditosque sermones requisisse: 'Italicus es an prouincialis?' se respondisse: 'nosti me, et quidem ex studiis.' ad hoc illum: 'Tacitus es an Plinius?'

Nothing has ever given me more pleasure than a story I recently heard from Cornelius Tacitus. He was describing how a Roman knight sat beside him at the last races. After a wide-ranging and learned discussion, the knight asked him, 'Are you an Italian or a provincial?' He answered, 'You already know me from your reading.' To which the knight replied, 'Are you Tacitus or Pliny?' (Plin. *Ep.* 9.23.2)

For Pliny the point of the story is that he and Tacitus were paired as the literary stars of the time. But what is striking for my purposes is the *non sequitur* with which Tacitus responds to the question about his origins. It looks as if the eminent senator might be trying to obfuscate his provincial roots.[124] Elsewhere he writes scathingly of

120 Syme 1999 ch. 7 claims that imperial literature does not show as much prejudice against provincials as one might expect (i.e. as much as he observed in contemporary England?), though he qualifies this by noting that so many surviving authors were provincials themselves and will have been wary of raising the topic of provincial extraction (p. 44). In any case there are numerous examples of slurs against provincial origins. See the examples collected by Farney 2007 pp. 234–6 and Hemelrijk 1999 pp. 317–18 n. 204.

121 See pp. 27–32.

122 For the self-presentation of *noui homines*, see Wiseman 1971 pp. 107–16. See Tac. *Agr.* 4.2 on Agricola's origins in Gallia Narbonensis and Syme 1999 ch. 7 for similar examples.

123 On Tacitus' origins, see Birley 2000 pp. 233–4 and Syme 1958 ch. 45.

124 So Farney 2007 pp. 235–6 ('evasive reply') and Syme 1958 pp. 619 ('a veiled answer') and 621. Syme pushed the interpretation of this second-hand anecdote further (surely too

the criminality of 'over-powerful provincials' (*praeualidi prouincialium*) and grants a senator a speech inveighing against the 'arrogance of provincials' (*prouincialium superbia*).[125] Whatever we make of Tacitus' attitude to provincials, it should be clear that the invention and proliferation of the noun *prouinciales* is implicated in a broader reconfiguration of the terms in which identity and status are negotiated by a self-professed imperial elite.

The socii *in the second century* CE

The emergence of the new noun *prouinciales* and the wider rhetoric of provinciality did not entail the obsolescence of the older *socii*. On the contrary, *socii* seems to have remained the more common of the two terms, at least in the discourses to which we have access. With the exception of the two Plinys, no first- or second-century author writing about the empire mentions *prouinciales* more often than *socii*.[126] As late as the 160s and 180s CE, provincials are still being described as *socii* by Fronto and Gellius. Fronto writes that the emperor's duties include 'curbing the faults of the allies

far) with the suggestion that the knight had already guessed, perhaps from his accent, that Tacitus is from either Southern Gaul or Northern Italy and is just trying to work out which (Syme 1999 pp. 73–4).

125 *exim Claudius Timarchus Cretensis reus agitur, ceteris criminibus, ut solent praeualidi prouincialium et opibus nimiis ad iniurias minorum elati* (Tac. *Ann.* 15.20.1). '*aduersus nouam prouincialium superbiam ... capiamus consilium*' (ibid. 4). See further p. 247.

126 Use of *socii* and *prouinciales* in the context of empire:

	socii	*prouinciales*
Tacitus	39	9
Pliny, *Letters*	14	–
Valerius Maximus	13	–
Suetonius	6	3
Quintilian	4	–
Seneca the Younger	3	1
Fronto	3	1
Asconius	2	1
Gellius	1	–
Pliny the Elder	–	4
Pliny, *Panegyricus*	–	6

Note: these figures exclude the use of *socii* in a private context ('associate', 'partner') and also Tacitus' use of *socii* to denote the *auxilia* in battle narratives.

with edicts'.[127] Gellius, writing about extortion trials, says that a senator 'who is speaking on behalf of the common interest and the well-being of the allies' should not waste his time on a *captatio beneuolentiae*.[128] The epigraphic evidence is unfortunately too limited to say more than that both terms were in use through the first and second centuries CE.[129]

In principle, the two terms ought to have had quite distinct functions, denoting two different categories that overlap but are not coextensive, namely non-citizen subjects of Rome (*socii*) and the inhabitants of the provinces (*prouinciales*). A reference to the *socii* ought to exclude provincial citizens, but encompass 'free peoples', allied kingdoms and other formally autonomous communities that would be excluded from the strict sense of *prouinciales*. Yet the distinction between the two terms seems to have become increasingly blurred – owing partly to a degree of indifference on the part of elite writers, partly to the continued lability of the term *socii* – to the extent that they are often treated as interchangeable in the second century CE.

Second-century authors do regularly contrast *socii* with *ciues*, showing that the term could still serve to denote specifically the non-citizen population of the empire.[130] Yet the *socii* appear so widely as the inhabitants of particular provinces and the subjects of provincial governors that it is hard to imagine that every use of the

[127] *sociorum culpas edictis coercere* (Fronto, *Ant. de eloquentia* 1.5). See pp. 213 and 229–32 on imperial edicts issued to the provinces. Fronto also refers to provincials as *socii* at *Parth.* 10 and *Ant. imp.* 1.2.4. Commenting on the latter passage, van den Hout 1999 p. 231 implies that *socii* is only applied to communities that enjoyed treaties with Rome. But this ignores the more expansive use of the term in Roman discourse in general and Fronto in particular (as evidenced by *Ant. de eloquentia* 1.5). Fronto uses *prouinciales* only once (*Amic.* 1.18.1).

[128] *alia* [sc. *principia conducunt*] *uiro ... pro utilitatibus publicis ac pro salute sociorum grauiter ac libere indignanti simul ac dolenti* (Gell. *NA* 6.3.18). Gellius does not use *prouinciales* at all.

[129] *Socii* appears in the Tiberian *SC de Cn. Pisone patre* (Eck, Caballos and Fernandez 1996 line 90), a first-century CE Corsican inscription commemorating harbour works for the benefit of 'citizens and allies' (*AE* 1982 441) and two second-century vows recorded by the Arval Brethren (*CFA* 85 and 87; see n. 89 above). *Prouinciales* appears in Claudius' speech on the admission of Gauls to the senate (Smallwood *GCN* 369 = *ILS* 212, II 5 and 7) and an inscription from Mauretania from the reign of Commodus advertising the construction of fortifications as indicative of the emperor's care for his *prouinciales* (*ILS* 396).

[130] See Plin. *Pan.* 33.1, Tac. *Dial.* 37.5, *Hist.* 3.33.2, *Ann.* 1.9.5, 1.11.4, 4.13.1, 4.38.3, 14.33.2 and Suet. *Ner.* 39.1. Several of these are quoted at p. 36.

term is intended to exclude the large number of provincial citizens. When Tacitus writes that the news that the province of Gallia Narbonensis had been surrounded by Otho's fleet moved the Vitellian general Valens with a concern to protect 'the allies' (*cura socios tuendi*, *Hist.* 2.28.1), that a governor of Africa ended his campaign against the rebel Tacfarinas more hastily than was in the interest of 'the allies' (*properantius tamen quam ex utilitate sociorum*, *Ann.* 3.74.3), that Gaius Silanus was prosecuted 'by the allies' for extortion (*repetundarum a sociis postulatum*, *Ann.* 3.66.1) and Publius Suillius was accused of having plundered 'the allies' when he governed the province of Asia (*direptos socios, cum Suillius provinciam Asiam regeret*, *Ann.* 13.43.1), when Suetonius says, in the passage quoted at the beginning of this chapter, that Augustus renewed the terms of the incumbent provincial governors to keep 'the allies' under control (*Aug.* 23.1), when Juvenal in his Eighth Satire warns his illustrious pupil 'Ponticus' not to abuse 'the allies' when he becomes a provincial governor (8.89, 99, 108 and 136) – in all these cases, it would be pedantic to insist that the reference to the *socii* always excludes the citizen population of these provinces. *Socii* seems to be the term of choice for a governor's subjects, whatever their legal status.

For the Younger Pliny, the distinction between the two terms seems to be a matter of tone and connotation, not scope of reference. In a striking example of selective usage, he employs *socii* exclusively in the *Panegyricus* and *prouinciales* exclusively in the *Letters*.[131] The two terms perform the same functions in their respective texts. This is most obvious in the fact that the African and Spanish provincials whom Pliny represented in the extortion court are called *prouinciales* in his letters, but *socii* in the *Panegyricus* – even though they must have included many Roman citizens.[132] This invites us to consider why the two terms are so carefully segregated in Pliny's work. The avoidance of

[131] *Socii* appears six times in the *Panegyricus*; *prouinciales* not at all. In contrast, *prouinciales* appears fourteen times in the *Letters*; *socii* never.

[132] *Prouinciales*: Plin. *Ep.* 2.11.2 and 10.3a.2; *socii*: *Pan.* 95.1. In the prosecution of Marius Priscus, Pliny was not representing the whole province of Africa but one city and a large number of individuals (*una ciuitas publice multique priuati*, *Ep.* 3.9.4). The city was Lepcis, a Roman *colonia*. In the prosecutions of Baebius Massa and Caecilius Classicus

prouinciales in the *Panegyricus* is probably due to its relative novelty. Pliny's speech makes a point of describing the world of the principate in the language of the Republican past in order to emphasise political continuity.[133] The use of *socii*, with its clear Ciceronian precedent, contributes to this recuperation of the past in a way that *prouinciales* could not. The fact that the *Letters* eschew *socii* for *prouinciales* is more difficult to explain, but it *might* (in so far as the *Letters* show a preference for plain vocabulary in narration) be a sign that the two words differed in register in this period, with *socii* being the more elevated.[134]

The works of Tacitus offer further evidence that the two terms could be used with the same scope of reference in this period. Discussing the loyalties of the province of Africa during the civil war between Vitellius and Vespasian, Tacitus writes that Vitellius' governorship of the province had been honest and popular, whereas Vespasian's had been scandalous and hated. The *socii* formed their estimates of them as emperors accordingly, he says, and the legionary legate Valerius Festus at first faithfully backed the preference of the *prouinciales* but later switched his allegiance.[135] Here Tacitus in his pursuit of *uariatio* employs *prouinciales* as a synonym for *socii*. Both serve to denote the population of the province as a whole. In another passage, Tacitus records that the imperial procurator of Asia was accused by the province (*prouincia*) and that Tiberius empowered the senate to sit in judgement, enjoining them to listen to the *socii*.[136] Elsewhere again, in a characteristic rejection of conventional terminology, he refers to the provincial councils as *concilia sociorum* ('councils of the allies'), eschewing

he was acting on behalf of the whole province on Baetica, presumably at the invitation of the provincial council. On the right of citizens to claim under the Julian *lex repetundarum*, see Brunt 1988 p. 527.

133 The rhetorical strategy is certainly not limited to Pliny, but it is a particularly distinctive feature of the *Panegyricus*. See Durry 1938 pp. 43–4.

134 On the vocabulary of the *Letters*, see Gamberini 1983 pp. 491–4, Sherwin-White 1966 pp. 5–6 and 16–18, Guillemin 1929 pp. 113–57 and Peter 1901 ch. 5.

135 *quippe integrum illic ac fauorabilem proconsulatum Vitellius, famosum inuisumque Vespasianus egerat: proinde socii de imperio utriusque coniectabant, sed experimentum contra fuit. ac primo Valerius Festus legatus studia prouincialium cum fide iuuit; mox nutabat* (Tac. *Hist.* 2.97.2–98.1).

136 *apud quos* [sc. *patres*] *etiam tum cuncta tractabantur, adeo ut procurator Asiae Lucilius Capito accusante prouincia causam dixerit, magna cum adseueratione principis non se ius nisi in seruitia et pecunias familiares dedisse … audirent socios* (Tac. *Ann.* 4.15.2).

the usual *concilium prouinciae*. He would hardly do so if *socii* necessarily excluded citizens, since many or most of the members of these councils were Roman citizens.[137] In Tacitus' narrative of the Batavian revolt of 69–70 CE, the Batavian chieftain Julius Civilis incites his countrymen to revolt by complaining that 'it is with the provinces' blood that the provinces are conquered' (*prouinciarum sanguine prouincias uinci*, *Hist.* 4.17.2) while another chieftain later tries to persuade them to make peace with Rome by reminding them how much better off they were than the Raeti, the Norici and the rest of Rome's 'allies' (*respicerent Raetos Noricosque et ceterorum onera sociorum*, Tac. *Hist.* 5.25.2). It is hard to imagine that these propositions are intended to differ in their scope of reference – that the second speaker, in using *socii* rather than *prouinciae*, is carefully excluding provincial citizens from consideration. The mention of Raeti and Norici, both peoples coextensive with provinces (and indeed provinces in which the Latin right and Roman citizenship were relatively widespread), suggests that he is thinking of provincials as a whole. Indeed any Batavian chieftain is likely to have been a Roman citizen himself.[138] The point is rather that *socii* and *prouinciales* function equally well in this context. They both serve to denote those who are regarded as the subjects of Roman rule. If there is a logic behind the choice of terms, it lies in their expressive, not referential, meaning. *Socii*, with its connotations of association rather than subjection, is a good word for a speaker who aims to reconcile his people to Roman rule, whereas *prouinciae*, which arguably evokes the whole oppressive apparatus of Roman administration and control, is the better word for a proponent of rebellion.

All this is indicative of a further slippage in the referential meaning of *socii* in this period. It appears not to be as closely tied to citizen status as it once was. A generic term for those who are regarded as the subjects of empire, its scope of reference has become vague and inconsistent. Juxtaposed with *ciues*, it refers narrowly to the non-citizen population. Used on its own, it can bear

[137] Tac. *Ann.* 15.22.1. On the provincial councils, whose members were drawn from the elite of each province, see Lintott 1993 p. 124.

[138] See Roymans 2004 pp. 62–3 on the Batavian Julii.

a much wider reference and include all provincials. This recalls its similar lability in Cicero's time, when it was capable of functioning both as a complement of *prouinciae*, excluding the provincialised population, and as an umbrella category subsuming them. In second-century texts it would be unwise to assume that so-called *socii* are always non-citizens. The intended scope of reference can only be deduced from the context, if at all.

The slippage by which *socii* becomes capable of embracing citizens as well as non-citizens and functioning as a synonym for *prouinciae* and *prouinciales* is further proof of the growing importance of a centre and periphery model of empire, in which the most important division is geographic rather than legal. But the inconsistent use of the term, with the scope for ambiguity it creates, also reveals a degree of indifference to the distinction between non-citizens (a legal category) and provincials (a geographic category), at least among these members of the imperial elite. For the jurist – and presumably for most provincial citizens – there was a world of difference between the two categories. But there was considerable overlap between them and it is perhaps not surprising that those close to the centre of power did not always trouble themselves over the distinction. From the perspective of a Pliny or a Tacitus, 'the provinces' and 'the allies' were equally their subjects.

Romans and allies

It should by now be clear that the label *socii* is a distinctive and enduring feature of the Roman imperial lexicon. Despite significant changes in the distribution of power and privilege within the empire and despite the emergence of a new discourse of provinciality, *socii* remains as central to the language of empire in the second century CE as it was three hundred years earlier. Its capacity to function as a synonym of *prouinciales*, entailing yet another extension of its scope of reference, is only the latest example of its remarkable capacity to accommodate itself to changing circumstances. Its prominence and longevity raise wider questions. What does it reveal about Rome's imperial culture that the language of alliance had such enduring appeal and relevance? Conversely, how did the normative expectations raised by the everyday repetition of this language constrain or channel the conduct of the men who exercised Roman power in the provinces? To have remained so central to imperial discourse for so long, the word must have both expressed and reinforced shared beliefs about Rome's imperial project.[139]

Its capacity to connote association rather than subjection was certainly important to its early success. *Socii* probably established itself early in the rhetoric of Roman diplomacy, providing a euphemistic label for subjection to Rome. Deployed first in Rome's dealings with her Italian subjects, it subsequently became a recurring trope in Rome's interactions with the Greek world in the third and second centuries BCE – often translated into the Greek σύμμαχοι.[140] If Livy's history is any guide, Roman statesmen used the language of alliance to idealise Roman power in contrast with the Hellenistic kingdoms. Where the kings had 'tributaries' (*stipendiarii*), Rome had 'allies'.[141] The label will also have been propagated within domestic political discourse by those who wished to champion the rights of Rome's provincial subjects or mobilise outrage at the conduct of provincial governors – whether in the extortion court or in the wider ad hominem attacks that pervaded Roman political discourse. The cumulative impact of these interventions is evident from *socii*'s wide currency as a label for provincials by the first and second centuries CE, with the duty of care it implies.

But the term has a second aspect. If *socii* implies association rather than *subjection*, it also suggests association rather than *integration*. In the Republican period, it resonated with Rome's preference for keeping dependent communities at arm's length rather than integrating them into Rome's political structure. The label 'allies' nicely captures the combination of dependence and separation that characterised the status of the Italians before their

[139] Peter Brunt is one of the few to have asked what might be at stake in the widespread use of the term: 'Perhaps the constant use of the term *socii* to describe provincials in itself indicates something about Roman attitudes to them; it could hardly have been totally divested of the nuance imparted by its other senses' (Brunt 1978 p. 319).

[140] See p. 38 on the *formula sociorum* and the use of σύμμαχοι in letters and *senatus consulta* addressed to Greek communities.

[141] For the kings' subjects as *stipendiarii*, see Livy 35.16.6, 37.53.3, 37.55.6, 38.39.7, 38.39.8.

enfranchisement and that of Rome's overseas subjects throughout the Republic. In his survey of the development of the Roman citizenship, Sherwin-White sees the use of *socii* at the time of the Social War as symptomatic of the exclusiveness of Roman politics in that period.[142] His narrative emphasises the changes in Roman practice thereafter – the process by which the subjects of empire were brought 'within the state'. But there is continuity too. The label *socii* – with its implications of association rather than integration – continues to be applied to provincials throughout the first two centuries CE, despite the structural changes in the empire which saw many provincials recruited to the citizenship and even the equestrian and senatorial elites. In a period where modern histories highlight political and cultural integration across the empire, Roman discourse continues to mark provincials as separate from the Roman state.

This aspect of *socii* takes on further significance in the light of the term's association with the revolt of the Italian allies in 91 BCE. First called the 'Marsic' or 'Italian War' (*bellum Marsicum* or *Italicum*), it was from the middle of the first century CE more commonly known as the 'Social War' (*bellum sociale*), because *socii* had been the usual label for the non-Latin Italians before their enfranchisement.[143] Later narratives blamed the war on Rome's unjust and short-sighted refusal to extend the citizenship to the Italians.[144] The Social War was remembered as the almost disastrous result of Rome's refusal to grant parity to the Italian *socii*. The continued use of *socii* as a label for provincials was thus always a potential reminder both of the Romans' history of niggardliness

[142] Sherwin-White 1973 pp. 186–9.

[143] *Bellum Marsicum* may have been the earliest term, but the evidence is extremely limited. *Bellum Italicum* is the most common title in Cicero and early imperial authors. While *bellum sociale* is attested as early as Cicero (Cic. *Font.* 41; cf. *bellum sociorum* at *2 Verr.* 5.8), it remains a rarer variant until the mid first century CE. Thereafter, however, it is the most common term for the war. See Plin. *HN* 2.199, 2.238, 3.70, 33.20, 33.55, Frontin. *Str.* 1.5.17, 2.4.16, 4.7.41, Tac. *Ann.* 6.12.3, Juv. 5.31, Gell. *NA* 15.4.3, Flor. 2.6.1. See further Brown 2003 pp. 96–102, Rosenberger 1992 pp. 35–9, and von Domaszewski 1924 pp. 1–10.

[144] For retrospective assessments of the justice of the Italian cause, see e.g. Vell. Pat. 2.15.2, Asc. p. 22.5–6 Clark and Flor. 2.6.3. (See Mouritsen 1998 on the anachronism of these later accounts in privileging demands for the citizenship over desire for independence as the motivation for the Italians' revolt.)

towards their dependants and of the possibility that those dependants might take matters into their own hands. Its persistence is indicative of the stubbornly exclusivist character of Roman political culture.

There is change on the horizon, though it lies beyond the chronological limits of this book. The evidence for the third century is little or non-existent, but it is clear that *prouinciales* has completely displaced *socii* in Roman discourse by the beginning of the fourth century CE. The change is obvious in historical prose. In marked contrast with Tacitus and Suetonius, Ammianus Marcellinus uses *prouinciales* nine times and *socii* not at all, while the *Historia Augusta* employs *prouinciales* thirty-three times and *socii* only twice.[145] *Prouinciales* are similarly ubiquitous, and *socii* entirely absent, in imperial pronouncements. From the late third century, whenever emperors wish to address the empire at large, they address themselves 'to the *prouinciales*'.[146] In the rhetoric of imperial munificence, emperors advertise their concern for the welfare of 'their provincials' (*prouinciales sui*).[147] Since even Italians were *prouinciales* following the provincialisation of Italy

[145] Both instances of *socii* in the *Historia Augusta* are in contexts where archaising language is particularly appropriate. The first is a senatorial letter celebrating the restoration of the senate to its ancient powers by the emperor Tacitus (*scirent omnes socii omnesque nationes in antiquum statum redisse rem populi Romani*, SHA *Tacitus* 12.1). The second is a prayer to the Capitoline gods (*date hoc senatui populoque Romano, date militibus, date sociis atque exteris nationibus*, SHA *Prob.* 12.7).

[146] From 315 CE at the latest, imperial constitutions are regularly addressed *ad prouinciales* or *ad uniuersos prouinciales* (see Mommsen and Meyer 1905 I pp. clxii–clxiii). The practice may well have begun earlier. While Diocletian's prices edict (301 CE), like all edicts (see p. 232), is a general pronouncement without a formal addressee, it does apostrophise its recipients as *prouinciales nostri* at one point in the preamble (Lauffer 1971 praef. 84–5).

[147] Assertions of the emperors' concern for *prouinciales nostri* can be found as early as the reign of Commodus (*securitati prouincialium suorum consulens*, *ILS* 396). They become widespread from the reign of Diocletian. See e.g *Cod. Iust.* 9.41.8.2 (*uniuersi prouinciales nostri* will benefit from restrictions on use of torture, 284 or 292 CE), *CIL* III 12134 (the emperors will put an end to the plundering of *prouinciales nostri* by the Caesariani, 305 CE), *FIRA* 94, 6–7 (the emperors act *consulentes securitati prouincialium nostrorum* in restricting the right of accusation, early fourth century), *CIL* III 13569, 45–6 (the emperors are confident that *prouinciales nostri* will rejoice that they have been provided for, early fourth century). In the 350s Magnentius advertises himself as *conseruator prouincialium et militum* on a whole series of Italian milestones (e.g. *AE* 1997 525). A few years later, Constantius II and Constantinus Gallus are styled *conseruatores rei publicae et omnium prouincialium* on another Italian milestone (*ILS* 737).

under Diocletian, the term no longer implies a dichotomy between Italy and the rest of the empire.[148] It has become a universal term for all the inhabitants of the empire. If there is a dichotomy in this period, it is between the military and the civil population, often styled *milites* and *prouinciales* respectively.[149] The obsolescence of *socii* is perhaps unsurprising after Caracalla's general grant of citizenship had made the distinction between citizens and non-citizens all but irrelevant. What is remarkable is how long the old category, with its implicit exclusion of the subject peoples from the Roman *res publica*, had outlasted the structures of the expansionist city state in which it originated.

This chapter has highlighted the importance of binary distinctions in the Roman lexicon of empire. *Socii*, *prouinciae*, *prouinciales*, *peregrini* – all these terms implicitly impose a dichotomy on the population of the empire, demarcating a class of subjects in opposition to an imperial centre, conceived variously as the citizen body, Italy or the Roman people. Though this list might appear to conflate legal, geographic and ethnic categories, Roman usage will not always bear such precise distinctions. *Peregrini* is capable of functioning as both ethnic and a legal category. *Socii* is even harder to pin down. It often serves to denote the non-citizen population of the empire, but it is sometimes used with much narrower reference (denoting some class of nominally autonomous peoples) or much wider reference (encompassing all provincials). Even *prouinciae* is, I suspect, often used without regard to the formal limits of provincial administration. These terms all perform similar functions in Roman discourse. They serve as labels for those who are regarded as the subjects of empire – those who benefit from or suffer under Roman rule, who pay tribute, and who need to be kept under control. They are all potential categories in opposition to which self-professed Romans can define themselves. Writing about empire often entails choosing between them, and choosing to use them in one sense rather than another. Ideological, rhetorical and

[148] Italians as *prouinciales*: *ILS* 8984 and *CIL* VI 1702. See Millar 1986 for the provincialisation of Italy under Diocletian.
[149] See *TLL* s.v. *prouincialis* p. 2344.14–50 for examples.

stylistic considerations are at least as important in these decisions as any notional differences in the terms' scope of reference. This is best exemplified by Cicero's strategic use of the label *socii* in the extortion courts. When representing provincials against their governor, he is eager to call them all *socii* in order to assert their right to Roman protection. But when he finds himself on the other side of the court, he has no qualms about using *socii* with a much narrower application, denying the aggrieved inhabitants of the provinces any status other than that of foreigners. It is also illustrated by Pliny's use of *socii* as a substitute for *prouinciales* in the *Panegyricus* in order to exploit its Ciceronian resonance. The choice of categories can itself be a rhetorical strategy, no less than the metaphors that are discussed in the following chapters.

The ubiquity of these categories illustrates the importance of binary divisions in Roman discourse about empire. Roman writers regularly divide the population of the empire into two classes, in the process eliding distinctions that must have been important to many provincials, including the distinctions between citizens and non-citizens in the provinces, between Latins and other non-citizens and between autonomous communities and the provincialised population. The fact that what are properly legal, geographic and ethnic categories are so often used for the same purpose and sometimes treated as interchangeable testifies to the complexity and fluidity of elite identity in the first and second centuries CE. Roman writers are certain of their superiority as members of an imperial people, yet they are often vague and inconsistent on where the line between rulers and ruled is to be drawn. This should not come as a surprise. It reflects the complexity of the underlying distribution of power and privilege in the Roman empire, which resists any simple dichotomy between privileged rulers and exploited subjects.

Although this vocabulary admits considerable variety and even inconsistency of usage in all periods, it is possible to observe some long-term shifts in its configuration. The first is the process by which these simple binaries displaced more complex taxonomies in the lexicon of empire. In Cicero, the binary distinction between citizens and allies coexists with a more differentiated terminology which highlights differences of status among Rome's various subjects and dependants. That vocabulary of dependence has by the first century CE been all but completely superseded by the use of generic categories such as *socii*, *prouinciae* or *gentes* to encompass all Rome's subjects. A second important development is the emergence of a discourse of provinciality. In the late first century BCE the key distinction in the discourse of empire is between citizens and non-citizens. The first century CE sees geography become a competing criterion of distinction. This can be seen both in the appearance and spread of the noun *prouinciales* and in the semantic slippage by which *socii* become capable of encompassing not just non-citizens but all provincials. In the first and second centuries CE, provincial citizens are increasingly bracketed with non-citizens and regarded as the subjects of empire. This is part of a new rhetoric of social exclusion in response to the progressive extension of the citizenship in this period.

The label *socii* emerges from this study as one of the most persistent and distinctive elements of the language of Roman imperialism. Evolving from a term for the Italians and *ciuitates liberae* to one for all non-citizen subjects and eventually all provincials, it is as common in the second century CE as it was in the second BCE. With its connotations of alliance, association and partnership, it reveals continuities in Roman imperial ideology across this period. Its use to denote the subject peoples implies some degree of moral obligation to them. But the label also implies association rather than integration. It defines Rome's subjects as separate from the Roman *res publica* – like the Italians before the Social War. Its persistence in Roman discourse is thus indicative of the continued exclusivism of Roman political culture in a period in which modern historiography emphasises processes of political and cultural integration.

2

MASTERS OF THE WORLD

respicite finitimam Galliam, quae in prouinciam redacta, iure et legibus commutatis, securibus subiecta perpetua premitur seruitute.

Look at nearby Gaul. Reduced to a province, its rights and laws changed utterly, made subject to the axes, it is crushed by unending slavery.

(Caes. *B Gall.* 7.77.16)

So speaks the Gallic rebel Critognatus in Caesar's *Gallic War.* The claim that subjection to Rome is tantamount to enslavement is typical of the rhetoric of Rome's enemies, at least as it is represented in Roman historiography. Caesar's Gallic speakers almost invariably represent the conflict with Rome as a struggle for freedom (*libertas*) against enslavement (*seruitus*).[1] Sallust's famous 'Letter of Mithridates' accuses the Romans of turning kings into slaves.[2] In Livy too, accusations of enslavement are the mainstay of anti-Roman rhetoric, ubiquitous in the speeches of dissatisfied Italian allies, rebellious barbarians and hostile kings.[3] Tacitus' rebels are no exception.[4] In short, describing the Romans' subjects as their 'slaves' is one of the most characteristic tropes of those who resist Roman power.

Many modern readers have seen such accusations of enslavement as a potentially damning critique of Roman power, giving the

[1] See also Caes. *B Gall.* 1.17, 1.51.3, 2.14, 3.8.3–4, 4.34.5, 5.27, 5.38, 7.1.2–5, 7.37, 7.38 and 7.71.

[2] *ex rege miserrumum seruorum effecere* (Sall. *Hist.* 4.69.8); *quem ... quia fama erat diuitem neque seruiturum esse, per Nicomedem bello lacessiuerunt* (ibid. 10); *postremus seruorum Archelaus* (ibid. 12); *omniaque non serua et maxume regna hostilia ducant* (ibid. 17).

[3] Italians: Livy 8.4.1–11 (Annius), 10.16 (Samnites). Rebels: 29.1.20–4 (Indibilis). Kings: 31.29.3–16 (Macedonians), 35.17.3–9 (Seleucids), 37.25.4–12 (Antiochus) 39.37 (Lycortas), 42.52.6–16 (Perseus).

[4] Tac. *Agr.* 30–2 (Calgacus); *Hist.* 4.14, 17 and 32 (Civilis), 4.64 (the Tencteri); *Ann.* 1.59, 2.10, 2.15 and 2.45 (Arminius), 3.40 (Florus and Sacrovir), 12.34 and 37 (Caratacus) and 14.35 (Boudicca).

lie to self-serving Roman rhetoric and exposing the brutal reality of Roman rule. To give a recent example, Andrew Riggsby's study of Caesar's *Gallic War* draws attention to the prominence of the slavery motif in the speeches of Caesar's Gauls and argues that this must have posed a problem for Roman readers: to accept the Gallic accusations of enslavement would be to condemn Roman expansion. He solves the apparent paradox by suggesting that Caesar leaves a way out, allowing Roman readers to reject Gallic claims that being ruled by Rome is a form of slavery.[5] Andrew Fear responds similarly to the complaints of the Caledonian chieftain Calgacus in Tacitus' *Agricola*, claiming that his accusations of enslavement by Rome would be unsettling for most Roman readers.[6]

Riggsby and Fear (and they are certainly not alone) take the idea of provincial slavery to be an inherently subversive trope – a challenge to Roman self-presentation and thus to the legitimacy of Roman power. It should not be forgotten, however, that this notionally hostile rhetoric is itself a Roman construct. Its relationship to the voices of those who rejected Roman rule is at best problematic. More importantly, we should not be misled by our own conviction that slavery is morally unjustifiable into presuming that to describe empire as enslavement is necessarily to condemn it. The connotations of a comparison with slavery must have been different in a culture where slavery was a feature of everyday life and where its legitimacy as an institution was never seriously challenged. In fact, this chapter will show, slavery plays a central role in Roman accounts of empire.[7]

The primary aim of the chapter is to demonstrate the pervasiveness of the language and imagery of slavery in Roman discourse

[5] 'To accept [their] rhetoric is to accept that the Aedui face a terrible fate, one much to be avoided' (Riggsby 2006 p. 182). 'Elsewhere however,' he claims, 'the equation is questioned' (ibid. 183). But he only cites one passage that in any way challenges the idea of slavery to Rome.

[6] 'It would have been impossible for Pliny [the Elder] to have written, or read with comfort, the impassioned denunciation of Roman Imperialism put in the mouth of the Caledonian Calgacus by Tacitus' (Fear 2011 pp. 28–9). Fear claims that Pliny, not Tacitus, is representative of 'the intellectual mainstream' of the period (p. 31).

[7] In the interest of clearly establishing that these tropes are not limited to hostile rhetoric, this chapter makes a point of excluding the many slavery metaphors in direct or indirect speech attributed to Rome's enemies and in passages clearly focalised through them.

about empire. This necessitates a wide-ranging approach, accumulating examples of the tropes of mastery and slavery from a wide range of genres and across a span of three hundred years (without exhausting the material available). To facilitate consideration of the range of functions of these metaphors, the survey is structured by the context of use, looking first at representations of conquest and revolt and then at representations of the ongoing condition of the provinces. This inevitably involves some movement back and forth between periods and genres. Jarring as these transitions may seem, they serve to underline the reach and longevity of these metaphors – a key theme both of this chapter and of the book as a whole. A more problematic consequence of the wide-ranging approach is the necessarily superficial engagement with individual texts and their particular agendas. A survey of this sort can only be a beginning. The next chapter will illustrate the value of a deeper analysis of these metaphors in their textual context. A close reading of three Tacitean revolt narratives will demonstrate that the idea of provincial slavery can be developed in different directions and to serve different purposes. For now, however, the priority is to map the distribution of these metaphors within Roman discourse, and to reflect on the implications for our understanding of both Roman imperial ideology and the ideology of slavery.

The language of slavery

This chapter focuses on a cluster of words, expressions and images closely associated with the domain of chattel slavery. At its core is the noun *seruus* ('slave') and its cognates, *seruitus* and *seruitium* ('slavery') and *seruire* ('to be a slave'). It includes their mutually entailing antonyms in the domains of freedom on the one hand (*liber, libertas*) and mastery on the other (*dominus*, *dominatio*, *dominari*). It extends to related images and symbols such as chains and the yoke.[8] Even when these words are used in other contexts, they always retain their connection with one another and with the

[8] The most important recent discussion of the language of slavery in Roman political discourse is Matthew Roller's analysis of debates about the legitimacy of the principate in the Julio-Claudian period (Roller 2001 ch. 4).

domain of chattel slavery. This is best evidenced by their clustering in political invective, which shows both that they constitute a coherent system of mutually reinforcing metaphors and that they possess an emotive force which must depend on their link to the experience of slavery. Particularly good examples are Cicero's *Philippics*, the speech of Macer in Sallust's *Histories* (3.48) and, in an imperial context, the speech of Calgacus in Tacitus' *Agricola*. Each of these texts builds a coherent system of metaphors from the terms for slavery (*seruus*, *seruitus*, *seruitium*, *seruire*), mastery (*dominus*, *dominatio*, *dominatus*, *dominare*), freedom (*libertas*, *liber*), the yoke (*iugum*, *ceruices*) and the *causa liberalis* (*uindex*, *uindicatio*, *uindicare*).[9]

Two common misconceptions about the meaning of *seruitus* and *seruire* need to be dispelled immediately. The first is the idea that *seruitus* is a technical term in political discourse. It is true that the subjection of a city to a tyrant or to a foreign power is often described as enslavement in both Greek and Latin.[10] But this does not mean that *seruitus* (or *douleia* in Greek) has some technical sense (such as 'political subjection') that is divorced from the connotations of slavery.[11] First, it is significant that it is in historiography and oratory

[9] The speech of Calgacus is analysed in detail at pp. 128–9.

[10] Brunt 1988 pp. 291–6 gives numerous examples. Raaflaub 2004 traces the origin of the trope to the fifth century BCE. He shows that 'those who use the word [*douleia*] … desire to characterize a given relationship of dependency as especially hated, feared, and reprehensible' (p. 130). On the Greek context, see further Tamiolaki 2010, Brock 2007 pp. 210–11, Welles 1965 and Gomme 1962.

[11] 'Political subjection': *OLD* s.v. *seruitus* § 2. Matthew Roller (2001 p. 232) puts it well when he criticises attempts (by Hammond 1963, Hellegouarc'h 1963 and Wirszubski 1950; cf. Arena 2007) to articulate a purely political definition of *libertas* in the context of domestic politics: 'it is incorrect to speak of *libertas* as being a "political idea" or having a "political meaning" … independent of its function as a category of social status and its embeddedness in the institution of chattel slavery'. This is all the more true of *seruitus* and its cognates. A genuine technical sense of *seruitus* that does deserve note is the legal concept of praedial *seruitutes* (the equivalent, but opposite, of common law 'easements', rights over another's land). Roman law allowed restrictions to be placed on the use of a property by its owner, either by preventing him from making certain uses of it or by compelling him to allow some other person to make certain uses of it. Common examples included on the one hand restrictions on building above a certain limit (*seruitus altius non tollendi*) or building so as to block a neighbour's light (*seruitus ne luminibus officiatur*) and on the other obligations to allow a neighbour to draw water through a property (*seruitus aquaeductus*) or to graze cattle on it (*seruitus pascendi*). See further Berger 1953 pp. 702–4 and Bannon 2009 on servitudes involving water rights. Even here the semantic link with chattel slavery is still present, as can be seen from the fact that the

that these terms are used – not in the technical language of treaties or law codes.[12] Exactly what constitutes *douleia* or *seruitus* is open to debate and disagreement; their application to a given political situation is always a rhetorical choice and never self-evident. More importantly, *douleia* and *seruitus* always retain the force of their connection with the domain of chattel slavery. As this chapter will show, the condition of *seruitus* to Rome is regularly associated with the wider language and imagery of slavery and contrasted with freedom (*libertas*) on the one hand and mastery (*dominatio*) on the other.

A second common misconception is that the verb *seruire* means no more than 'to serve'. On the contrary, it is an integral part of the language of chattel slavery. With an indirect object it means 'to serve someone as a slave'; used absolutely, *seruire* means 'to be a slave'. A freedman in Petronius' *Satyricon* boasts that he was born a king's son. Why then had he been a slave, he is asked (*quare ergo seruiuisti*)? Because he gave himself into slavery (*seruitus*) in the hope of becoming a Roman citizen through manumission (*Sat.* 57). Pliny the Younger writes disparagingly of a senator who was a cruel master, though his own father had been a freedman. He says that the senator had forgotten – or perhaps remembered too well – that his father had been a slave (*seruisse patrem suum*, *Ep.* 3.14.1). A free person who allows himself to be owned as a slave because he is unaware of his own status (for example because he was exposed as a child) is called in Roman law a *liber homo bona fide seruiens*.[13] The close semantic link between *seruire* and *seruus* is nicely illustrated by a staple of the declamation schools – the question of what happens to a debtor condemned to serve his creditor as a slave until he pays off his debt (*seruire dum soluerit*) if the creditor dies and frees his slaves in his will. A debtor serves as a slave (*seruit*). Is he then a slave (*seruus*), and so to be freed?[14]

implicit metaphor is often extended through the use of other elements of the language of slavery: with one property being said *seruitutem debere*, *seruire* or *seruiens esse* to the other.

[12] Neither *douleia* nor *seruitus* (or their cognates) appear as a term for subjection in the texts assembled by Bengtson and Werner 1975 and Schmitt 1969 in their survey of the treaties of the ancient world.

[13] Berger 1953 p. 562 and Buckland 1908 pp. 331–52.

[14] See Quint. *Inst.* 5.10.60 and 7.3.26–7 and [Quint.] *Decl. min.* 311.

Like all good topics of debate, the question has no definitive answer.

It is true, however, that the verb is sometimes used in a more abstract sense – notably in the opposition between *seruire* and *imperare* ('rule') that is so common in Roman discourse.[15] 'We must distinguish', writes Cicero in the *Republic*, 'different forms of ruling and being subject (*et imperandi et seruiendi sunt dissimilitudines cognoscendae*, Cic. *Rep.* 3.37). Where a Greek writer would have used *archein* and *archesthai*, Cicero uses *imperare* and *seruire*.[16] He goes on to describe these different forms of being subject (*seruire*), one of which turns out to be the subjection of a slave to a master.[17] In other words, *seruire* is made to denote subjection in general, with the result that slavery ends up being only one of several modes of *seruire*. So central is slavery to Roman conceptions of power that when Latin looks for a generic terminology of subjection, it often finds it in the language of slavery. It follows that the idea of chattel slavery is not necessarily equally prominent in every instance of *seruire* and its cognates. Metaphors of enslavement form a continuum from the obvious to the relatively latent. A single word may be less striking than a complex of mutually reinforcing metaphors. The verb *seruire* is perhaps less marked than the concrete noun *seruus*.

Nevertheless, the connection between *seruire* and *seruus* is often made explicit by other references to the experience of slavery. In any case, it is always there to be recuperated. The best proof of this is the sensitivity with which the verb is used – and more often avoided – in domestic political discourse. There it is almost always limited to invective, precisely because it connotes a servile form of submission. Cicero complains to Atticus about the political climate: 'We are pressed on all sides and we no longer refuse to be

[15] For the pairing of *seruire* and *imperare* as antonyms, see e.g. Cic. *Leg. Man.* 41, *Rep.* 3.21, 3.37, *Amic.* 82, Sall. *Cat.* 20.17, *Hist.* 1.55.10, Hor. *Sat.* 2.7.81, *Epist.* 1.10.47, Livy 30.16.7, 45.32.4, Sen. *De ira* 2.15.4, *De vita beata* 7.8.2, *Ben.* 2.20.2, *Ep.* 66.32, 85.32, 116.1, Pub. *Sent.* A.41, [Sen.] *Monita* 58, Curt. 7.10.16, Plin. *HN* 6.182, Quint. *Inst.* 9.3.95.

[16] So Dumont 1983 p. 118 and Ferrary 1974 763 n. 2.

[17] *sed et imperandi et seruiendi sunt dissimilitudines cognoscendae. nam, ut animus corpori dicitur imperare, dicitur etiam libidini; sed corpori, ut rex ciuibus suis, aut parens liberis; libidini autem, ut seruis dominus, quod eam coercet et frangit* (Cic. *Rep.* 3.37).

slaves (*neque iam quo minus seruiamus recusamus*). We fear death and exile as if they were greater evils, though they are far lesser' (*Att.* 2.18.1). A declaimer has Cicero defiantly boast 'let our descendants know that the state could be Antony's slave (*Antonio seruire*), but Cicero could not' (Sen. *Suas.* 6.1). In Lucan Cato the Censor grieves for the fate of his descendant who would not be a slave (*non seruituri nepotis*, Luc. 6.790). All these texts derive their emotive force from the servile associations of *seruire*.

Finally, it is important to acknowledge the complexities and contradictions of Roman visions of slavery. These cannot be reduced to a stereotype.[18] Any generalisation about Roman attitudes to slaves can only be an oversimplification of a complex discourse. Moses Finley well observed that Greek and Roman practices of slavery are founded on a central ambiguity and paradox – the self-evidently problematic assumption that a slave was a thing and not a person.[19] Recent work on Latin literature has illustrated the significance of this central paradox for literary representations of slavery.[20] Other contradictions abound in Roman discourse about slavery. Slaves are imagined to be immoral, criminal beings; yet the faithful slave (*seruus fidelis*) is a commonplace of literature.[21] Slaves are assumed to be stupid; but the clever slave (*seruus callidus*) is another topos.[22] Roman texts often insist that

[18] One problematic aspect of Matthew Roller's recent and important analysis of the paradigm of slavery in representations of the principate (Roller 2001 ch. 4) is that he does precisely this. See e.g. his reading of metaphors of *seruitus* on the basis of a 'stereotype' of slavery at pp. 226–7 (cf pp. 236–7 and 287) Because he takes the master–slave relationship to be a stereotype, he treats all metaphors derived from this domain as interchangeable: they all draw on the same conception of slavery; they all have the same affective and ethical implications (see especially pp. 227). This does not do justice to the complexity of the Roman discourse of slavery.

[19] Finley 1980 ch. 3. See especially p. 99: 'Roman lawyers may have linked slaves and animals in noxal actions and in other property contexts; but no one could for a moment have forgotten that the differences were fundamental.' On the paradox as embodied in Roman law, see Buckland 1908 pp. 10–72 on 'the slave as *res*' and pp. 73–238 on 'the slave as man' (with Crook 1967 pp. 55–7).

[20] See McCarthy 2000 esp. pp. 21–2 on the importance of this 'crux of slavery' ('that slaves become useful only when they can combine two contradictory attributes') for Plautine comedy and Fitzgerald 2000 pp. 6–8 on 'living with contradiction' ('it is more fruitful to see the master's experience of slavery in terms of such conflicts than in terms of fixed attitudes').

[21] Slaves are morally inferior, criminal beings: Bradley 1994b pp. 143–4, Brunt 1988 pp. 287–8 and Bradley 1984 pp. 26–31. Faithful slaves: Vogt 1974 ch. 7.

[22] On this tension, see especially Hopkins 1993.

master–slave relations are necessarily adversarial and that slaves can only be ruled through fear.[23] Yet there are many accounts of bonds of affection between masters and slaves.[24] To become a slave is a personal catastrophe; but the condition of slavery also has its attractions in the fantasies of the Roman elite.[25] Given these contradictions, we should not expect metaphors of slavery to be all of a kind. By looking closely at the different visions of slavery embedded in particular metaphors, this chapter will illustrate the many facets of slavery, the variety of slavery metaphors and the difficulty of pinning down their affective and ethical connotations.

Conquerors and slaves

Historiography is a good place to begin since it is the source of the 'rebel' rhetoric with which this chapter opened. A closer look will demonstrate that Roman expansion is regularly figured in terms of enslavement not only by rebel speakers but also by the narrative voice. Caesar represents Gallic resistance to Rome as a struggle for freedom and against enslavement. He explains his awareness of the ever-present danger of mass revolt with the sententious observation that it is human nature to 'desire freedom and hate the condition of slavery' (*libertati studere et condicionem seruitutis odisse*, *B Gall.* 3.10.3). He thus frankly acknowledges that subjection to Rome is a servile, and so inherently hateful, condition. Later he attributes the momentum of Vercingetorix's great revolt to a 'shared resolve to lay claim to freedom' (*consensio libertatis uindicandae*, ibid. 7.76.2). This is the language of the *causa liberalis*, the judicial procedure by which someone who was wrongly enslaved could be claimed as free (*uindicatio in libertatem*).[26] The trope is common

[23] See Roller 2001 p. 226 on the presumptively adversarial nature of master–slave relations.

[24] Vogt 1974 ch. 5.

[25] Fitzgerald 2000 (especially chs. 2 and 5) explores fantasies of enslavement as a privileged position, showing how aspects of the slave's condition (such as freedom from the demands of self-restraint) could be imagined as attractive by the Roman elite.

[26] On the *causa liberalis* see Watson 1975 pp. 96–7 and Buckland 1908 pp. 652–72. Technically the de facto slave could not argue his own case and had to be championed by someone of undisputed free status (the *uindex libertatis*). See Livy 3.39.7 for a similar attribution of agency to the 'slave'.

in Roman political invective, with various factions claiming to free the Roman people from enslavement by their rivals.[27] Here the same figure is applied to the Gaul's struggle against Rome.

A fragment of Sallust's *Histories* refers to 'a race that was fierce in battle and unaccustomed to slavery' (*genus armis ferox et seruitii insolitum*, *Hist.* 2.39) – cited by a fourth-century grammarian as an example of constructions with *insolitus*. The fragment is usually ascribed to Sallust's account of the campaign against the Isaurians in Book 2. The *seruitium* referred to is probably subjection to Rome. Even Livy can represent submission to Rome as a form of slavery. Explaining why Cato the Elder faced a greater challenge than his predecessors in conquering Spain, he writes:

eo maiorem habebat difficultatem in subigendis hostibus quam qui primi uenerant in Hispaniam, quod ad illos taedio imperii Carthaginiensium Hispani deficiebant, huic ex usurpata libertate in seruitutem uelut adserendi erant.

The reason that he had more difficulty in subduing the enemy than those who first arrived in Spain was that the Spanish deserted to them because they were tired of Carthaginian rule, whereas it was his task to reclaim them as slaves, so to speak, after they had been living as free men. (Livy 34.18.1–2)

This is again the language of the *causa liberalis*, this time from the master's perspective. The *uindicatio in seruitutem* was the process by which a master could assert his rights over a slave.[28] As Livy presents it, the Spanish had been acting as if they were free and it was Cato's task to assert the Romans' lawful authority over their slaves.[29] Livy's *uelut* highlights the metaphor at the same time that it apologises for it: this is language proper to the domain of chattel slavery.[30] It is worth emphasising that mastery is here invoked as a paradigm of rightful authority. Justice is eventually done and the slaves reduced to their proper condition.

[27] See e.g. *RGDA* 1 with Hellegouarc'h 1963 pp. 550–5 and Roller 2001 pp. 214–15.

[28] On the *uindicatio in seruitutem* in particular, see Livy 3.44–8 with Ogilvie 1965 pp. 482–3.

[29] *Usurpare* denotes a unilateral action to take possession of something. Although it can be used of both lawful and unlawful acts (see *OLD* s.v. § 1), the context implies the latter here.

[30] On the frequent use of *uelut* to qualify novel metaphors in classical prose, see Mayer 2001 p. 102 and Oakley 1997–2005 IV pp. 322 with *OLD* s.v. § 3.

Tacitus regularly represents conquest by Rome as enslavement. In the *Agricola*, he describes Rome's cultivation of the minor king Cogidumnus as typical of its established policy of using kings as 'tools for enslaving others' (*instrumenta seruitutis*, *Agr.* 14.1). This is followed by the notorious claim that the British did not realise that their adoption of Roman ways (rhetoric, the toga, architecture and dining) was really part of their enslavement (*pars seruitutis*, ibid. 21.2). In the *Annals*, he writes of popular regret that Tiberius had jealously prevented Germanicus from following up his many victories against the Germans by crushing them with slavery (*seruitio premere*, *Ann.* 2.73.2).

The representation of conquest as enslavement is not limited to historiography. Cicero's *Pro Flacco* provides a particularly striking example of the trope. One of the accusations against Cicero's client, the former governor of Asia, was that he had broken precedent in forbidding the Jews to send contributions to their temple. Cicero's response is to denigrate the Jews as a barbaric and hostile people, so that he can claim that their resentment of Flaccus is really ground for commendation.[31] His scathing attack on the Jewish race ends with the claim that their defeat by Rome illustrates how little the gods care for them:

> quam cara dis immortalibus esset docuit, quod est uicta, quod elocata, quod serua facta.[32]
>
> Just how dear [that race] is to the immortal gods was shown by the fact that it was defeated, farmed out [i.e. to the *publicani*], made a slave. (Cic. *Flac.* 69)

Cicero is referring to Pompey's intervention in Judaea in 63 BCE. Describing this as enslavement (*serua facta*) is meant to be humiliating. It is the final salvo in Cicero's attempt to disparage Flaccus' Jewish critics. Yet Pompey did not annex Judaea as a province; instead he left it as an allied kingdom under the Hasmonean ethnarch Hyrcanus, although it was required to pay tribute.[33] If

[31] See further p. 47 and Barclay 1996 pp. 286–8.

[32] *Serua facta* is a sixteenth-century emendation by François Dubois (Franciscus Sylvius) to the transmitted *seruata*, which makes little sense here. *Serua facta* is printed by Clark (OCT, 1909) and Boulanger (Budé, 1938). Fruechtel (Teubner, 1932) prints *serua*, following Angelius.

[33] See Smallwood 1976 pp. 27–30.

this state of relative autonomy constitutes enslavement, what is the condition of the provinces subject to direct Roman rule?

The yoke of Roman rule

The conquest of foreign peoples is often described in terms of breaking animals to harness. The verbs *domare*, *perdomare*, *subigere*, *frangere* and *coercere* – all regularly used of taming animals – are widespread in accounts of Roman expansion.[34] Since slaves are often assimilated to domesticated animals, these animalising metaphors resonate with the broader language of enslavement.[35] The link is particularly strong in the case of the imagery of the *iugum*. The yoke that was forced on the necks of draught animals to attach them to plough or vehicle was a potent symbol of slavery.[36] The close association between slavery and the yoke is nicely illustrated by a famous passage preserved in the Elder Seneca's collection of declamations, which cynically argues that Cicero had no reason for not subjecting himself to Mark Antony by begging his forgiveness:

[34] For *domare* ('to subdue (animals) by taming, domesticate, break in', *OLD* s.v. § 1; cf. *TLL* 1943.72–1944.60), see e.g. Sall. *Hist.* 3.1, Livy 38.37.4, 43.18.2, Vell. Pat. 2.108.2, 2.117.3, Tac. *Hist.* 5.9.1, *Ann.* 14.29.2, Suet. *Aug.* 21.1, 81.1 and Flor. 1.11.8, 1.37.6, 1.39.7. For *perdomare* ('to tame (esp. wild animals) thoroughly, break in', *OLD* s.v. § 1; cf. *TLL* 1280.73–1281.3 and 1281.14–23), see e.g. Sall. *Hist.* 1.11; Livy 8.13.8, 28.12.12, 39.2.6, 39.29.5, 41.17.1, 45.43.4; Vell. Pat. 2.90.1, 2.95.2, 2.97.4; Plin. *Ep.* 2.7.2; and Tac. *Hist.* 5.1.1, *Ann* 3.47.4, 4.5.1. For *subigere* ('to drive under a yoke', 'to break in, tame an animal', *OLD* s.v. § 3b and 4; cf. the passages cited there), see e.g. Cic. *Font.* 13; [Caes.] *B Gall* 8.46.1; Sall. *Cat.* 2.2; Hor. *Carm.* 2.1.23; Livy 2.49.2, 8.13.8, 28.43.14, 30.9.2, 34.18.1; Tac. *Agr.* 33.3, *Hist.* 5.9.1, *Ann.* 4.51.3; and Flor. 1.11.8. For *frangere* ('to reduce to obedience, break in', *OLD* s.v. § 11b; cf. *TLL* 1249.27, 1251.20–4), see e.g. Caes. *B Gall.* 1.31.7, Livy 9.19.4, Vell. Pat. 1.12.1, Val. Max. 6.4.1, Tac. *Ann.* 14.31.2 and Flor. 1.33.9. For *coercere* ('to keep under physical control (horses, etc.)', *OLD* s.v. § 5; cf. *TLL* 1435. 43–61), see e.g. Livy 8.2.11; Sall. *Iug.* 91.7; Tac. *Hist.* 5.9.2, *Ann.* 3.41.1, 4.5.2; and Suet. *Aug.* 21.

[35] On the animalisation of slaves in Roman culture and literature see especially Bradley 2000.

[36] See the many references to the servile yoke (*iugum seruile*) or yoke of slavery (*iugum seruitutis*), including Cic. *Rep.* 2.46 and *Phil.* 1.6, Val. Max. 8.9.2e, Sen. *De ira* 2.14.4 and Just. *Epit.* 6.9.7, 11.14.7 and 15.4.12. It is worth noting that, as well as symbolising oppression and coercion (see Nisbet and Hubbard 1970 p. 373 on the oppressive character of the ancient yoke), the yoke could also provide a powerful image of partnership, e.g. in marriage (because the Greeks and Romans used a double yoke). See ibid. pp. 373–4 and 398 and Nisbet and Hubbard 1978 pp. 80–1 on its use in erotic contexts.

nam quod ad seruitutem pertinet, non recusabit; iam collum tritum habet. et Pompeius illum et Caesar subegerunt. ueteranum mancipium uidetis.

As for slavery, he will not refuse it. His neck is already chafed. Both Pompey and Caesar drove him under the yoke. You are looking at a slave of long standing. (Sen. *Suas.* 6.12)

Here the language of chattel slavery (*seruitus*, *mancipium*) is seamlessly interwoven with the imagery of the yoke (*collum tritum*, *subigere*).

References to 'accepting the yoke' (*iugum accipere*, *recipere*, etc.) are common in accounts of Roman conquest.[37] In his history of Rome's expansion, Velleius Paterculus says that it was between the First and Second Punic Wars that Sardinia was securely yoked to the empire (*certum recepit imperi iugum*, 2.38.2). Valerius Maximus describes Scipio Africanus' achievement in defeating Hannibal as fixing the yoke to the neck of conquered Carthage (*deuictae Karthaginis ceruicibus inposito iugo*, 6.9.2). Manilius writes similarly that Carthage's conquered turrets had accepted the yoke (*accepisse iugum*, 4.40). Livy says that the campaigns of T. Sempronius Gracchus in the early second century BCE induced the peoples of Celtiberia to accept the yoke (*iugum accipere*, 40.49.1). Elsewhere, a Roman general chides an ambassador from the Seleucid king Antiochus III for thinking he is in any position to negotiate with Rome after his defeat in the Syrian War:

non solum frenis, sed etiam iugo accepto, quae disceptatio ex aequo, cum imperium patiendum sit, relicta est?

You have taken not just the bit but the yoke. What place is left for discussion on equal terms, when you must endure our command? (Livy 37.36.5)

[37] It is worth distinguishing the image of yoking an animal to a plough or chariot from that of forcing a defeated enemy to bend and pass beneath an arch formed by a spear suspended horizontally between two upright spears, an archaic Italian practice referred to as 'sending beneath the yoke' (*sub iugum mittere*). On the latter see especially Paul. Fest. 92 and Livy 3.28.10–11 with *TLL* s.v. *mittere* 1184.10–30 and Kissel 1997 and, on its possible ritual significance, Versnel 1970, Wagenvoort 1947 and Warde Fowler 1913. There is an obvious potential for interaction between the two senses of *iugum*. Florus, for example, says that Cincinnatus, summoned from his plough to lead a Roman army against the Aequi, defeated them and – so as not to abandon his imitation of rural labour – sent them beneath the yoke *like cattle* (*uictos, ne quid a rustici operis imitatione cessaret, more pecudum sub iugum misit*, 1.5.13). This represents the sending of the Aequi beneath the 'yoke' as a literal yoking (and constitutes an implicit aetiology of the *sub iugum missio* which explains it as a borrowing from agricultural practice).

Scipio turns to the imagery of mastering animals – the bit (*frena*) and the yoke (*iugum*) – to convey the Seleucids' total subjection to Roman power. He wants them to be under no illusion as to their position: they have placed themselves entirely at Rome's mercy.

Slave and animal imagery are similarly interlaced in descriptions of Roman conquest in the poetry of praise. When the Spanish Cantabri (against whom Augustus campaigned from 27 to 16 BCE) first appear in Book 2 of Horace's *Odes*, he writes of the 'Cantabrian who has not been taught to bear our yoke' (*Cantabrum indoctum iuga ferre nostra*, *Carm.* 2.6.2). After their (supposed) conquest, he writes:[38]

seruit Hispanae uetus hostis orae
Cantaber sera domitus catena

The old enemy from the edge of Spain, the Cantabrian, serves us as a slave. The chain has tamed him at last. (ibid. 3.8.21–2)

The idea that the Cantabri are beasts to be tamed returns in *domitus*. This time it is combined with explicit reference to slavery in the verb *seruit* and the reference to chains – a common punishment for recalcitrant slaves. The Cantabri return one more time, when Horace exclaims that the 'once untameable' Cantabrian (*Cantaber non ante domabilis*) is now in awe of Caesar (ibid. 4.14.41).

Claudius is praised in the same terms for his conquest of Britain. The series of epigrams in the Latin Anthology entitled 'The Praise of Caesar' (*Laus Caesaris*) celebrates Britain's subjection to the yoke.[39] One boasts that Britain 'has lowered its neck to bear the weight of an unaccustomed yoke' (*subdidit insueto colla premenda iugo*).[40] The elaborate metaphor evokes the yoke in all its physicality: the yoke itself, the neck that must be placed beneath it, and the terrible weight – suggested by the adjective *insuetum* and the verb *premere* (to press or crush). Another epigram professes wonder at how quickly Britain lowered its once free neck to the

[38] Nisbet and Rudd 2004 ad loc. date the poem to 25 BCE, after the initial campaign of 27–25 but some ten years before the final defeat of the Cantabri at the hands of Agrippa in 16 BCE.

[39] *Anth. Lat.* I 417–24 Shackleton-Bailey. On the *Laus Caesaris*, wrongly attributed to Seneca in the *Anthology*, see further Barrett 2000 and Breitenbach 2009.

[40] *Anth. Lat.* I 424. 8 Shackleton Bailey.

conqueror (*libera uictori quam cito colla dedit*).[41] *Colla dare* again suggests an animal submitting to the yoke. In a mock funeral dirge for Claudius in Seneca's *Apocolocyntosis*, which presumably parodies the language of the Claudian court, the mourners praise him for commanding the Britons and Brigantes to give their necks into Roman chains (*dare Romuleis colla catenis iussit*).[42] This time the reference to chains (*catenae*) rather than a yoke evokes slavery even more explicitly. In the *Octavia*, Claudius is again praised – this time without irony – for having been the first to impose the yoke on the Britons (*Britannis primus imposuit iugum*).[43]

Statius writes in very similar terms of the young Vettius Bolanus' campaigns in Armenia under Nero:

quippe ille iuuentam
protinus ingrediens pharetratum inuasit Araxen
belliger indocilemque fero seruire Neroni
Armeniam.

At the very moment that he entered manhood, he embarked on war and invaded quiver-bearing Araxes and Armenia, which would not learn slavery to fierce Nero. (Stat. *Silv.* 5.2.31–4)

Like a difficult slave, Armenia is *indocilis seruire*: it will not be tamed by its master.[44] Hence the need for a violent lesson. Martial acclaims Domitian's 'victory' over Dacia in similar terms. Writing of the tomb of Cornelius Fuscus, a praetorian prefect killed in an earlier expedition into Dacia and apparently buried there, he says:

non timet hostilis iam lapis iste minas;
grande iugum domita Dacus ceruice recepit
et famulum uictrix possidet umbra nemus.

That slab no longer fears hostile threats.
The Dacian, his neck tamed, has accepted the mighty yoke.
A conquering shade possesses the servile grove. (Martial 6.76.4–6)

Domita ceruice emphasises the physicality of the process of taming, *grande* the burden of the yoke. The Dacian landscape has been

41 *Anth. Lat.* I 418.4 Shackleton Bailey.
42 ... *Britannos ultra noti* | *litora ponti* | *et caeruleos scuta Brigantas* | *dare Romuleis colla catenis* | *iussit*... (Sen. *Apocol.* 12.3).
43 *Octavia* 41.
44 See *TLL* s.v. *docilis* 1767.32–44 for its application to animals.

enslaved (*famulus nemus*). As the latter claim illustrates, claims of Roman mastery are not limited to conquered peoples but also extend to the natural world. This is particularly true of rivers. Ovid rejoices that the waters of the Rhine have been reduced to slavery (*famulae aquae*, *Fast.* 1.286). Martial makes the same boast of the Danube (*famulae Histri aquae*, 5.3.1–2). A Roman inscription from Dacia boasts that Roman *uirtus* can tame (*domare*) anything since even the swift Danube has been put beneath the yoke (*sub iugum*, *AE* 2004 1182).

This evidence for the widespread deployment of the language and imagery of slavery in accounts of Roman conquest has parallels in other media. Throughout this period, visual representations of Roman victories in both public and private contexts abound in images of dejected captives – men, women and even children prostrated and in chains.[45] Whether we take these as representations of particular acts of enslavement or as a trope for the condition of the defeated peoples (and they are surely both), they constitute a visual analogue to the metaphors of enslavement discussed here. The ritual of the triumph celebrated conquest in similar terms. The victorious general was preceded by chained captives and by representations of the cities, peoples and landscapes he had conquered.[46] Ovid offers a rare insight into the appearance of these triumphal images. In his exile poetry, he twice imagines that Augustus will celebrate a triumph for his German conquests (a triumph he may not even hear of, let alone see). Both poems describe an image of Germania being carried in the triumphal procession. In both cases she is represented as a captive:

crinibus en etiam fertur Germania passis,
 et ducis inuicti sub pede maesta sedet,
collaque Romanae praebens animosa securi
 uincula fert illa, qua tulit arma, manu.

See! Even Germania is carried there, her hair in disarray. She sits despondent beneath the foot of the invincible leader. She offers her proud neck to the Roman axe and bears chains in the hand that once bore arms. (Ov. *Tr.* 4.2.43–6)

[45] See especially de Souza 2011, Bradley 2004 and Ferris 2000.
[46] Captives: Östenberg 2009 ch. 3 and Beard 2007 ch. 4. Representations: Östenberg 2009 ch. 4 and Beard 2007 ch. 5.

Sic fera quam primum pauido Germania uultu
ante triumphantis serua feratur equos.

So may wild Germania soon with fearful face be carried as a slave before your triumphing horses. (Ov. *Pont.* 2.8.39–40)

In Ovid's eyes, the iconography of the triumph reduces Germania to a slave (*serua*). These representational strategies which assimilate conquest to enslavement reflect – and also work to legitimise – the mass enslavements that often accompanied Roman conquest.[47]

Rebels and slaves

The metaphor of enslavement is not limited to the moment of conquest. Revolt is another context in which the language of slavery often comes to the fore. Particularly striking is a series of speeches attributed to Roman generals which seek to incite Roman indignation by representing Rome's rebellious subjects as recalcitrant slaves. The first is a speech Livy assigns to Cato the Censor, dispatched to Spain to consolidate Roman control after a series of native revolts in the decade following the expulsion of the Carthaginians from the peninsula. On the eve of the first battle against the Spanish rebels, he says:

imperium nobis citra Hiberum amissum est. hoc armis et uirtute reciperetis oportet, et nationem rebellantem magis temere quam constanter bellantem iugum quo se exuit accipere rursus cogatis.

We have lost our control of this side of the Ebro. You must recover it with your weapons and your courage. You must force this tribe – opportunistic rebels rather than obdurate enemies – to submit again to the yoke that it has cast off. (Livy 34.13.8–9)

In typically Roman fashion, Cato insists that a foreign people has only one chance to wage war (*bellare*) against Rome; once it has submitted, any further conflict can only be revolt (*rebellio*, literally 'fighting again') and should be met with both force and contempt.

47 The literary evidence for mass enslavement is catalogued by Volkmann 1990. Bradley 2004 highlights the importance of the visual evidence. See also Bradley 1994b pp. 33–4 and Bradley 1987 (especially p. 57).

As rebels the Spanish deserve no respect: their resistance is a sign of recklessness (*temeritas*) not determination (*constantia*). They are like animals who have thrown off the yoke (*iugo se exuere*) and need to be broken to it again (*accipere cogere*).[48] Cato's masterly rhetoric is echoed by the narrator in the description of the challenges Cato faced in reclaiming the Spanish as slaves, quoted earlier, which follows at 34.18.1–2.

The same contempt for those who have once subjected themselves to Rome and later rebel can be found in a speech that Livy attributes to Publius Scipio (the father of Africanus) during the Second Punic War. Before a battle with Hannibal, he tells his men that the Carthaginian general was born the 'tributary, subject and slave of the Roman people' (*uectigalis stipendiariusque et seruus populi Romani*) and so cannot be a serious threat (Livy 21.41.7). (This is of course a tendentious interpretation of Carthage's relationship to Rome in the aftermath of the First Punic War.) He goes on to encourage his men to fight their Carthaginian enemies as if they were their slaves:

itaque uos ego, milites, non eo solum animo quo aduersus alios hostes soletis, pugnare uelim, sed cum indignatione quadam atque ira, uelut si seruos uideatis uestros arma repente contra uos ferentes.

And so, soldiers, I want you to fight not just with the spirit you show against other enemies but with outrage and anger, as if you were seeing your slaves suddenly taking up arms against you. (Livy 21.41.10)

Scipio wants his men to feel the same outrage at this rebellion as they would at a slave revolt. Scipio's rhetoric can be traced back to Polybius' earlier version of this speech, in which Scipio tells his troops that they have nothing to fear since the Carthaginians 'have paid much tribute and have for a long time been all but their slaves (μόνον δ' οὐχὶ δουλεύοντες)'.[49] But Livy's version pushes the metaphor considerably further. Where Polybius stops just short of describing the Carthaginians as slaves (μόνον δ' οὐχὶ), Livy refers

[48] For other descriptions of revolt as shaking off the yoke of Roman rule, cf. Plin. *Pan.* 11.5, where hostile tribes shake off the yoke (*iugum excusserant*) under Domitian (only to be put in their place by Trajan) and Flor. 1.30.2, where Macedonia under Andriscus shakes off the yoke (*iugum excutit Macedo*) in the Fourth Macedonian War.

[49] πολλοὺς δ' ἐξενηνοχότες φόρους, μόνον δ' οὐχὶ δουλεύοντες αὐτοῖς ἤδη τοσούτους χρόνους (Polyb. 3.64.4).

to Hannibal as a slave without qualification, substitutes the concrete noun *seruus* for the participle δουλεύοντες, and adds the exhortation to see this as a slave revolt.

A speech from Cassius Dio's history makes a similar appeal to masterly contempt for rebellion.[50] Confronting Boudicca's revolt in Britain in 60 CE, the Roman general Gaius Suetonius Paulinus exhorts his men to despise the rebellious Britons as slaves:

μάλιστα μὲν οὖν ἔγωγε νικήσειν ἡμᾶς ἐλπίζω καὶ τῇ παρὰ τῶν θεῶν συμμαχίᾳ ... καὶ τῇ πατρῴᾳ ἡμῶν ἀνδρίᾳ ... καὶ ταῖς ἐμπειρίαις ... τῷ τε ἀξιώματι (οὐ γὰρ ἀντιπάλοις τισὶν ἀλλὰ δούλοις ἡμετέροις συμβαλοῦμεν, οὓς καὶ ἐλευθέρους καὶ αὐτονόμους ὄντας ἐνικήσαμεν).

I have the highest hopes of victory, because of our alliance with the gods ... because of our inherited courage ... because of our experience ... and because of our rank (for we are fighting not against equal adversaries but against our own slaves, whom we defeated even when they were free and independent). (Dio 62.11.3)

Like Livy's Scipio, Paulinus tells his men that the Britons are their subjects and therefore their slaves (δοῦλοι). He assumes that the Britons are necessarily even weaker in their present state of slavery than they were when they were free. The inherent superiority (ἀξίωμα) of free men over slaves will guarantee victory. In other words, Paulinus seeks to convince his men of their invincibility by identifying empire with slavery – a sphere of domination where resistance is (he believes) both despicable and futile.

These are only representations of the rhetoric that might be used in such contexts, but it is significant that they share recourse to the paradigm of enslavement to condemn uprisings against Rome. The trope mobilises contempt for, and outrage at, resistance to Rome; it reaffirms Roman self-confidence; and it legitimates – even demands – Roman violence. Like ornery beasts and troublesome slaves, rebels respond only to force.[51] The masterly rhetoric of these Roman commanders has its parallels in what we know of

[50] See n. 101 below for Dio's place in the Roman historiographical tradition.

[51] Cf Said 1993 p. xii on similar tropes in modern imperial cultures: 'the disturbingly familiar ideas about flogging or death or extended punishment being required when "they" misbehaved or became rebellious, because "they" mainly understood force or violence best'.

Roman practice in suppressing revolts. There is ample evidence, especially from Palestine, that the Romans regularly crucified captured rebels – a punishment normally reserved for slaves.[52] In any case, the alternative to crucifixion was often enslavement.[53]

The *populus dominus*

Although metaphors of enslavement are particularly widespread in descriptions of conquest and revolt, they are certainly not limited to those contexts. Slavery can also provide a paradigm for ongoing subjection to Roman rule. Many epithets are used to mark Rome as an imperial power in the triumphalist rhetoric of Latin literature. The Roman people is often styled the conqueror (*uictor, domitor, pacator*) and ruler (*princeps, imperator, moderator, arbiter*) of the world (*omnes gentes* or *orbis terrarum*).[54] But the most common epithet is *dominus* (master). This holds true from the first century BCE to the third CE and across all genres. Cicero repeatedly styles the *populus Romanus* as 'master of all peoples' (*dominus omnium gentium*), a boast that is echoed in Suetonius (*dominus gentium populus*) and Florus (*Romani gentium domini*).[55] Livy, Velleius Paterculus and Valerius Maximus all call Rome 'mistress of the world' or 'mistress of the peoples' (*ciuitas domina orbis terrarum, ciuitas gentium*

[52] For crucifixion as a slave penalty, see p. 125 n. 2. Aubert 2002 pp. 120–7 concludes that 'crucifixion was a normal way to execute rebels' (p. 122). The evidence he cites is largely limited to Judaea, where crucifixion is well attested (see e.g. Joseph. *BJ* 2.75, 306 and 308, 3.321, 5.289 and 449–51 and 7.201–2; *AJ* 17.295 and 20.102 and *Vit.* 420–1 with Kuhn 1982 pp. 724–36 and Hengel 1978 pp. 46–50). But Tacitus suggests that crucifixion was in store for Boudicca's British rebels (*Ann.* 14.33.2 with pp. 124–7). It is also significant that bandits (*latrones*) seem to have been crucified in several provinces (Aubert pp. 119–20), since resistance to Rome was often classed as banditry (*latrocinium*). See *Dig.* 49.15.24 and Grünewald 2004 ch. 2. On the brutality with which resistance was repressed, see also Brunt 1990 pp. 314–16 (focusing on the first century BCE) and cf. Harris 1979 pp. 50–3.

[53] For the enslavement of rebels (like other captives), see e.g. Caes. *B Gall.* 7.89.5 and Joseph. *BJ* 3.305, 6.420, 7.118. See further n. 47 above.

[54] *Victor*: Cic. *Phil.* 3.35, 6.12, *Planc.* 11, *Dom.* 90, *De or.* 2.76, Sen. *Control.* 2.1.5 Sen. *Ben.* 5.15.6, Plin. *HN* praef. 16, 36.118, Juv. 2.73 and 162, Flor. 1.44.3 and 2.1.2; *domitor*: Plin. *HN* 36.118; *pacator*: Sen. *Ben.* 5.15.6. *princeps*: Cic. *Planc.* 11, Livy praef. 3, 34.58.8, 42.39.3; *imperator*: Cic. *Dom.* 90, Sall. *Iug.* 31.20; *moderator*: Sall. *Hist.* 1.55.11; *arbiter*: Flor. 2.6.7.

[55] Cic. *Leg. agr.* 2.22, *Planc.* 11, *Phil.* 6.12 (and cf. *Dom.* 90); Suet. *Calig.* 35.3, Flor. 2.26.14. Cf. also [Sall.] *Ad Caes. sen.* 2.5.5 (*populus qui dominus erat*).

domina, urbs gentium domina).[56] Horace, Ovid and Martial dub Rome the 'mistress city' (*domina Roma, domina urbs*).[57]

Jupiter's famous prophecy of Rome's future greatness in Virgil's *Aeneid* is similarly couched as a promise of *mastery*:

> mecumque fouebit
> Romanos, rerum dominos gentemque togatam:
> sic placitum. ueniet lustris labentibus aetas
> cum domus Assaraci Pthiam clarasque Mycenas
> seruitio premet ac uictis dominabitur Argis.

And [Juno] will join me in favouring the Romans, masters of the world, the togate race. So it is ordained. As the years slip by, there will come a time when the house of Assaracus will crush Phthia and renowned Mycenae with slavery, and be master of conquered Argos. (Verg. *Aen.* 1.281–5)

Aeneas' descendants are promised mastery over the world in general (*rerum domini*) and the Greeks in particular (*dominabitur Argis*). Enslavement (*seruitium*) awaits the Greek cities – and it will be a harsh experience, as the violence of the verb *premere* ('crush') suggests. The trope of crushing the conquered with slavery (*seruitio premere*), employed by Caesar in the epigraph to this chapter and Virgil here and echoed by later authors, deserves more attention as a counterweight to the more often cited Virgilian injunction to spare those who submit (*parcere subiectis*, *Aen.* 6.853).[58] Jupiter's prophecy recalls and inverts Hector's prediction of the fall of Troy and Andromache's enslavement in the *Iliad*.[59] So too Apollo's later prophecy of the mastery destined for the house of Aeneas (*domus Aeneae cunctis dominabitur oris | et nati natorum et qui nascentur ab illis*, 3.97–8) reworks a promise that Homer's Poseidon makes to Aeneas (with *dominabitur* translating ἀνάξει).[60] The repeated metaphors of Roman mastery are thus part of the

[56] Livy 38.51.4, Vell. Pat. 2.29.4, Val. Max. 7.3.1.

[57] Hor. *Carm.* 4.14.44, Ov. *Am.* 2.14.16, *Met.* 15.447 (with Bömer 1969–86 ad loc.) and *Pont.* 4.5.7 (with Helzle 1989), Mart. 1.3.3, 3.1.5, 9.64.4, 10.103.9 and 12.21.9. See also Christ 1938 pp. 83–9.

[58] Cf Caes. *B Gall.* 7.77.16 (*perpetua premitur seruitute*), *Anth. Lat.* 1 424.8 Shackleton Bailey (*subdidit colla premenda iugo*) and Tac. *Ann.* 2.73.2 (*Germanias seruitio premere*).

[59] See Hom. *Il.* 6.448–65 with Kenney 1979 225 n. 13.

[60] νῦν δὲ δὴ Αἰνείαο βίη Τρώεσσιν ἀνάξει | καὶ παίδων παῖδες, τοί κεν μετόπισθε γένωνται (Hom. *Il.* 20.307–8). See Heyworth 1993.

Aeneid's complex engagement with the Homeric poems.[61] But they also resonate with a wider rhetoric of mastery (such as Cicero's *dominus populus*) and must, in so canonical a text, have had a significant impact on later Roman self-fashioning.[62]

Rome is still being represented as a masterly power a century later in Silius Italicus' epic on the Second Punic War. He styles Italy the 'master land' (*terra dominans*, *Pun.* 4.228). The Romans' imperial ambitions lead to war with those, like Veii, that refuse to accept the yoke (*acceptare iugum*, *Pun.* 7.41). Their rivalry with Carthage is a contest to see who will master the world. In challenging Rome, Carthage is seeking 'to claim the reins of power and to place a new yoke on the world' (*rerum deposcere frenos | et terris mutare iugum*, *Pun.* 3.226–7). Before the final battle at Zama, Hannibal declares, 'we fight for the world, which will today receive its master' (*certatus nobis hodie dominum accipit orbis*, *Pun.* 17.337).

Slaves to Rome

These assertions of Roman mastery have their counterpart in a rhetoric of provincial slavery. Cicero, for example, warns his brother Quintus that the Greeks have been trained to flattery by their long enslavement (*diuturna seruitus*, *Q Fr.* 1.1.16), by which he presumably means their subjection first to the kings and then to Rome. Elsewhere he claims that the Greeks chose to be slaves to the Romans rather than to rule over others (*seruire populo Romano quam imperare aliis maluisse, Leg. Man.* 41). Cicero sometimes applies the paradigm of slavery somewhat more narrowly, to define a particular mode of submission to Rome. This can be seen in a comment he makes while contrasting the nature of domestic and foreign conflicts in the *Fourth Catilinarian*:

hostes alienigenae aut oppressi seruiunt aut recepti beneficio se obligatos putant; qui autem ex numero ciuium dementia aliqua deprauati hostes patriae semel esse

[61] Cf. also *unde genus Longa nostrum dominabitur Alba* (*Aen.* 6.766), *aduentare uirum et partis petere agmen easdem | partibus ex isdem et summa dominarier arce* (7.69–70).

[62] Suetonius tells us that Augustus turned to Virgil's promise of mastery (*Romanos rerum dominos gentemque togatam*) in order to rebuke the Roman people for their failure to wear the toga in the Forum (*Aug.* 40.5).

coeperunt, eos, cum a pernicie rei publicae reppuleris, nec ui coercere nec beneficio placare possis.[63]

Foreign enemies are either crushed and serve us as slaves or admitted [to our friendship] and consider themselves bound to us by the favour. But citizens, once they have been corrupted by some madness and become enemies of their country, cannot be subdued with force or appeased with favours, even when you have prevented them from overthrowing the state. (Cic. *Cat.* 4.22)

Cicero's point is that the hostility of citizens, unlike that of foreigners, is unending – and hence that his own victory over Catiline was won at a higher personal cost than were the victories of those who fought foreign foes. What matters for my purposes is that he distinguishes two ways in which Rome's foreign enemies are pacified: some serve as slaves (*seruiunt*); others are bound by their own sense of moral obligation for Roman benefactions (*beneficio se obligatos putant*). The latter phrase reflects the ethic of reciprocity, which is discussed further in Chapter 4. What defines slavery in this contrast is its coercive aspect (*oppressi*; *ui coercere*). It provides the paradigm for the condition of those peoples whose obedience to Rome depends on the threat of force.

Cicero's *Verrines* suggest a slightly different contrast between servile and other forms of subjection. Explaining why earlier generations of Romans (unlike Verres) had refrained from expropriating the civic art of Greek states, Cicero writes:

etenim mirandum in modum Graeci rebus istis, quas nos contemnimus, delectantur. itaque maiores nostri facile patiebantur haec esse apud illos quam plurima: apud socios, ut imperio nostro quam ornatissimi florentissimique essent; apud eos autem quos uectigalis aut stipendiarios fecerant tamen haec relinquebant, ut illi, quibus haec iucunda sunt quae nobis leuia uidentur, haberent haec oblectamenta et solacia seruitutis.

For the Greeks take extraordinary pleasure in [their public works of art] which we despise. And so our ancestors readily allowed them to retain as much of them as possible. In the case of the allies, this was to ensure that they would reach the heights of magnificence and splendour under our rule. As for those who had been made tributary and tax-paying, they left them these at least so that they, who take such delight in things that seem trivial to us, might have them as a distraction and consolation for their enslavement. (*2 Verr.* 4.134)

[63] On *recepti*, see p. 165 n. 26.

Here Cicero divides the Greeks into allies (*socii*) and tributary peoples (*uectigales aut stipendiarii*) and describes the condition of the latter as enslavement (*seruitus*).[64] Hence the need for petty concessions that make their life more bearable. Here it is not coercion but the exaction of tribute that constitutes enslavement. This is an even wider-reaching definition, given that the vast majority of provincial communities paid tribute. (And this in a speech delivered on behalf of provincials and propounding a relatively benign vision of empire.[65]) Both these passages take for granted the servile condition of most of Rome's subjects, even if a privileged few are imagined to enjoy a less coercive and degrading form of association with Rome.

More than a century later, Tacitus and Pliny the Younger are still describing the condition of the provinces in these terms. Tacitus applies the language of slavery to ongoing Roman rule as well as to conquest. In the *Annals* he writes that Boudicca's revolt spread to any British tribes who had not yet been broken by enslavement (*nondum seruitio fracti*), thus identifying the condition of the provinces as *seruitium* (*Ann.* 14.31.2). In the *Agricola*, he claims that the Gauls of his own time have lost their martial spirit with their liberty (*amissa uirtute pariter ac libertate*, *Agr.* 11.4). These are not the Gauls of Caesar's conquests but those of the early second century CE. Yet they are still being represented as having lost their freedom – that is, as slaves. When Tacitus observes that the British have been 'broken to obedience but *not yet* to slavery' (*iam domiti ut pareant, nondum ut seruiant*), the implication of *nondum* is that servility is the inevitable end result of submitting to Rome (*Agr.* 13.1). All three of these passages develop a distinctively Tacitean vision of the emasculating effects of subjection to Rome, discussed further in Chapter 3.

Tacitus' contemporary Pliny too describes Roman rule as enslavement. A particularly striking example can be found in a passage of the *Panegyricus* praising Trajan's management of the grain supply:[66]

[64] See p. 42 n. 67 for Cicero's use of *socii* to denote a privileged few subject communities, here those cities that were immune from tribute.

[65] On the idealised vision of empire in the *Verrines*, see p. 45 and pp. 192–3.

[66] See also *Pan.* 31.3 and 31.6 (discussed at p. 172) and *Ep.* 8.24.4 (discussed at pp. 99–101).

hic alternis commeatibus orientem occidentemque connectit ut ... omnes gentes discant quanto libertati discordi seruientibus sit utilius, unum esse cui seruiant.

[This emperor] binds together East and West with alternating commerce so that ... all peoples can learn how much more profitable it is for those who are slaves to dissentious freedom to be slaves to one master only. (Plin. *Pan.* 32.2)

In the same breath that he extols the benefits of Roman rule, Pliny asserts that all Rome's provinces are slaves to the emperor (*seruiant*). The literal sense of *seruire* is emphasised here by the paradoxical pun of being slaves to freedom (*libertati seruientes*). Pliny implies that freedom can only be an illusion for the peoples of the empire since those who appear to enjoy it are really its slaves. If slavery is inevitable, the emperor is the better master. The metaphor is particularly significant because the *Panegyricus* is a text that is acutely sensitive to the symbolics of power in general and to the paradigm of slavery in particular.[67] Trajan is repeatedly praised for not behaving like a master to his fellow citizens, as Domitian is accused of doing.[68] He is called 'father' not 'master' (*non de domino sed de parente loquimur*, 2.3). This passage shows that Trajan may relate to the citizens as a father, but he is a master to the provinces.[69] There is more to be said about this passage, which will feature again in the discussion of relations of exchange in Chapter 4. For now, it is

[67] The perception and representation of power is of central importance in the *Panegyricus*. Pliny praises the appearance of equality between emperor and citizens, e.g. in social etiquette (*Pan.* 24 and 49) and the layout of the Circus (51), and valorises even the *pretence* of freedom (*liberae ciuitatis simulatio*, 63.5) and the fiction of senatorial participation in power, praising Trajan for urging the senate to 'take responsibility for the empire *as if* they had a share in it' (*capessere quasi communis imperii curas*, 66.2). Bartsch 1994 pp. 148–87 is particularly acute on the centrality of such 'make-believe' for the *Panegyricus*.

[68] Pliny repeatedly describes Rome's enslavement by Domitian. See e.g. *Pan.* 2.5, 45.3, 63.6 and 85.2. Trajan behaves like a father: *Pan.* 2.3, 2.5, 21.4, 45.3 and 53.1.

[69] Pliny is quite clear that Trajan's behaviour as father rather than master and his care for the appearance of equality are both aspects of his relationship to Roman citizens. It is his concern for the freedom of *citizens* that distinguishes Trajan from bad emperors (*Pan.* 2.3–5). It is to *citizens* that he behaves like a father to his children (21.4). It is *citizens* whom he greets with proper courtesy (24.2). It is *citizens* who will be able to return the emperor's gaze in the newly restored Circus (51.3–5). Readers who have translated *ciues* as 'subjects' (notably Radice's Loeb throughout and Durry 1938 p. 44) ignore the opposition between *ciues* and *socii* in Roman discourse in general and the *Panegyricus* in particular (see Chapter 1 with *Pan.* 33.1). Pliny's portrait of the ideal emperor is at the same time an assertion of a special relationship between the emperor and the citizen body – a relationship that is not necessarily available to the other inhabitants of the empire.

enough to note Pliny's unabashed description of the condition of the provinces as enslavement.

The illusion of freedom

How can these claims of Roman mastery be reconciled with the Roman rhetoric of freedom that will be familiar to any reader of Polybius or Livy? The Romans made extensive use of the trope of freedom during their rise to mastery of the Mediterranean. It played a particularly important role in their dealings with the Greek world, where it can be traced back to the end of the Second Macedonian War and T. Quinctius Flamininus' famous proclamation of Greek freedom at the Isthmian games of 196 BCE: 'The senate of the Romans and Titus Quinctius the proconsul, having defeated King Philip and the Macedonians, leave the following peoples free (ἐλεύθεροι), without garrisons, without tribute and subject to their ancestral laws: the Corinthians, Phocians, Locrians, Euboeans, Phthiotic Achaeans, Magnesians, Thessalians and Perrhaebians.'[70] This Roman proclamation was redeploying a long-established trope of Hellenistic diplomacy. The rhetoric of *eleutheria* had been employed by the kings for centuries.[71] Roman statesmen continued to profess their regard for freedom throughout the second century. Roman claims to be the champions of Greek freedom figured prominently in the wars against Nabis (195 BCE), Antiochus III (192–189), Perseus (172–167) and the Achaean League (146).[72] A letter of Q. Fabius Maximus to the Achaean city of Dyme from

[70] 'Ἡ σύγκλητος ἡ Ῥωμαίων καὶ Τίτος Κοΐντιος στρατηγὸς ὕπατος, καταπολεμήσαντες βασιλέα Φίλιππον καὶ Μακεδόνας, ἀφιᾶσιν ἐλευθέρους, ἀφρουρήτους, ἀφορολογήτους, νόμοις χρωμένους τοῖς πατρίοις, Κορινθίους, Φωκέας, Λοκρούς, Εὐβοεῖς, Ἀχαιοὺς τοὺς Φθιώτας, Μάγνητας, Θετταλούς, Περραιβούς' (Polyb. 18.46.5). Cf. Livy 33.32.5 and Plut. *Flam.* 10.4. For the enabling *senatus consultum* providing for the liberation of the Greek cities, see Polyb. 18.44.2–7, App. *Mac.* 9.3 and Diod. Sic. 28.13. On the origins and development of this rhetoric of freedom, see Dmitriev 2010 and also Walsh 1996, Gruen 1984 pp. 145–51 and Ferrary 1988 pp. 58–63.

[71] For the Greek precedents see in general Dmitriev 2010 chs. 1–3 and also Raaflaub 2004 on the Persian Wars and Peloponnesian War, Welles 1965 and Seager and Tuplin 1980 on the King's Peace and the early fourth century, Jones 1940 pp. 96–7 on Alexander, Jones 1940 p. 97 and Gruen 1984 pp. 134–6 on the Successors and Gruen 1984 pp. 134–6 and Walsh 1996 pp. 358–62 on royal rhetoric in the third and second centuries.

[72] See further Dmitriev 2010 chs. 6–9 and Gruen 1984 pp. 147–52.

c. 144 BCE justifies harsh reprisals against an anti-Roman faction on the grounds that they had acted contrary to 'the freedom given in common to the Greeks'.[73] Though the vast majority of the evidence comes from the Greek East, enough survives to show that the Romans also spoke of 'freedom' in the West. A bronze tablet from Alcántara recording the *deditio* of a Spanish tribe in 104 BCE seems to have stated that the tribe was declared free (*liberi*) by the Roman commander after it had satisfied Roman demands.[74]

It should be obvious, however, that this is the instrumental language of diplomacy. It is in no way incompatible with the use of the tropes of mastery and slavery in domestic political discourse. In any case, there is a significant shift even in the language of diplomacy from the end of the second century BCE. The general rhetoric of 'freedom' gives way to the use of 'freedom' as a term to refer to the juridical status of particular communities. The 'freedom' of a city usually entailed some combination of exemption from the governor's jurisdiction, freedom from the billeting of troops and, for a few, immunity from tribute.[75] It was a privileged status to be won, preserved or lost by individual communities. A famous rescript of Octavian to the Samians refuses their request to be granted 'freedom' on the grounds that 'it is not just for the greatest of all favours to be granted arbitrarily and without cause'.[76] Many provincial communities were never 'free'. Others that had once enjoyed this status lost it during the civil wars or under Augustus. By the beginning of the first century CE 'freedom' was a rare privilege among the non-citizen communities of the empire.[77] Several 'free' cities had their privileges revoked by subsequent emperors. New grants were rare. The most significant exception was Nero's 'liberation' of the whole province of Achaea in 67 CE. In imitation of Flamininus he issued his edict at the Isthmian games, proclaiming 'all you Greeks who inhabit Achaea and the land previously [known as] the Peloponnese, accept

[73] *RDGE* 43, 15–16. For the date, see Ferrary 1988 pp. 186–99.

[74] *eos L(ucius) Caesius C(ai) [f(ilius) imperator liberos] esse iussit* (Richardson 1986 pp. 199–201 = *AE* 1986 304, 7–8). *Liberos* here is a conjecture, but a compelling one in this context. See Richardson 1986 p. 200. On *deditio* see further pp. 186–9.

[75] On the status and privileges of *ciuitates liberae* under Rome, see the papers in *Mediterraneo Antico* 2 (1999) and Lintott 1993 pp. 36–40.

[76] *A&R* 13, 4. See further p. 236.

[77] See Jones 1940 pp. 129–31 for a survey of free cities in the Principate.

freedom and immunity'.[78] He boasted that other emperors had freed (ἠλευθέρωσαν) cities, but he alone had freed a province.[79] But Achaea's freedom was soon revoked by Vespasian.[80]

The convention of describing these relatively rare privileges and immunities in terms of 'freedom' has inevitable implications for the condition of other communities. If these privileged communities are 'free', the implication is that other non-citizen communities were not. The loss of these privileges is regularly described as the loss of freedom.[81] Several Roman writers take the rhetoric of the free city to its logical conclusion by styling this 'enslavement'. Thus Florus describes the annexation of Macedonia following the Third Macedonian War as punishing it with 'enslavement' (*Macedoniam seruitute multauit*, 1.30.5). Cassius Dio describes the revocation of the freedom of both Cyzicus and Lycia as 'enslavement' (δουλοῦν).[82] Among the younger Pliny's *Letters* is one written to a certain Maximus, who was being sent to Achaea to reform the troubled internal affairs of the *ciuitates liberae* there (*Ep*. 8.24).[83] Pliny urges Maximus to remember the gravity of his mission. Nothing is more precious than freedom (*quid libertate pretiosius?*, ibid. 7). It would be shameful if the cities lost their privileged status, substituting *slavery* for freedom (*quam turpe,*

[78] πάντες οἱ τὴν Ἀχαΐαν καὶ τὴν ἕως νῦν Πελοπόννησον κατοικοῦντες Ἕλληνες λάβετ' ἐλευθερίαν ἀνισφορίαν (Oliver 296 = Smallwood *GCN* 64, 12–14) The Peloponnese was evidently one of the many places that were renamed by Nero. Cf Suet. *Ner.* 55 with Dittenberger's note at *SIG*³ 814 n. 6.

[79] πόλεις μὲν γὰρ καὶ ἄλλοι ἠλευθέρωσαν ἡγεμόνες, [Νέρων δὲ ὅλη]ν ἐπαρχείαν (ibid. 26–7).

[80] Suet. *Vesp*. 8.4, Paus. 7.17.3–4. According to Pausanias, Vespasian accused the Greeks of having forgotten how to be free (ἀπομεμαθηκέναι φήσας τὴν ἐλευθερίαν τὸ Ἑλληνικόν, Paus. 7.17. 4).

[81] *redditur Rhodiis libertas, adempta saepe aut firmata, prout bellis externis meruerant aut domi seditione deliquerant* (Tac. *Ann.* 12.58.2). *urbium quasdam, foederatas sed ad exitium licentia praecipites, libertate priuauit* (Suet. *Aug* 47.1). *Cyzicenis in ciues R. uiolentius quaedam ausis publice libertatem ademit* (*Tib*. 37.3). *Lyciis ob exitiabiles inter se discordias libertatem ademit* (*Claud.* 25.3). *Achaiam, Lyciam, Rhodum, Byzantium, Samum libertate adempta in prouinciarum formam redegit* (*Vesp*. 8.4).

[82] τούς τε Κυζικηνούς, ὅτι Ῥωμαίους τινὰς ἐν στάσει μαστιγώσαντες ἀπέκτειναν, ἐδουλώσατο (54.7.6), τούς τε Λυκίους στασιάσαντας, ὥστε καὶ Ῥωμαίους τινὰς ἀποκτεῖναι, ἐδουλώσατό (60.17.3).

[83] See Whitton 2010 p. 137 on how this letter contributes to the thematisation of slavery in Book 8 as a whole. Other work on this letter has focused on its reworking of Cic. *Q Fr.* 1.1 and *Flac.* (see Cova 1972 and Zucker 1928), rather than its metaphors of freedom and slavery.

si ... libertas seruitute mutetur, ibid. 8). He goes on to exhort Maximus to hold himself to even higher standards than he did in his previous office, as quaestor in Bithynia:

quo magis nitendum est ne in longinqua prouincia quam suburbana, ne inter seruientes quam liberos, ne sorte quam iudicio missus, ne rudis et incognitus quam exploratus probatusque humanior melior peritior fuisse uidearis.

And so you must make all the more effort so as not to seem to have been more humane, more noble, and more competent in a distant province than in one close to Rome, among slaves rather than free men, when appointed by lot rather than selection, when inexperienced and unknown rather than when tried and proven. (Plin. *Ep.* 8.24.9)

Maximus' new responsibility for the free cities of Achaea is contrasted with his earlier quaestorship in Bithynia. The distinction between *seruientes* and *liberi* is thus a distinction between the provincials he administered in these two roles: not just between Bithynians and mainland Greeks, but between ordinary provincial communities and the more privileged free cities.[84] The freedom of the *liberae ciuitates* implies that the rest of Rome's subjects are like slaves (*seruientes*). Thus the rhetoric of freedom serves to reinforce rather than contradict the idea that Rome's subjects are her slaves. Freedom is the exception, not the rule.

Of course, the freedom enjoyed even by the 'free cities' was a limited one. Many modern scholars have described it as a fiction.[85] The incongruity of the terminology was not lost on the Romans themselves. Cicero observes to Atticus that Greeks value the privileges of a free city because they *think* that these constitute freedom – implying that he does not.[86] Tacitus writes of 'those cities that are *called* free' (*quae ciuitatium liberae uocantur*, *Ann.*

[84] Bithynia contained at least three free cities (Amisus, Chalcedon and Trapezus, Jones 1940 p. 130), but they would have been exempt from the authority of the governor and his staff.

[85] See e.g. Sherwin-White 1973 p. 177: 'Rome's benevolent protectorate over the original category of "free states" quickly changed to the control of a master.'

[86] Cicero is writing about the edict he promulgated as governor: *multaque sum secutus Scaevolae, in iis illud in quo sibi libertatem censent Graeci datam, ut Graeci inter se disceptent suis legibus ... Graeci uero exsultant quod peregrinis iudicibus utuntur. 'nugatoribus quidem' inquies. quid refert? tamen se autonomian adeptos putant* (Cic. *Att.* 6.1.15).

15.45.1). Pliny, in the same letter to Maximus, suggests that the freedom enjoyed by the privileged free cities is only an illusion:

habe ante oculos … Athenas esse quas adeas, Lacedaemonem esse quam regas; quibus reliquam umbram et residuum libertatis nomen eripere durum ferum barbarum est. uides a medicis, quamquam in aduersa ualetudine nihil serui ac liberi differant, mollius tamen liberos clementiusque tractari.

Remember that it is Athens that you go to, Sparta that you will rule. To strip them of the remaining shadow and title of freedom would be harsh, savage, barbaric. You see that free men are treated more gently and more humanely by physicians, though slaves and free men do not differ in their illnesses. (Plin. *Ep.* 8.24.4–5)

Pliny writes that the liberty that these cities enjoy is a mere *umbra et nomen*. But he also implies that it is valued by the Greeks, saying that it would be cruel to destroy it. The idea of Greek freedom is a fiction maintained for the benefit of a Greek audience, one that can be dispensed with when Romans discourse among themselves.

Later perspectives

The longevity of the tropes of Roman mastery and provincial slavery is surprising, given the ongoing political, social and cultural integration of the provinces in this period.[87] One might have expected these processes to have made the language of slavery increasingly irrelevant, even jarring. Yet the metaphors of mastery and enslavement are just as prominent in the works of Statius, Silius Italicus, Pliny and Tacitus and as they are in those of Horace, Virgil, Cicero and Caesar. Moreover, there is some evidence to suggest that they become even more prominent in the late second and early third centuries CE.[88]

No earlier work of Roman historiography, except perhaps Tacitus' *Agricola* (see Chapter 3), uses the metaphor of enslavement to Rome as intensively as Florus' *Epitome Taken from Titus*

[87] On the transformation of the provinces, see pp. 15–16.

[88] What follows is a compressed version of Lavan 2013, which argues that the works of Florus, Cassius Dio, Justin and Herodian reveal a new emphasis on the masterly aspect of Roman power in both Latin and Greek historiography of the second and third centuries CE, and links this to broader changes in the political culture of the empire.

Livius of All the Wars of 700 Years (the title under which it has been transmitted to us), written in the mid to late second century CE.[89] Florus' sequential history of all Rome's wars from its foundation to the reign of Augustus emphasises the power and violence of Roman expansion. The Roman conquest of Italy is compared to a disease (*contagium*) that overcomes its victims one by one (1.3.8). When the Romans cross into Sicily after conquering mainland Italy, they are likened to a forest fire leaping across a river (*more ignis*, 1.18[2].1–2). But the dominant metaphor is one of enslavement, with Florus' narrative turning again and again to the language of slavery (*seruitus*, *seruire*, *dominus*, *dominare*, *dominatio*) in its description of the extension of Roman power from the Romans' fifth-century victories over their Italian neighbours through to Augustus' conquests on the Rhine and Danube. Resistance to Rome is a struggle for freedom. The Spanish, Florus writes, were never able to unite to defend their freedom (*libertatem tueri*, 1.33.3) against the Romans. The Belgae fight fiercely for theirs (*pro libertate pugnantes*, 1.45.4). Defeat brings enslavement. I have already mentioned Florus' description of Macedonia's incorporation as a province as being punished with enslavement (*seruitute multauit*, 1.30.5). Elsewhere, he complains that Pompey did not go far enough in enslaving Armenia, merely imposing the partial slavery (*seruitus*) of accepting rulers imposed by Rome (2.32.43).[90] Florus' Romans are a master people. The Latins support the Tarquins in their attempt to return to Rome because they would like to see the Romans reduced to slavery at home, though they are masters abroad (*ut populus qui foris*

[89] This Florus may or may not be the same Florus who was a poet, friend of Hadrian and possibly also the author of the dialogue *Vergilius orator an poeta*. See further Bessone 1993 (favouring the single Florus thesis), Baldwin 1988 (more guarded) and Courtney 1993 pp. 381–2 and Jal 1967 I pp. cxiii–cxiv (agnostic). The best internal evidence for the date of the work is the statement in the preface that it was 'not much less than 200 years from Augustus to our age' (I praef. 8). Since this could be referring to Augustus' birth (63 BCE) or death (14 CE) or any important date in between, this is consistent with a date as early as 138 CE or as late as 214 CE. The current consensus – relying heavily on circumstantial evidence – is that it was written under Hadrian (Baldwin 1988 pp. 139–42 and Jal 1967 I pp. civ–cxi) or, possibly, Antoninus Pius (Bessone 1993).

[90] *Armenios ... in hoc unum seruitutis genus Pompeius adsueuerat, ut rectores a nobis acciperent* (2.32.43). *in hoc unum seruitutis genus* implies that Armenia's enslavement is only partial – and, by implication, insufficient.

dominabatur saltim domi seruiret, 1.5.1).[91] Reflecting on the civil conflicts that followed Rome's defeat of Carthage, Florus wonders whether Rome might not have been better off limiting her ambitions to being master in Italy (*dominans in Italia*, 1.47.6). Asked by a German tribe who they are, a Roman army responds with the boast 'Romans, the masters of nations' (*Romani gentium domini*, 2.26.14). Florus even coins 'the Roman mastery' (*dominatio Romana*, 2.14.8) as a synonym for the *imperium Romanum*.[92]

Two passages offer a particularly brutal vision of the experience of enslavement to Rome. Describing the long and difficult process of subduing Spain, Florus writes:

plus est prouinciam retinere quam facere. itaque per partes iam huc iam illuc missi duces, qui ferocissimas et in id tempus liberas gentes ideoque impatientes iugi multo labore nec incruentis certaminibus seruire docuerunt.

It is harder to hold on to a province than to create one. And so generals were sent throughout [Spain], now here, now there. With much toil and not without bloody conflict, they taught these most savage peoples – hitherto free and so defiant of the yoke – to be slaves. (Flor. 1.33.8)

The Spanish would not at first accept the yoke of Roman rule (*impatientes iugi*), but they were eventually taught to be slaves (*seruire docuerunt*). Like slaves or draught animals, Rome's subjects are broken to service. The fact that this is Spain – a land that is repeatedly singled out for praise by Florus and the birthplace of the emperors Trajan and Hadrian – makes the metaphor of enslavement all the more striking.[93] Later, Florus recounts the difficulties that Augustus faced in consolidating Roman control over the northern provinces:

[91] Florus here makes a Latin wish out of what is a Roman complaint about the Late Republic in the pseudo-Sallustian *Letter to Caesar* – that the Roman people, which had once been master (*dominus*) of other nations, has made itself a community of slaves (*priuatim sibi quisque seruitutem peperit*) ([Sall.] *Ad Caes. sen.* 2.5.5).

[92] *quodque in annua caeli conuersione fieri solet, ut mota sidera tonent ac suos flexus tempestate significent, sic tum Romanae dominationis, id est humani generis, conuersione penitus intremuit omnique genere discriminum, ciuilibus, externis, seruilibus, terrestribus ac naualibus bellis omne imperii corpus agitatum est* (2.14.7–8). See further Lavan 2013 on this difficult sentence, in which the unprecedented *dominatio Romana* can be construed as meaning 'mastery over Rome' as well as 'the Roman mastery'.

[93] See Jal 1967 I p. cxiii n. 3 for Florus' repeated praise of Spain.

noua quippe pax, necdum adsuetae frenis seruitutis tumidae gentium inflataeque ceruices ab imposito nuper iugo resiliebant.

Peace was still a new experience. Their proud and haughty necks, not yet accustomed to the harness of slavery, struggled against the yoke that had recently been forced upon them. (Flor. 2.21[12].2)

Again Florus combines the language of slavery (*seruitus*) with the imagery of breaking animals (*frena*, *ceruices*, *iugum*). The physicality and violence of the image is striking: the yoke is forced upon them (*impositum*); their necks recoil from it (*resilire*). This is a powerful and uncompromising evocation of the violence of Roman conquest.

Florus is of course describing conquests which took place several centuries in his past, not the empire of his own time. Yet it is nevertheless significant that, despite writing from the vantage point of the second century CE, he still sees enslavement as the telos of Roman expansion. Moreover, his language implies that slavery is the permanent condition of Rome's subjects. The northern provinces were hard to subdue because their inhabitants were *not yet* (*necdum*) accustomed to slavery. The implication is that they are now more docile. Similarly, the implication of *docuerunt seruire* in the previous passage is that the Spanish have now learned their lesson.

A partial explanation for Florus' distinctive use of the metaphor can be found in his personification of the *populus Romanus*. This is the governing trope of the work, which traces the stages of that life from infancy to old age.[94] The recurring metaphors of provincial slavery have gone uncommented, but they must work to reinforce this personification by representing the *populus Romanus* as enjoying personal relations with other peoples. The image is reinforced by Florus' occasional, but equally distinctive, use of the language of patronal and familial relations.[95] Rome is the 'mother and parent' of Italy (*mater ac parens*, 2.6.5); Ostia is Rome's 'client and nursling' (*cliens et alumna*, 2.9.12); the Numidian kingdom is 'under the protection and in the *clientela*' of the senate and people of Rome (*in fide et clientela*, 1.36.3). Collectively, these metaphors

[94] See especially Alonso-Nuñez 1982. [95] See further pp. 201–2 and 206–7.

drawn from social life, which represent the *populus Romanus* variously as mother, patron and master of its subjects, contribute to the trope of personification. While this goes some way towards explaining the frequency of these metaphors, it does not explain the focus on slavery in particular, which is by far the dominant metaphor for Roman rule in the work as a whole. Parallels in other historians of the period suggest that this is part of a wider phenomenon.

The language and imagery of slavery are similarly widespread in the descriptions of imperial powers from Assyria to Rome in Justin's *Epitome of Trogus*. This reworking of the *Philippica* of Pompeius Trogus, a universal history of the Greek world written in Latin during the reign of Augustus, was probably composed in the late second or early third century CE – though it may be as late as the fourth.[96] In Justin, submission to foreign rule is repeatedly described as *seruitus* and the loss of *libertas*; empire is *dominatio*.[97] Particularly striking are the repeated references to the yoke of slavery (*iugum seruitutis*). Philip II forces Macedonian rule like the yoke of slavery on the necks of Greece and Asia (*ceruicibus ueluti iugum seruitutis inponeret*, 6.9.7). The Persians accept the yoke of slavery (*iugum seruitutis*) under Alexander (11.14.7). After his death, India shakes the yoke of slavery from its neck (*ceruicibus iugo seruitutis excusso*, 15.4.12). Philip V of Macedon objects to being dictated to by Greeks, who had once been forced beneath the yoke of Macedonian rule (*sub iugum Macedonici imperii subactos*,

[96] Most estimates have placed it in the late second or early third centuries (see the survey at Syme 1988 pp. 359–61), but the evidence is limited. The most compelling argument is based on the fact that Justin introduces the ethnography of the Parthians with the remark that the Parthian empire 'now' shares the world with the Roman empire (41.1.1). This would be odd in a text written after the displacement of the Arsacid Parthians by the Sassanian Persians in the 220s. But the argument is far from conclusive. An iconoclastic paper by Ronald Syme has drawn attention to some distinctive vocabulary (*stagare*, *adtaminare* and *aduncare*) to argue for a much later date, around 390 CE (Syme 1988). His argument is endorsed by Barnes 1998, who also adduces an instance of *ducatus* which, he argues, must postdate Diocletian's reforms in 260. The case for an earlier date is restated by Yardley 2000, Yardley in Yardley and Heckel 1997 pp. 8–13 and Develin in Yardley and Develin 1994 p. 4.

[97] Subjection to an imperial power as *seruitus*: 6.5.1, 6.9.7, 8.1.3, 11.14.7, 15.4.12, 30.3.9; *seruire*: 41.1.5; loss of *libertas*: 9.3.11, 12.1.6, 24.1.2, 30.3.7, 32.1.2, 32.1.3, 41.6.3. Revolt as a *uindicatio in libertatem*: 13.5.5, 36.1.10. Empire as *dominatio*: 8.2.2, 9.3.11, 24.1.7, 32.1.2. The imperial power as *dominus*: 5.6.6, 8.4.7.

30.3.9). He says that they should be accounting for their conduct to their master, not asserting their freedom (*quibus prius sit seruitutis ratio reddenda quam libertas uindicanda*, ibid.). Rome's empire, when it finally appears at the end of the work, is no different:

nec prius perdomitae prouinciae iugum Hispani accipere potuerunt, quam Caesar Augustus perdomito orbe uictricia ad eos arma transtulit populumque barbarum ac ferum legibus ad cultiorem uitae usum traductum in formam prouinciae redegit.

The Spanish could not accept the yoke of a tamed province before Caesar Augustus had tamed [the rest of] the world, carried his victorious arms to Spain, used the law to convert a wild and barbarous people to a more civilised way of life, and reduced them to the form of a province. (Just. *Epit.* 44.5.8)

As in Florus, Roman rule is a yoke (*iugum*) imposed on the provinces. I do not wish to make too much of this problematic text. Besides the uncertainty surrounding its date, there is the problem of attributing language to Justin as opposed to Trogus (though it is now clear that Justin has substantially reworked his source).[98] Nevertheless this text suggests that Florus may not have been alone in using the language of enslavement more extensively than earlier Latin historians.

A more robust parallel is to be found in the *Roman History* of the senator and historian Cassius Dio, written in the second or third decade of the third century CE.[99] Though he writes in Greek, Dio was a prominent member of the imperial elite.[100] He belonged to one of the leading families of the province of Bithynia. His father was a senator and consul. Dio himself moved to Rome around 180 CE, probably about eighteen years of age, to join the senate. He governed the provinces of Africa, Dalmatia and Pannonia Superior

[98] Jal 1987 drew attention to Justin's efforts to create an autonomous work of his own. See further Yarrow 2006 pp. 110–16, Yardley and Heckel 1997 pp. 11–13 and Yardley and Develin 1994 pp. 5–6. See also Yardley 2003 chapter 5 and Yardley and Heckel 1997 pp. 337–41 on parallels with first- and second-century authors (notably Apuleius), which are presumably Justin's own work.

[99] Although Dio tells us that he spent ten years researching his work and a further twelve writing it (73[72].23.5), the precise dates are uncertain. Dio's *History* ends with his second consulship in 229 CE, after which he retired to his native Nicaea in ill health (80 [79].5.1), at the age of around 65. Millar 1964 pp. 28–32 has him writing between 207 and 219 CE with some minor later additions. Barnes 1984 argues persuasively for a later date, 220–31 CE or perhaps slightly later.

[100] On Dio's biography, see further Swain 1996 pp. 401–8, Barnes 1984 pp. 241–5 and Millar 1964 pp. 5–27.

(a major command, second only to Syria among the imperial provinces) and was an official *amicus* of many or all of the Severan emperors. He ended his career with a prestigious second consulship as the emperor's colleague in 229 CE. Dio knew Latin literature and his work draws upon the Roman historiographical tradition as well as its Greek counterpart.[101] His history provides invaluable evidence for the representation of the imperial project by the senatorial elite a century after Tacitus and Pliny.

Like Florus, Dio regularly represents Roman expansion as a project of enslavement. Early in Rome's history, Coriolanus enslaves the city of the Volsci (δουλώσας, 5.18.2). In the first century BCE the people of Crete, who had never before had a foreign master (δεσπότης ὀθνεῖος), are enslaved (κατεδουλώθησαν) by Metellus Creticus (36.19.3). In a rousing speech to his men, Caesar rehearses the names of the countless peoples ruled by Rome, saying 'we are now their masters' (δεσπόζομεν, 38.38.4). His forces enslave the Gallic Veragri (ἐδουλώσατο, 39.5.4) and Vercingetorix's rebels (ἐδουλώσατο, 40.42.1). In the civil wars, Pompey is criticised for allying himself with Eastern peoples whom he himself had previously enslaved (δουλωθεῖσι, 41.13.3) to Rome. Under Augustus, Egypt is enslaved in 30 BCE (ἐδουλώθη, 51.17.4),[102] as are the Spanish Cantabri and Astures in 22 BCE (ἐδουλώθησαν, 54.5.2). Following their own enslavement (δούλωσις, 53.7.1) the Pannonians bring slavery (δουλεία, 54.20.2) on the people of Noricum by involving them in their doomed rebellion of 16 BCE. The Maritime Alps are enslaved in 14 BCE (ἐδουλώθησαν, 54.24.3); and in 9 CE Germanicus enslaves some unfortunate place in Dalmatia (ἐδουλώσατο, 56.15.1). The metaphor of enslavement is not limited to the period of conquest. When Cyzicus and the Lycian league are deprived of their privileged status as 'free' communities by Augustus and Claudius respectively, both are described as being 'enslaved' (ἐδουλώσατο, 54.7.6 and 60.17.3) – implying that the normal state of the subject communities is slavery. When the people of Arabia first

[101] See e.g. Swain 1996 pp. 403–4.

[102] Reinhold 1988 ad loc. suggests that the metaphor 'reveals Dio's understanding of the harsh administration imposed on Egypt'. But this is to ignore the ubiquity of the language of slavery in Dio's description of Roman rule.

enter his narrative, they are introduced as 'the Arabians who are *now* slaves to the Romans' (Ἀραβίων μὲν τῶν νῦν τοῖς Ῥωμαίοις δουλευόντων, 37.15.1). Here the metaphor of slavery is applied not to the past, but explicitly to Dio's own time.

Dio's widespread use of δουλοῦν and the wider language of slavery constitutes a break with the representation of Roman rule in earlier Greek historiography. Claims that the Romans enslave their subjects are certainly common in speeches ascribed to Rome's enemies.[103] But such language is almost never found in the narrative voice or the rhetoric of Roman speakers, as it is in Dio. Other imperial powers – Persians, Hellenistic kingdoms and Carthaginians – are sometimes described as aiming at mastery, but not Rome.[104] Together, Polybius, Diodorus, Dionysius and Appian can offer only a handful of parallels for Dio's repeated description of Roman conquest as enslavement. Polybius says that Rome's constitution is superior to Sparta's for those who value 'being rulers and masters' (ἐπικρατεῖν καὶ δεσπόζειν) of many peoples (6.50.3). In his narrative of the Second Punic War, he gives P. Scipio (the father of Africanus) a speech in which he exhorts his men to have no fear of the Carthaginians since they have long been 'all but their slaves' (μόνον δ' οὐχὶ δουλεύοντες αὐτοῖς, 3.64.4, cited earlier). Diodorus Siculus says that the defeat of the Achaean League in 146 BCE deprived the Greeks of their ἐλευθερία (32.26.2). But these parallels are few and far between. Of all earlier Greek historians, only Josephus comes close to Dio. In his *Jewish War*, both Roman speakers and Jews who favour accommodation with Rome (including Josephus himself) describe subjection to Rome as enslavement. For example, the future emperor Titus couches an appeal to the Jewish rebels as that of a 'gentle master' (πρᾶος δεσπότης, 6.350) and reminds them that even the

[103] See e.g. Polyb. 9.37.7 (Acarnian ambassador), 11.5.1 (Rhodian ambassador) and 24.13.4 (Philopoemen), Diod. Sic. 32.26.4 (Achaean *strategos*), Dion. Hal. *Ant. Rom.* 5.61.4 (Latins) and 15.8.3 (Samnites), Joseph. *BJ* 7.76–8 Germans), 254–5 (Sicarii) and 323–4 (Eleazer) and App. *Mith.* 70 (Mithridates).

[104] Polybius describes Carthage as ruling like a master (δεσποτικῶς ἄρχειν) in Spain (10.36.7) and Macedon as enslaving (καταδουλοῦσθαι; cf. δουλεύοντας) Chalcis and Corinth (38.3.4). In Diodorus, the Persians, Macedonians and Antigonids all enslave (καταδουλοῦσθαι) other peoples (2.1.5, 2.34.4, 19.87.2) and the Carthaginians' tributaries are enslaved (δουλοῦσθαι) by them (25.10.3). Appian writes of Greek cities being slaves (δουλεῦσαι) to Pontus (*Mith.* 83).

Germans are slaves to the Romans (δουλεύοντας ἡμῖν, 6.331). Elsewhere, he assures his Roman soldiers that the Jews have already learnt to be slaves (δουλεύειν), and so will be easily defeated (6.42).[105] I have suggested elsewhere that these speeches are drawing on a characteristically Jewish conception of slavery as the paradigm for submission to God in order to align Roman power with divine authority.[106] In any case it is significant that the metaphor of enslavement to Rome never appears in the narrative voice in Josephus. In short, what survives of earlier Greek historiography offers nothing comparable to Dio's extensive use of the language of slavery – particularly the verb δουλοῦν – to describe incorporation into the Roman empire.

Setting aside for a moment the specific case of Roman power, it is of course true that the trope of describing foreign rule as enslavement can be traced back to the origins of Greek historiography. Herodotus describes subjection to Persia as enslavement and resistance to Persia as a struggle for freedom.[107] In Thucydides, the language of slavery is applied to Athens as well as to Persia, establishing a potential link between the two imperial powers.[108] But it is significant that the trope is almost entirely limited to the rhetoric of Athens' enemies (where it is ubiquitous). It is used by Athenian speakers only on a handful of occasions – and never in dialogue with their subjects.[109] Not even in the notoriously frank 'Melian dialogue' do the Athenians represent themselves as masters.[110] More importantly, the language of enslavement is, with only two exceptions, markedly absent from the narrative

[105] For the many further metaphors of slavery in the rhetoric of Titus, Agrippa II and Josephus himself, see p. 8 n. 25 and Lavan 2007 pp. 26–31.

[106] Ibid. [107] See e.g. Hdt. 1.94, 1.169 and 1.174 with Tamiolaki 2010 ch. 1.

[108] See e.g. Tamiolaki 2010 p. 110 on the parallel between Athens and Persia established by the use of δουλοῦν. On the use of δουλεία and cognates to refer to Athenian rule in Thucydides, see especially Tamiolaki 2010 ch. 2, Raaflaub 2004 pp. 129–30, Rood 1998 pp. 238–9 n. 50, de Ste Croix 1972 p. 36, de Romilly 1963 pp. 86–8 and Meritt, Wade-Gery and McGregor 1939–53 pp. 155–7.

[109] See Thuc. 6.84.3 (Euphemus tells the Camerinaeans that the Ionians and islanders brought δουλεία upon themselves), 8.46.3 (Alcibiades tells Tissaphernes that Athens and Persia should be fellow masters (ξυγκαταδουλοῦν)) and 8.48.5 (Phrynicus tells his fellow Athenians that an oligarchic coup will not make the allies any more willing to be Athens' slaves (δουλεύειν)).

[110] The Melians describe Athens' subjects as slaves (Thuc. 5.86, 92, 100), but the Athenians eschew such language and instead call their subjects ὑπήκοοι (91.1) or ἀρχόμενοι (91.1, 95). The contrast is noted by Raaflaub 2004 p. 130.

voice. Most recent scholarship has highlighted this discrepancy between the language of the speeches and that of the narrative, concluding that Thucydides sees little value in the trope as a tool of historical interpretation.[111] Nevertheless, though the trope of enslavement to Athens is not endorsed by the narrator, it is not rejected either; and it is used so frequently by Athens' enemies that it cannot be ignored by any reader of the text. Moreover, the two instances in which the language of slavery does figure in the narrative voice are potentially more significant than has been allowed. The first occurs in the passage in which Thucydides traces the development of Athenian power from hegemony to empire (1.98). Describing Naxos' attempt to break from the Delian League and its subsequent conquest by Athens, he says that this was the first allied city to be enslaved (ἐδουλώθη, 1.98.4) contrary to custom.[112] The second occurs in Book 7. Describing the reversal in Athens' fortune after the defeat at Syracuse, he notes the irony that instead of coming to enslave others (δουλωσόμενοι) the Athenians were leaving in fear of suffering the same fate themselves (7.75.7). Although these are only two examples, they take on particular importance because they frame the period of Athenian dominance. The former describes Athens' first significant encroachment on the autonomy of its allies; the latter comes just after the defeat at Syracuse has marked the end of Athens' imperial ambitions. In both cases Thucydides uses the verb δουλοῦν – precisely the word that is most distinctive in Dio. Dio's representation of Roman expansion as enslavement could thus be read as a move to take a Thucydidean perspective on his own state – one that is not afraid to expose the raw power relations that underlie empire.[113] Yet the parallels in Florus, and the fact that the immediate precedent lies not in Greek but in Latin historiography, suggests that there is more to this than the Thucydidean intertext.[114]

[111] So Tamiolaki 2010 ch 2, esp. pp. 104, 112 and 125, Raaflaub 2004 p. 129 and Rood 1998 pp. 238–9 n. 50.

[112] On the escalation constructed around the series Eion, Scyros, Karystos and Naxos in 1.98.4 see Tamiolaki 2010 p. 123 and Rood 1998 p. 238.

[113] This would not be Dio's only engagement with Thucydides. On the broader topic of Dio's use of Thucydides, see Swain 1996 pp. 405–6 and Millar 1964 p. 42.

[114] Herodian is another third-century Greek historian to make distinctive use of the trope of enslavement to the Romans. See Herodian 2.9.12 (τῶν ὑπ' ἄρκτῳ Ῥωμαίοις δουλευόντων ἐθνῶν) and 3.2.8 (Ῥωμαίοις δοῦλα γεγένηται) with Lavan 2013.

At the very least, these three texts reveal the persistence and continued relevance of the slavery trope well into the third century CE. They also suggest that metaphors of provincial enslavement may have become even *more* prominent in this period. The difference is one of degree in the case of Florus, who uses the trope more widely than earlier Roman historians; but it is certainly a difference of kind in the case of Dio, who is almost unprecedented among Greek historians in employing δουλοῦν and its cognates in describing Roman expansion. I have argued elsewhere that this apparent intensification in the rhetoric of Roman mastery and provincial slavery might reflect two broader developments in Roman political culture.[115] First, it is surely no accident that this is also the period in which *dominus*, an appellation studiously avoided by Augustus and Tiberius, was becoming established as one of the emperor's conventional epithets. An imperial elite that styled the emperor as master were all the more likely to represent themselves as masters of the world. The proliferation of references to Roman mastery is probably also a sign of negative reactions to the ecumenical processes at work in the second century CE, which were eroding the significance of the distinction between citizens and non-citizens and centre and periphery, culminating in Caracalla's grant. The language of these texts suggests that at least some Romans sought to reaffirm the idea of an empire divided between a master people and its enslaved subjects. In a period from which few Latin texts survive (compared to the rich evidence from the early second and the fourth centuries), this is limited but valuable evidence for the persistence of an exclusivist voice in Roman political culture.

Empire and slavery

Far from being limited to the rhetoric of Rome's enemies, metaphors of Roman mastery and provincial enslavement pervade Latin literature, transcending genre boundaries, spanning the three centuries covered here, and becoming if anything more prominent by the end of the period. Although they are particularly widespread in

[115] Lavan 2013.

accounts of conquest and revolt, they can also be found in descriptions of ongoing Roman rule. A long line of Roman senators – Caesar, Cicero, Pliny, Tacitus, Cassius Dio – represent themselves as the masters of the empire and regard some or all of the population of the provinces as being in a state of servile subjection. It should by now be obvious that this does not in itself imply moral condemnation of Rome's empire or sympathy with its subjects.[116] This should not come as a surprise. After all, slavery is a ubiquitous and largely unquestioned feature of Roman society. Although the abuses of individual masters are criticised, no surviving Roman text seriously challenges the ethical foundations of slavery as an institution.[117]

It is worth pausing at this point to review the diversity of the metaphors surveyed in this chapter. They cannot be reduced to a single, stereotypical vision of the servile condition. Although slavery is often viewed as an oppressive and hateful state, metaphors of enslavement to Rome are also compatible with claims of Roman beneficence. Pliny the Younger claims that the provinces are better off being slaves to the emperor than being independent (*Pan.* 32.2) and Justin says in the same sentence that Spain accepted the yoke of Roman rule and that it was civilised by it (*ad cultiorem uitae usum traductum*, 44.5.8). Slavery is often a degrading and humiliating condition, as when Cicero seeks to mobilise contempt for the Jewish people by describing it as having been enslaved by Rome (*serua facta*, Cic. *Flac.* 69) or Livy's Scipio exhorts his men to despise Hannibal since he was born their tributary and slave (*uectigalis stipendiariusque et seruus populi Romani*, 21.41.7).

116 *Pace* Roller 2001, who claims that the language of slavery has fixed 'ethical overtones' – that it necessarily implies a (critical) 'ethical and affective commentary' on the power relations to which it is applied (see especially pp. 129, 213, 223 and 227). This may be true when the model of slavery is projected on to the principate (though even that is contestable; see n. 137 below), but it is certainly not true of its use in contexts such as Roman rule over the provinces.

117 Garnsey 1996, the best discussion of ancient attitudes to, and theories of, slavery as an institution, takes issue with the conventional wisdom that the ethical foundations of slavery were never seriously questioned in the ancient world, though he sets the bar low by arguing against a 'universal, passive acceptance of the institution'. He concludes that there was some criticism of slavery as an institution, but acknowledges that 'overt critiques of slavery are on the surface few, weak and isolated' (p. 11). It is also significant that none of his meagre crop of attacks on slavery as an institution (ch. 6) emerge from Latin literature in my period.

But there is no such implication of degradation when Cicero in the *Verrines* describes how his Sicilian clients have slaved for Rome:

patiemini, iudices, ab sociis, ab aratoribus populi Romani, ab eis qui uobis laborant, uobis seruiunt, qui ita plebem Romanam ab sese ali uolunt ut sibi ac liberis suis tantum supersit quo ipsi ali possint, ab his per summam iniuriam, per acerbissimas contumelias plus aliquanto ablatum esse quam natum sit?

Judges, will you allow the allies, the farmers of the Roman people, those who labour and slave for you, who are so eager for the Roman plebs to be fed by them that they and their children are left only as much as they need to be fed themselves – will you allow them, by the greatest injustice and bitterest insult, to be robbed of considerably more than they produced? (*2 Verr.* 3.102)

Here the language of slavery serves not to degrade the Sicilians but to emphasise their total commitment to feeding Rome. The idea of servile service implicit in *seruiunt* resonates with the self-denial described in the following sentence. One might compare the metaphor of the wet nurse (*nutrix*) sometimes applied to the provinces that supplied Rome with grain. Cicero says that Cato used to call Sicily the 'wet nurse of the Roman people' (*nutrix plebis Romanae Siciliam*, *2 Verr.* 2.5). Valerius Maximus describes Sicily and Sardinia as 'the kindly wet nurses of the city' (*benignissimae urbis nostrae nutrices*, 7.6.1c). The *nutrix*, regarded with affection perhaps but nevertheless commonly a slave, provides a useful paradigm for Rome's dependence on provincial resources.[118] As these passages illustrate, the slave's absolute and unconditional subordination to the master can provide a powerful paradigm not just of degradation and abasement but also of self-denying, self-abnegating service. The latter vision of slavery proved particularly productive in early Christian discourse, where it can be seen at work in the idea that Christians are slaves to God (just as the former vision underlies the rhetoric of slavery to sin).[119] It can also be seen

[118] On *nutrices* in Roman society, see Bradley 1994a, Bradley 1986.

[119] Work on metaphors of slavery in early Christian writings has produced some of the most insightful studies of Greek and Roman conceptions of slavery. Martin 1990 pp. 50–1 shows that slavery provided Christian writers with paradigms both of moral and social degradation and of unconditional obedience and self-sacrificing devotion to others. See also Combes 1998 p. 42 on the connotations 'of degradation and abasement, of loss of self will and of forced captivity and misery' that underlie the idea of slavery to sin and the connotations 'of devotion and submission, merging of identity with and absolute dependence on the master' that inform the idea of slavery to Christ.

at work in the ideal of the ruler enslaved to the state, as voiced by Tiberius in his dictum that a good emperor 'should be the slave of the senate and the citizen body' (*senatui seruire debere et uniuersis ciuibus*, Suet. *Tib.* 29).[120]

That said, many if not most of these metaphors of provincial enslavement do construct slavery to Rome as a coercive and oppressive relationship.[121] Particularly evocative are the recurring image of a yoke forced upon unwilling necks,[122] the emphasis on the crushing experience of slavery (*seruitio premere*),[123] and the references to chains.[124] In Caesar, slavery is explicitly a hateful condition (*omnes autem homines natura condicionem seruitutis odisse*, Caes. *B Gall.* 3.10.3); in Cicero, it is a wretched state that requires consolation (*ut haberent oblectamenta et solacia seruitutis*, Cic. 2*Verr.* 4.134). All these texts highlight the oppressive aspect of enslavement to Rome. Yet there is no indication that they imply condemnation of Roman rule or sympathy with Rome's subjects. On the contrary, they celebrate Roman success. These texts show that mastery can provide a normative model for Roman rule even when it is recognised as a coercive mode of domination. Parallels can be found in philosophical discussions of self-mastery. Cicero, for example, writes that the best part of the soul should 'wear down'/'break' (*fatigare*) the worse and weaker parts in the same way that masters 'wear down'/'break' their slaves – animalising language which highlights the violence underlying masterly control, even as it invokes it as a normative model of authority.[125]

[120] For the trope of slavery to the laws or the state, see further Béranger 1975 pp. 35–8.

[121] See further pp. 163–6 on coercion as the defining feature of mastery as a mode of control.

[122] Note especially *iugum quo se exuit accipere rursus cogatis* (Livy 34.13.9), *Karthaginis ceruicibus inposito iugo* (Val. Max. 6.9.2), *Britannis imposuit iugum* (*Octavia* 41), and *ab imposito nuper iugo resiliebant* (Flor. 2.21[12].2).

[123] *perpetua premitur seruitute* (Caes. *B Gall.* 7.77.16), *Mycenas seruitio premet* (Verg. *Aen.* 1.284–5), *Germanias seruitio premere* (Tac. *Ann.* 2.73.2) and *Britannia subdidit colla premenda iugo* (*Anth. Lat.* 1 424.8 Shackleton Bailey).

[124] *seruit . . . Cantaber domitus catena* (Hor. *Carm.* 3.8.21–2) and *Britannos dare Romuleis colla catenis iussit* (Sen. *Apocol.* 12.3).

[125] *domini autem seruos ita fatigant, ut optima pars animi, id est sapientia, eiusdem animi uitiosas imbecillasque partes, ut libidines, ut iracundias, et perturbationes ceteras* (Cic. *Rep.* 3.37).

The presumptive legitimacy of master–slave relations in a society of masters is best evidenced by those texts that explicitly invoke mastery as a paradigm of *rightful* authority. When Livy's Scipio urges his men to fight the Carthaginians with the same outrage they would feel against rebellious slaves (21.41.10), he is invoking slavery as the model of a relationship where resistance is despicable. When Livy the narrator represents Rome's long struggle to subdue Spain as the assertion of a master's legal rights over slaves who have been usurping free status (34.18.2), mastery provides a paradigm of legitimate authority that must be affirmed against the slaves' unlawful attempts to free themselves from it.

An even more elaborate example can be found in the debate about the expediency of justice in the third book of Cicero's *Republic*. This debate seems to have centred on the question of whether empire – and Rome's empire in particular – was just as well as expedient. Unfortunately, most of the text has been lost, so we are heavily dependent on excerpts and summaries in later writers. It appears that Cicero's first speaker, Lucius Furius Philus, argued that neither individuals nor communities can be successful without committing injustice, and supported his argument with the example of the Roman empire.[126] According to Augustine, the counter-argument, voiced by Scipio Aemilianus' close friend Gaius Laelius, also centred on a discussion of Roman rule:

> et quoniam, cum prius ageretur pro iniustitiae partibus contra iustitiam et diceretur nisi per iniustitiam rem publicam stare gerique non posse, hoc ueluti ualidissimum positum erat, iniustum esse, ut homines hominibus dominantibus seruiant; quam tamen iniustitiam nisi sequatur imperiosa ciuitas, cuius est magna res publica, non eam posse prouinciis imperare: responsum est a parte iustitiae ideo iustum esse, quod talibus hominibus sit utilis seruitus, et pro utilitate eorum fieri, cum recte fit, id est cum improbis aufertur iniuriarum licentia, et domiti melius se habebunt, quia indomiti deterius se habuerunt; subditumque est, ut ista ratio firmaretur, ueluti a natura sumptum nobile exemplum atque dictum est: 'cur igitur Deus homini, animus imperat corpori, ratio libidini ceterisque uitiosis animi partibus?' plane hoc exemplo satis edoctum est quibusdam esse utilem seruitutem, et Deo quidem ut seruiatur utile esse omnibus.

[126] Lactant. *Div. inst.* 5.16.2–3 and August. *De civ. D.* 19.21. On Philus' speech, see further Glucker 2001, Ferrary 1988 pp. 351–63, Büchner 1984 ad loc. and Ferrary 1977.

When the case for injustice against justice was made first [i.e. by Philus] and it was argued that a state cannot exist or be administered except through injustice, great emphasis was placed on the point that it is unjust for some men to be slaves and others to be their masters, and that no imperial city, which has a wide dominion, can command provinces unless it pursues that very injustice. The response on behalf of justice [i.e. by Laelius] was that it [i.e. ruling over provinces] was just because slavery is expedient for such men and that it is in their own best interest when it is rightly established, that is when wicked men are deprived of the freedom to do wrong and when they will be better off conquered because they were worse off unconquered. To strengthen that argument, a fine example is added, drawn from nature as it were, and stated as follows: 'Why is it that God commands man, the soul rules the body, and reason rules the desire and the other defective parts of the soul?' This example is clearly sufficient to show that slavery is expedient for some and that slavery to God is expedient for all. (August. *De civ. D.* 19.21)

Whereas Philus had argued that empire must be unjust since servile subjection (*homines hominibus dominantibus seruire*) is unjust and an imperial city (*imperiosa ciuitas*) cannot rule provinces without reducing them to slavery, Laelius responded by arguing that enslavement is expedient and thus just for some men, namely those who would act unjustly if they were free.[127] A passage quoted verbatim elsewhere by Augustine asserts that the mastery (*dominatus*) of the better over the worse is a natural principle.[128] Another excerpt, preserved this time by the grammarian Nonius (and unfortunately truncated), seems to draw a distinction between just and unjust forms of slavery: 'For there is a kind of unjust slavery (*seruitus*), when men who are capable of ruling themselves are subject to another. But when those men are slaves (*famulantur*) who . . .'.[129] Nonius (who was interested only in the use of

[127] On the overall structure of Laelius' speech see further Ferrary 1988 pp. 363–81, Dumont 1983 and Ferrary 1974. Enough excerpts from the speech survive to show that Augustine's summary is only a partial one. As well as arguing for the justice of ongoing Roman rule (as Augustine suggests here), Laelius also discussed the causes of war and argued that all Rome's wars had been just (see *Rep.* 3.34 and 35). The defence of these two different aspects of Roman imperialism has been noted by Erskine 1990 p. 192 and Ferrary 1988. Dumont 1983 p. 123 suggests the possibility that the two arguments were conflated in a punitive theory – that *bellum iustum* justified the enslavement of the defeated because of their wickedness.

[128] *an non cernimus optimo cuique dominatum ab ipsa natura cum summa utilitate infimorum datum* (*Rep.* 37, cited by August. *C. Iulianum Pelag.* 4.12.61).

[129] *est enim genus iniustae seruitutis, cum ii sunt alterius, qui sui possunt esse. cum autem hi famulantur*... (*Rep.* 37).

famulantur) does not give the rest of the sentence, but Cicero presumably went on to say that when the slaves are those who cannot rule themselves, slavery is just.

Laelius' speech evidently contained some sort of justification of empire as a form of just enslavement. However, the analogy between empire and slavery must have been more complex than Augustine suggests in the passage quoted above. He elsewhere quotes another passage in which Laelius distinguishes between paternal and masterly modes of ruling and explicitly classes the authority of 'kings, generals, magistrates, senates and assemblies' over *both* citizens *and* allies (*socii*) as an example of the former.[130] There is thus an apparent contradiction in what survives of Laelius' defence of empire: it seems to have contained both a defence of empire as a form of just enslavement and an assertion that Rome related to its allies as a father rather than a master. The key to the paradox probably lies in the semantics of *socii*, which is often used in a narrow sense in Cicero to denote the more privileged dependent communities as opposed to the provinces.[131] The best way of making sense of what survives of Laelius' discourse is to assume that he distinguished two modes of imperial rule in general (and Roman rule in particular) and justified them separately.[132] Rome rules some peoples like slaves and others like children. The two forms are complementary, not mutually exclusive. This idea of two

[130] *paulo post enim: sed et imperandi et seruiendi sunt dissimilitudines cognoscendae. nam, ut animus corpori dicitur imperare, dicitur etiam libidini; sed corpori, ut rex ciuibus suis, aut parens liberis; libidini autem, ut seruis dominus, quod eam coercet et frangit; sic regum, sic imperatorum, sic magistratuum, sic patrum, sic populorum imperia ciuibus sociisque praesunt, ut corporibus animus. domini autem seruos ita fatigant, ut optima pars animi, id est sapientia, eiusdem animi uitiosas imbecillasque partes, ut libidines, ut iracundias, et perturbationes ceteras.* ('A little later, [Cicero/Laelius] says: "The different modes of both ruling and being subject must be distinguished. For the soul is said to rule both the body and desire. But it rules the body like a king rules his fellow citizens or a parent his children, whereas it rules desire like a master rules his slaves, in that it curbs and breaks it. The rule of kings, generals, magistrates, senates and assemblies over citizens and allies is like the rule of the soul over the body. But masters dominate their slaves in the same way that the best part of the soul, that is reason, dominates its flawed and weaker parts, such as desire, anger and other disruptive emotions", Cic. *Rep.* 3.37 = August. *C. Iulianum Pelag.* 4.12.61.) See Dumont 1983 on Cicero's reworking of Arist. *Pol.* 1254b here.

[131] See pp. 42–3.

[132] Garnsey 1996 p. 41 and Ferrary 1988 pp. 371 and 377 reach a similar conclusion, without considering Cicero's habit of sometimes using *socii* with a restricted sense, which further strengthens the case.

imperial modes has parallels in the account of empire in Aristotle's *Politics* (an important influence on Laelius' speech);[133] it is also consistent with the two passages already discussed in which Cicero distinguishes between two modes of submission to Roman rule.[134] This text is, it must be said, an oddity in Roman discourse about empire. There is no evidence that the philosophical justification of empire deployed by 'Laelius' here influenced Cicero's descriptions of Roman rule outside the *Republic* or those of later Roman authors.[135] But it is a further illustration of mastery's potential to provide a paradigm of legitimate authority.

Thus far I have emphasised the presumptive legitimacy of master–slave relations in Roman society. There is of course one major exception which I have so far ignored – the discourse of what we might call 'domestic' politics. That is a context in which mastery is a highly charged and deeply problematic paradigm of authority from the Republic through to the Principate. The politics of both *optimates* and *populares*, the ambitions of the triumvirs, the power of the emperors – all these are condemned by their critics as aspirations to mastery.[136] Rarely in this domain do those in power so overtly

[133] Criticising Lycurgus for having established a system of military training whose only object was to establish despotic rule over Sparta's neighbours, Aristotle claims that 'the proper object of practising military training is not in order that men may enslave those who do not deserve slavery (καταδουλώσωνται τοὺς ἀναξίους), but first so that they may themselves avoid becoming enslaved to others; second to seek rulership (ἡγεμονία) for the benefit of the subject people, but not for the sake of worldwide mastery (δεσποτεία); and third to hold masterly power over those who deserve to be slaves (δεσπόζειν τῶν ἀξίων δουλεύειν)' (Arist. *Pol.* 1333b–1334a). While states should not seek mastery over the whole world, there are peoples who should be ruled as slaves. Cf Plutarch's statement that Aristotle tried to persuade Alexander to act as leader of the Greeks, but master of the barbarians (τοῖς μὲν Ἕλλησιν ἡγεμονικῶς τοῖς δὲ βαρβάροις δεσποτικῶς χρώμενος, Plut. *De Alex. fort.* 329b). Here we have the same contrast between *hegemonia* and *despoteia*, but this time the extent of the two spheres is explicitly delimited. Thus it seems that, like Cicero's Laelius, Aristotle distinguishes between two modes of imperial rule. Some peoples deserve relatively enlightened rule; but others need to be ruled like slaves.

[134] Cic. *2 Verr.* 4.134 and *Cat.* 4.22. See pp. 93–5.

[135] It is notable that there is no sign of Laelius' masterly and paternal modes in Cicero's famous description of Roman rule at *Off.* 2.27, which instead constructs an ad hoc (and distinctly Roman) contrast between *imperium* and *patrocinium* (see pp. 194–5). Laelius' speech is almost unique in its deployment of a theory of natural slavery in this period (cf. Garnsey 1996 ch. 3). Isaac 2004 pp. 183–6 and 192–3 exaggerates the importance of theories of natural slavery for Roman imperial ideology.

[136] On claims of enslavement in Republican political discourse, see Manuwald 2007 II p. 428, Achard 1981 pp. 321–2 and Hellegouarc'h 1963 p. 559; for the Principate, see the extensive discussion in Roller 2001 ch. 4.

style themselves as masters, and the dominated as their slaves.[137] The recurring language of Roman mastery and provincial slavery *is* surprising if we expect Cicero to describe relations with the *socii* in the same terms that he uses to describe political relations within the citizen body – or Tacitus and Pliny to describe the subjection of the provinces in the same terms they describe relations between the emperor and the aristocracy. But this is clearly a mistaken assumption. Empire is a different domain, where the language of mastery and slavery can be used widely and apparently unproblematically of the subject population. This is perhaps partly a matter of perspective. The affective connotations of slavery metaphors must depend on whether the relationship is being imagined from the perspective of the master or the slave. It is one thing for these Roman men, accustomed to the habits of mastery, to imagine themselves the masters of their empire, another to imagine themselves the slaves of a fellow citizen or an emperor.

No prospect of freedom

No discussion of slavery would be complete without considering the possibility of manumission. Although we have no firm quantitative evidence for its prevalence, it is clear that manumission was an important element of the Roman practice of slavery. At least for a privileged category of skilled slaves, slavery might well be a temporary condition.[138] The freed slave (*libertus*) not only acquired the legal privileges of freedom but was also, provided appropriate form was followed, immediately inducted into the citizen body (albeit with certain disadvantages), a policy that made Roman slavery truly distinctive to Greek observers like Dionysius of Halicarnassus.[139] This represents a dramatic transformation in status and honour: passage from the most despised directly into one of the more privileged categories of Roman society. Given the widespread representation of conquest as enslavement, manumission would seem to offer an obvious and attractive metaphor for the integration and

[137] Rarely, but certainly not never. See Lavan 2013 for a short discussion of early experiments in a more masterly style, and their fruition in the second and third centuries CE.

[138] On the scale of manumission, see Mouritsen 2011 pp. 120–41.

[139] Dion. Hal. *Ant. Rom.* 4.22.4–23.7.

incorporation of conquered peoples into the empire. Yet it is strikingly absent from Roman accounts of empire. The few times that the metaphor of manumission is used in an imperial context, it is Hellenistic monarchs, not the Romans, who are the former masters – and the freedman proves a problematic paradigm.

One example is the creative diplomacy of Prusias II of Bithynia, who found himself in an uncomfortable position in the aftermath of the Third Macedonian War because he had remained neutral rather than siding with Rome. Several sources record that he represented himself as Rome's freedman in one or more encounters with Roman officials – even going so far as to shave his head and wear the *pilleus* (the felt cap worn by a freed slave).[140] This was an attempt to rewrite the history of his uncomfortably close relations with the recently defeated Perseus of Macedon by portraying himself as Perseus' slave, freed by the Roman people.[141] He achieved his aims at the time (even securing some territorial gains), but his posturing as a *libertus* was not remembered favourably by later writers. Almost all of the accounts represent Prusias in extremely pejorative terms. His behaviour is condemned by Polybius, Livy, Diodorus Siculus, Plutarch and Appian as shameful, unbecoming to a king, effeminate, obsequious and laughable.[142]

The trope of manumission from an imperial power recurs in Livy, in a speech he attributes to Perseus' father, Philip V of Macedon. The king describes his former subjects as freedmen in a speech delivered before a Roman commission sent to Greece in 185 BCE to investigate a host of complaints against him. He is angrily denying accusations laid against him by the Thessalians, who had been subject to Macedon before they were freed by Rome at the end of the Second Macedonian War:

insolenter et immodice abuti Thessalos indulgentia populi Romani, uelut ex diutina siti nimis auide meram haurientes libertatem: ita seruorum modo praeter

[140] Polyb. 30.18, App. *Mith.* 2, Diod. Sic. 31.15, Dio 20.69, Livy 45.44.5–20, Plut. *De Alex. fort.* 336E (confusing Nicomedes with Prusias).

[141] So Braund 1982 pp. 353–4.

[142] It is not possible to pin the problem specifically on Prusias' self-presentation as freedman. His inventiveness – and the historians' censure – extended to a wider range of symbolic gestures: imitating Roman dress and behaviour more generally (wearing the toga and *calceus*, speaking Latin), performing *proskynesis* in the senate and hailing the senators as 'saviour gods'.

spem repente manumissorum licentiam uocis et linguae experiri et iactare sese insectatione et conuiciis dominorum.

The Thessalians [he said] were shamelessly and wantonly abusing the generosity of the Roman people. Long thirsty, as it were, they were drinking too eagerly the strong wine of freedom. Like slaves freed suddenly and unexpectedly, they were trying out their freedom of speech and tongue and were making a show of themselves by attacking and insulting their masters. (Livy 39.26.7–8)

Philip invokes the *libertus* here as a paradigm not of integration but of insubordination. In what is another revealing expression of the ethic of mastery, he appeals to the Romans as fellow masters, inviting them to share his contempt for freed slaves who are disrespectful and troublesome.

No text known to me applies the model of manumission to Rome's subjects. Their slavery is never represented as anything other than a permanent condition. This silence about the possibility of manumission may say something about elite ambivalence towards freedmen and the notion of transformation from slave to free (as suggested by these two examples).[143] It certainly reveals a lack of interest in processes of integration and incorporation in the provinces.[144]

Metaphors of mastery and enslavement pervade Roman accounts of empire. In historiography from Caesar to Cassius Dio, in the oratory and letters of both Cicero and Pliny the Younger, in lyric and epic from Horace and Virgil to Statius and Silius Italicus, provincial submission is represented as enslavement and Roman rule as mastery. The idea of slavery to Rome manifests itself in a complex of coherent and mutually reinforcing metaphors: mastery (*dominatio* and cognates), enslavement (*seruitus* and cognates), the loss of freedom (*libertas*), the chains (*catenae*), harness (*frena*)

[143] We should not forget that the texts we are looking at are traces of an elite discourse where manumission is often regarded as a problematic or incomplete transformation. Tacitus, for example, repeatedly insinuates that freedmen retain their slavish nature (p. 151 n. 68). Mouritsen 2011 ch. 2 is an excellent discussion of the ideological problems raised by the practice of manumission in Roman society.

[144] On the surprising lack of interest in narratives of cultural integrations, see further p. 15 n. 46.

and yoke (*iugum*) of slavery, the assertion of freedom (*uindicatio in libertatem*) and countervailing assertion of a master's rights (*uindicatio in seruitutem*). Although they are particularly widespread in accounts of conquest and revolt, these tropes are also applied to the ongoing condition of the provinces. Far from being marginalised by the progressive political and cultural integration of the empire over the course of the first two centuries CE, the vision of a world divided into masters and slaves becomes if anything more prominent by the end of the period. To return to the subject with which this chapter began, it is far from obvious that Roman readers of any period would have been troubled by, or impelled to reject, the equation of empire and slavery in the rhetoric of Critognatus and other (imagined) rebels.

No account of Roman imperial ideology can afford to ignore the pervasive language of enslavement. This masterly style is an important counterpoint to the more benign and beneficent rhetoric discussed in Chapters 4 and 5 and so often emphasised in modern scholarship. It is particularly significant that so many of these texts stress the oppressive character of enslavement to Rome. It reveals the extent to which empire was acknowledged to be a coercive and adversarial relationship. More broadly, the persistent intrusion of the language of slavery (even in its less marked forms) into descriptions of Roman rule and provincial subjection illustrates that discourse about empire was not subject to the same constraints as discourse about domestic politics. The willingness to describe empire in terms that would not normally be applied to the political relations of the emperor, aristocrats and the citizen body marks empire as a distinct political domain subject to its own norms. The very aristocrats who decry any encroachment on their own liberty assert their collective mastery over Rome's conquered subjects.

These descriptions of empire as enslavement also speak to the ideology of slavery. The range of contexts in which they are deployed reveals the different facets of slavery in the Roman imagination – for example its capacity to provide a paradigm of self-denying service as well as one of degradation and abjection. Cumulatively, however, they illustrate the centrality of coercion to the Roman vision of slavery. They also show that slavery can provide a normative paradigm for other power relations even as an avowedly coercive institution. We should never allow our conviction that slavery is unjust to blind us to the master's ethic that underlies Roman discourse.

3

EMPIRE AND SLAVERY IN TACITUS

ad septuaginta milia ciuium et sociorum iis, quae memoraui, locis cecidisse constitit. neque enim capere aut uenundare aliudue quod belli commercium, sed caedes patibula ignes cruces, tamquam reddituri supplicium, at praerepta interim ultione, festinabant.

It has been established that around 70,000 citizens and allies perished in the places which I mentioned. No one was taken captive or sold into slavery; there was none of the trafficking usual in war. Instead there was hurried slaughter, whipping-posts, burning, crosses. It was as if they knew they would be punished and seized revenge while they could.

(Tac. *Ann.* 14.33.2)

This is Tacitus' description of the massacre of the inhabitants of Londinium, Verulamium and Camulodunum by Boudicca's rebels in 60 CE. Most readers have interpreted the violence that the Britons inflict on their captives as a sign of their barbarism, standing in stark contrast to the civilisation represented by Rome.[1] But this is to miss the point. The violence on display here is entirely familiar: this is how Romans punished their slaves. The reference to crosses is the giveaway. Crucifixion was the conventional method of executing slaves. Even if it was sometimes inflicted on

[1] Some examples: 'Used though we are to horrors and bestiality in our modern world, we still cannot read his words without revulsion' (Webster 1978 p. 94). 'His account of the sack of London with its stark silver Latin account of the atrocities perpetrated there, *caedes, patibula, ignes, cruces*; *Annals* 14.33, shows the Britons reverting to barbarian type' (Fear 1997 [non pag.]). The Britons 'inflict inappropriate punishment, rejecting the norms of civilised warfare' (Braund 1996 p. 136). Roberts 1988 does not address this passage specifically, but argues that an antithesis between civilisation and savagery is central to the structure of the Boudicca narrative. The two other surviving accounts of the revolt, in the *Agricola* and in Cassius Dio, do describe the sacking of the cities as barbaric and transgressive: *nec ullum in barbariis ingeniis saeuitiae genus omisit ira* (Tac. *Agr.* 16.1), φόνον ἀμύθητον ... ὡς ἔφην, εἰργάσατο. ... οὐδὲν τῶν δεινοτάτων ἔστιν ὅ τι οὐκ ἐγίνετο (Dio 62.7.1). But neither of these accounts mention crucifixion. Compare Dio's much more lurid description of the terrible and bestial deaths (δεινότατον καὶ θηριωδέστατον) inflicted on the Roman noblewomen (62.7.2–3).

non-citizens and even citizens of lower social standing (*humiliores*), it was always regarded as a characteristically servile punishment.[2] The *patibulum* was also typical of the punishment of slaves. It was a wooden beam to which victims were tied with their arms outstretched in order to be beaten or scourged.[3] The burning of captives (*ignes*) has a similar significance, as various forms of burning were regularly used in the torture of slaves.[4] *Caedes* is a little harder to pin down in the context of slavery. In Tacitus it usually means 'slaughter' or 'killing'.[5] But it can also mean 'whipping' (Roman lashes were made to cut deep), another typically servile form of punishment.[6] Far from being barbaric, *caedes patibula ignes cruces* are forms of violence that are institutionalised in Roman society. Indeed the punishment of slaves was a service industry, as revealed by an Early Imperial inscription from

[2] Aubert 2002 pp. 110–28 shows that crucifixion was normally reserved for slaves. When it was applied to others (e.g. poisoners, deserters, pirates and rebels) it constituted 'a conscious attempt to treat them as slaves' (114). It was a *seruile supplicium* (Val. Max. 2.7.12; cf. Tac. *Hist.* 2.72.2 and 4.11.3). See further Kuhn 1982 (esp. 719–23), Hengel 1978 pp. 51–73, Hitzig 1901 and Mommsen 1899 pp. 919–20.

[3] See especially Plaut. *Mil.* 360, *Mostell.* 56 and Dion. Hal. *Ant. Rom.* 7.69.1–2, with Parente 1979 and Brecht 1949. The *patibulum* could also, when attached to a vertical post, serve as the crossbar for crucifixion.

[4] Jackson's Loeb translates *ignes* as 'arson' here, but this is to miss both that what is being described here is the deaths that the British inflicted on their captives and that the noun *ignes* refers to the torture of people much more often than to the burning of property. See Tac. *Ann.* 15.57.1 (*at illam non uerbera, non ignes, non ira torquentium peruicere*) and the examples collected at *TLL* 291.37–44, 54–5 and 61–3. (cf *TLL* 291.75). Many forms of burning are attested in the torture of slaves (pitch, metal plates, torches, wax, candles, etc.). See e.g. *AE* 1971 88 = Gardner and Wiedemann 1991 no. 22 (the *lex libitinaria*), II, 12–13, with Murgatroyd 1980 p. 162, Wiseman 1985 p. 6 and Bradley 1994b p. 166. Torture, from which those of free status were normally immune, was always seen as a characteristically servile form of punishment. Cf. Tac. *Ann.* 3.50.1 (*seruiles cruciatus*) and Suet. *Aug.* 27.4 (*seruilem in modum torsit*) with Garnsey 1970 pp. 143–5. On the use of burning as a penalty in Roman law, see further Mommsen 1899 p. 923.

[5] Gerber and Greef 1903, s.v. *caedes*.

[6] For *caedes* meaning *uerbera* or *uerberatio*, see the examples at *TLL* s.v. *caedes* 52.17–22. *Caedere* is the usual verb used of whipping (ibid. s.v. *caedere* 58.52–59.26). Roman whips were made to cut deep (Wiseman 1985 pp. 5–6). Whipping was a common punishment for slaves (Bradley 1994b p. 166, Wiseman 1985 pp. 5–6 and Bradley 1984 pp. 119–20). Like the other characteristically servile punishments, whipping was sometimes inflicted on non-citizens and even, in a later period, on citizens of lower status (*humiliores*). See Garnsey 1970 pp. 139–41 and Mommsen 1899 pp. 981–5. Yet it was consistently regarded as a servile punishment. Cf *uerbera seruilia* (*Dig.* 49.14.12) and μάστιξιν αἰκισάμενοι καθάπερ ἀνδράποδον (Dion. Hal. *Ant. Rom.* 9.40.4), and especially Saller 1991 pp. 151–4 (who notes 'the special potency of the symbolic act of beating hinged on its association with slavery'). Roller 2001 pp. 262–4 argues that vulnerability to such corporal punishment is central to aristocratic conceptions of what it meant to be a slave.

Puteoli regulating the fees charged by undertakers (*libitinarii*) for a range of services, including the torture and execution of slaves and criminals for private households and public magistrates.[7]

Tacitus is always sensitive to the inherently servile nature of particular penalties, especially when they are inflicted on non-slaves.[8] It must therefore be significant that the Britons avenge themselves on their Roman conquerors in the same way that masters punish their slaves. The symbolic import of this violence is given point by the suggestion that their haste was caused by their awareness of impending punishment (*tamquam reddituri supplicium at praerepta interim ultione*). The Britons seem to know they are going to be punished, which is why they hurriedly seize revenge. The word order, which describes the future punishment before the present revenge, suggests that the Britons are seeking vengeance in advance for the punishment that is to come. They inflict on the Romans the punishments they expect to receive themselves – punishments fitting for criminal slaves. I will return to the question of how this functions within the broader context of Tacitus' narrative. For now, it is enough to illustrate Tacitus' subtle and provocative development of the familiar idea that the Romans' provincial subjects are their slaves.

The previous chapter traced the use of slavery as a metaphor for empire across a range of genres and over the period from Cicero to Cassius Dio. The broad approach was necessary in order to draw any conclusion about the characteristic tropes and structures of Roman discourse. But it inevitably ran the risk of ironing out inconsistencies and glossing over the particular agendas of individual texts. This chapter aims to address these potential problems by working with a much narrower focus. It concentrates on three of Tacitus' accounts of provincial resistance in order to look

[7] *AE* 1971 88 = Gardner and Wiedemann 1991 no. 22. If the contracting party wants the slave punished on a *crux* or *patibulum*, we are told, the undertaker should provide the bars and rope (II, 8–10). He is also to provide pitch, wax, tapers and anything else that is required for punishment or torture (ibid. 12–13). The contracting party is to pay for the floggers (ibid. 10).

[8] See e.g. *sumptum de eo supplicium in seruilem modum* (Tac. *Hist.* 2.72.2). *Asiaticus (is enim libertus) malam potentiam seruili supplicio expiauit* (*Hist.* 4.11.3). *neque carcer neque laqueus, ne seruiles quidem cruciatus in eum suffecerint* (*Ann.* 3.50.1). *raptus in locum seruilibus poenis sepositum manu Statii tribuni trucidatur* (*Ann.* 15.60.1).

more closely at how and why these texts represent rule by Rome as slavery. It begins by considering the representation of conquest as enslavement in the *Agricola* before illustrating the quite different ways in which the idea of provincial *seruitus* is reworked for the Gallic–Batavian revolt in *Histories* 4–5 and Boudicca's revolt in *Annals* 14. Besides highlighting the differences between these three representations of provincial slavery, this chapter will also demonstrate that all three descriptions of resistance to Rome are embedded in, and inseparable from, the broader narratives of which they are parts. It will become clear that Tacitus is not so much interested in provincials in their own right as in how their experience can be used to illuminate important aspects of Roman culture, society and politics.[9] This is an important caveat for any attempt to use these texts to illuminate ideologies of empire.

The *Agricola*

Even a cursory reading will reveal the prominence of the language of slavery in the account of Agricola's governorship of Britain that is the centrepiece of the *Agricola*.[10] The ethnographic survey with which it begins represents Rome's provincial subjects as living in a condition of slavery, saying that the Gauls lost their courage when they lost their freedom (*amissa uirtute pariter ac libertate*, 11.4) and that the same has happened to those Britons who have been conquered. Roman rule is again identified with enslavement when Tacitus claims, with regard to Rome's support for King Cogidumnus, that it is an old and long-established custom of the Roman people to use kings to enslave others (*uetere ac iam pridem recepta populi Romani consuetudine, ut haberet instrumenta seruitutis et reges*, 14.1). In the short account of Boudicca's revolt, the Britons discuss the evils of slavery (*mala seruitutis*, 15.1), seek inspiration from German success in shaking off the yoke

[9] The seminal discussion of how Tacitus' accounts of *res externae* mirror the concerns of his Roman narrative is Keitel 1978. See also Roberts 1988 (which laid the ground for this chapter's analysis of Tacitus' Calgacus and Boudicca) and Gilmartin 1973.

[10] This reading of the *Agricola* reworks Lavan 2011.

(*sic Germanias excussisse iugum*, 15.3) and attack Camulodunum because it was the seat of slavery (*sedem seruitutis*, 16.1).

The much-cited account of Agricola's efforts to promote Roman culture in Britain (21) concludes with the notorious barb that the Britons mistook for civilisation what was really part of their enslavement (*idque apud imperitos humanitas uocabatur, cum pars seruitutis esset*, 21.2). Many readers who have been troubled by the implication that Agricola was responsible for the enslavement of Britain have sought to contain and disarm the closing reference to *seruitus* by distinguishing the aspects of Roman culture promoted by Agricola (temples, forums, houses) from the vices adopted by the Britons of their own accord (porticoes, baths and elegant dinner parties) and seeing their enslavement as the result of those luxuries rather than Roman rule *per se*.[11] But such attempts to exculpate Rome in general or Agricola in particular from the charge of enslavement fly in the face of the recurring descriptions of Roman rule as slavery elsewhere in the *Agricola* – and the fact that luxury is only *part* (*pars*) of their *seruitus* here. Indeed Tacitus later explicitly ascribes masterly rhetoric to Agricola himself, when he records that his father-in-law once said that it would have been easy to conquer Ireland and thereby deny the Britons even the sight of freedom.[12]

The language of slavery reaches a crescendo in Calgacus' speech before the battle of Mons Graupius. The British chieftain is addressing the massed Caledonians, for whom the day will bring either revenge or enslavement (*ultionem aut seruitium expectantes*, 29.3). He promises that this day will be the beginning of freedom for all Britain (*initium libertatis toti Britanniae*, 30.1). He congratulates his fellow Caledonians for having no experience of slavery (*seruitutis expertes*, 30.1), for being so remote from Rome's empire that even their eyes are uncorrupted by the contagion of mastery (*contactus dominationis*) since they cannot see the coast of the servile Gauls (*litora seruientium*, 30.2), and for being the last of the free (*libertatis extremi*, 30.2). He complains

[11] See Braund 1996 pp. 161–5 for a recent version of this argument.

[12] *saepe ex eo audiui legione una et modicis auxiliis debellari obtinerique Hiberniam posse; idque etiam aduersus Britanniam profuturum, si Romana ubique arma et uelut e conspectu libertas tolleretur* (24.3).

that their children and friends are conscripted to be slaves elsewhere (*alibi seruituri*, 31.1). Real slaves (*nata seruituti mancipia*) have it better: they are sold once and then fed by their masters, whereas Britain has to pay for her slavery (*seruitus*) daily and feed herself (31.2). The Britons will be the prey of their fellow slaves (*conserui*) in the old slave-gang that is the world (*orbis terrarum uetus famulatus*, 31.2). Calgacus laments that provincials, once Rome's enemies and now her slaves (*serui*), spill their blood in the service of Roman mastery (*dominatio*, 32.1). But he promises that the Gauls will remember their old freedom (*libertas*, 32.3). Finally, he warns them that defeat will bring tribute, labour in the mines and the other punishments suffered by slaves (*ceterae seruientium poenae*, 32.4).

The *Agricola* is certainly not unique in describing conquest by Rome as enslavement. But it is nevertheless remarkable for the sheer concentration of these metaphors within such a short space. However, it is essential to recognise that the language of slavery is not limited to the narrative of Agricola's governorship of Britain (*Agr.* 10–39), but also plays an important role in the framing account of Domitianic Rome (*Agr.* 1–9, 39–46). The preface introduces the theme of slavery when it describes the senate as having plumbed the depths of *seruitus* under Domitian (*sicut uetus aetas uidit quid ultimum in libertate esset, ita nos quid in seruitute*, 2.3). It goes on to promise a future work that will provide a record of that former state of enslavement (*prior seruitus*, 3.3). The imagery of slavery to the emperor returns towards the end of the work when Agricola, returning to Rome after his successes in Britain, is granted only a brief reception before being lost in the crowd of slaves (*turba seruientium*, 40.3).

It is now more than forty years since J. H. W. G Liebeschuetz insisted on the thematic unity of the *Agricola* in an important article.[13] Yet it is still all too common for readers to approach the account of the conquest of Britain without considering its relationship to the Roman narrative in which it is embedded.[14] Moreover,

[13] Liebeschuetz 1966.

[14] Clarke 2001 explicitly excludes the Roman frame from her focus (p 112). Although Evans 2003 acknowledges some parallels between senate and Britons (p. 276), the rest of

not even Liebeschuetz's article does justice to the elaborate system of parallels that connects provincial subjection to Rome and senatorial subjection to Domitian in Tacitus' account.[15] This chapter will show that the two accounts are inextricably linked and demonstrate that Tacitus' description of the conquest of Britain cannot be understood in isolation from his overarching concern with the political situation in Rome. It will also highlight the thematic importance of slavery and slavishness for the *Agricola* as a whole.[16] In Liebeschuetz's formulation, what unites the different parts of the Agricola is a concern for 'the consequences of subjection' (p. 136). His avoidance of the word 'enslavement' is curious given the prominence of the language of slavery in the *Agricola*.[17] The distinction is significant because enslavement in the *Agricola* is more than a synonym for subjection. It is a moral condition – a state of mind and spirit. Tacitus turns to the

the article treats the British narrative as an unproblematic document of Flavian (*sic*) imperial ideology. Rutledge 2000 largely ignores the Roman narrative in order to explore the *Agricola* as an imperialist text. To read this inward-looking text for insights into Roman imperialism is, I will argue, to miss the point. Braund 1996 recognises the importance of approaching the *Agricola* as an organic whole, but his analysis of the British narrative is undermined by a surprisingly uncritical reading of the Roman narrative, which sees Agricola as an unambiguously positive paradigm of behaviour under domination (pp. 162–3 and 172). Many readings of the Roman narrative suffer from the opposite fault. Thus Haynes 2006 focuses almost exclusively on Rome (apart from a brief mention of Britain at 165–6). Whitmarsh 2006 stands out for its even-handed treatment of the two spheres of domination.

15 Note his surprisingly cautious conclusion: 'The *Agricola* as a whole does not leave the impression that it was designed to bring out a parallel between the rule of the Caesars over the Romans and that of the Romans over their subjects' (Liebeschuetz 1966 p. 138). Liebeschuetz's article only scratches the surface of the parallels between the two narratives. When his insights have been acknowledged by others (Sailor 2008 p. 98, Whitmarsh 2006 p. 306 and McGing 1982 p. 22), they have not been developed much further. Many of the correspondences discussed here have never been acknowledged, let alone adequately interpreted. This chapter aims to show their importance for any attempt to understand the *Agricola* as a whole.

16 The concept of slavishness or servility has received surprisingly little attention in recent readings of the *Agricola*. Haynes 2006 p. 154 has some suggestive remarks, in the context of *Agr.* 2.3, about slaves not having histories. Sailor 2004 p. 154 observes that *inertia* in the same passage has servile associations; Sailor 2008 p. 64 (again on 2.3) connects *patientia* with servitude. But none of these pursues the theme of slavishness further.

17 In focusing attention on slavery and slavishness as well as freedom, this chapter is aligned with Roller 2001 (especially pp. 214–33) in its critique of the recurring tendency to assert a compartmentalised, political sense of *libertas* remote from the lived reality of slavery (see further pp. 76–7). Such attempts to compartmentalise Tacitean *libertas* include Morford 1991, Vielberg 1987, Percival 1980, Ducos 1977, Benario 1964, Hammond 1963, Jens 1956 and Wirszubski 1950 pp. 160–7.

psychology of slavery (as he imagines it) to explain the persistence of domination in both Rome and Britain.

Slavishness

From the outset, slavery is an inward as well as an outward condition. When *seruitus* is first mentioned in the preface, it is associated with submissiveness and silence:

dedimus profecto grande patientiae documentum; et sicut uetus aetas uidit quid ultimum in libertate esset, ita nos quid in seruitute, adempto per inquisitiones etiam loquendi audiendique commercio.

We certainly gave clear proof of our submissiveness. Just as the past age witnessed the extremes of liberty, so we have seen the extremes of slavery. Even the intercourse of speaking and listening was taken from us by spies. (Tac. *Agr.* 2.3)

The conjunction '*et*' connects the statement that the senate plumbed the depths of slavery to the preceding description of senatorial *patientia*.[18] *Patientia* is a distinctly Roman concept whose wide range of meanings has been teased out by Robert Kaster (they include endurance, patience, forbearance, passivity and submissiveness). Although it can be a virtue in the face of forces of nature, *patientia* is always problematic in the world of social relations. Submission to the will of another implies a differential of power and so raises the spectre of servility. 'Insofar as it entailed inactivity in the face of *iniuria* and *contumelia* – insofar as it entailed turning the other cheek – it looked uncomfortably like the *patientia* of a slave.'[19] Kaster's arguments are certainly borne out elsewhere in Tacitus' works, where *patientia* is regularly glossed as a distinctively servile trait.[20] In the *Agricola*, *patientia* is explicitly associated with *seruitus* both here and when Boudicca's rebels complain of the evils of slavery (*mala seruitutis*), saying that their *patientia* has gained them nothing but harsher treatment (15.1). The defeat of that revolt sees the province returned to its former state of *patientia*

[18] Sailor 2008 p. 64 too notes the connection between *seruitus*, *patientia* and silence here.

[19] Kaster 2002 p. 144.

[20] *Ann.* 3.65.3 (*seruientium patientia*), 12.50.2 (*quamuis seruitio sueti patientiam abrumpunt)*, 14.26.1 (*seruilis patientia*) and 16.16.1 (*patientia seruilis*).

(16.2). All this suggests that the senate's *patientia* is a slavish submissiveness.[21]

The senate's enslavement is also connected, by the ablative absolute that follows, to the loss of 'the intercourse of speaking and listening' (*loquendi audiendique commercio*). The next sentence goes on to lament the senate's loss of voice (*uox*) and its silence (*tacere*). When the slavery motif recurs at the end of the preface it is again associated with silence, since the slavery of the past (*prior seruitus*) is contrasted with the novice speech (*rudis uox*) of the present (3.3).[22]

My point is that these opening references to senatorial enslavement construct slavery as a moral condition by associating it with submissiveness and silence. To these we might add the passivity (*inertia*, *desidia*) that Tacitus describes when explaining the difficulty of resuming intellectual activity in 3.1 (a passage I return to below).[23] Together these traits imply the loss of the ability – and even the will – to resist. This is a vision of the servile condition to which both Roman and British narratives will repeatedly return.

Making slaves

The British narrative describes provincial subjection to Rome in very similar terms. Like Domitian's senate, Rome's subjects are reduced to a state of slavish submission:

plus tamen ferociae Britanni praeferunt, ut quos nondum longa pax emollierit. nam Gallos quoque in bellis floruisse accepimus; mox segnitia cum otio intrauit,

[21] Leeman 1973 p. 203 suggests that their *patientia* is the Stoic virtue *karteria*, but this is unconvincing given its association with *seruitus* here, at 15.1 and in the *Annals*. When Tacitus later says that it is the willingness to endure *iniuriae* that distinguishes slavery from mere obedience (13.1), this is further confirmation that submissiveness is a characteristically servile trait. *Patientia* further hints at sexual exploitation, which was also part of the slave's lot. So Sailor 2004 p. 154 n. 46 and Evans 2003 pp. 173–4. On the sexual connotations of *patientia* see Adams 1982 pp. 189–90 and, for Tacitus, *Ann.* 6.1.2 (*tuncque primum ignota antea uocabula reperta sunt sellariorum et spintriarum ex foeditate loci ac multiplici patientia*). On the sexual exploitation of slaves, see Harper 2011 ch.7, Williams 1999, Bradley 1984 pp. 116–18, Kolendo 1981 and Finley 1980 pp. 95–6.

[22] See Sailor 2008 p. 64 on the connection between speech and freedom in the *Agricola*. Strocchio 1992 surveys Tacitus' use of silence more widely.

[23] On *inertia* in the *Agricola*, see further Jens 1956 pp. 332–8.

amissa uirtute pariter ac libertate. quod Britannorum olim uictis euenit: ceteri manent quales Galli fuerunt.

The Britons show greater spirit, since they have not yet been softened by a long peace. For we have read that the Gauls too used to excel at war. But then passivity came with inaction; and they lost their courage with their freedom. The same happened to those Britons who were conquered some time ago; the rest remain as the Gauls once were. (Tac. *Agr.* 11.4)

This passage stresses the transformational effects of Roman rule. The provincials have been softened (*emollierit*) and emasculated (*amissa uirtute*) by enslavement to Rome (*amissa libertate*) and the peace it brings (*pax*). The enervating effects of peace are a commonplace of Hellenistic and Roman thought.[24] What Tacitus does here is to identify peace with slavery. Peace is an aspect of enslavement to Rome, just as *inertia* is an aspect of the senate's enslavement under Domitian. Like other aspects of slavery it works to engender a disposition towards passivity. Inaction (*otium*) has bred passivity (*segnitia*) – a claim that should remind us of the senate's *inertia* and *desidia* in the preface (3.1).

'They lost their manhood/courage with their freedom' (*amissa uirtute pariter ac libertate*). Tacitus' pithy *sententia* recalls the Homeric adage that 'far-thundering Zeus takes away half a man's worth (ἀρετή) when the day of slavery overcomes him'.[25] The idea that slavery is an emasculating condition plays an important role in ancient ideologies of slavery. But it is a perspective that has been marginalised by modern fascination with Aristotle's theory of natural slavery. It is worth remembering that the idea of slavishness does not presuppose a genetic theory – that slaves can be made, as well as born.[26] This conception of slavish character as the *result* of enslavement is central to the *Agricola* as a whole.

In Tacitus, the degeneration into slavishness is gradual, not instantaneous. He returns to the idea that servility is produced by enslavement slightly later in the ethnography:

[24] See Fraenkel 1957 pp. 212–13 with *TLL* s.v. *otium* 1179.48–73 and s.v. *pax* 870.7–23 for Roman examples (and cf. Tac. *Agr.* 15.3, *Germ.* 14.2 and 36.1 and *Hist.* 1.88.2).

[25] ἥμισυ γάρ τ' ἀρετῆς ἀποαίνυται εὐρύοπα Ζεὺς | ἀνέρος, εὖτ' ἄν μιν κατὰ δούλιον ἦμαρ ἕλῃσιν (Hom. *Od.* 17.322–3). Plato treats this passage as paradigmatic of one common conception of slavery (*Leg.* 777a).

[26] On this aspect of the Roman ideology of slavery, see now Mouritsen 2011 ch. 2, esp. pp. 22–5.

ipsi Britanni dilectum ac tributa et iniuncta imperii munia impigre obeunt, si iniuriae absint: has aegre tolerant, iam domiti ut pareant, nondum ut seruiant.

The Britons themselves are not slow to comply with the levy, tribute and the other obligations imposed by the empire – provided they are not treated unjustly. Injustice they do not bear lightly. They have been broken to obedience, not yet to slavery. (Tac. *Agr.* 13.1)

Men have to be broken or tamed (*domiti*) into servile obedience (*ut seruiant*). The Britons may have been enslaved (11.4), but they have not yet been reduced to the depths of slavishness.[27] Yet the *nondum* implies it is only matter of a time. Servility is the inevitable end result of being broken to Roman rule. The same idea of a gradual, but inevitable, process of degeneration can be seen in the reference to *not yet* being softened by peace in the previous passage (*ut quos nondum longa pax emollierit*, 11.4). It is worth noting that what distinguishes slavery (*seruire*) from mere obedience (*parere*) here is the willingness to endure *iniuriae*. This servile disposition meekly to accept injustice recalls the *patientia* of the proem. Like Domitian's senate, Rome's tamed subjects will endure the unendurable.

In its enervating effects, enslavement is like a disease. A. D. Leeman has highlighted the series of medical metaphors in Chapter 3 of the proem, which represent the senate as recovering from the debilitating disease that was Domitian's reign – notably *redit animus* (of regaining consciousness) and *remedia* (remedies).[28] The metaphor returns in the British narrative when the British leader Calgacus congratulates his countrymen for living out

[27] If there seems to be an inconsistency (in that the Britons are not yet slaves here), it is because slavery in the *Agricola* is both an outward (social) and an inward (moral) condition. As psychological states, freedom and slavery form a continuum, not a simple polarity – as is implied by the reference to extremes of freedom and slavery in the preface (*sicut uetus aetas uidit quid ultimum in libertate esset, ita nos quid in seruitute*, 2.3). The Britons have been enslaved in the first sense, but they have not yet reached the depths of slavery in the second sense. They are not (yet) as slavish as Rome's other provincial subjects – notably the Gauls. The distinction returns when Calgacus congratulates the remote Caledonians for not even being able to see the shores of slaves (*seruientium litora*, 30.2). This is presumably in contrast to the southern Britons who do indeed look on the shores of Gaul. (So Ogilvie and Richmond 1967, Heubner 1984 and Furneaux 1896–1907.) The implication is that the southern Britons (whom the Caledonians can see) are not yet *seruientes*. Again it is the Gauls who are truly slavish.

[28] Leeman 1973 pp. 203–5. On the importance of medical metaphors elsewhere in Tacitus, see especially Woodman 2006.

of sight of Roman rule and thus keeping their eyes 'pure of the contagion of mastery' (*a contactu dominationis inuiolatos*, 30.2). The condition of provincial slavery is like a disease that can infect those who so much as look upon it. Calgacus resumes the metaphor a little later when he describes his people as 'unimpaired and unconquered' (*integri et indomiti*, 31.4). So long as they are unconquered they remain *integri* – whole and healthy.[29] These disease metaphors resonate with the idea of enslavement as a debilitating condition.

Servile complicity

Slavishness in the *Agricola* is not just produced by domination; it also serves to perpetuate it. Both the Roman and the British narratives explore how the dominated become complicit in their own subjection. Part of the problem is that slavery is a seductive condition. Describing the difficulty of resuming the practice of historiography after the silence of Domitian's reign, Tacitus writes of the pleasures of inaction:

> et ut corpora nostra lente augescunt, cito extinguuntur, sic ingenia studiaque oppresseris facilius quam reuocaueris: subit quippe etiam ipsius inertiae dulcedo, et inuisa primo desidia postremo amatur.

> As our bodies grow slowly but are quickly extinguished, so it is easier to crush our faculties and spirit than it is to revive them. For the very pleasure of passivity steals over us and we come to love the indolence which we once despised. (Tac. *Agr.* 3.1)

Inertia (idleness/passivity) may at first have been forced on the senate against its will. But pleasure (*dulcedo*) soon replaces disgust, as the inherent pleasure of inaction overcomes their better nature.[30] The seductions of slavery recur in the British narrative in

[29] See the passages cited at *OLD* s.v. *integer* § 10 ('unimpaired by ill health or disease').

[30] Leeman 1973 pp. 203–5 interprets *ipsius inertiae dulcedo* as suggesting 'the lethargic euphoria of the ill patient'. But his exclusive focus on disease does not give slavishness and its seductions their due. Most subsequent readings of the passage have followed Leeman. So Haynes 2006 p. 158 and Sailor 2004 p. 154. The latter acknowledges the description of 'moral corruption and collapse', noting perceptively its representation 'of not doing anything, of letting other people do things to us, and, worst of all, of enjoying it', but focuses on the idea of effeminacy rather than servility.

the famous passage describing Agricola's encouragement of the adoption of Roman practices by the Britons:

sequens hiems saluberrimis consiliis absumpta. namque ut homines dispersi ac rudes eoque in bella faciles quieti et otio per uoluptates adsuescerent, hortari priuatim, adiuuare publice, ut templa fora domos extruerent, laudando promptos, castigando segnis: ita honoris aemulatio pro necessitate erat. iam uero principum filios liberalibus artibus erudire, et ingenia Britannorum studiis Gallorum anteferre, ut qui modo linguam Romanam abnuebant, eloquentiam concupiscerent. inde etiam habitus nostri honor et frequens toga; paulatimque discessum ad delenimenta uitiorum, porticus et balineas et conuiuiorum elegantiam. idque apud imperitos humanitas uocabatur, cum pars seruitutis esset.

The following winter was spent on a very sound policy. The aim was to use the pleasurable life to accustom to peace and leisure men who were scattered and uncivilised and therefore always ready for war. He encouraged individuals and assisted communities in the construction of temples, forums and houses, praising the energetic and rebuking the indolent. Thus competition for honour made compulsion unnecessary. Moreover, he educated the sons of the chieftains in the liberal arts and praised the talents of the Britons over the learning of the Gauls. As a result, those who used to spurn the Latin language began to covet its eloquence. Even our dress acquired prestige and the toga became ubiquitous. Little by little they strayed to the seductions of vice – porticoes, baths and the refinements of dining. In their ignorance they called this culture, when it was part of their enslavement. (Tac. *Agr.* 21.1–2)

If the Britons end up in a state of slavery (*seruitus*), their own desires play a central role in their subjugation. It is pleasure (*uoluptates*) that accustoms them to peace and leisure; desire (*concupiscere*) that makes them study Roman oratory. It is particularly telling that these Britons learn to covet the Latinity they once rejected. This mirrors the moral corruption described in the proem, by which senators came to love the idleness they once despised (3.1). These Britons are just as complicit in their own degeneration. The point of these two passages is that there is an inherent attractiveness to the servile condition (a conceit that is not unique to the *Agricola*).[31] Both senators and Britons are corrupted by this pleasure to the point of forgetting their own best interests.

[31] Fitzgerald 2000 ch. 2 discusses the attractions of slavery in the imagination of the Roman elite, exploring how some aspects of the slave's condition – notably freedom from the demands of self-restraint – could be imagined as dangerously attractive.

The pernicious consequences of enslavement extend even further. The *Agricola* insists that it is in the nature of slaves to prey on each other. It is always other slaves who enforce the master's authority. When Calgacus seeks to convince his countrymen of the necessity of confronting Rome, he tells them that they are the newest slaves in Rome's household and reminds them of the abuse inevitably suffered by new slaves at the hands of their fellows:

ac sicut in familia recentissimus quisque seruorum etiam conseruis ludibrio est, sic in hoc orbis terrarum uetere famulatu noui nos et uiles in excidium petimur.

As in a household the newest slave is always the sport even of his fellow slaves, so in the long-standing slave-gang that is the world we are new and worthless and so are being hounded to death. (Tac. *Agr.* 31.2)

A little later, Calgacus encourages his countrymen by reminding them of the preponderance of provincials in Rome's armies. He promises them that adversity will dissolve the Roman army:

nisi si Gallos et Germanos et (pudet dictu) Britannorum plerosque, licet dominationi alienae sanguinem commodent, diutius tamen hostes quam seruos, fide et adfectu teneri putatis.

Unless you believe that Gauls and Germans and – shameful though it is to say it – many Britons, who though they give their blood for foreign mastery were nevertheless enemies longer than they have been slaves, are bound by loyalty and affection. (Tac. *Agr.* 32.1)

Calgacus laments the fact that these slaves (*serui*) spill their blood in the service of Roman mastery (*dominatio*). In this slave-gang, it is slaves who enforce the masters' will. Calgacus goes on to promise that they will remember who they are and where their interests lie, but of course they do not. Such blindness is characteristic of the servile condition as it is presented elsewhere in Tacitus.[32] The battle narrative that follows confirms that the Romans exercise their powers by proxy. The Roman legions play no role in the fighting. They are stationed in the rear, while it is the auxiliary cohorts – whose ethnic origins are clearly marked

[32] Cf Pomeroy 2005 p. 148 on *libido seruitii* (servile whim) in Tacitus: 'enslavement does not so much rob its victim of choice as replace it with mere whim, with no thought for the common good'. See also Edwards 1993 pp. 195–8 for the importance of the idea that slaves are ruled by sensual pleasure in the broader Roman discourse of slavery.

(*Batauorum cohortes ac Tungrorum*, 36.1; *Bataui*, 36.2) – who fight Rome's battle.[33] The later stages of the fighting are described as a vast and awesome spectacle (*grande et atrox spectaculum*, 37.2). The entertainment (*spectaculum* is often used of the arena and the theatre) is for the benefit of the Roman legions as much as the Roman reader.

Such provincial complicity in Roman domination has its parallel in the senate's involvement in the suppression of resistance to Domitian, which Tacitus acknowledges in a famous passage at the end of the work:

> mox nostrae duxere Heluidium in carcerem manus; nos Maurici Rusticique uisus <adflixit>; nos innocenti sanguine Senecio perfudit. Nero tamen subtraxit oculos suos iussitque scelera, non spectauit: praecipua sub Domitiano miseriarum pars erat uidere et aspici.

> Soon ours were the hands that led Helvidius to the cell; it was us whom Mauricius and Rusticus struck with their gaze; it was us whom Senecio drenched with his innocent blood. At least Nero hid his eyes; he ordered outrages but did not watch them. The worst of our miseries under Domitian was to watch and be observed. (Tac. *Agr.* 45.1–2)

The insistent repetition of *nostrae* and *nos* underscores the senate's complicity in these horrors, recalling the provincials' complicity in the enslavement of Britain.[34] There is a further echo of the British narrative in the description of Domitian's gaze that follows. Here too, the real oppressor looks on while the oppressed persecute each other. Again we find that the Britons have been acting out the plight of the senatorial class under Domitian.

It should by now be clear that enslavement has a particular thematic importance in the *Agricola*. Throughout the work, slavery is associated with a set of slavish traits which includes compliance (*patientia*), passivity (*inertia* or *segnitia*) and silence. Such slavishness is represented both as the inevitable result of enslavement and as working to perpetuate it. The *Agricola* draws on this implicit

[33] Most commentary on this passage has focused on the frequency of, and the rationale for, this form of deployment. See Ogilvie and Richmond 1967 ad loc. Regardless of its historicity, this account of Roman military practice resonates with the description of senatorial complicity in the purges of Domitian's reign.

[34] The importance of senatorial complicity as a theme of the *Agricola* has been highlighted by Liebeschuetz 1966 pp. 133–4 and Haynes 2006.

psychology of slavery in order to explain the interdependence of domination and slavishness in both Rome and Britain. Like slaves, both senators and provincials are not just broken but corrupted by the experience of subjugation. They lose their will to act; they submit to any and all forms of abuse; they become blind to their real interests – even to the extent of becoming complicit in their own subjection.

Britain and Rome

Because the plight of the British under Rome is made to mirror that of the senate under Domitian, Tacitus' representation of the provincials who resist or submit to Roman rule constitutes an oblique commentary on senatorial resistance to the emperor. The figure of Calgacus is particularly significant. His angry and defiant speech before the final battle takes on wider import in the context of the *Agricola*'s insistence on its own status as a speech act after the enforced silence of Domitian's reign.[35] Even more striking is his condemnation of a policy of accommodation to Roman rule:

sed nulla iam ultra gens, nihil nisi fluctus ac saxa, et infestiores Romani, quorum superbiam frustra per obsequium ac modestiam effugias.

There is no people beyond us, nothing but the sea and the rocks and – deadlier still – the Romans. Obedience and restraint offer no escape from their arrogance. (Tac. *Agr*. 30.3)

Obsequium ac modestia ('obedience and restraint') are the very same words used to describe Agricola's conduct under Domitian in what is often regarded as the political manifesto of the work:[36]

sciant, quibus moris est inlicita mirari, posse etiam sub malis principibus magnos uiros esse, obsequiumque ac modestiam, si industria ac uigor adsint, eo laudis excedere, quo plerique per abrupta sed in nullum rei publicae usum ambitiosa morte inclaruerunt.

[35] Where Tacitus offers only a record of enslavement after the fact (*memoria prioris seruitutis*, 3.3), Calgacus testifies to Roman enslavement in the present. Note also that Boudicca's rebels reject the *patientia* that Tacitus and his colleagues endured (15.1~2.3). Of course, both instances of defiant speech prove futile.

[36] On *obsequium* as the middle course between *seruitus* and *libertas* in Tacitus, see especially Vielberg 1987 ch. 3.

Those who are accustomed to admire transgression should know that even under bad emperors men can become great. Obedience and restraint can, if they are combined with diligence and spirit, attain to the same heights of glory more often reached by those who have won fame through an ostentatious death – a difficult path, but one that is of no benefit to the state. (Tac. *Agr.* 42.4)

Calgacus condemns the very values for which Agricola is praised.[37] His language thus aligns him with those who would prefer an ostentatious death to a policy of restraint and accommodation – presumably Thrasea Paetus, Helvidius Priscus and their like. By identifying the Stoic opposition with Calgacus, the *Agricola* associates their policy of resistance with the barbarian and thus the irrational.[38] Their defiance is condemned as ultimately futile (*in nullum rei publicae usum*). Calgacus' stubbornness proves fatal when the ensuing battle sees the destruction of his people and the devastation of their land.

But this can only be half the story. The *Agricola*'s rejection of outright defiance in favour of a policy of *obsequium ac modestia* is not without ambivalence. There is a degree of sympathy for those who resist, both Roman and British, and the idealisation of Agricola and the course he espouses leaves room for doubt and equivocation.[39] Several readers have drawn attention to Agricola's implication in the enslavement of Britain.[40] But, as the previous chapter has shown, it is far from certain that Roman readers would have found the representation of conquest as enslavement as disquieting as we do. More obviously problematic is the hint that even

37 The striking echo has not always received the attention it deserves. Ogilvie and Richmond 1967 do not even acknowledge it in their commentary on the passage. Among the few to comment on it are Sailor 2008 p. 98, Whitmarsh 2006 p. 316, Rutledge 2000 p. 89 and McGing 1982 p. 23.

38 My reading of Calgacus as a paradigm of defiance that is attractive but nevertheless futile and thus irrational owes much to the reading of Boudicca in *Annals* 14 by Roberts 1988. The figure of Boudicca plays much the same role in *Annals* 14 that Calgacus does in the *Agricola* – though Tacitus exploits her gender in order to further reinforce the connection between resistance and irrationality.

39 Whitmarsh 2006 is the best account of the ambivalence of the *Agricola*'s political and ethical message. 'The *Agricola* is an ambiguous text. It dramatizes a position of quietist *obsequium*, enacts a rhetoric of compliance; but in doing so, it points up the array of choices, exposes the roads not taken' (p. 324). See also Haynes 2006, Clarke 2001 p. 134 and Liebeschuetz 1966.

40 Haynes 2006 pp. 165–6, Whitmarsh 2006 p. 306, Dench 2005 p. 85, Evans 2003 p. 276, and Clarke 2001 p. 109.

Agricola shares in the slavishness common to senators and provincials:

mox inter quaesturam ac tribunatum plebis atque ipsum tribunatus annum quiete et otio transiit, gnarus sub Nerone temporum, quibus inertia pro sapientia fuit, idem praeturae tenor et silentium; nec enim iurisdictio obuenerat.

The time between being quaestor and tribune of the people and even the year of the tribunate itself he passed in peace and leisure, since he understood the nature of Nero's reign – a time when inaction counted as wisdom. His praetorship had the same character and silence, since he was not allotted judicial responsibility. (Tac. *Agr.* 6.3–4)

Agricola's *inertia* may be pragmatic and his *silentium* a matter of chance (in that his praetorship involved no judicial duties), but it is still surprising to find him indulging in two failings which featured prominently in the earlier description of the senate's slavishness under Domitian (3.1, 3.2).[41] The discordant note is reinforced by the comment that Agricola passes his tribunate in 'peace and leisure'. *Quies et otium* is precisely the mechanism that Agricola will later use to pacify the Britons, in the famous account of his promotion of Roman culture discussed earlier (*ut homines dispersi ac rudes ... quieti et otio per uoluptates adsuescerent*, 21.1).[42] The end result there is enslavement (21.2). It is also the same passive posture that Domitian's intimates will press on Agricola at the end of his career when they persuade him to excuse himself from the governorship of Africa or Asia, to which he would normally have been entitled, by praising 'peace and leisure' (*quietem et otium laudare*, 42.1). The parallels suggest that Agricola's policy of withdrawing himself from public life aligns him to some extent with the servile senate and with the provincials who slavishly submit to Roman rule. Despite his virtues, he does not entirely escape the slavishness that results from living under domination.

This reading has illustrated the many verbal and thematic parallels that bind the *Agricola*'s narrative of Roman conquest in Britain to the description of Domitianic Rome in which it is embedded. The two accounts are structured around a shared set of

[41] Haynes 2006 p. 163 seizes upon Agricola's *inertia* here, but surprisingly neglects his *silentium*.

[42] Whitmarsh 2006 pp. 319–20 too notes the echo.

polarities – submission and resistance, silence and speech, passivity and action, masculinity and effeminacy, self-indulgence and self-control, oblivion and memory – all of which are encompassed within a broader, governing opposition between slavishness and freedom. No reading of the *Agricola* can afford to ignore the interweaving of the two narratives. The problem is particularly acute for readers who are tempted to see the British narrative as a straightforward document of Roman imperialism.[43] In the context of the work as a whole, it is the relationship between emperor and senate that occupies centre stage. The British narrative provides a space for exploring the political, cultural and moral crisis Tacitus sees confronting his own society.[44] To read it for insights into Roman imperialism is, in many ways, to miss the point. At the very least, we have to acknowledge that the *Agricola*'s particular perspective on the nature of empire is developed for the specific purpose of exploring the analogies between the condition of the provinces under Rome and that of the senate under Domitian.

The Batavian revolt (*Histories* 4–5)

Much of the fourth and what survives of the fifth book of Tacitus' *Histories* is devoted to the revolt in the German and Gallic provinces in 69–70 CE. In Tacitus' account, the revolt is instigated by the Batavian chieftain Julius Civilis, who stirs up his countrymen by representing Roman rule as enslavement. He complains of the evils of slavery (*seruitii mala*, 4.14.2) and tells them that they are no longer being treated like allies but like slaves (*mancipia*, ibid.). He then incites the Gauls to join the revolt, chiding them for calling a wretched slavery (*misera seruitus*) 'peace' (4.17.2) and exhorting them to take up arms against their common masters (*communes dominos*, ibid.). He later persuades a Gallic noble (Alpinius Montanus) to join him by rebuking his people (the Treveri) for

[43] See e.g. Shumate 2006 ch. 3, Evans 2003 and Rutledge 2000, all of whom treat Tacitus' text as a representative expression of Roman imperial ideology.

[44] Cf. Roberts 1988 p. 131 on the Boudiccan revolt in *Annals* 14: 'The reader of the *Annals* is more likely to apply the model of imperial oppression established for Britain to the Roman context than vice-versa; Rome will be perceived as the tenor, Britain the vehicle, though, of course, in principle the two are capable of mutual revelation.'

their slavish spirit (*seruientium animae*, 4.32.2). Later, the Ubii of Cologne, who have so far remained loyal to Rome, are urged to join the revolt, tear down the fortifications of slavery (*munimenta seruitii*, 4.64.2) that are their walls, expel their Roman masters (*domini*, 4.64.3) from their city and forget their enslavement (*seruitutis oblitus*, ibid.). When, after a series of Roman successes, the Batavians eventually decide to abandon their revolt, their rhetoric takes a fatalistic turn. It is just not possible for the whole world to be freed from slavery by a single people (*ab una natione totius orbis seruitium depelli*, 5.25.1). If they have a choice of masters (*dominorum electio*), they decide, it is more honourable to be the slaves of Roman emperors than German women (referring to the German prophetess Veleda).

The narrative of *Histories* 4–5 also includes a Roman counter-rhetoric in two speeches delivered by Roman generals to rebellious Gallic communities. It is significant that neither makes any attempt to contradict the rebels' claims that subjection to Rome is a form of slavery. The first speech is a defiant but unsuccessful attempt by C. Dillius Vocula, legionary legate and de facto commander of the army in Germany, to dissuade two Gallic tribes, the Treveri and Lingones, from joining Civilis' revolt (4.57.1–2). Far from contradicting the rebel rhetoric of freedom, Vocula appropriates the metaphor of slavery in an attempt to cow them into submission. He warns the Gauls that they have rebelled only because their masters have treated them too gently (*quia molle seruitium*); once they have been punished they will be reconciled to Rome (4.57.2).[45] Vocula's rhetoric is ultimately ineffective. The Treveri and Lingones defect to Civilis and Vocula himself is murdered by a legionary deserter. But the rebels' success is checked by the arrival of Q. Petilius Cerialis with a new army. The majority of the Gallic tribes decide to make peace and the remainder are defeated in battle. It is at this point that Cerialis makes his famous speech to the now reconquered Treveri and Lingones (4.73–4). He chides them for letting themselves be seduced by Civilis' rhetoric of freedom into ignoring his ulterior motives and forgetting the benefits of Roman rule. Much has been written about Cerialis'

[45] See further pp. 238–9.

description of the benefits of empire. Where earlier commentators tended to take his justification of Roman rule at face value,[46] more recent criticism has focused on its ironies. The first half of the speech seeks to expose the dishonesty of German appeals to *libertas* by asserting that their real desire was to enslave the Gauls:

acciti auxilio Germani sociis pariter atque hostibus seruitutem imposuerant. … libertas et speciosa nomina praetexuntur; nec quisquam alienum seruitium et dominationem sibi concupiuit ut non eadem ista uocabula usurparet.

Summoned to help, the Germans had imposed slavery on their allies and enemies alike … They use liberty and other attractive words as a covering. But no one ever lusted after the enslavement of others and mastery for himself without making use of those very words. (Tac. *Hist.* 4.73.2–3)

Cerialis' unmasking of German pretexts invites a critical reading of his own later claims about Roman rule. The reader is primed to see the *speciosa nomina* in what follows.[47] But it is worth observing that Cerialis' account of Roman rule is not as flattering as some would suggest. He never claims that the Gauls are anything other than Rome's slaves now. On the contrary, he describes Roman rule in precisely those terms when he advises the Gauls to resign themselves to their masters' luxury and greed (*luxum uel auaritiam dominantium tolerate*, 4.74.2). Like Vocula, Cerialis implies that the Gauls are indeed slaves.[48]

While the language of slavery is widespread in rebel and even Roman rhetoric, however, it is entirely absent from the narrative voice. In this respect *Histories* 4–5 is very different to the *Agricola*. Even in the speeches, metaphors of enslavement are often conflated with the language of kingship (*regnum*) and imperial power (*imperium, imperitare*). The Gauls hope to shrug off their enslavement

46 See Benario 1991 p. 3341, with bibliography.

47 So Haynes 2004 p. 44, Haynes 2003 p. 168, Keitel 1993, Ternes 1990, Bastomsky 1988.

48 The harsh dichotomy implied by the language of slavery and mastery is reinforced by the description of the Gauls as *uicti* at the end of the speech: *proinde pacem et urbem, quam uicti uictoresque eodem iure obtinemus, amate colite* (Tac. *Hist.* 4.74.4). This sentence simultaneously promises them a share in empire and reminds them that their relationship to Romans is still that of *uicti* to *uictores*. Like the slave, the *uictus* – whose impotence is a recurring figure in Roman literature and iconography – is a powerful paradigm of subjection. See e.g. de Souza 2011, Bradley 2004 and Ferris 2000 on images of the conquered in Roman art.

(*seruitium*) and desire to become *rulers* themselves (*imperitare*, *Hist*. 4.25.3). Civilis talks of freedom but aims at *kingship* (*regnum*, 4.17.6). Cerialis variously accuses the Germans of aiming at mastery (*dominatio*, 4.73.2 and 3) and *kingship* (*regnum*, 4.73.2 and 74.2). This suggests that the text is not particularly invested in the specificity of slavery as opposed to other forms of domination. Where the *Agricola* ascribes special importance to slavery as a mode of domination with its own distinctive logic, the *Histories* is more interested in the use of freedom and slavery as tropes of a self-serving style of political rhetoric.

As with the *Agricola*'s account of the conquest of Britain, this narrative of events in the provinces has a wider significance. The Batavian revolt serves to explore and develop many of the themes already raised by the *Histories*' Roman narrative. It describes provincials liberating themselves from Roman rule only to fall victim to discord (*discordia*) and thus self-destruction.[49] The link between *libertas* and *discordia* is an important theme of the *Histories* as a whole. The Gauls and Germans find themselves in the same trap as the Roman senate, as Galba has described it earlier in the *Histories* – they cannot bear to be reduced to slaves, but they cannot endure true liberty either (*nec totam seruitutem pati possunt nec totam libertatem*, 1.16.5). When at the end of *Histories* 4 Cerialis tells the Gauls that they should be prepared to endure (*tolerare*) their masters' faults, this echoes the speech at the beginning of the same book in which Eprius Marcellus advises the senate to endure (*tolerare*) whatever emperors they get.[50] Cerialis' closing appeal for them to pursue the safe path of obedience (*obsequium*) rather than the self-destructive course of defiance (*contumacia*) also speaks to the Roman narrative, in which these are key words.[51] Similarly, when the Batavians eventually realise that a choice (*electio*) of masters is the best they can hope for (5.25.2),

[49] For the responsion between the Batavian revolt and the Roman narrative of *Histories* 1–4, see especially Keitel 1993. Cf. Haynes 2003 pp. 148–77 and Hose 1998.

[50] Cerialis: *quo modo sterilitatem aut nimios imbris et cetera naturae mala, ita luxum uel auaritiam dominantium tolerate* (4.74.2). Marcellus: *bonos imperatores uoto expetere, qualiscumque tolerare* (Tac. *Hist*. 4.8.2). See further Keitel 1993.

[51] *ne contumaciam cum pernicie quam obsequium cum securitate malitis* (4.74.4). On *obsequium* and *contumacia* in Tacitus' Roman narratives, see especially Vielberg 1987 chs. 3 and 6.

they echo Galba's earlier claim that the selection (*eligi*) of a master is the closest Romans can come to freedom (1.16.1).[52] The Batavian revolt is thus embedded in the *Histories*' broader meditation on the impossibility of escape from domination.

Like Calgacus, Civilis is more than just a rebel against Rome. But his ulterior motives – the gap between his public rhetoric of freedom and his private desire for power – give him a very different paradigmatic value. He is an opportunist who exploits the emotive appeal of *libertas* for his own purposes. The speech in which he promises the Gauls freedom (4.17.2–5) is tellingly juxtaposed with the claim that he was hoping to make himself king (*regno imminebat*, 4.17.6). It is characteristic of the *Histories* that promises of freedom are always deferred as one master replaces another.[53] In the *Agricola*, Domitian's dominance is a given; the only choice for senators is whether to pursue a course of servile acquiescence or one of outright confrontation – or to attempt to find a safe but honourable path between them. In the opening books of the *Histories*, on the other hand, imperial power is always up for grabs, with a series of opportunistic pretenders making their bids for the purple. Civilis is just another contender. Indeed his name is almost too good to be true, coming as it does after the *bellum ciuile* of *Histories* 1–3.[54] Tacitus repeatedly suggests that this revolt blurs the line between *bellum ciuile* and *bellum externum* – that it is just another instalment in the long series of internal conflicts.[55] Where

52 Batavians: *sibi non tributa, sed uirtutem et uiros indici. proximum id libertati; et si dominorum electio sit, honestius principes Romanorum quam Germanorum feminas tolerari* (5.25.2). Galba: *sub Tiberio et Gaio et Claudio unius familiae quasi hereditas fuimus: loco libertatis erit quod eligi coepimus* (*Hist.* 1.16.1). See Keitel 1993.

53 Compare the Gauls, who hope to free themselves and then rule over others (*arma sumpsere spe libertatis et, si exuissent seruitium, cupidine imperitandi, Hist* 4.25.3), and the Tencteri, who urge the Ubii to liberate themselves from Roman rule and hope to rule others (*seruitutis oblitus populus aut ex aequo agetis aut aliis imperitabitis*, 4.64.3). Cf. Haynes 2003 pp. 158–9.

54 So O'Gorman 1995 and Haynes 2003 p. 148.

55 Promised in the proem (*trina bella ciuilia, plura externa ac plerumque permixta, Hist.* 1.2.1) and alluded to in Book 2 (*principium interno simul externoque bello parantibus fatis*, 2.69.1), the blurring of foreign and civil war is delivered in Book 4: *mixta belli ciuilis externique facie* (4.22.2). Hence the significance of Civilis describing himself both as another Hannibal and another Sertorius – the one a foreigner, the other a Roman (4.13.2). However, readers have been too quick to ascribe this motif to the fact that the Gauls are provincials and (some of them) Roman citizens – as if provincial revolt was obviously a form of civil war (so Shumate 2006 pp. 113–14, Pomeroy 2003 and

Calgacus provides a paradigm of heroic but futile resistance, Civilis embodies the opportunism of those who contest the legitimacy of one emperor only to put themselves in his place. Both have a paradigmatic significance for the Roman narratives in which they are embedded.

The Boudiccan revolt (*Annals* 14)

Tacitus' *Annals* offer a series of analogues to Calgacus and Civilis: Arminius in Books 1–2, Florus and Sacrovir in Book 3, Caratacus in Book 12 and Boudicca in Book 14 – all northerners who struggle to free their peoples from enslavement to Rome. The rest of this chapter focuses on the last of these, because Tacitus' account of the Boudicca revolt of 61 CE, the centrepiece of *Annals* 14, makes the most sustained use of the metaphor of enslavement. Again it is essential to recognise that this narrative of provincial resistance has a broader significance within the work in which it is embedded. Like Calgacus, Boudicca is a figure whose rejection of Roman rule invites comparison with senatorial defiance at Rome. Her significance as a paradigm of resistance has been well described by Michael Roberts.[56] He shows that the language of *libertas* and *seruitus* aligns the British rebels with those senators who defy the emperor. But he also demonstrates that the Britons are represented as feminine rather than masculine, emotional rather than disciplined, and savage rather than civilised in contrast with their Roman foes. By implication, senatorial resistance is open to the same negative characterisation: 'Expressions of resistance in Neronian Rome can appropriately be associated with the emotional

O'Gorman 1995 pp. 124 and 128). None of the other Tacitean revolts are described in these terms – not even the Gallic revolt led by Julius Sacrovir and Julius Florus (*Ann.* 3.40–7), both obviously Roman citizens, or that of Tacfarinas, who had served in the Roman army (*Ann.* 2.52, 3.20–1, 3.73–4, 4.23–6). If we look closely at Tacitus' representation of the boundary between war and civil war, we find that what makes the difference is the presence of units of the Roman army – and particularly their standards – on the rebel side: *hinc ueteranarum cohortium signa, inde depromptae siluis lucisque ferarum imagines, ut cuique genti inire proelium mos est, mixta belli ciuilis externique facie obstupefecerant obsessos* (*Hist.* 4.22.2). It is the desertion of the Batavian cohorts and later the Vitellian legions, not provincial revolt *per se*, that makes this a quasi-civil war in Tacitus' eyes.

[56] Roberts 1988. All quotations are from p. 127.

and the female, for they depend on an unrealistic and irrational estimate of the relationship between ruler and ruled ... The only rational ... reaction to such a disparity of power is acquiescence.' But (as in the *Agricola*) the message is not without ambivalence: 'Such a sensible course lays itself open, all too readily, to the charge of *seruitium*.'

There is more to be said about the function of slavery in this narrative. Like the *Agricola*, *Annals* 14 abounds in the language and imagery of slavery. The tribes that rebel are those 'who were not yet broken by enslavement' (*nondum seruitio fracti*, 31.2), an allusion to the debilitating effects of enslavement familiar from the *Agricola*.[57] They resolve to recover their freedom (*resumere libertatem*, ibid.). They are confirmed in their purpose by their hatred for the Roman colonists at Camulodunum who had evicted them from their land, calling them captives and slaves (*captiuos seruos appellando*, 31.3). They are also incensed by the new temple of Claudius, which they see as a bastion of eternal mastery (*arx aeternae dominationis*, 31.4). Boudicca later calls on her countrymen to avenge her loss of freedom (*libertatem amissam*, 35.1) and promises that the gods will help redeem her from slavery (*uindictae adesse*, 35.2).[58]

From the outset, however, Tacitus blurs the line between metaphorical and real enslavement. This is immediately evident in his description of the events that sparked the revolt – the abuse inflicted on the family of the Iceni king Prasutagus following his death:

> rex Icenorum Prasutagus, longa opulentia clarus, Caesarem heredem duasque filias scripserat, tali obsequio ratus regnumque et domum suam procul iniuria fore. quod contra uertit, adeo ut regnum per centuriones, domus per seruos uelut capta uastarentur. iam primum uxor eius Boudicca uerberibus adfecta et filiae stupro uiolatae sunt; praecipui quique Icenorum, quasi cunctam regionem muneri accepissent, auitis bonis exuuntur, et propinqui regis inter mancipia habebantur.

Prasutagus, king of the Iceni and famous for his long wealth, made the emperor and his own two daughters his heirs. He thought that such obedience would protect his kingdom and family from injustice. But events proved otherwise – so much so that

[57] Note that *fractus* also connotes effeminacy (*OLD* s.v. *fractus* § 4 and *frango* § 8).

[58] Because of the two senses of *uindicta*, Boudicca is calling on the gods both to avenge her (*OLD* § 2) and to free her from slavery (§ 1).

his kingdom was plundered by centurions and his household by slaves, as if they had been taken in war. First, his wife Boudicca was punished with the whip and his daughters were violated by rape. Then, as if [the Romans] had received the whole country as a gift, the most prominent of the Iceni were stripped of their ancestral property and the king's kinsmen were treated like slaves. (Tac. *Ann.* 14.31.1)

Here provincial enslavement becomes a reality. The dead king's family and friends are treated like slaves (*inter mancipia habebantur*). His wife is whipped (*uerberibus adfecta*) – a punishment normally reserved for slaves.[59] The rape of his daughters has a similar significance. They are described as *stupro uiolatae*, *stuprum* being a specifically Roman concept implying more than rape. It is the 'violation of the sexual integrity of *freeborn* Romans'.[60] The symbolic significance of these offences is underlined in Boudicca's later speech to the rebels:

sed tunc non ut tantis maioribus ortam regnum et opes, uerum ut unam e uulgo libertatem amissam, confectum uerberibus corpus, contrectatam filiarum pudicitiam ulcisci.

But now [she said] she was seeking vengeance, not as a woman of such noble birth for her kingdom and wealth, but rather as an ordinary woman for the freedom she had lost, for her body exhausted by the lash, and for her daughters' violated honour. (Tac. *Ann.* 14.35.1)

When Boudicca complains of her loss of freedom (*libertatem amissam*), she is not just describing subjection to Rome, as is conventional in rebel rhetoric. She is also referring to concrete, personal grievances. She reminds us that her body was violated by servile punishments (*confectum uerberibus corpus*) and that her daughters' sexual integrity was similarly abused (*contrectatam filiarum pudicitiam*).[61] Like *stuprum* earlier, *pudicitia* is a loaded word, denoting the 'physical inviolability of *free* Roman citizens'.[62] In short, the offences against Prasutagus' family – the de facto enslavement of his kinsmen, the whipping of his wife, the

[59] See n. 6 above.

[60] Williams 1999 p. 96 (the emphasis is mine). The rape need not have been described as *stuprum*. *Raptus* and *uis* are less loaded alternatives.

[61] Roberts 1988 p. 126 does not see the connection between her lost *libertas* and the physical abuse.

[62] Williams 1999 p. 99 (again the emphasis is mine).

rape of his daughters – constitute violations of the privileges of freedom. These freeborn provincials have been treated like slaves.

These transgressions are clearly problematic. The boundary between slave and free is central to Roman social order. The reader's sympathies are further engaged (if they share Tacitus' aristocratic values) by the contrast between the nobility of the victims and the servile status of some of their oppressors (*domus per seruos ... uastarentur*).[63] The language in which the rape is described has the same effect. The references to *stuprum* and *pudicitia* elide the cultural divide between these Britons and Roman readers, inviting sympathy for them as for any wronged member of the Roman elite.[64]

These outrages in the provinces have a broader significance in Tacitus' narrative. The Roman officials who thus trample on the rights of the freeborn reveal the extent to which Roman society has been corrupted by power. The rape is particularly significant. Throughout the Roman historiographical tradition, unrestrained lust and sexual violence are symbols of tyranny. In Livy, for example, the rape of Lucretia by Tarquinius Superbus (1.57–60) and the attempted rape of Verginia by Appius Claudius (3.44–54) are the concrete signs that excessive power has corrupted the kings and the decemvirate respectively.[65] Like those paradigmatic examples of sexual violence, this provincial rape is symptomatic of the dysfunction of Roman political culture. But here it is not a case of a few individuals being corrupted by their personal power, but of Romans in general being corrupted by their power as an imperial people.[66] Similar degeneration is visible in the behaviour of the colonists at Camulodunum:

[63] It is also significant that the grievances are focalised through Prasutagus himself rather than the women involved (a point well made by Braund 1996 p. 134). The victims of the rape are identified only as his daughters. Even Boudicca is at first presented as his wife (*uxor eius*), rather than the disturbingly autonomous figure she will subsequently become.

[64] *Stuprum* is occasionally used in contexts that do not involve freeborn Romans. But where it is so used, it always retains connotations of moral transgression. See Williams 1999 p. 98.

[65] See further Beard 1999, Moore 1993, Joshel 1992 and Philippides 1983.

[66] Tacitus' transposition of rape to the imperial periphery is already anticipated by Livy, whose fourth decade includes an account of the rape of a Galatian noblewoman by a nameless centurion, itself closely linked to the earlier rapes of Lucretia and Verginia (Livy

quippe in coloniam Camulodunum recens deducti pellebant domibus, exturbabant agris, captiuos, seruos appellando, fouentibus impotentiam ueteranorum militibus similitudine uitae et spe eiusdem licentiae.

For the men recently settled at the *colonia* of Camulodunum were forcing [the Britons] from their homes and driving them from their fields, calling them captives and slaves. The army encouraged the veterans' lawlessness because they had a similar way of life and because they looked forward to taking the same liberties themselves. (Tac. *Ann.* 14.31.3)

Their conduct is attributed to unrestrained power (*impotentia*), while the serving soldiers anticipate a similar freedom to act without restraint (*licentia*).[67] That the British are abused as slaves is thus a sign of the dysfunction of Roman society.

The Boudiccan narrative concludes with the dispatch of Nero's freedman Polyclitus to settle the situation in Britain. Tacitus invites the reader to see him through British eyes. The Britons cannot understand the power of freedmen in Roman culture. How, they ask, can the men who defeated them submit to slaves (*seruitiis oboedirent*, 14.39.2)? The Britons call the imperial freedman a slave. Though it is attributed to barbarians here, the assimilation of freedmen to slaves is typical of aristocratic Roman discourse.[68] It is no accident that the narrative ends by highlighting the power of 'slaves' in Roman society. Powerful slaves also feature at the beginning, when Prasutagus' property is looted by centurions and *serui* (14.31.1). The framing examples of servile power are the inverse of the abuse of Prasutagus' family. These are two sides of the same coin – representing on the one hand the erosion of the privileges of the free and on the other the increasing power of slaves. These are problems that preoccupied the senatorial elite in

38.24). Like Tacitus, Livy uses the Roman terms *stuprum* (38.24.3) and *pudicitia* (38.24.10) to describe this foreign rape. On this story and its link to the earlier rape narratives, see Langlands 2006 pp. 109–14: Livy's story is set in the context of 'an expanding Roman empire and the spread of moral corruption that is one of its unwelcome consequences' (ibid. pp. 109–10).

67 *Impotentia* indicates power exercised without self-control or constraint. In Tacitus it is characteristic of powerful women such as Livia and Agrippina. See Goodyear 1972–1981 ad 1.4.5. For *licentia*, freedom without responsibility or self-control, see Braund 2009 p. 181.

68 For other examples of freedmen classed as *serui*, see Treggiari 1969 pp. 265–6. Tacitus in particular frequently insinuates that one has only to scratch the surface of a freedman to find the slave beneath. See e.g. *Hist.* 2.92.3, 4.11.3, 5.9.3, *Ann.* 2.12.3, 4.23.1, 13.6.3, 15.54.4.

imperial Rome. Even senators could, at the emperor's whim, be deprived of the privileges of freedom and subjected to arbitrary physical violence. At the same time, they resented the power and prestige enjoyed by imperial slaves and freedmen.[69] The abuses that Tacitus describes in Britain reflect what he sees as a similar breakdown of the boundary between slave and free at the centre of the empire.

There is a further complication. Boudicca's revolt (*Ann.* 14.29–39) is in Tacitus' narrative followed almost immediately by the murder of the urban prefect Pedanius Secundus by one of his slaves and the senatorial debate this provoked (14.42–5). Roman law provided that, when a master was killed, any of his slaves who were in the house at the time were to be put to death.[70] The application of the law was controversial in this case because Secundus had no fewer than four hundred slaves in his household. In Tacitus' account, the plebs and some senators call for leniency but the eminent jurist C. Cassius Longinus gives a speech in defence of the traditional penalty. His arguments win the day and Secundus' slaves are put to death, though his freedmen are spared. The juxtaposition of these two accounts of resistance and suppression invites us to consider how they relate to each other. There are many ways in which the latter account of responses to servile violence invites a rereading of the provincial revolt that precedes it. Perhaps most striking is the implicit commentary on any sympathy the reader may have felt for the British rebels.

Tacitus records two explanations for why the slave murdered his master – either he had been cheated of a promise of manumission or he saw him as a rival for the love of another slave (42.1). Neither reflects well on Secundus. Whatever the circumstances of the

[69] Cf. Roller 2001 pp. 262–4 on elite anxiety about corporal punishment and pp. 264–72 on the threat from slaves and freedmen.

[70] On the legal regime (especially the *SC Silanianum*) see Harries forthcoming and Gamauf 2007 p. 148 with bibliography. Discussion of the Tacitean narrative has largely focused on the question of whether or not Tacitus agreed with the views expressed by Cassius. Kajanto 1969 is confident that he did; Ginsburg 1993 argues that Cassius' speech is undermined both by Tacitus' narrative and by weaknesses in its own rhetoric. (I for one believe that the fact that Cassius' opponents are aligned with the plebs is a sign of where the narrator's sympathies lie.) Neither considers how this account of servile violence relates to the preceding description of provincial revolt.

murder, the Roman plebs were strongly opposed to the punishment of so many innocent slaves, and their concerns were shared by a minority of senators (42.2). But Cassius speaks for the senatorial majority when he calls for the traditional penalty to be applied. He defends it on the grounds that the old ways are best and that fear is the only means by which slaves can be kept under control. He is particularly scathing towards those who suggested that the murder might have been justified:

an, ut quidam fingere non erubescunt, iniurias suas ultus est interfector, quia de paterna pecunia transegerat aut auitum mancipium detrahebatur? pronuntiemus ultro dominum iure caesum uideri.

Was the murderer avenging wrongs done to him, as some are not ashamed to imagine, because he had made a contract about his ancestral fortune or he was being deprived of an inherited slave? Let us go ahead and rule that the killing of a master was justified! (Tac. *Ann.* 14.43.4)

The suggested justifications are phrased in a way that reveals their absurdity. Slaves could not own property or be party to a contract (*transigere*) – let alone inherit (*paterna, auitum*). *Dominum iure caesum* is presented as an oxymoron: the murder of a master, Cassius implies, can never be justified.[71] He rebukes his fellow senators for thinking that a slave might have legitimate grievances (*iniuriae*): they should be ashamed (*erubescunt*) of such a fabrication (*fingere*). The aristocratic Cassius has nothing but contempt for those who sympathise with the slaves and their grievances. In Tacitus' narrative, it is primarily the plebs who feel such sympathy (42.2 and 45.1). This must problematise any sympathy the reader may have felt for the British rebels. Are we supposed to be caught showing a vulgar sympathy for the servile provincials? Perhaps. After all, the Britons are represented as themselves expecting to be punished like rebellious slaves and taking their revenge accordingly (as discussed at the beginning of this chapter).[72] Much is left unsaid in this ambiguous and allusive narrative. Judgement is left to the reader. But at the very least it should be clear that *Annals* 14 presses the reader to think hard about whether provincials are like slaves – and whether they should be treated accordingly.

[71] The phrase *iure caesum uideri* is a legal formula. See Koestermann 1963–8 ad loc.
[72] Tac. *Ann.* 14.33.2. See p. 126.

The trope of representing empire as enslavement may be a commonplace in Roman discourse, but it is one that can be developed in quite different directions. This chapter has shown the varied ways in which Tacitus deploys the metaphor of enslavement in three narratives of resistance to Roman rule. The account of the conquest of Britain in the *Agricola* is dense with the language and imagery of slavery. Behind the repeated references to enslavement lies an implicit psychology of slavery which is used to explain how Roman rule perpetuates itself. Once conquered, Rome's subjects lose the ability, and even the will, to resist. In contrast, the narrative of the Batavian revolt in *Histories* 4–5 makes only limited use of slavery metaphors. Its main concern is with the instrumental use of the rhetoric of freedom by those who seek to replace one master with another. The language of slavery returns to prominence in Boudicca's revolt in *Annals* 14, but the focus there is not so much on the psychological aspects of domination as on the fragility of the boundary between slaves and free in a world corrupted by power. Tacitus blurs the line between metaphorical and real slavery, by showing British nobles being treated as slaves by their Roman masters. The contrasts between these three narratives reveal the potential diversity of superficially similar metaphors of provincial enslavement.

This chapter has also stressed that all three narratives are inextricably linked to the broader narratives in which they are embedded. The subjugation of Britain in the *Agricola* reproduces the symbiosis of domination and slavishness that Tacitus sees at work in Domitianic Rome. The Batavian revolt reaffirms the impossibility of escape from domination. That of Boudicca reflects the erosion of the privileges of freedom under Nero. The three successive rebels also have a paradigmatic significance. Calgacus and Boudicca embody both the attractions and the folly of the outright defiance shown by Helvidius Priscus, Thrasea Paetus and their supporters. Civilis exposes the opportunism of would-be emperors whose appeals to *libertas* mask their own appetites for absolute power. These narratives of provincial revolt speak to the relationship of senate and emperor at least as much as they do to that of the provinces and Rome. The provinces are made to function as a mirror for the political, social and cultural problems of the

Roman elite. This complicates any attempt to treat them as straightforward examples of an imperial ideology.

Tacitus may be an extreme case in the complex architecture of his narrative.[73] But it must be true of many other accounts of empire in Roman literature that they too are implicated in the idiosyncratic projects of the works in which they are embedded. These texts often have their own agendas, purveying particular visions of Roman rule for particular purposes, purposes that sometimes have little to do with empire itself. But this insight does not negate the value of the wider perspective provided by Chapter 2. Whatever the differences between them, each of Tacitus' narratives draws on, and contributes to, a wider discourse of provincial slavery. What it does do is to illustrate the need to engage with these texts at two levels – both as exemplars of a broader discourse and as individual texts.

[73] Cf Henderson 1989 p. 172 on the *Annals*' similarity to Virgil's *Aeneid*: '"the same" monumental energy of concentrated writing in self-responsion across a vast domain'.

4
BENEFACTORS

sed antequam arma inciperent, misere legatos amicitiam obsequiumque memoraturos, et mansura haec si nullo nouo onere temptarentur; sin ut uictis seruitium indiceretur, esse sibi ferrum et iuuentutem et promptum libertati aut ad mortem animum.

But before taking to arms, they sent envoys to recall their friendship and obedience and to say that these would continue so long as they were not put to the test with any new burden. But if slavery was imposed upon them as upon a conquered people, they said, they possessed weapons, youth and a spirit eager for freedom or death.

(Tac. *Ann.* 4.46.2–3)

The tribes in the mountainous interior of Thrace revolted in 26 CE, apparently out of resentment at the conscription of their men for service in the Roman army. According to Tacitus, they first sent envoys to complain about how they were being treated. They insisted (or so he tells us) that their bond to Rome was one of friendship (*amicitia*) and objected to being reduced to a condition of slavery (*seruitium*).[1] Two points are worth noting here. First, their complaints fall on deaf ears. The governor plays for time, assembles an army and then crushes the rebels. Neither he nor the narrator sees fit to insist that what Rome expected from the Thracians was anything other than slavery. Second, when these Thracians insist upon their status as friends, they do not pretend that this is a relationship of equals. Their friendship is combined with obedience (*obsequium*). It is a salutary reminder that slavery is not the only mode of subjection in Roman society. Legal freedom is compatible with many forms of dependence, subordination and even exploitation.

1 As with all rebel speeches in Roman historiography, this is a Roman construct. It is a poor guide to whatever rhetoric the Thracian embassy may have used at the time.

The Thracians' friendship with Rome bears comparison with the similarly unequal friendship that Sallust's Sulla promises the Mauretanian king Bocchus when persuading him to switch sides in the war against Jugurtha:

populo Romano iam a principio imperi melius uisum amicos quam seruos quaerere, tutiusque rati uolentibus quam coactis imperitare.

The Roman people had [he said] from the very beginning of their empire preferred to acquire friends rather than slaves, and thought it safer to rule over willing rather than coerced subjects. (Sall. *Iug.* 102.6)

Sulla claims that Rome prefers to have friends (*amici*) rather than slaves (*serui*).[2] But the following sentence shows that this is not an equal friendship. The Romans prefer voluntary to enforced submission – but in either case they *command* (*imperitare*). Sulla goes on to boast that 'the Roman people has never been bested in favours' (*numquam populum Romanum beneficiis uictum esse*, ibid. 11). This is a double-edged claim. It promises Bocchus that he will gain more than Rome does from their relationship. But it is also an assertion of Roman superiority, since the exchange of favours (*beneficia*) played an important role in creating and reinforcing relations of dependence in Roman society.

It is this rhetoric of benefaction which this chapter takes as its subject. Its focus is not so much on the concrete claims made about the beneficial effects of Roman rule (indeed Rome's 'favours' are often left unspecified), as on the language in which they are couched – the rhetoric of favours and obligation.[3] It will show that such claims of Roman generosity are always also assertions of Roman dominance and of the moral obligation of Rome's dependants. The chapter begins with a brief survey of the role of *beneficia* in constructing hierarchy in Roman society. It goes on to illustrate three recurring themes of Roman discourse about empire: the moral obligation that Roman favours impose on their recipients; the juxtaposition of rule by fear and rule by favours as the two possible

[2] Rome had a long history of forming 'friendships' with other peoples. On the role of friendship (*amicitia*, φιλία) in Roman diplomacy during the period of expansion, and its roots in Hellenistic practice, see Gruen 1984 ch. 2 and now Burton 2011.

[3] See Fear 1996 pp. 16–23 for a survey of the claims about for the benefits of Roman rule. Nutton 1978 discusses Greek perspectives.

modes of imperial control; and representations of peoples on the periphery of the empire as submissively begging favours from Rome. The end of the chapter provides a close reading of a passage of Pliny's *Panegyricus* that foregrounds the issue of Roman dependence on provincial resources and the problems it poses for the idea of Roman superiority. This text nicely illustrates the intimate connection between exchange and power in the Roman imagination.

This chapter, like the book as a whole, is focused on the relationship between a self-professed Roman elite and the peoples they regarded as their subjects or dependants. Much excellent work has been done on the importance of *beneficia* to the practice and ideology of the monarchical system instituted by Augustus.[4] A wide range of imperial decisions were regularly described as *beneficia* and seen as personal favours – not just grants of money, land and goods, but also appointments to office, grants of status, legal exemptions and even judicial decisions.[5] Dependence on such favours – especially appointment to office – bound the senatorial and equestrian elite to the emperor, while their ability to broker lesser imperial favours for their own dependants bolstered their own powers of patronage. But these imperial *beneficia* are not the concern of this chapter, which focuses instead on the use of the rhetoric of *beneficia* to describe the dominance of an imperial people. It will show that the trope is particularly prominent in the Late Republic, with Cicero and Sallust representing the Romans as binding other peoples to them through their benefactions, but can also be found in Imperial authors.

The ideology of exchange

The rhetoric of favours draws its force from the reciprocity ethic that underpinned Roman social life. Roman writers lived in a world

[4] See especially Saller 1982 ch. 2 on the dependence of the senatorial and equestrian elites on personal favours obtained directly or indirectly from the emperor and Roller 2001 ch. 3 on the importance of gift exchange to the construction, negotiation and sometimes contestation of imperial authority.

[5] See especially Saller 1982 pp. 41–2 on the range of decisions referred to as *beneficia*.

where their status and autonomy were always under threat from the possibility of being unable to reciprocate in what J. E. Lendon has called the 'economy of favours' and Ramsay MacMullen the 'web of favours given or owed'.[6] The letters of Cicero, Pliny and Fronto and the poems of Horace, Statius and Martial amply illustrate the constant exchange of gifts, both large and small, among the Roman elite.[7] As in other societies where gift exchange plays so prominent a role, great emphasis was placed on the principle of reciprocity. The recipient of a favour was expected to strive to reciprocate, while in the meantime acknowledging his or her obligation to the benefactor.[8] Although favours could be exchanged within a relationship of equals, they often worked to create relations of dependence when the exchange was not balanced over time. Even Seneca's treatise *On Favours*, a text which propounds an idealised vision of a horizontal web of favours that binds together a society of equals, acknowledges the potential for unbalanced exchange to create and reinforce relations of dependence.[9]

Favours were rarely given or received without an eye for how they would be perceived by others. Even if etiquette frowned on a benefactor who trumpeted his own generosity, the recipient was expected to demonstrate his gratitude by advertising the favour received and his debt to the benefactor.[10] A substantial favour demanded a show of deference and humility.[11] Hence some were

6 Lendon 1997 p. 64, MacMullen 1988 p. 121.

7 See Bowditch 2001 on Horace; Nauta 2001 on Statius and Martial. Verboven 2002 Part II and Saller 1982 ch. 4 provide a broader overview of the wide range of goods and services exchanged as gifts.

8 The ideology of exchange in Roman culture has been discussed extensively. See especially Griffin 2003, Verboven 2002 pp. 35–48, Bowditch 2001 ch. 1, Roller 2001 ch. 3 (esp. pp. 195–8), Lendon 1997 pp. 63–9, Dixon 1993, Saller 1982 pp. 15–22 and Michel 1962 pp. 449–601.

9 Griffin 2003 (esp pp. 97 and 101–2) rightly notes Seneca's focus on horizontal relationships and his vision of the exchange of favours as a source of social cohesion. But Seneca repeatedly alludes to the potential for favours to elevate the benefactor over the recipient. See e.g. *Ben.* 5.2.1, 6.35.2–4, 6.40.2 and 7.26.3.

10 For one perspective on the proper manner of granting and accepting favours, see Sen. *Ben.* 2.

11 See Roller 2001 p. 197 for the expression of the *gratus animus* through symbols of social subordination.

loath to be seen to accept a favour, for fear that they would be seen as dependants.[12] Others were reluctant to see their own favours repaid, lest their prestige be diminished.[13] Favours were not just a source of honour and prestige; they were also seen as a source of real power. Benefactors are said to 'bind' their beneficiaries through their favours (*beneficio obligare*, *obstringere* and *deuincire*); favours are sometimes represented as chains (*uincula*).[14] The proverbial wisdom of Publius Syrus warned that 'to accept a favour is to sell your freedom' (*beneficium accipere libertatem est uendere*, Pub. *Sent.* B5). The power ascribed to favours can also be seen in the double aspect of the Latin word *gratia*, which denotes not only the gratitude shown by the recipient of a favour, but also the influence enjoyed by the benefactor. In the latter sense, it is often paired with other words for power – *auctoritas*, *dignitas*, *honos*, *nobilitas* and *potentia*.[15]

I set aside for the moment the question of how the language of favours relates to the relationship between *patronus* and *cliens*. The spate of recent work on the role of patronage in Roman society has obscured some important distinctions between *clientela* and other relations of dependence in the economy of favours – distinctions that are important in the Roman imagination even if they are of limited use in analysing Roman society. These distinctions will be explored in the next chapter. For now I am concerned with the broader rhetoric of favours. This chapter explores the role played in discourse about empire by the characteristically Roman assumption that exchange – and particularly asymmetrical exchange – both creates and reflects hierarchical relations.

[12] See e.g. Cic. *Planc.* 73 (*ceteri uera beneficia etiam minora dissimulent, ne obligati esse uideantur*), *Off.* 2.69 (*qui se locupletes honoratos beatos putant ii ne obligari quidem beneficio uolunt*), Sen. *Ben.* 2.23.1 (*sunt quidam qui nolint nisi secreto accipere*).

[13] See e.g. Sen. *Ben.* 2.17.6 (*multi sunt tam prauae naturae, ut malint perdere quae praestiterunt quam uideri recepisse, superbi et imputatores*).

[14] For *beneficio obligare*, *obstringere* and *deuincire* see pp. 161–3. For the image of being chained by favours, see e.g. Cic. *Planc.* 72 (*maximis beneficii uinclis obstrictus*), Livy 7.30.2 (see n. 16 below), [Quint.] *Decl. maiores* 9.21 (*tenacioribus beneficiorum uinculis fatear esse constrictum*).

[15] See the examples cited by Hellegouarc'h 1963 p. 206. See further Moussy 1966.

The bonds of gratitude

Livy's account of Roman expansion attributes particular importance to benefaction as a source of Roman authority. The Romans are repeatedly represented as benefactors whose favours give them a claim to the loyalty and obedience of her beneficiaries. Roman favours bind and subordinate their recipients. When Campanian ambassadors appeal to Rome for assistance against the Samnites in 343 BCE, they stress how deeply indebted they will be if Rome comes to their aid. So great a *beneficium* will secure their friendship with a strong chain (*uinculum*) and would make them subject and beholden (*subiecti atque obnoxii*) to the Romans.[16] When the city of Demetrias seems inclined to side with Antiochus III against Rome in 192 BCE, Roman ambassadors rebuke its inhabitants, declaring that 'while all Greece was beholden (*obnoxia*) to the Romans for the *beneficium* of freedom, this was all the more the case for their city' (which Rome had freed from a Macedonian garrison).[17] Interceding to prevent the incarceration of L. Cornelius Scipio in 187 BCE, the tribune Tiberius Gracchus recalled how he had bound (*deuinxit*) Eumenes, Rhodes and all the cities of Asia with the favours of the Roman people after the defeat of Antiochus.[18] In his account of the Third Macedonian War, Livy notes the perversity of the many Greek cities who cheered Perseus' early success against Rome despite being bound (*obligati*) by great favours from the Romans.[19] Those who fail to fulfil their supposed obligations to their Roman benefactors are condemned as *ingrati*.[20]

[16] *quam* [sc. *amicitiam*] *si secundis rebus nostris petissemus, sicut coepta celerius, ita infirmiore uinculo contracta esset; tunc enim, ut qui ex aequo nos uenisse in amicitiam meminissemus, amici forsitan pariter ac nunc, subiecti atque obnoxii uobis minus essemus. nunc, misericordia uestra conciliati auxilioque in dubiis rebus defensi, beneficium quoque acceptum colamus oportet, ne ingrati atque omni ope diuina humanaque indigni uideamur* (Livy 7.30.2–3). See Oakley 1997–2005 II p. 295 on the use of *obnoxius* to describe the condition of someone who has received a great *beneficium*.

[17] *cum totam Graeciam beneficio libertatis obnoxiam Romanis esse, tum eam ciuitatem praecipue* (Livy 35.31.8).

[18] *regem Eumenem, Rhodios, alias tot Asiae urbes deuinxerit populi Romani beneficiis* (Livy 38.60.6).

[19] *ingentibus Romanorum obligati beneficiis* (Livy 42.63.1). Cf. the allowance Rome makes for the Greek cities that withdrew from a proposed alliance with Rome because they were bound (*illigati*) by Macedonian *beneficia* (Livy 32.22.11; cf. 32.19.6–7).

[20] See the further examples compiled by Gruen 1984 I pp. 172–3.

The Magnesians, for example, are rebuked by Flamininus for being reluctant to side with Rome against Antiochus despite their debt to Rome. 'Raising his hands to heaven he called on the gods to witness the ungrateful and faithless spirit (*ingratus ac perfidus animus*) of the Magnesians'.[21] Later in the war, the Boeotians who also sided with Antiochus are chastised by Acilius Glabrio for their ungrateful spirit (*ingratus animus*) towards the Romans after favours that were so great and so recent.[22]

Although it is usually Rome that acquires dependants through its benefactions, a particularly good illustration of the political significance of *beneficia* casts Rhodes as the (would-be) benefactor. In Livy's account of the negotiations at the end of the Syrian War, Eumenes II of Pergamum warns the senate not to accede to Rhodes' request that Antiochus' Greek subjects be freed. Eumenes claims that the Greek cities would attribute this *beneficium* to Rhodes and that the favour would be so great that it would make them her de facto subjects:

agent enim causam ciuitatium Graecarum, et liberari eas dicent debere. quo impetrato, cui dubium est, quin et a nobis auersuri sint non eas modo ciuitates, quae liberabuntur, sed etiam ueteres stipendiarias nostras, ipsi autem tanto obligatos beneficio uerbo socios, re uera subiectos imperio et obnoxios habituri sint?

For they will plead the cause of the Greek cities and say that they should be freed. Does anyone doubt that once this has been granted they will take from us not only those cities that are to be freed, but even those that have long paid tribute to us? Or that those who are bound by so great a favour will be their allies in name, but in reality subject to their power and beholden to them? (Livy 37.53.3–4)

If Rhodes is seen to have secured the freedom of these cities, they will be not just beholden to it (*obnoxii*) but effectively subject to its power (*subiecti imperio*) – despite being nominally independent allies.[23]

[21] *Quinctius quidem adeo exarsit ira ut manus ad caelum tendens deos testes ingrati ac perfidi animi Magnetum inuocaret* (35.31.13). Cf. 35.39.7: *altercatio inde non sermo fuit, cum Romanus ut ingratos increparet Magnetas imminentesque praediceret clades.*

[22] *castigati . . . Boeoti ob ingratum in tantis tamque recentibus beneficiis animum erga Romanos* (36.20.4).

[23] Hence Antiochus' insistence in 196 BCE that Smyrna and Lampsacus could only be free if it was clear to them and to others that they had been freed by him and not by their own efforts (Livy 33.38.6). Cf. Polybius' account in which Antiochus tells a Roman envoy that the autonomous cities of Asia ought to receive their *eleutheria* from himself, not from Rome (Polyb. 18.51.9).

Eumenes' argument illustrates how *beneficia* become a source of power in a world governed by the ethic of reciprocity. A favour of sufficient magnitude will dissolve a community's autonomy, leaving it obliged to comply with the will of its benefactor.

Cicero's *Verrines* offer another striking example of the power attributed to favours. Cicero claims that the people of Sicily submitted to the depredations of governors like Verres because they felt it was their duty to do so, given the magnitude of the favours they had received from the Romans:

magistratuum autem nostrorum iniurias ita multorum tulerunt ut numquam ante hoc tempus ad aram legum praesidiumque uestrum publico consilio confugerint . . . sic a maioribus suis acceperant, tanta populi Romani in Siculos esse beneficia ut etiam iniurias nostrorum hominum perferendas putarent.

They showed such forbearance in the face of the injustices committed by many of our magistrates that they have never before now sought refuge as a community in the sanctuary of the law and in your protection . . . They had learned from their ancestors that the favours which the Roman people had bestowed on the Sicilians were so great that they considered they should even endure injustice from our men. (Cic. *2 Verr.* 2.8)

This is of course part of Cicero's strategy of idealising the character of his Sicilian clients. The people of Sicily are, he says, more like Romans than Greeks – and the Romans of old at that (*2 Verr.* 2.7). Their careful regard for their obligations to Rome is evidence of their virtue. But Cicero's conceit is also typical of the rhetoric of Roman benefaction in its vague and sweeping reference to Roman favours – favours which are left unspecified and located in the distant past, but which are nevertheless sufficient to place their professed beneficiaries under an inescapable and unending obligation to the Roman people.[24]

Fear and favours

In the short overview of Roman history with which he begins his *War with Catiline*, Sallust claims that the Romans had until the

[24] For further assertions of the Romans' moral authority and power as benefactors, see e.g. Cic. *2 Verr.* 3.123 and 5.115, *Balb.* 20, *Deiot.* 6 and 36, Caes. *B Gall.* 1.35.2, *B Hisp.* 42.3, *B Alex.* 33.4, Sall. *Iug.* 14.8, Vell. Pat. 2.20.2 and 2.38.5, Val. Max. 5.1a and 9.13.2e, Tac. *Ann.* 3.60.3.

fall of Carthage always 'exercised power more through favours than through fear' (*beneficiis magis quam metu imperium agitabant*, Sall. *Cat.* 9.5). A similar claim about Rome's distaste for coercion appears in a speech that Livy attributes to Scipio Africanus following the expulsion of the Carthaginians from Spain in the Second Punic War. The Roman general exhorts the Spanish to appreciate the benefits of being ruled by Rome:

uniuersos bonum animum habere iussit: uenisse enim eos in populi Romani potestatem, qui beneficio quam metu obligare homines malit exterasque gentes fide ac societate iunctas habere quam tristi subiectas seruitio.

He bade them all to be of good spirits. For, he said, they had come into the power of the Roman people, which preferred to bind men with generosity rather than fear and to have foreign peoples attached by loyalty and alliance rather than subjected to grim slavery (Livy 26.49.8).

The implicit comparison here is with Carthage, the imperial power from which Rome has just wrested control of Spain. Like Sallust, Livy's Scipio constructs an opposition between two modes of ruling, one based on favours (*beneficia*), the other on fear (*metus*), in order to assert Rome's exceptionalism as an imperial power. It is worth observing that both these texts leave a space for fear in the exercise of Roman power. Sallust's claim applies to the past; the implication is that the empire of his own time no longer lives up to this standard (cf. *Cat.* 11.7). And he does not say that Rome renounced rule by fear, merely that it took second place to rule by favours. Scipio says that Rome prefers (*malit*) to avoid rule through fear, implying that it is not always possible to do so. Moreover, both texts see favours as a source of power. In Sallust *beneficia* and fear are both modes of exercising imperial power (*imperium agitare*); in Livy they are both ways of binding (*obligare*) to Rome those peoples who have come into her power (*in potestatem*).

The contrast between coercion and benefaction is a topos of Roman political discourse. It is perhaps most familiar from works such as Cicero's *De officiis* and his *Philippics* which insist that fear is never a secure source of authority (with an eye to

Caesar and Antony respectively).[25] But Cicero's focus in those works is on domestic politics, and even he acknowledges that there are other contexts in which coercion is the best means of control:

sed iis, qui ui oppressos imperio coercent, sit sane adhibenda saeuitia, ut eris in famulos, si aliter teneri non possunt.

But harshness certainly must be applied by those who are using their authority to control subjects that have been forcefully subjugated – for example by masters against slaves, if they cannot be controlled in any other way. (Cic. *Off.* 2.24)

Cicero cites slavery as one such context, but it is evidently not the only one. Other passages suggest that empire is another sphere where Cicero sees a place for rule by coercion. Consider the contrast that Cicero draws between foreign and domestic conflicts in the *Fourth Catilinarian* (already discussed in Chapter 2):

hostes alienigenae aut oppressi seruiunt aut recepti beneficio se obligatos putant; qui autem ex numero ciuium dementia aliqua deprauati hostes patriae semel esse coeperunt, eos, cum a pernicie rei publicae reppuleris, nec ui coercere nec beneficio placare possis.

Foreign enemies are either crushed and serve us as slaves or admitted [to our friendship] and consider themselves bound to us by the favour. But citizens, once they have been corrupted by some madness and become enemies of their country, cannot be subdued with force or appeased with favours, even when you have prevented them from overthrowing the state. (Cic. *Cat.* 4.22)

Cicero distinguishes two different ways in which Rome pacifies its foreign enemies (his point being that neither mode is effective against treasonous citizens). Some serve as slaves (*seruiunt*); others are allies, friends or clients (depending on how one construes *recepti*).[26] The former mode is based on force (*oppressi*; *ui coercere*). The latter depends on benefaction and the ethic of reciprocity (*beneficio se obligatos putant; beneficio placare*). The

[25] See Cic. *Phil.* 1.33 and 2.112, *Off.* 2.23, 24 and 25. Cf. Cic. *Cat.* 1.16–17, Plin. *Pan.* 49.3 and Tac. *Agr.* 32.2.

[26] The use of *recepti* without an adverbial phrase is unusual, but it is retained by Clark (OCT, 1905) and Maslowski (Teubner, 2003), though the latter notes the variant *recepti in amicitiam* as 'possibly correct'. The unqualified *recepti* must be understood as meaning something like 'accepted as allies' (*recepti in societatem*), 'admitted into friendship' (*recepti in amicitiam*), or 'taken under protection' (*recepti in fidem*). See p. 186 for the connotations of clientage in the latter two expressions.

contrast is familiar, but Cicero here uses it to articulate a distinction *within* the empire, without suggesting that either mode is more characteristic of Roman rule. The two modes are similarly combined when Sallust decries the intractability shown by the African city of Capsa, which had served as a base for Jugurtha. Its inhabitants were, he said, 'a flighty and fickle people, which could be controlled neither through favours nor through fear' (*neque beneficio neque metu coercitum*, Sall. *Iug.* 91.7). Like Cicero, Sallust suggests that both coercion and benefaction have a place in the Roman imperial repertoire.

All of these texts see a fundamental distinction between two forms of power – one based on fear and coercion and exemplified by slavery, the other based on the sense of obligation created by favours. For some texts that make a case for Roman exceptionalism, the latter constitutes a distinctly Roman style of relating to other states. For others the contrast is used to articulate a distinction within the Roman empire. Rome rules through both fear and favours, the choice between them being dictated by circumstance and the character of particular peoples. In both cases benefaction is a form of power – a means of ruling (*imperium agitare*), binding (*obligare*) and controlling (*coercere*) subjects.

To beg a favour

To have to ask for a *beneficium* is the ultimate humiliation in the economy of favours. Seneca said that '"I ask" (*rogo*) is an unpleasant word, burdensome, to be spoken with downcast face' – and complained that many of his peers enjoyed having a crowd of petitioners (*rogantium turba*).[27] 'Cato preferred to die than beg (*rogare*)', wrote the declaimer Quintus Haterius.[28] The intransitive use of *rogare* in these texts is revealing. It shows that the very act of requesting is seen as a symbolic expression of submission and

[27] *molestum uerbum est, onerosum, demisso uultu dicendum, rogo* (Sen. *Ben.* 2.2.1). Cf. ibid. 2.1.4 (*nulla res carius constat, quam quae precibus empta est*). *Rogantium turba:* ibid. 2.5.1.

[28] *Cato, solus maximum uiuendi moriendique exemplum, mori maluit quam rogare (nec erat Antonium rogaturus)* (Sen. *Suas.* 6.2). The point is that if Cato could not bring himself to beg Caesar (for his life), Cicero should not beg Antony, of all people.

deference. Augustus draws on this association between requests and submission when he boasts in his *Res gestae* that foreign peoples had sought the friendship of Rome (*amicitiam petere, appetere*).[29] The same appeals for Roman friendship are recorded in the later accounts of Suetonius and Florus.[30] Horace acclaims the fact that the Scythians and Indians 'seek answers' (*responsa petunt*) from Rome.[31]

Statius exploits the same symbolism to point out that opportunities for conquest still remain:

> nondum in gremio Iouis Indica laurus,
> nondum Arabes Seresque rogant.
>
> The Indian laurel is not yet in Jupiter's lap;
> The Arabs and Chinese do not yet beg. (Stat. *Silv.* 4.1.41–2)

'They do not yet beg' (*nondum rogant*). The intransitive use of the verb *rogare* focuses on the act of petitioning. What the Arabs and Chinese might ask for is irrelevant; what matters is that they abase themselves by begging a favour. It is the gesture of deference that is demanded of Rome's neighbours. When Pliny in his *Panegyricus* praises Trajan for having restored Rome's superiority after years of weakness under Domitian, he uses the same expression to describe the state to which the tribes beyond the frontier have been returned:

> rogant, supplicant; largimur, negamus, utrumque ex imperii maiestate; agunt gratias, qui impetrauerunt; non audent queri, quibus negatum est.
>
> They beg and supplicate; we grant and deny [their requests], in both cases as befits the majesty of our empire. Those who gain what they desire thank us; those who are denied do not dare to complain. (Plin. *Pan.* 12.2)

[29] *nostram amicitiam appetiuerunt per legatos Bastarnae Scythaeque et Sarmatarum qui sunt citra flumen Tanaim et ultra reges, Albanorumque rex et Hiberorum et Medorum* (*RGDA* 31.2). *ad me rex Parthorum Phrates Orodis filius filios suos nepotesque omnes misit in Italiam non bello superatus, sed amicitiam nostram per liberorum suorum pignora petens* (ibid. 32.2). By alternating between the first person singular and the first person plural, the Augustan text uses these embassies to illustrate both Augustus' personal prestige and that of the Roman people: *ad me missae sunt, ad me confugerunt, ad me misit, me principe, a me petitos* ~ *nostram amicitiam appetiuerunt, amicitiam nostram petens, expertae sunt populi Romani fidem* (ibid. 32–3).

[30] *qua uirtutis moderationisque fama Indos etiam ac Scythas, auditu modo cognitos, pellexit ad amicitiam suam populique Romani ultro per legatos petendam.* (Suet. *Aug.* 21.3, where *ultro* emphasises the deference inherent in the request). *nam et Scythae misere legatos et Sarmatae amicitiam petentes* (Flor. 2.34.62).

[31] *iam Scythae responsa petunt, superbi | nuper et Indi* (Hor. *Carm. saec.* 55–6).

Again the intransitive use of *rogare*, this time combined with *supplicare*, highlights the submissive posture of the petitioner. The similar use of *largiri* and *negare* emphasises the Romans' power to give and deny. This imagined ritual of entreaties granted or rejected affirms Roman dominance. All these texts focus on the same symbolically significant behaviour. They are also all concerned with peoples on the periphery of the empire. Evidently the association between petitioning and dependency proved particularly useful in conceptualising and representing the workings of Roman power beyond the frontiers. It allowed Roman writers to see Roman superiority and authority even in the absence of clear control.

Pliny on empire and dependency

A close reading of another passage of Pliny's *Panegyricus* will provide a further illustration of the fundamental importance of exchange for Roman conceptions of power. The passage in question is Pliny's account of how Trajan saved Egypt from the effects of a drought (*Pan.* 30–2). Pliny begins with a narrative of the drought and the emperor's intervention (30), before expounding the deeper significance of Trajan's actions, claiming that the drought was actually a blessing in disguise because it brought glory to the emperor (31). He then widens his focus to the empire as a whole, claiming that all the provinces are indeed fortunate in being ruled by Rome (32.1–3), before reverting to Egypt to beseech its gods not to test the emperor's generosity by failing to produce again (32.3–4). At first glance, the point of the passage might seem to be the emperor's concern for the welfare of the provinces. Indeed it contains a famous assertion of the benefits of Roman rule, which is often quoted out of context:

> quam nunc iuuat prouincias omnes in fidem nostram dicionemque uenisse, postquam contigit princeps, qui terrarum fecunditatem nunc huc, nunc illuc, ut tempus et necessitas posceret, transferret referretque, qui diremptam mari gentem, ut partem aliquam populi plebisque Romanae, aleret ac tueretur!

> How fortunate for all the provinces to have come into our trust and power, now that there is an emperor who transports the bounty of the lands back and forth, as the needs of the moment demand, and who feeds and protects an overseas people as if it were part of the Roman people and plebs. (Plin. *Pan.* 32.1)

But there is more at stake in Pliny's account. This is a text that focuses attention on the flow of resources between Rome and its provinces and asks what that flow implies about the real location of power in the imperial relationship. When Pliny praises Trajan for his management of Egypt's drought, it is for having revealed the true nature – as Pliny would have it – of the imperial relationship.[32]

It used to be said that Rome was dependent on Egypt:

percrebuerat antiquitus, urbem nostram nisi opibus Aegypti ali sustentarique non posse.

It had long been widely held that our city could not be fed and supported without Egypt's resources. (Plin. *Pan.* 31.2)

But Trajan has revealed that the opposite is true:

mirum, Caesar, uideretur, si desidem Aegyptum cessantemque Nilum non sensisset urbis annona: quae tuis opibus, tua cura usque illuc redundauit, ut simul probaretur et nos Aegypto posse et nobis Aegyptum carere non posse.

It may seem astonishing, Caesar, that the city's grain supply did not feel Egypt's idleness and the Nile's slackening. Thanks to your resources and your diligence it was so overflowing that it was proved simultaneously both that we can survive without Egypt and that Egypt cannot survive without us. (Plin. *Pan.* 31.5)

It is Egypt that cannot survive without Rome. Trajan's achievement is to have punctured the myth that the Romans (Pliny's *nos*) are dependent on their province. Particular stress is laid on the question of who feeds whom. People used to think that Rome was *fed* by Egypt (*ali*, 31.2). Egypt prided herself on *feeding* Rome (*pasceret*, 31.2) but later has to learn that what she provides to Rome is not *food* but tribute (*non alimenta se nobis, sed tributa praestare*, 31.3). In contrast, the emperor does *feed* Egypt (*aleret*, 32.1). The claim that Egypt feeds Rome is a loaded one, given the symbolic importance of food-giving in Roman culture. Patrons, local elites, and emperors all granted food to dependants.[33] *Alimenta* (31.3) is a particularly pointed way of describing food-giving. It is the

[32] Isaac 2004 pp. 360–1 notes that the 'exhibition of anger' in this passage is motivated by a 'fear of dependence on the subject nations'. But he does not explore the deeper logic of its analysis of imperial power.

[33] On the social and political significance of food-giving, see especially Woolf 1990 pp. 212–16. Damon 1997 shows the centrality of food to Roman representations of the patron–client relationship.

technical term for the support owed by the *paterfamilias* to certain types of dependants – the very young, the very old and *liberti*.[34] It is also the word for the programme set up by Nerva and Trajan to feed the children of Italian communities and is used by Pliny earlier in the *Panegyricus* to describe the grain distributed by the emperor to the urban plebs (usually called the *frumentatio*).[35]

Pliny reveals that Roman prestige is at stake in these questions about dependency by repeatedly figuring his account in terms of honour and shame. He introduces his narrative of the drought by claiming that Egypt once boasted (*gloriata est*) of her self-sufficiency.[36] The fact that Egypt supplied food to Rome only increased Egyptian arrogance:

superbiebat uentosa et insolens natio, quod uictorem quidem populum, pasceret tamen; quodque in suo flumine, in suis nauibus uel abundantia nostra uel fames esset.

That haughty and arrogant people prided themselves on the fact that the people that had conquered them was nevertheless fed by them, and that whether we had plenty or famine depended on their river and their ships. (Plin. *Pan.* 31.2)

Roman dependence spurs the Egyptians to act above their station (that being the essence of *superbia*).[37] But the emperor's actions have restored Roman prestige:

ita beneficio tuo, nec maligna tellus, et obsequens Nilus Aegypto quidem saepe, sed gloriae nostrae numquam largior fluxit.

34 Kubitschek 1894 and Saller 1994 p. 114.

35 On the *alimenta* scheme, see Woolf 1990. The *frumentatio* is called *alimenta* at *Pan.* 26.3.

36 Egypt claimed to owe nothing to external forces, not even the natural forces of the heavens (*nihil … deberet*, 30.1). She relied only on her own resources (*proprio amne*, [sc. *aquas*] *quas ipsa devexerat*, 30.1). But the drought forces Egypt's proud sense of autarky to give way to recognition of dependence. Failed by the Nile, Egypt turns in vain to the forces of nature that she had previously ignored (30.3) and is finally forced to invoke the aid of the emperor (*opem Caesaris invocavit*, 30.5). The moment she makes this appeal and acknowledges her dependence, the crisis is averted (30.5).

37 Although characteristically a vice of those of high status (cf. Hellegouarc'h 1963 pp. 439–41), inferiors too can be guilty of *superbia*. See e.g. Cic. *Att.* 8.4.1 with Fabre 1981 pp. 238–9 on the *superbia* of freedmen. As the connection with *super* suggests, the essence of *superbia* lies in overstepping one's proper place. Cf Isid. *Etym.* 10.248 (*superbus dictus quia super uult uideri quam est; qui enim uult supergredi quod est, superbus est*). Crushing *superbia* is one aspect of the Roman imperial project as memorably articulated by Virgil (*Aen.* 6.853). See further pp. 246–7.

And so, thanks to your benefaction, the earth was not grudging, and propitious Nile – though it may often have flowed more generously for Egypt – never flowed more generously for our glory. (Plin. *Pan.* 31.6)[38]

At the same time, Egypt has been shamed (*pudebat*, *erubescebat*, 31.6). Roman glory is earned at Egypt's expense.

By confronting the question of whether or not the Romans are dependent upon, and even fed by, their province and explicitly linking this to issues of status and honour, Pliny is clearly conceptualising empire in terms of the economy of favours. The reciprocity ethic that underlies Pliny's reflection on imperial dependency is also evident in the solutions he offers to the problem, which serve to reassert Roman dominance in the face of imagined provincial *superbia*. Most obviously, he reverses the asymmetry of exchange by emphasising what the provinces receive from Rome and the emperor, thus representing Rome, not Egypt, as the dominant giver. Not only have Egypt's contributions been returned (*refudimus* ... *copias, recepit frumenta* ... *messes reuexit*, 31.3), but Egypt has actually been saved from destruction (31.6). The emperor is also repeatedly described as a benefactor.[39] The much-cited declaration of the benefits of Roman rule (32.1–3, quoted earlier) must also be understood in this context. It is an assertion that it is the provinces which benefit from, and are dependent upon, the redistribution of resources within the empire. The symbolism of food-giving, subversively appropriated by the Egyptians at the beginning of the passage, is normalised here: it is the emperor who feeds and protects (*aleret ac tueretur*) the provinces. The shift of perspective to encompass the whole empire (*prouincias omnes*) is significant because it shows that Trajan's actions are framed not only in the particular context of Rome's relationship

[38] Although the overall sense is clear, the syntax of this sentence has caused problems. The difficulty lies in construing *obsequens* and *Aegypto*. Betty Radice's Loeb reads *obsequens* as belonging only in the first clause, and takes *Aegypto* as dependent on it: 'Thus by your gracious aid the earth has not begrudged her fruits, and if the Nile has often shown herself more propitious to Egypt, it has never flown more generously for our glory.' But it is better to take *obsequens* as an epithet (as often of deities – cf. *OLD* § 2b and Durry 1938 ad loc.) and the contrasting pair of datives *Aegypto quidem* ... *sed gloriae nostrae* as both dependent on *largior fluxit* – as translated here and in Durry's Budé.

[39] See the references to imperial *bonitas* (Plin. *Pan.* 30.5), *beneficium* (31.6) and *benignitas* (32.2 and 3).

to Egypt (always a special case) but also in the wider context of its relationship with, and potential dependence on, the provinces as a whole.[40]

Pliny also suggests some alternative ways of conceptualising the flow of resources within the empire. He repeatedly uses the language of slavery to describe provincial submission (as discussed in Chapter 2):

sciat se non esse populo Romano necessariam et tamen seruiat.[41]

Let [Egypt] know that she is not necessary to the Roman people, but let her slave for us all the same. (Plin. *Pan.* 31.3)

actum erat de fecundissima gente, si libera fuisset.

That most fertile race would have perished, if it had been free. (ibid. 31.6)

hic alternis commeatibus Orientem Occidentemque conectit, ut, quae ubique ferunt quaeque expetunt opes gentes, discant inuicem capiant, quanto libertati discordi seruientibus sit utilius unum esse, cui seruiant.

[This emperor] binds together East and West with alternating commerce so that both those peoples who produce resources and those who require them learn and understand in turn how much more profitable it is for those who are slaves to dissentious freedom to be slaves to one master only. (ibid. 32.2)

Egypt is the slave of the Roman people (*seruiat*); she is no longer free (*libera*); all the provinces are slaves to the emperor (*seruiant*). The juxtaposition of these repeated assertions of provincial slavery with claims of Roman beneficence is one of the striking features of this passage. It begins to make sense only when we see that the whole passage is focused on the question of whether Rome is dependent on its provinces. Asserting the provinces' servile status reaffirms Roman superiority by putting the provinces in their place.

[40] Egypt had a special place in the Roman imperial system and Egyptians were disadvantaged compared to other provincials, notably by being barred from access to Roman citizenship (citizens of Alexandria excepted). See Sherwin-White 1966 ad Plin. *Ep.* 10.6. On the complex and ambivalent place of Egypt in the Roman imagination, see Vout 2003. This may have been further complicated in the Trajanic period by the Flavians' close association with Egypt and particularly the gods Isis and Serapis (see Liebeschuetz 1979 p. 181).

[41] This sentence puns on the two different meanings of *necessaria*. On one level the sentence is about dependence: Egypt is not 'necessary' to Rome. But it is also about how the imperial relationship should be represented: Egypt is Rome's slave, not its 'kinswoman' (*OLD* s. v. *necessarius* § 6).

It also serves to defuse the problem posed by Rome's dependence on provincial grain by identifying empire with a domain where asymmetrical exchange is less problematic. Although the ethic of reciprocity has implications for all forms of social relations, it is nevertheless true that the calculus of *beneficia* works very differently within the family, and particularly between master and slave, than among free men.[42] Because of the slave's duty to serve his master, relations between slaves and masters are not governed by the same logic of gift exchange that characterises relations among the free.

Pliny's insistence that Egypt sends Rome tribute not food (31.3) is yet another way of redefining the context in which resources flow to Rome. It asserts that Egypt is a defeated nation and that its grain is Rome's right by conquest.[43] So too is the idea of indebtedness introduced at the end of the passage, when Pliny warns Egypt not to test the emperor's generosity again (32.3). He insists that it should consider itself eternally in Rome's debt:

non quidem reposcimus fenus: putet tamen esse soluendum, fallacemque unius anni fidem omnibus annis omnibusque postea saeculis tanto magis, quia non exigimus, excuset.

We are not calling in the interest, but it should consider the debt outstanding. Let it make good the broken faith of that one year over all the years and all the ages to come – all the more so since we do not demand it. (Plin. *Pan.* 32.4)

Pliny claims not to expect repayment, but he is demanding recognition of the debt. Whatever Rome receives will only be its due. Gender provides another code for articulating provincial dependency when Pliny claims that the emperor saved Egypt from shame (at its own failure) as much as from starvation:

pudebat sterilitatis insolitae nec minus erubescebat fame, quam torquebatur; cum pariter a te necessitatibus eius pudorique subuentum est.

[Egypt] was ashamed of this unexpected infertility and was no less embarrassed by the famine than tortured by it. You restored not only her needs but also her modesty. (Plin. *Pan.* 31.6)

[42] Lendon 1997 pp. 64–5 and Saller 1982 p. 23 show that the principle of reciprocity could be applied to a wide range of social relations.
[43] On the ideological importance of tribute, see p. 51 n. 95.

The references to *sterilitas* and blushing invite a gendered reading, emphasised in Latin by the feminine gender of the noun *Aegyptus*. Egypt is imagined as a woman whose modesty has been saved by her male protector – another domestic analogy that helps to put arrogant Egypt in her place. Within a relatively short space Egypt is represented as slave, subject, debtor and woman. All these metaphors work to reconfigure the nature of exchange within the empire. They reaffirm Roman superiority in the face of what might appear to be dependency on provincial resources.

What makes Pliny's account of the Egyptian drought so interesting is that it reveals the intimate connection between power and exchange in the Roman imagination. There is nothing remarkable in the fact that Pliny praises Trajan for alleviating the Egyptian drought (little goes unmentioned in the *Panegyricus*). What is interesting is the reason why he thinks it is praiseworthy – not because it benefited the provinces but because it punctured a myth of Roman dependency. Pliny turns Trajan's management of the drought in Egypt into a Roman solution to a distinctively Roman problem.

Exchange plays a central role in the construction and representation of power relations throughout Roman culture. 'Relations of domination are created, sustained and challenged by giving and receiving in particular ways', as Matthew Roller has concisely put it.[44] This chapter has shown that the discourse of empire is no exception. Authors from Cicero to the Younger Pliny represent the Romans as bestowing *beneficia* on their grateful dependants. These widespread references to Roman benefactions (the details of which are often vague and unspecified) are not a sign of Roman altruism. They are assertions of supremacy – proclaiming Roman dominance in the economy of favours while simultaneously asserting a moral obligation on the part of Rome's dependants. Their ideological significance is highlighted by Pliny's reflection on imperial dependency. Since relations of exchange are considered to be inextricably intertwined with hierarchies of power and status, Rome's dependency on provincial resources becomes a sensitive

[44] Roller 2001 p. 131.

issue. Roman honour demands that the subject peoples be dependent on Roman generosity, and the flow of resources – particularly grain – to the centre jars with the image of Rome as an imperial power.

The benefactor is an important alternative to the paradigm of mastery in Roman discourse. Where the master's power is founded on coercion and fear, that of the benefactor rests on an ethic of reciprocity. In the context of empire, the contrast is sometimes deployed in a rhetoric of Roman exceptionalism – as when Livy's Scipio and Sallust's Sulla assert that Rome prefers to rule through *beneficia* than through fear. Elsewhere, however, the contrast serves to highlight differences within Rome's empire: Rome controls some subjects through generosity, others through (masterly) coercion. Elsewhere again, the power of exchange is used to conceptualise Rome's less obvious dominance over the peoples on the periphery of its empire. In all cases, benefaction is represented as a mode of control. How this rhetoric of Roman favours relates to the more specific idea of *clientela* is the subject of the next chapter.

5

PATRONS AND PROTECTORS

si sibi Antiochus pulchrum esse censet, quas urbes proauus belli iure habuerit, auus paterque numquam usurpauerint pro suis, eas repetere in seruitutem, et populus Romanus susceptum patrocinium libertatis Graecorum non deserere fidei constantiaeque suae ducit esse.

If Antiochus thinks it reflects well on him to seek to re-enslave cities which his great-grandfather held by right of war [but] his grandfather and father never treated as their possessions, the Roman people too considers it a mark of its good faith and constancy not to abandon the patronal duty it has undertaken with respect to the freedom of the Greeks.

(Livy 34.58.10–11)

In Livy's account of negotiations with ambassadors of the Seleucid king Antiochus III shortly before the outbreak of the Syrian War in 193 BCE, the Roman consular Quinctius Flamininus seeks to discomfit the ambassadors by contrasting Roman and Seleucid motives in dealing with Greece. Whereas Antiochus seeks to re-enslave the Greek cities (*eas repetere in seruitutem*), Flamininus claims, Rome has undertaken the *patrocinium* of their freedom. *Patrocinium* denotes the protection a Roman patron afforded his clients, both individuals and communities, in the law courts and in other contexts.[1] Livy's Flamininus uses the word to evoke a more benevolent relationship than the slavery (*seruitus*) that is subjection to Antiochus. This trope raises important questions in the context of this book. How important is the paradigm of patronage for Roman discourse about empire? How does it relate both to the language of slavery discussed in Chapters 2 and 3 and to the rhetoric of *beneficia*

[1] *Patrocinium suscipere* is often used metaphorically in the context of arguing for an idea or cause (Cic. *2 Verr.* 4.81, *Nat. D.* 1.6, *Rep.* 3.8, *Phil.* 7.3; Ov. *Pont.* 1.2.67–8), which suggests that it is particularly associated with defending a client in court. But the phrase is also used of patronage more widely, e.g. of undertaking to be patron of a community (*pat[rocinium] succipere coloniae*, *ILS* 6105).

discussed in the previous chapter? These are among the issues explored in this chapter, which traces representations of subjects as clients from the Late Republic to the second century CE. Of course many provincial and Italian cities were clients in a more concrete sense, attached by bonds of patronage to individual members of the Roman elite. But it is something else to use patronage as a metaphor for the dominance of the imperial people. It is this conceptual and rhetorical move that is my subject here.

I am certainly not the first to consider the significance of patronage for Roman conceptions of empire. But work to date has largely been confined within the terms of a debate about Roman expansion in the Middle Republic. The seminal contribution was Ernst Badian's claim that the domestic practice of patronage explains the forms of Roman imperialism in the Middle Republic, especially the preference for informal connections over formal treaties.[2] I will not enter into this dispute, although I do believe that the ubiquity of patronal power structures in Roman society goes some way towards explaining both this comfort with extra-legal arrangements and the apparent lack of interest in the distinction between the inhabitants of the provinces and those of nominally independent cities and kingdoms (as evidenced in the use of *socii*). Instead I want to expand the focus to consider a number of broader issues which this debate has obscured.

It is a testament to Badian's continued influence that the chronological focus has remained almost exclusively on the Middle Republic. Later authors such as Cicero and Livy have been valued for what they can reveal about conceptions of empire in the earlier period, not for what they tell us about their own.[3] This chapter

[2] 'The latter [permanent clientship] was probably the way in which educated Romans in the second century considered the relations of Rome with at least some other states' (Badian 1958 p. 6). 'There had grown up a system of informal connexion with free states . . . the elastic obligations of which fitted into Roman habits of social thought which we know as *clientela*' (ibid. p. 68). Cf. ibid. pp. 41 and 53. The germ of the idea was already present in Sherwin-White 1973 pp. 187 (pp. 161–2 of the 1939 edition): 'Here [in the conception on *clientela*] is to be found the essence of the peculiarity in the relation of Rome to her allies of the higher grades.' Badian's many critics include Gruen 1984 ch. 5, Lintott 1981b pp. 61–2, Harris 1979 p. 135 n. 2 and Bleicken 1964. His argument has been reasserted with some refinements by Rich 1989. Ferrary 1997b pp. 113–17 attempts to find a middle ground.

[3] The analysis of patronage metaphors at Eilers 2002 pp. 186–9 focuses on 'interstate relations in the Republic' and complains that oft-cited passages of Cicero, Livy and Proculus date from a 'later period' (p. 188). Ferrary 1997b pp. 113–17 regrets that the

treats the usage of the Late Republic and Principate as a subject in its own right. A second limitation of past scholarship is that it has privileged *cliens* and *patronus* and the abstract nouns *clientela*, *patrocinium* and *patronatus* as the markers of a patron–client relationship. This chapter pays more attention to the fluidity and indeterminacy of patronal language by considering the different semantic ranges of each of these words, while also casting the net wider to consider a range of closely related expressions often used periphrastically to denote the status of a client (*in fide esse*, etc.) – not to mention the rhetoric of favours discussed in Chapter 4.[4] The third and greatest weakness of existing work is its exclusive focus on patronage. In the quest for a simple answer to the question of whether or not Romans considered empire a form of patronage, an inordinate amount of attention has been devoted to debating whether patronal language is used literally or metaphorically – as if marking this language as metaphorical would render it insignificant.[5] It should by now be clear that patronage is at best one of several models for representing Rome's relationship to its dependants. The important question is not whether Romans considered empire to be a form of patronage, but rather how patronage worked

evidence of Livy is 'anachronistic' for the period he is interested in. Gruen 1984 p. 176 similarly complains that 'Livy has taken liberties … The language is anachronistic' (cf. also p. 159). Harris 1979 p. 135 n. 2 concludes that 'there is no secure evidence that Romans used terminology specifically belonging to *clientela* for their international relations *in the Middle Republic*' (my emphasis).

4 Rich 1989 pp. 128–30 takes an important step in this direction by considering references to *amicitia*, *beneficia*, *officia*, *gratia* and, especially, *fides*. However his brief analysis does not give sufficient attention to the differences between the language of *clientela* and the broader language of *amicitia*, nor does it engage with the semantic differences between *in fidem uenire/accipi* (very common, particularly in the context of surrender) and *in fide esse* (rarely used of foreign peoples outside Cicero and Livy).

5 This has been a long and unproductive controversy. 'To speak of "client states" is to use a metaphor', declares Sherwin-White 1973 p. 188 (first published in 1939). Badian 1958 p. 42 n. 2 disagrees: 'Sherwin-White … makes the very misleading inference that … *clientela* … is, in the international sphere, only a metaphor.' But Harris 1979 p. 135 n. 2 concurs with Sherwin-White on 'the metaphorical character of the term', as does Gruen 1984 p. 162 (who agrees that there is 'no clear acknowledgment' that empire is a form of patronage). Rich 1989 p. 124 renews the dispute: 'It has been claimed that when the Romans did use the terminology of *clientela* in their interstate relations they did so metaphorically. This is a misconception.' Ferrary 1997b pp. 113–17 thinks it necessary to insist that patronal language is explicitly metaphorical. So too does Eilers 2002 p. 188, who concludes that the evidence 'suggests not that the Romans really regarded their subjects as clients, but that from time to time they might use the patron-client relationship for analogy, comparison or metaphor' (cf. ibid. p. 187 'a metaphor only').

as one of several competing models for the imperial relationship. Lastly, where past studies of the subject have offered catalogues of examples, this chapter provides close readings of individual passages. It explores the particular work the patronage metaphor is doing in each context in order to elucidate how and why Rome's subjects are imagined to be like clients.

The chapter begins with a short discussion of *patrocinium* and *clientela*, complex and elusive concepts which are too often treated as self-evident. The next section discusses the close relationship between surrender and clientage in Roman culture, which is typified by the expression *in fidem uenire*. The chapter goes on to discuss two contexts in which patronal language is particularly prominent – Ciceronian invective and Livy's representation of Roman diplomacy. The following section demonstrates that there are further examples of the language of *clientela* scattered throughout Roman discourse about empire, but that no other surviving Roman author uses them to the same extent as Cicero or Livy. It explores the significance of this contrast, taking the opportunity to consider what might be at stake in the choice between the more specific language of *clientela* and the broader, and more widespread, rhetoric of exchange, benefaction and obligation. A final section demonstrates the relative rarity of what might seem to be an obvious alternative paradigm for Roman power – the authority of a parent.

The language of *clientela*

First a word on terminology. Any study of patronage in Roman culture must grapple with some problems of definition. Richard Saller's groundbreaking work demonstrated the value of analysing Roman social relationships in terms of their structure rather than the language in which they are described. Starting with a structural definition of patronage (an ongoing relationship of reciprocal exchange, personal rather than commercial in nature, between two parties of unequal status), he illustrated the ubiquity of such relationships in the society of the Principate, many of them couched in the language of friendship (*amicitia*) rather than *clientela*.[6] Most subsequent accounts of Roman patronage have followed this model.[7] For a study of metaphor, however, what matters is how the Romans themselves imagined their social world – emic rather than etic categories, in the terminology of anthropology. As we will see, the Roman concepts of *clientela*, *patrocinium* and *patronatus* cannot be reduced to Saller's structural definition of patronage.

The Roman categories are themselves more problematic than one might think. Latin has no single word for patronage as an institution or practice. Instead it offers a cluster of words and expressions – including *patronus*, *patrocinium* and *patronatus*; *cliens* and *clientela*; *in fide esse, in fidem uenire* and *in fidem recipere* – which intersect and overlap but are not quite congruent in their application.[8] The usage of *patrocinium* and *patronatus* is a notable example of the lack of congruence. The patron's bond to his *liberti* (freedmen) is always called *patronatus* and never *patrocinium*, whereas the bond to freeborn *clientes* is always called *patrocinium* and never *patronatus*. Yet the two nouns are used interchangeably of the bond to client communities and *collegia*. I call this lexical cluster 'the language of *clientela*' at the risk of exaggerating both its coherence and the homogeneity of the relationships it is used to describe.

One striking feature of this vocabulary is the range of different relationships to which it is applied. These include relations between freed slaves and their former masters,[9] between cities or *collegia*

6 For the definition, see Saller 1982 p. 1: 'First, it involves the reciprocal exchange of goods and services. Secondly, to distinguish it from a commercial transaction in the marketplace, the relationship must be a personal one of some duration. Thirdly, it must be asymmetrical, in the sense that the two parties are of unequal status and offer different kinds of goods and services in the exchange.' This definition is followed by Wallace-Hadrill 1989a pp. 3–4, with the added proviso that the relationship be voluntary and not legally enforceable.

7 See e.g. Winterling 2008, Nauta 2001, Deniaux 1993 and Wallace-Hadrill 1989a.

8 While considerable attention has been given to the meaning of *patronus* and *cliens* (see especially White 1993 pp. 30–4, Saller 1989 pp. 54–7, Brunt 1988 pp. 395 and 417, Saller 1982 pp. 9–10 and Neuhauser 1958), surprisingly little work has been done on the semantics of the other words and phrases in this cluster.

9 On patrons and freedmen see especially Andreau 1993, Fabre 1981 and Treggiari 1969. The former master is called a *patronus* (*TLL* 782.43–783.40) – indeed the jurists largely restrict the use of the word to that context (*Dig*. 2.4.8.1, with Brunt 1988 p. 408 n. 74). His rights over his former slave are called the *ius patronatus* (see esp. *Dig* 37.14), the same word used to describe the bond between municipalities and *collegia* and their patrons

and the patrons they expected to protect their interests,[10] between defendants (and more rarely plaintiffs) and the orators who pleaded on their behalf,[11] and between other freeborn *clientes* and the wealthy and powerful individuals to whom they attached themselves. The language of *clientela* is flexible indeed if it can encompass relationships with both individual and collectivities, both the extra-legal dependence of the free *cliens* and the legally enforceable dependence of the *libertus*, and both the highly formalised bonds with *liberti* and communities and the much less formalised connection with individual *clientes* (more on this below). The shared idiom suggests that, despite their differences, all these relationships have a certain coherence in the Roman imagination that distinguishes them from other relations of dependence.

It would be natural to expect that it was the bond between *patroni* and their individual, freeborn *clientes* that provided the conceptual core of this cluster of relationships. But *clientes* are themselves a slippery category – one in which *clientela* blurs into other modes of dependency. The bond between *patronus* and *cliens* may well have its origins in Rome's early history and presumably evolved over the intervening period, but for that early history we

(see n. 10 below). While *liberti* are rarely if ever called *clientes*, they are probably included in generalising references to a noble's *clientelae* (e.g. *nobilitas divitiae clientelae*, Cic. *Part. or.* 87; *gloriam dignitatem clientelas*, [Sall.] *Ad Caes. sen.* 2.11.3).

10 On patrons of cities (and provinces), see Nicols 1990, 1988, 1980a, 1980b and 1979, and Harmand 1957 and, for the East, Eilers 2002, Ferrary 1997a and Touloumakos 1988. For patrons of *collegia*, see van Nijf 1997 ch. 2, Clemente 1972 and Waltzing 1895–1900 I pp. 416–46. Like individual *clientes*, communities are said to be under the protection (*in fide*) of their *patronus* (e.g. Cic. *Planc.* 97 [twice], *Scaur.* 27, *Fam.* 13.65.2, *Q Fr.* 2.13 (12).3) and to enjoy their *patrocinium* (*TLL* s.v. *patrocinium* 774.64–775.7) and *patronatus* (*TLL* s.v. *patronatus* 780.37–54; cf. the many references to *tabulae patronatus* and the *honos patronatus*). Although communities rarely refer to themselves as the *clientes* of their *patronus* (one exception is the *collegium* of *decatrenses* at Puteoli [*ILS* 1226]) – they regularly describe themselves as being in his *clientela* (Nicols 1980b pp. 550–1) and are presumably encompassed in references to a man's *clientes* or *clientelae*.

11 On *patrocinium* in the courts see especially David 1992, who rightly insists that legal patronage is one instance of a general model of patronage (esp pp. 56, 68, 76, 167, 168–9). The orator who undertakes to plead for someone (especially for a defendant or a provincial community in an extortion trial) is regularly styled *patronus* (cf. *TLL* s.v. *patronus* 785.33–787.6 with Neuhauser 1958); their service is called *patrocinium*, the same word used to describe the protection provided by patrons to both individuals and client communities (*TLL* s.v. *patrocinium* 775.10–43). Those whose case they argue can be described, and describe themselves, as *clientes* (Cic. *Scaur.* 26, *Brut.* 97, *De or.* 1.51 and 174; Caecina at Cic. *Fam.* 6.7.4, Vatinius at *Fam.* 5.9.1 and Pompey at Sen. *Controv.* 7.2.6).

are almost entirely dependent on a few accounts produced in the first century BCE and later. It would be unwise to take these as anything more than myths that explain, legitimise or criticise practices of patronage in their own time.[12] Even for the historical period, there is much debate about the prevalence and importance – whether social, economic or political – of *clientes* in Roman society.[13] The uncertainty extends to the fundamental question of what (if anything) distinguished *clientes* from the wider circle of dependants. Many scholars have explained the condition of the *cliens* in terms of gift-debt.[14] The reciprocity ethic is certainly important to the ideology of *clientela*: much of the moral authority of the *patronus* derives from the perception that he has granted *beneficia* beyond the capacity of the *cliens* to repay. It would be wrong, however, to assume that *all* relations of dependency and obligation that arise within the economy of favours are relations of *clientela*. Many of the bonds so created are more transient and involve less social subordination. Cicero in his *De officiis* explicitly distinguishes between *clientela* and other forms of dependence:

at qui se locupletes, honoratos, beatos putant, ii ne obligari quidem beneficio uolunt ... patrocinio uero se usos aut clientes appellari mortis instar putant.

Those who consider themselves men of wealth, distinction and rank do not even want to be bound by a favour ... but they consider accepting patronage or being called clients tantamount to death. (Cic. *Off.* 2.69)

[12] Accounts of the origins of patronage: Cic. *Rep.* 2.16, Dion. Hal. *Ant. Rom.* 2.9.2–10.4, Plut. *Rom.* 13.1–6 and Serv. ad *Aen.* 6.609. Uncritical readings of these texts have rightly been challenged by Verboven 2002 pp. 55–61, Drummond 1989 p. 91 and Wallace-Hadrill 1989b pp. 67–8.

[13] Rouland 1979 locates the apogee of the *clientela* system in the second century BCE and sees a drastic decline in its political significance thereafter (though he notes that it continued to play an important social and economic function). Eilers 2002 p. 16 suggests that 'real' *clientes* are relatively uncommon throughout the historical period. Brunt 1988 pp. 382–442 too sees a decline in the importance of clientage by the Late Republic, but suggests a resurgence in the Principate (esp. pp. 439–40), as does White 1993 p. 32. Garnsey 2010 and Verboven 2002 argue for its continued social and economic importance at all times. Further disagreement concerns the extent of individual clientage outside the city of Rome (cf. Rouland 1979 esp. pp. 422–5 with the critique of Brunt 1988 p. 282 n. 1).

[14] 'Patronage, in the Roman sense, exists when true reciprocity of favours has ceased' (Lendon 1997 p. 67). 'It is precisely when gifts far exceed the recipient's ability to reciprocate that his gift-debt becomes chronic and he is rendered a client' (Roller 2001 p. 198).

The adverb *uero* draws a contrast between being bound by a favour (*beneficio obligari*) and the condition of the *cliens* (*patrocinio uti*, *clientes appellari*). The latter is evidently a more extreme form of dependence, and thus all the more repugnant to the great and the good. Not all relations of asymmetrical exchange are relations of *clientela*. *Clientela* is embedded in the economy of favours, but not reducible to it.

It is not easy to see where the line is drawn. Unlike the *libertus*, the *cliens* is not a category that is defined and prescribed by law. The bond between *patronus* and *cliens* is extra-legal and depends entirely on convention and social pressure.[15] Whereas patronal connections with client communities were initiated by a formal agreement and often confirmed by bronze tablets displayed in the city and the patron's home, there does not seem to have been any similar formalisation of the bond between *patronus* and *cliens*.[16] There is certainly no convincing evidence for the solemn ritual of *applicatio* posited by some scholars to fit elaborate, legalistic theories of *clientela*.[17] Instead, the essence of *clientela* seems to lie in the public displays of deference with which the *cliens* was expected to repay the *beneficia* of the patron, particularly in the social rituals of the *salutatio*, *adsectatio* and

[15] The category *cliens* is strikingly absent from Roman law. The only known exceptions in the Late Republic are the restrictions on patrons and clients testifying against each other in the Gracchan *lex de rebus repetundis* (*RS* 1, 10 and 32–3) and the *lex de ambitu* (implied by Plut. *Mar.* 5.4). *Clientes* are mentioned only five times in the Digest (7.8.3, 9.3.5.1, 33.9.3.6, 47.2.90). *Pace* Eilers 2002 pp. 9–10, these passages do not imply that *clientes* constituted 'a clearly delineated social category'; the category need be no more precise than the *amici* and *universi quos circa se habet* in whose company *clientes* appear at *Dig*. 33.9.3.6.

[16] See Eilers 2002 pp. 23–37 and Nicols 1980b on the initiation of city patronage and the *tabulae patronatus*.

[17] A ritual of *applicatio* was postulated by von Premerstein 1900 p. 32 and Mommsen 1864–79 I pp. 360–2. They are followed by Gelzer 1969 pp. 67–9, Rouland 1979 pp. 95–8 and 270 (who terms it *applicatio/deditio*), Freyburger 1986 pp. 155–8 and Eilers 2002 p. 21 (calling it 'self-commendation'). The principal evidence cited are the formulae at Ter. *Eun*. 886–7 and 1039 (despite their inconsistency, not to mention the possibility they translate a Greek idiom (see Barsby 1999 ad loc.)), the obscure reference to a *ius applicationis* at Cic. *De or.* 1.177 and recurrent phrases such as *deditio* or *receptio in fidem* and *se commendare*. The inadequacies of this evidence have been demonstrated by Verboven 2002 p. 53 and Badian 1958, 7–9 and 291 n. B. Even Rouland 1979, who insists that the ritual existed in Terence's time, admits there is no evidence for such formalisation by the first century BCE (p. 466).

conuiuium.[18] Yet mere attendance at these rituals is not enough to define the *cliens*, since they all admitted a wider range of dependants (and indeed equals).[19] Nor is it simply a matter of rank, as some have suggested, since the evidence suggests that equestrians and even senators could be *clientes*.[20] The bond between *patroni* and *clientes* is a relationship that is discursively constructed. *Clientes* are those who behave, and are treated, as *clientes* in their interactions with their more powerful friends – not least by using the terms *clientes* and *patroni*. The language of *clientela* is at least partly constitutive of the relations to which it refers.

Even those who professed to be *amici* might leave themselves open to the accusation of being a *cliens* if they appeared overly dependent or deferential. As the passage of Cicero quoted earlier implies, the difference between *clientela* and lesser forms of dependence can come down to perceptions. Cicero claims that the privileged would rather die than be *called* clients (*clientes appellari*). In a similar context, Seneca talks of those who fear being *considered* clients (*opinionem clientium timent*).[21] It would seem that the economy of favours gave rise to a continuum of relations of dependence between free men, that relations of avowed *clientela* lay at one end of that spectrum, and that there was a further grey area within which the applicability of the label *cliens* might be a matter for debate. The connections between poets and

[18] On the public avowal of dependence expected of the client, see especially Verboven 2003, Saller 2000 p. 839, Dixon 1993 pp. 453–4 and Rouland 1979 pp. 484–8, 515–16.

[19] On the *salutatio*, the morning reception in the great houses, see Goldbeck 2010, Winterling 1999 pp. 138–42, Saller 1989 pp. 57–8, Rouland 1979 pp. 266–8, 484–5, 515 and Friedlander 1919–201 pp. 226–7. See especially Cicero, *Comment. pet.* 35–6 and Sen. *Ben.* 6.33.3–34.5, with Saller 1982 p. 129, for the wide range of dependants and equals who might attend. For the crowd that accompanied the Roman noble in public (*adsectatio*), especially in the Late Republic, see Rouland 1979 pp. 485–8 (and cf. Sen. *Tranq.* 9.12.4 and *Ep.* 22.9 for continuities in the Principate). Cic. *Mur.* 68–72 and Cicero, *Comment. pet.* 34–8 illustrate the wide range of attendance.

[20] The view that it is a matter of rank has been advanced most recently by Winterling 2008, who tries to explain away evidence that knights and senators could be *clientes* by claiming that the language of *clientela* is only applied to relations within the senatorial and equestrian orders by derogatory extension of its normal usage. The clearest evidence to the contrary are the provisions of the *lex de repetundis* which imply that a provincial governor (by definition a senator) might be the client (*in fide*) of another senator (*RS* 1, 10). See Verboven 2002 p. 52 and Saller 1989 pp. 52–3 for further evidence.

[21] Sen. *Ben.* 2.23.3.

their more powerful supporters must often have fallen into this space, where the degree of asymmetry in the relationship and hence the nature of the dependence were open to debate. Thus the long and sometimes bitter debate as to whether or not they were (regarded as) *clientes* is misguided in so far as it has aimed at a definitive answer.[22] To call someone a *cliens* is to make a claim about the whole context of his relationship with the other party – to claim that it conforms to what is ultimately an ideal model of patron–client relations.[23]

This chapter adopts the working assumption that there is sufficient ideological coherence to what I call the language of *clientela* to distinguish it from the broader rhetoric of favours discussed in Chapter 4. The distinction may be of limited analytical use in describing Roman social practice, in so far as it imposes a false dichotomy on what is ultimately a continuum of relations of dependence, but it is one that matters in the Roman imagination. The language of *clientela* unites an otherwise heterogeneous cluster of relationships and distinguishes them from other relations of dependence. The distinctive character of these bonds of *patrocinium* and *clientela* must lie in several shared features. These presumably include permanence (distinguishing them from other, more transient relations of obligation in the economy of favours), clear asymmetry (unlike relations of dependence that preserved an illusion of equality) and the particular moral obligations it imposes on *both* parties (and not just the dependent party). But it will be one of the goals of this chapter to look closely at the figurative use of this language in order to test its

[22] See especially Bowditch 2001, Nauta 2001, White 1993, Gold 1987, Saller 1983 and White 1978. Because of inconsistencies in the use of the term 'patron', this debate has conflated three different questions: (i) whether the poets or their contemporaries would describe these relationships in the language of *clientela*, (ii) whether these relationships fit the sociological model of patron–client relations (the dispute turning on the duration of, and the degree of asymmetry in, the relationship), and (iii) whether these relationships fit the model of 'artistic patronage' provided by seventeenth-century France and eighteenth-century Britain (the issue being the extent of active direction and continued material support). This is not to mention the problems entailed in taking poetic representations as evidence for the poet's life and social relations.

[23] Verboven 2002 pp. 57–61 similarly concludes that what unites the heterogeneous cluster of relations called *clientela* is a common ideal model, which he suggests is defined by its supposed origins in archaic Roman practice. He dubs this the 'myth of patronage'.

coherence and to explore further what it is that defines *clientela* in the Roman imagination.

Surrender and clientage

The most obvious – but also the most complex – connection between empire and *clientela* in Roman discourse is the common trope of describing foreign peoples who surrender to Rome as coming into *fides* (*in fidem uenire*, etc.). The *fides* is variously and inconsistently that of the Roman general, the Roman people or left unqualified.[24] No English translation can quite do justice to the phrase, which encompasses all of 'trusting to the good faith of', 'coming under the protection of' and 'coming into the power of'. While this particular expression (*in fidem uenire*) is largely limited to the context of surrender, it is part of a wider cluster of constructions with *fides* which are normally used of the patron–client relationship. 'To be in someone's *fides*' (*in fide alicuius esse*) is to be their client. 'Those in *fides*' *(qui in fide sunt*) can serve as a periphrasis for *clientes* even in a legal text such as the Gracchan extortion law (*RS* 1, 10 and 13). Similar expressions are used to describe becoming a client (*in fidem se dare, ad fidem alicuius applicare*) and accepting a client (*aliquem in fidem accipere* or *recipere*).[25] The connection between surrender and clientage is particularly obvious in references to accepting surrender, which is often described as 'taking into *fides*' (*in fidem accipere* or *recipere*) – precisely the expressions used to describe accepting a man as a client.[26]

In fidem uenire is only one of several different expressions, including *in potestatem uenire* and *in dicionem uenire*, used to

[24] Livy's inconsistent usage is typical: surrender into the *fides* of the Roman people: Livy 32.2.5, 34.35.10, 38.31.6, 39.54.7, 42.8.5, 45.4.7; into the *fides* of the general: 7.19.1, 10.43.8, 37.6.6, 37.32.9; into both: 37.45.3; unspecified: 8.26.7, 26.40.14 and 37.9.7. Rich 1989 p. 129 n. 3 rightly concludes (*pace* Badian 1958 p. 156) that these expressions are too inconsistent to be reduced to a rule.

[25] For *in fide esse, ad fidem applicare, in fidem recipere*, etc., see the many examples cited at *TLL* s.v. *fides* 663.67–75 with the discussion at Brunt 1988 p. 406, Freyburger 1986 pp. 71–2, Badian 1958 p. 1 and Fraenkel 1916 pp. 193–6.

[26] Accepting surrender described as *in fidem accipere/recipere*: e.g. Caes. *B Gall.* 2.15.1, 4.22.3, Plin. *HN* 7.97, *ILS* 140, 11 and 35, and Tac. *Ann.* 2.24.3 (cf. 2.22.2) and 3.73.2.

describe the surrender of foreign peoples. In Roman practice, surrender (*deditio*) involved a formal verbal exchange between the Roman commander and representatives of the surrendering community. Much about the practice of *deditio* is, and is likely to remain, obscure. We are dependent for most of our knowledge on the narratives of Polybius and especially Livy, historians writing at several removes from the practice of Roman commanders in the field. We do not even know whether *fides* was mentioned in the ritual of *deditio* itself. Our firmest evidence for a *deditio* is a bronze tablet from Alcántara recording the surrender of a Spanish tribe in 104 BCE. The bronze records that the tribe first 'surrendered' (*[se] dedit*) and the Roman commander then 'received' them (*accepit*).[27] Unfortunately the tablet is damaged at precisely the point where it might have specified whether they were being received into *fides*, *dicio* or *potestas*.[28] Our only evidence, shaky though it is, for the full verbal exchange is Livy's account of the *deditio* of the Latin city of Collatia to Tarquinius Priscus in the late seventh or early sixth century BCE. The king asks the city's representatives: 'Are you envoys and orators sent by the people of Collatia to surrender yourselves and the people of Collatia?' They respond: 'We are.' 'Is the people of Collatia its own master (*in sua potestate*)?' 'It is.' 'Do you surrender (*dedere*) yourselves and the people of Collatia, the city, fields, water, boundaries, temples, belongings, everything both divine and human, into my power (*dicio*) and that of the Roman people?' 'We do surrender (*dedimus*).' 'Then I accept (*recipio*).'[29] There is no mention of *fides* in this *deditio* formula. Instead the people of Collatia consign themselves and all that they possess to Roman *dicio*. Livy uses a very similar formula when describing the *deditio* of Capua in the fourth century BCE. The

[27] *populus Seanoc[orum se ...] dedit. L(ucius) Caesius C(ai) f(ilius) imperator postquam [—] accepit, ad consilium retolit quid eis im[perandum] censerent* (Richardson 1986 pp. 199–201, 2–5 = AE 1986 304).

[28] The lacuna before *accepit* (see above) has been variously restored as *eos in deditionem*, *eos in fidem*, *eos in dicionem*, *eos in potestatem* and just *deditionem*.

[29] *rex interrogauit: 'estisne uos legati oratoresque missi a populo Collatino ut uos populumque Collatinum dederetis?' – 'sumus.' – 'estne populus Collatinus in sua potestate?' – 'est.' – 'deditisne uos populumque Collatinum, urbem, agros, aquam, terminos, delubra, utensilia, diuina humanaque omnia, in meam populique Romani dicionem?' – 'dedimus.' – 'at ego recipio'* (Livy 1.38.1–2).

Capuans too surrender themselves and all they possess to Roman *dicio*.[30] In a Plautine account of a *deditio*, the defeated are described as consigning themselves to the *dicio* and *arbitratus* of the victors – not their *fides*.[31] However, some texts which also seem to be quoting or paraphrasing the formula of *deditio* speak of *potestas* rather than *dicio*, while others (including the famous account of the *deditio* of the Aetolians to M'. Acilius Glabrio in 191 BCE) do mention *fides*.[32]

The variety of different expressions used to denote *deditio*, together with the wide range of contexts in which *deditiones* are attested (ranging from surrender after defeat to proactive appeals for Roman protection), led early scholars to posit at least two distinct modes of *deditio* – *deditio* proper (sometimes termed *deditio in potestatem*), a form of unconditional surrender which left the defeated entirely at the mercy of their Roman conquerors, and *deditio in fidem*, which committed the Romans to the good treatment and protection of the *dediti*.[33] But Roman usage is too inconsistent to support such a distinction. *Fides*, *dicio*, *potestas* are used interchangeably and sometimes together in references to *deditio*.[34] All the evidence supports Heuss's conclusion that the Romans knew only one mode of *deditio*, which always involved the foreign people renouncing its sovereignty and placing itself entirely in Roman power until the Roman commander decided its future status – though the degree of severity or favour that he might be expected to show must have depended on the circumstances of the *deditio*.[35] Heuss also suggested that the proper formula for a *deditio* provided

[30] *itaque populum Campanum urbemque Capuam, agros, delubra deum, diuina humanaque omnia in uestram, patres conscripti, populique Romani dicionem dedimus* (7.31.4).

[31] *deduntque se, diuina humanaque omnia, urbem et liberos in dicionem atque in arbitratum cuncti Thebano poplo* (Plaut. *Amph.* 258–9).

[32] *Potestas*: e.g. Livy 8.19.12 (*orare se consulem ut bellum ab innoxio populo abstineat; agros, urbem, corpora ipsorum coniugumque ac liberorum suorum in potestate populi Romani esse futuraque*) and Caes. *B Gall.* 2.31.3 (*se suaque omnia eorum potestati permittere dixerunt*). *Fides*: e.g. Livy 36.28.1 ([sc. *dixit*] *Aetolos se suaque omnia fidei populi Romani permittere*; cf. Polyb. 20.10.2) and Caes. *B Gall.* 2.3.2 (*Remi . . . legatos . . . miserunt, qui dicerent se suaque omnia in fidem atque potestatem populi Romani permittere*).

[33] See e.g. Täubler 1913 pp. 14–28.

[34] This is well demonstrated by Gruen 1982 pp. 53–4.

[35] Heuss 1933 pp. 60–9, upheld by Dahlheim 1968 pp. 25–43 and Nörr 1989.

for surrender into the *fides et dicio* of the Romans.[36] But this is only a hypothesis. Indeed, it may well be misguided to attempt to define a fixed formula for the ritual of *deditio*. Roman practice may have been just as inconsistent as its representation in the historians. The key point for my purposes is that *in fidem uenire*, *in potestatem uenire*, *in dicionem uenire* all refer to the same practice. *In fidem uenire* is only one of several different ways of figuring the ritual of *deditio*. Where it differs is in its expressive meaning. It retains its connection to *clientela*, the quintessential *fides* relationship. The use of *fides* rather than *potestas* or *dicio* assimilates the condition of the surrendering community to that of a client. It implies that the Romans' absolute power over the peoples who have surrendered to them is tempered by a moral obligation to protect their welfare.

If *in fidem uenire* is only one of several ways of figuring surrender, it is also an expression that is capable of extending beyond the specific context of *deditio*. Livy, for example, has the Roman senate explain to a Samnite embassy that the Romans have a different kind of relationship with the Campanians than they do with the Latins because the Campanians 'came into *fides* not through a treaty, but through surrender' (*non foedere sed per deditionem in fidem uenissent*, 8.2.13). This sentence would be nonsensical if *in fidem uenire* just meant 'surrender'. The implication is that Latins, though they are Rome's allies and have not performed *deditio*, have nonetheless also 'come into Roman *fides*'. Here *deditio* is only one way of 'coming into Roman *fides*' – that is, entering a state of dependency. The Younger Pliny in his *Panegyricus* exclaims on the good fortune of all the provinces in 'having come into our *fides* and *dicio*' (*quam nunc iuuat prouincias omnes in fidem nostram dicionemque uenisse*, *Pan*. 32.1).[37] Florus writes that the inhabitants of the Etruscan city of Volsinii, conquered in 265 BCE, were the last of the Italians to 'come into *fides*' (*postremi Italicorum in fidem uenere Volsinii*, 1.16.1). In both cases *in fidem uenire* is used loosely of a large number of peoples to denote submission to Roman power, not to refer to a particular act of *deditio*. The key point is that *in fidem uenire* is not a technical term tied to the practice of *deditio*, but figurative language capable of

[36] Heuss 1933 p. 64. [37] On this passage, see further pp. 168–74.

being used more widely. Whether or not a particular foreign people described as 'coming into *fides*' performed a formal *deditio* can only be deduced from the context, if at all.

The question of the connection between surrender and clientage is further complicated by Cicero's testimony that it was the custom of the forefathers (*mos maiorum*) for Roman generals to become the patrons of defeated cities and tribes who had surrendered to them.[38] It is significant that this is a statement about the past, not his present. The most recent analysis of the phenomenon, by Claude Eilers, identified only three probable examples of generals becoming patrons of peoples they had conquered, all from the third and second centuries BCE, and concluded that the practice had been abandoned by the Late Republic.[39] Others have questioned its historicity outright, given the paucity of evidence.[40] Whatever we make of Cicero's claim, it would seem that there is a deep-rooted association between surrender and clientage in Roman culture, with foreign peoples who surrender to Rome often being described as coming into Roman *fides* – language which assimilates them to the status of clients. The connection also operates in the opposite direction. Clients are sometimes represented as 'surrendering' themselves to the patrons, with *dedere* being used of voluntary entry into *clientela*. Thus Aulus Gellius glosses clients as 'those who have surrendered (*dediderunt*) themselves into our protection and patronage'.[41] In the end, the question of the connection between *deditio* and *clientela* exposes the limits of our knowledge about both institutions.

Cicero on Rome's *patrocinium orbis terrae*

Beyond this widespread use of *in fidem uenire*, the most systematic deployment of patronal language to describe the imperial project is

[38] *et cum iis, quos ui deuiceris consulendum est, tum ii, qui armis positis ad imperatorum fidem confugient, quamuis murum aries percusserit, recipiendi. in quo tantopere apud nostros iustitia culta est, ut ii, qui ciuitates aut nationes deuictas bello in fidem recepissent, earum patroni essent more maiorum* (Cic. *Off.* 1.35). Note the use of the historic perfect (*culta est ut … essent*) rather than the pure perfect or present.

[39] Eilers 2002 ch. 2. [40] Verboven 2003 and Gruen 1984 p. 163.

[41] *qui sese … in fidem patrociniumque nostrum dediderunt* (Gell. *NA* 5.13.2). Cf. [sc. *Thais*] *in clientelam et fidem nobis dedit se* (Ter. *Eun.* 1039).

to be found in Ciceronian invective, especially the speeches against Verres. The first of these, the so-called *Divinatio in Caecilium*, was not part of the prosecution proper but an assertion of Cicero's right to conduct the prosecution in the face of an attempt to pre-empt him by one of Verres' allies. This speech aims to establish Cicero's credentials as both the better orator and the advocate expressly desired by the communities of Sicily. At the same time, it also seeks to justify his embarking on such a prosecution relatively late in his career by presenting the prosecution of Verres as a laudable duty rather than the breach of aristocratic solidarity it might seem to be.[42] One of Cicero's strategies is to valorise the act of championing Rome's subjects by making it characteristic of an idealised past:

clarissimi uiri nostrae ciuitatis temporibus optimis hoc sibi amplissimum pulcherrimumque ducebant, ab hospitibus clientibusque suis, ab exteris nationibus, quae in amicitiam populi Romani dicionemque essent, iniurias propulsare eorumque fortunas defendere.[43]

The most eminent men of our state, during the best period of its history, counted it their most honourable and splendid achievement to protect from injury, and maintain in prosperity, their guests and clients, the foreign peoples who had been received into the friendship and power of the Roman people. (Cic. *Div. Caec.* 66)

Cicero praises the aristocrats of old for protecting (which, we will see, is the defining duty of the patron) not just their own dependants but also those of the Roman people. The implication is that Roman nobles should afford the same protection to all Rome's subjects that they do to their own personal dependants. A similar effect is achieved when Cicero describes the extortion law as the *patrona* of Rome's subjects:

etenim cum lex ipsa de pecuniis repetundis sociorum atque amicorum populi Romani patrona sit, iniquum est non eum legis iudicique actorem idoneum

[42] See Vasaly 2002 pp. 87–8 and Steel 2001 pp. 22–3 on Cicero's predicament and the rhetoric of the *Div. Caec.*

[43] The unusual use of the accusative after *esse in* has led some editors to emend the clause: *amicitia ... dicioneque* (Eberhard), <*receptae*> *essent* (Novak), *uenissent* (Ursini). But it is rightly retained by Peterson (OCT, 1917). The use of *in* with the accusative to denote 'place where' is characteristic of the style of Roman laws (Crawford 1996 I 18). Lintott 1992 p. 111 suggests plausibly that Cicero is here alluding to the text of a lost *de repetundis* law.

maxime putari quem actorem causae suae socii defensoremque fortunarum suarum potissimum esse uoluerunt.

Since the very extortion law is the patron(ess) of the allies and friends of the Roman people, it is unjust that the man they most wished to plead their cause and defend their affairs is not considered the best fitted to carrying out the law and the prosecution. (Cic. *Div. Caec.* 65)

By styling the law the *patrona* of Rome's *socii atque amici*, Cicero again implies that Rome's subjects are like clients, in the sense of having a right to protection. These allusions to a collective patronal duty to Rome's subjects are among the strategies pursued by the *Divinatio in Caecilium* in order to persuade the Roman jurors to see this prosecution as the admirable performance of a duty rather than an opportunistic attack on a peer.

The representation of the Sicilians as clients with a claim to Roman protection is developed in the *Verrines* proper. The third speech opens with a brief history of Rome's relationship with Sicily which states that 'Sicily was the first of all foreign peoples to place itself in the friendship and good faith of the Roman people' (*omnium nationum exterarum princeps Sicilia se ad amicitiam fidemque populi Romani applicauit*, 2 *Verr.* 2.2). This is language normally used in the context of the patron–client relationship. *Se ad fidem alicuius applicare* means to place oneself into a patron's *clientela*.[44] It is much more striking than the familiar references to surrender as coming into, or being received into, Roman *fides* (*in fidem uenire, recipi*). The collocation *amicitia fidesque* is also significant. Cicero elsewhere uses the formula of his own personal clients, writing for example of taking one Apollonius, a freedman of P. Crassus, into his *fides* and friendship (*in fidem atque amicitiam recipere*) after Crassus' death.[45] The few instances of *amicitia fidesque* outside Cicero also occur in the context of *clientela*.[46]

44 See n. 25 above.

45 *dignior uisus est quem in fidem atque amicitiam meam reciperem* (Cic. *Fam.* 13.16.2). See also Cicero's description of his relationship to C. Trebatius Testa: *te ex adulescentia tua in amicitiam et fidem meam contulisses* (Cic. *Fam.* 7.17.2).

46 At *B Alex.* 23.2 it is used of the Alexandrians becoming Caesar's clients (*in Caesaris fidem amicitiamque uenturi*). When Caesar describes the dependence of the Bellovaci on the Aedui in these terms (*Bellouacos omni tempore in fide atque amicitia ciuitatis Haeduae fuisse*, *B Gall.* 2.14.2), this is one of several examples of his using the language of *clientela* to describe relations of dependence among the Gallic tribes (see n. 70 below).

Cicero's reference to the 'friendship and good faith of the Roman people' is almost unparalleled outside the *Verrines*, but it recurs four more times in those speeches.[47] Cicero says that Rome took the cities of Sicily into its friendship and good faith (*Siciliae ciuitates ... in amicitiam fidemque accepimus*, 2 *Verr.* 3.12). Cities which remained loyal during the Punic War are twice described as remaining permanently in the friendship and good faith of the Roman people (*quod semper in amicitia fideque mansissent*, 2 *Verr.* 2.90; *ciuitates ... quae in amicitia fideque populi Romani perpetuo manserant*, 2 *Verr.* 5.83). The citizens of one Sicilian city are given voice as proudly proclaiming that they have always relied on the friendship and good faith of the Roman people (*nos semper ... amicitiam fidemque populi Romani secuti sumus*, 2 *Verr.* 5.124). The repeated references to Sicily's coming into, and being in, Roman friendship and *fides* assimilate the Romans' relationship to their province to that of a patron and client. The fact that Cicero nowhere else uses these expressions in the context of empire suggests that they must be doing particular work here. Chapter 1 has already shown that the *Verrines* use the label *socius* widely in order to emphasise Rome's obligation to the Sicilians as a whole. Representing the Sicilians as Rome's clients asserts a similar claim to Roman protection. Both these rhetorical choices contribute to the particularly benevolent vision of empire constructed by the *Verrines*.

The patronal imagery of the *Verrines* recurs in the later attack on the character of his enemy Publius Clodius Pulcher in the *De domo sua*. One of Clodius' many crimes, Cicero tells us, was his treatment of Ptolemy, king of Cyprus:

qui cum lege nefaria Ptolomaeum, regem Cypri, fratrem regis Alexandrini, eodem iure regnantem causa incognita publicasses, populumque Romanum scelere obligasses, cum in eius regnum bona fortunas patrocinium huius imperi inmisisses,

[47] The one exception is also in Cicero and serves a similar function. Writing of the Galatian tetrarch Deiotarus who supported Pompey against Caesar, Cicero says: *fidem secutus amicitiamque populi Romani functus sit officio* (Cic. *Div.* 2.78). Siding with Pompey, Cicero implies, was the act of a faithful client of the Roman people. The point is to vilify Caesar's subsequent treatment of Deiotarus. As in the *Verrines*, Rome's injured subject is represented as a wronged client.

cuius cum patre auo maioribus societas nobis et amicitia fuisset, huius pecuniae deportandae et, si ius suum defenderet, bello gerendo M. Catonem praefecisti.

By an impious law you confiscated without trial the kingdom of Ptolemy, king of Cyprus, brother of the king of Alexandria and possessed of the same right to kingship. You implicated the Roman people in the crime when you unleashed the *patrocinium* of this empire on the kingdom, property and fortunes of a man whose father, grandfather and ancestors were our allies and friends. Then you put Marcus Cato in charge of carrying off his wealth and – if he were to stand up for his rights – waging war on him. (Cic. *Dom.* 20)

The use of *patrocinium* has worried editors – unnecessarily.[48] *Patrocinium* denotes the duties of a *patronus*, particularly in his role as protector. *Patrocinium inmittere* (to unleash the patronage) is an oxymoron. Heir to a long alliance, Ptolemy ought to be able to count on Roman power for protection; instead he finds that power unleashed against the very things it ought to be defending. By dubbing the empire a *patrocinium* at the very moment that it is exploited by one avaricious Roman in order to rob one of its old allies, Cicero draws attention to the gap between ideal and reality.

A final example comes from the *De officiis*.[49] It is in this work that Cicero famously describes Rome's empire as a *patrocinium* of the world:

uerum tamen quam diu imperium populi Romani beneficiis tenebatur, non iniuriis, bella aut pro sociis aut de imperio gerebantur, exitus erant bellorum aut mites aut necessarii, regum, populorum, nationum portus erat et perfugium senatus, nostri autem magistratus imperatoresque ex hac una re maximam laudem capere studebant, si prouincias, si socios aequitate et fide defendissent. itaque illud patrocinium orbis terrae uerius quam imperium poterat nominari.

[48] See the violent objections of Shackleton Bailey 1979 p. 264. He proposes emending to *praeconium* (cf. *latrocinium* (Naugerius) and *patrimonium* <*uim*> (Nägelsback), with Shackleton Bailey's criticisms). Clark (OCT, 1905) and Peterson (OCT, 1911) retain *patrocinium*; Maslowski (Teubner, 1981) follows Shackleton Bailey.

[49] I set aside another possible example because of its obscurity. In the *Republic*, Cicero's Scipio introduces the people of Massilia as *clientes nostri*, when using them to illustrate his claim that popular freedom is impossible under an aristocracy (Cic. *Rep.* 1.43). Harris 1979 p. 135 n. 2, Gelzer 1969 p. 88 and others have explained this as a reference to a formal patronage relationship between the city and the Scipios, though there is no other evidence for such a connection. The alternative is to see it as another example of Rome's subjects being described as her clients (reading the first person plural as 'we Romans' rather than 'we Scipios'). Indeed Gruen 1984 p. 159 cites this as the most obvious example of the *clientela* metaphor (so too Zetzel 1995 ad loc.). But it is not at all clear what purpose such a metaphor might have in a passage that is concerned with the Massilians' domestic politics, not with their relationship to Rome.

But as long as Roman supremacy was maintained through generosity and not abuse, wars were fought either on behalf of the allies or to maintain our power, wars were settled leniently or as necessity dictated, the senate was a safe harbour and refuge for kings, peoples and tribes, and our magistrates and generals thought that the greatest glory lay in fairly and faithfully defending the provinces and allies. And so it could have been more truthfully called a *patrocinium* of the world than an *imperium*. (Cic. *Off.* 2.26–7)

The paradigm of *clientela* plays a central role in this famous example of self-congratulatory Roman rhetoric. In Cicero's time, the phrase *imperium Romanum* had not yet developed the concrete sense of a territory ruled by Rome.[50] When Cicero says that what is called Rome's *imperium* would be better named a *patrocinium*, he is contrasting two forms of authority familiar from Roman civic life: the almost unlimited coercive power of the highest magistrates (*imperium*) and the authority of a patron (*patrocinium*), which is tempered by a duty to protect his clients. The ground is laid for the patronal ideal by the preceding emphasis on Rome's role as defender – fighting on behalf of the allies (*bella pro sociis gerebantur*) and defending the allies (*socios defendissent*). But it is important to note that this idealised vision of Roman rule is located in the past, not in Cicero's own time, and that here too Cicero's idealising rhetoric has a polemical purpose. The *De officiis* is a damning attack on Caesar.[51] This particular passage goes on to describe the abuse of Rome's allies in recent generations, culminating in an account of Caesar's triumphal celebration of the capture of Massilia (Marseille), a long-standing ally of Rome which had resisted him on his march to Spain (ibid. 2.28). Cicero condemns Caesar by contrasting his treatment of Rome's subjects with a patronal model situated in an idealised past.

From the *Verrines* to the *De officiis*, Cicero turns to the language of *clientela* in order to articulate a particular vision of empire that stresses Rome's obligations to its subjects. But we should not forget that these descriptions of empire are embedded in particular projects of persuasion. In the *Verrines*, Cicero is trying to persuade his Roman jury to convict a fellow Roman noble of extortion in the

50 See pp. 52–3.
51 On politics and anti-Caesarianism in the *De officiis* see Dyck 1996 pp. 29–36 and Long 1995.

provinces. In the later speeches, he is aiming to vilify the provincial conduct of his opponents and enemies. It is worth remembering that Cicero was quite capable of purveying a very different vision of Rome's obligations when he found himself on the other side of the *de repetundis* court later in his career.[52]

Livy on Roman *patrocinium*

Livy is a second author who makes particularly extensive use of the language of patronage and clientage in characterising Roman power. Like other authors, he regularly uses the trope of coming into Roman *fides*, often – but not always – to refer to *deditio*.[53] I have already mentioned his description of a treaty and *deditio* as two different manners of 'coming into *fides*' (8.2.13, cited above). In his narrative of the Second Punic War, Bruttian tribes who defect to Hannibal but later switch sides again, are represented as 'returning to the *fides* of the Roman people' (*in fidem populi Romani redierunt*, Livy 25.1.2). Another rebel Italian lures a Roman general into a trap by pretending that his countrymen are on the brink of restoring their allegiance to Rome and that a few encouraging words from the Roman are all that is needed for the whole Lucanian people to be in Roman *fides* and alliance (*ut omne nomen Lucanum in fide ac societate Romana sit*, 25.16.14). In these and similar passages, 'being in Roman *fides*' is synonymous with allegiance to Rome. The cumulative effect of the repeated references to *fides* is to suggest a patronal aspect to Roman power.

Livy is more distinctive in his references to Roman guardianship (*tutela*). An early example can be found in the speech attributed to Publius Cornelius Scipio before the battle of the Ticinus during the Second Punic War. He condemns the Carthaginians for their ingratitude in attacking Rome after the Romans had treated them as

[52] See pp. 46–8 on the defence speeches.

[53] When it comes to reconstructing the forms of Roman imperialism from Livy's narrative, the ambiguity inherent in the references to *in fidem uenire* (which may or may not refer to a formal *deditio*) is compounded by the unreliability of some explicit references to *deditio*. See e.g. Oakley 1997–2005 II pp. 286–9 on the doubtful historicity of Livy's account of the *deditio* of Capua in the fourth century BCE.

being under their guardianship (*tutelae nostrae duximus*) during the Mercenary War.[54] But it is in the narrative of Roman expansion into the Greek world that the language of *tutela* come to the fore. It features in the debate among the Roman commissioners that preceded the 'liberation' of Greece in 195 BCE. The urgent concern was the threat posed by the Seleucid king Antiochus III now that Philip V of Macedon had been defeated:

Quinctius liberandam omnem Graeciam . . . nihil contra ea de libertate urbium alii dicebant: ceterum ipsis tutius esse manere paulisper sub tutela praesidii Romani quam pro Philippo Antiochum dominum accipere.

Quinctius said that all Greece should be set free . . . The others did not contradict him on the subject of the cities' freedom. But they said that it was safer for the cities themselves to remain a while under the guardianship of a Roman garrison than to receive Antiochus as a new master in place of Philip. (Livy 33.31.8–10)

When Flamininus calls for the liberation of Greece (meaning, by the conventions of Hellenistic diplomacy, that it be relieved of tribute and garrisons), the others argue for a middle ground.[55] Their rhetoric exploits a contrast between the enslavement implied by *dominus* and the dependency suggested by *tutela* to make a continued Roman presence seem more palatable in comparison to Seleucid occupation. The contrast between *tutela* and *seruitus* recurs in a Roman rebuke to the Rhodians for their mistreatment of Lycia, which had been assigned to them in the aftermath of the Syrian War:

nec Lycios Rhodiis nec ullos alii cuiquam, qui nati liberi sint, in seruitutem dari placere; Lycios ita sub Rhodiorum simul imperio et tutela esse, ut in dicione populi Romani ciuitates sociae sint.

The senate [they said] did not approve of the Lycians being enslaved to the Rhodians – or of any people that was born free being enslaved to another people. The Lycians were simultaneously under the power and the guardianship of the Rhodians in the same way that the allied communities were under the authority of the Roman people. (Livy 41.6.11 12)

The senate implies that the Romans regards their 'allies' as being not just under their control, but also under their *tutela* – and that the

[54] *tutelae deinde nostrae duximus, cum Africo bello urgerentur* (Livy 21.41.12).
[55] On freedom in Hellenistic diplomacy see p. 97 n. 71.

Rhodians should treat their subjects in the same way, not as slaves. Livy's senate employs the same rhetoric of *tutela* in the aftermath of the Third Macedonian War:

omnium primum liberos esse placebat Macedonas atque Illyrios, ut omnibus gentibus appareret arma populi Romani non liberis seruitutem, sed contra seruientibus libertatem adferre, ut ... in libertate gentes quae essent, tutam eam sibi perpetuamque sub tutela populi Romani esse ... crederent.

The very first decision was that the Macedonians and Illyrians should be free so that it would be clear to all peoples that the arms of the Roman people did not bring enslavement to the free but rather freedom to the enslaved – so that the peoples who were free would believe that their freedom would be eternally safe under the guardianship of the Roman people. (Livy 45.18.1–2).

The rhetoric of *tutela* asserts Roman authority while disavowing any aspiration to mastery. It acknowledges that the Romans have dependants while denying that they have slaves. The idea of *tutela* is strictly distinct from that of *patrocinium*. It refers to the role of the *tutor*, the guardian assigned to women and children who had lost their *paterfamilias*.[56] Yet there is an obvious affinity between the patron and guardian in their roles as protectors of the weak. The language of *tutela* is sometimes applied to patrons. When Suetonius describes Sparta as being *sub tutela Claudiorum* (*Tib.* 6.2), he presumably means that it was in their *clientela*.[57] Livy's references to Roman *tutela* thus resonate with the broader references to Roman *fides* and *patrocinum*.

By far the most famous patronal metaphor in Livy is that quoted at the beginning of this chapter – Flamininus' claim that Rome has undertaken the role of patron of Greek freedom (*patrocinium libertatis Graecorum*) whereas Antiochus III seeks to reclaim them as slaves (*eas repetere in seruitutem*). It should by now have become apparent that many of Livy's patronal metaphors occur, as here, in the rhetoric of Roman diplomacy. Throughout Livy's history, Rome's enemies accuse her of enslaving her subjects, while Rome's ambassadors claim to offer *patrocinium* or

[56] Sachers 1948. *Liberti* under the age of 20 and all *libertae* were also subject to *tutela* (Gai. *Inst.* 1.165 with Duff 1928 pp. 43–4).
[57] Cf. Livy. 25.29.6 (*incolumesque Syracusas familiae uestrae sub clientela nominis Marcellorum tutelaque habendas tradas?*).

tutela and to champion *libertas*.[58] But it would be doing Livy an injustice to read the latter as a straightforward presentation of his own views. We know that Roman readers valued Livy's narrative particularly for the quality and appropriateness of its speeches.[59] The sophisticated reader is supposed to appreciate the rhetorical skills of the various parties – but not necessarily to be convinced by any of them.

Flamininus' exchange with Antiochus' ambassadors Menippus and Hegesianax is a particularly good example of Livy's knowing presentation of the claims and counterclaims of diplomacy. Menippus is the first to speak, complaining that Antiochus is being treated like a conquered enemy rather than an equal ally (34.57.6–11). Flamininus insists that Rome's demands are not open to negotiation (34.58.1–3). When Hegesianax asks whether Rome has any sense of honour (34.58.4–8), Flamininus retorts that if it is a question of honour, Rome's wish that the Greek cities be free is surely more laudable than Antiochus' desire to enslave them (34.58.8–13). It is here that he claims that Rome has undertaken the *patrocinium* of Greek freedom. At this point Hegesianax hesitates because he finds himself unable to deny that 'the more honourable cause was the one that was fronted by the sign (*titulus*, an inscribed notice) of freedom rather than that of slavery' (*honestiorem causam libertatis quam seruitutis praetexi titulo*, 34.59.1). The verb *praetexere* with its connotations of covering and concealment invites us to see the instrumental nature of Roman appeals to 'freedom'.[60] Livy then punctures the debate. Publius Sulpicius, the oldest Roman present, interrupts impatiently with a 'let's talk straight' (*quin mittimus ambages?*, 34.59.1). This Roman has no time for rhetorical subterfuge. He eschews talk of Greek freedom for a bare demand that Antiochus accept Rome's conditions (34.59.2).

58 For the condemnation of Roman rule as *seruitus* by Italian allies, rebels and hostile kings, see p. 73.

59 Quint. *Inst.* 10.1.101. Cf. the compilation of Livian speeches mentioned at Suet. *Dom.* 10.3.

60 Briscoe 1981 ad loc. insists that *praetexi* does not imply doubt and is determined only by the metaphorical use of *titulus*. But *praetexere* is regularly used of specious rhetoric (cf. *OLD* § 3 'cloak' and § 4 'put forward as pretext'). The same verb is used by Cerialis in Tacitus' *Histories* to denounce German pretexts for invading Gaul: *libertas et speciosa nomina praetexuntur* (Tac. *Hist.* 4.73.4, on which see pp. 143–4).

It is a further sign of Livy's interest in these strategies of persuasion that it is Greek speakers who subsequently pick up this patronal rhetoric, for their own purposes. Flamininus' claim that the Roman empire is a *patrocinium* is echoed several books later in a speech by Rhodian ambassadors in the aftermath of the defeat of Antiochus. Seeking to persuade the Romans not to cede the cities they have captured from Antiochus to Eumenes of Pergamum but to leave them independent, the Rhodians remind the Romans of their promise to be the patrons of the Greeks:

gentis uetustissimae nobilissimaeque uel fama rerum gestarum uel omni commendatione humanitatis doctrinarumque tuendam ab seruitio regio libertatem suscepistis; hoc patrocinium receptae in fidem et clientelam uestram uniuersae gentis perpetuum uos praestare decet.

You have undertaken to protect from enslavement to the kings the freedom of the people that is oldest and noblest – both in the fame of its achievements and in the excellence of its culture and learning. It is a fine thing that you never fail in this patronal duty to the entire people that you have accepted under your patronage and protection. (Livy 37.54.17)

The Rhodians claim that the Romans have accepted the Greek people as their clients – *in fidem et clientelam recipere* being a common way of referring to accepting a client.[61] They call on them to do their patronal duty (*patrocinium praestare*) by defending (*tueri*) their clients. The idea of Roman *patrocinium* is useful for the Rhodians because it implies a moral obligation on the part of the dominant party. It is an assertion as much of Roman responsibility as it is of Greek dependence and subordination.[62] The Rhodians thus exploit Flamininus' rhetoric to their own advantage. Nor is this the only time that Livy represents foreign speakers trying to use Roman rhetoric to manipulate Roman behaviour.[63]

61 Expressions such as *in fide clientelaque esse, in fidem clientelamque recipere, accipere, se dare* and *se conferre* are used of both individual clients and client communities. Individuals: Ter. *Eun.* 1039, Cic. *Rosc. Am.* 93 and 106. Communities: Livy 26.32.8 and 37.54.17. The phrase *in fidem clientelamque recipere* appears in 23 of the 30 *tabulae patronatus* analysed by Nicols 1980b.

62 Ferrary 1997b p. 114 notes rightly of this passage that '*patrocinium* is used to evoke a Roman undertaking to protect Greek liberty, not a form of Roman hegemony; the *officium* alluded to is that of the *patronus*'.

63 Other examples of provincials trying to manipulate Rome by appropriating the Roman rhetoric of freedom include the citizens of Henna at Livy 24.37.6–7.

It is worth noting that the Polybian passage on which the Rhodian speech is based (Polyb. 21.22–3) makes no use of patronal language in any form. These tropes are apparently a Livian addition. The same may well be true of the reference to Roman *patrocinium* in Flamininus' earlier speech, though the relevant passage of Polybius is not extant for comparison.[64] (It is not inconceivable that this is an allusion to Cicero's distinctive description of the Roman empire as a *patrocinium orbis terrae* in the *De officiis*.[65]) There is certainly no evidence for the rhetoric of *tutela* in those passages for which Polybian parallels exist.[66] It would be unwise to assume that Livy is a reliable guide to the tropes of Roman rhetoric in the second century BCE. It is enough for my purposes, however, that Livy thought that these were the tropes that Roman speakers might have – or should have – used in these contexts. He sees in the language of *patrocinium* and *tutela* a means of idealising Roman power in contrast with that of the kings, implying that the Romans acknowledge a moral duty towards their dependants and can be relied on to protect them.

Beyond Cicero and Livy

It should by now be clear that both Cicero and Livy make repeated use of the language of *clientela* in order to underline Rome's obligations to her dependants, though neither author is necessarily committed to the paradigm as anything more than a rhetorical strategy. Patronage is not, however, the dominant paradigm for Roman rule that a reading of these two authors might suggest. Beyond the references to coming or being accepted into Roman *fides*, more elaborate metaphors of Roman patronage and provincial clientage are remarkably rare in other authors.

One exception is Florus' description of the Numidian kingdom as Rome's client in his account of the Jugurthine War. Explaining

64 So Ferrary 1997b p. 114, Gruen 1984 p. 176 and Tränkle 1977 pp. 125–6, *pace* Rich 1989 p. 126 n. 1.
65 For other allusions to Cicero in Livy, see Oakley 1997–2005 ad 6.18.5 and 8, 6.41.4–10 and 8.35.7.
66 Contrast Livy 33.31.10 with Polyb. 18.45.9–12 and Livy 41.6.11–12 with Polyb. 25.4.5.

Jugurtha's caution in moving to seize the Numidian kingdom from his half-brothers, Florus claims that he was even more afraid of Rome than he was of his rivals, since the Numidian kingdom 'was in the *fides* and *clientela*' of the senate and people of Rome.[67] The collocation *in fide et clientela* is common in references to the condition of personal clientage.[68] The patronal metaphor speaks to the special relationship between Rome and the Numidian kingdom which had been forged during the Second Punic War. Like the many slavery metaphors in the narrative, it also contributes to Florus' project of personifying the *populus Romanus*.[69]

A second example is the analogy drawn by the Early Imperial jurist Proculus in order to describe the condition of 'allied and free peoples' (*populi foederati et liberi)*, a relatively privileged category of non-citizen community, within the empire of the first century CE. Proculus' concern is to explain why all peoples who have a treaty with Rome are considered 'free' – even those whose treaty has a so-called *maiestas* clause, requiring them 'courteously to maintain the superiority' (*maiestatem comiter conseruare*) of the Roman people:

hoc enim adicitur, ut intellegatur alterum populum superiorem esse, non ut intellegatur alterum non esse liberum: et quemadmodum clientes nostros intellegimus liberos esse, etiamsi neque auctoritate neque dignitate neque uiribus nobis pares sunt, sic eos, qui maiestatem nostram comiter conseruare debent, liberos esse intellegendum est.

For this [clause] is added to show that the one people is superior, not to show that the other is not free. Just as we understand that our clients are free even if they are inferior to us in influence, standing and power, so those who are obliged to 'courteously maintain our superiority' should also be understood to be free. (*Dig*. 49.15.7.1)

To explain how peoples who have formally acknowledged their inferiority to Rome can nevertheless be considered free, he adduces the example of clients, who are inferior to their patrons in every

[67] *hic, auo Masinissa et Micipsa patre per adoptionem, cum interficere fratres statuisset agitatus regni cupiditate, nec illos magis quam senatum populumque Romanum, quorum in fide et clientela regnum erat metueret, primum scelus mandat insidiis* (Flor. 1.36.3). Elsewhere, Florus calls Ostia Rome's 'client and nursling' (*cliens et alumna urbis Ostia*, 2.9.12).

[68] See n. 61 above. [69] See pp. 104–5.

way but are nonetheless free men, not slaves. Looking back to Chapter 2, it is worth noting that Proculus is discussing a relatively small and privileged group within the empire. The implication is that the provincialised population is not free.

These are isolated examples. The rest of Latin literature offers nothing to compare with the deployment of patronal metaphors in Cicero and Livy. Indeed, Julius Caesar is an example of an author who seems to go out of its way to *avoid* describing Roman rule in such terms. His *Gallic War* repeatedly turns to *clientela* in order to describe relations of dependence among the Gallic tribes. Dependent tribes are described variously as the *clientes*, part of the *clientela*, or under the protection (*in fide*) of more powerful neighbours.[70] Yet that language is never applied to Rome's dependants, who are instead described as being *in dicione* or as slaves.[71] For Caesar, it seems, *clientela* provides the model for a distinctly un-Roman style of foreign relations.

Scholarship to date has stressed the rarity of patronal metaphors and so played down the significance of patronage for Roman representations of empire.[72] Various explanations have been proposed. Badian, who found himself forced to admit the relative paucity of patronal metaphors in Latin literature despite his conviction that 'educated Romans' conceptualised their relationship with at least some foreign peoples in terms of the patron–client relationship, suggested that Roman texts avoided the language of clientage because it implied inferiority and Romans wanted to spare their subjects' feelings.[73] More recently, John Rich has explained the infrequency of patronal metaphors on the grounds that the model of *patrocinium* is only appropriate to systems of

70 *clientes*: Caes. *B Gall.* 1.31.6, 4.6.4, 5.39.3 and 6.12.4; *clientela*: 6.4.5 and 6.12.2; *in fide*: 2.14.2, 6.4.2, 7.5.2.

71 *in dicione*: 2.34.1. For the language of slavery, see pp. 80–1.

72 The evidence is 'surprisingly thin and contradictory' (Eilers 2002 p. 188). 'If patronage of Roman aristocrats over foreign communities is well attested, the idea of patronage of the Roman people over those communities is, *pace* Badian, both quite unusual and metaphorical' (Ferrary 1997b pp. 115). 'The number of passages in our sources in which patron/client terminology is used of Roman interstate relations is certainly very small' (Rich 1989 p. 124). Even Badian felt obliged to qualify his claim that patronage was the model that educated Romans used to think about empire with an acknowledgement of an 'avoidance of the term in official documents' (Badian 1958 p. 7).

73 Badian 1958 pp. 6–7.

power where there could be a multiplicity of patrons and therefore makes little sense in the context of a world dominated by Rome.[74] But these accounts fail to acknowledge – let alone explain – the fact that Cicero and Livy *do* make repeated use of *clientela* as a paradigm for Roman rule. Nor do they address the wide currency of the broader rhetoric of favours, which was discussed in the last chapter.

To understand the distinctive use of patronal metaphors in Cicero and Livy, we must pay closer attention both to their rhetorical context and to the particular connotations of the language of *clientela* in comparison with the broader rhetoric of favours. Previous discussions of the terms *patronus*, *cliens* and their cognates have focused on the inequality that these terms imply. It has even been claimed that they have pejorative connotations and were thus avoided in 'polite society', which preferred to describe the condition of clientage in the language of friendship.[75] But the focus on inequality risks obscuring other features which define *clientela* in the Roman imagination. The most significant shared feature of the metaphors of clientage examined in this chapter has been an emphasis on the patron's obligations to the client – particularly the duty to protect and defend him. When Cicero and Livy turn to the specific language of *clientela*, it is not to assert provincial inferiority but rather to affirm a Roman duty to care for and protect the dependent peoples. This is an important difference from the broader rhetoric of favours. As Chapter 4 has shown, texts that deploy the language of benefaction and obligation tend to do so in order to assert Roman superiority or their dependants' obligations. A glance at Livy will show that the metaphors of *patrocinium* and *tutela* are almost exclusively used to make claims about what Rome's dependants can expect from her, whereas references to

74 Rich 1989 p. 127.

75 Saller 1982 pp. 9–11. Saller tries to explain why the language of *clientela* is so rare in literature (where relations of dependence are more often described in terms of *amicitia*) when it is relatively common in honorific inscriptions. His explanation is that the labels of patronage were considered offensive 'in polite society' and were therefore avoided by the superior party although they were used by inferiors. But this is not an entirely satisfactory explanation. It remains hard to understand both why inferiors would identify themselves as clients if the language was so offensive and why the Roman elite do not more often describe third parties as clients where there is no risk of giving offence.

Roman *beneficia* usually serve to remind Rome's dependants of the loyalty and deference they owe their benefactors.

Because the language of *clientela* makes a much stronger claim about the obligations of the dominant party than does the language of *beneficia*, the two lend themselves to different uses. This is the key to the distinctiveness of Cicero and Livy. Both authors employ patronal metaphors for particular rhetorical purposes. It is in political invective that Cicero appeals to *patrocinium* as the paradigm of how Rome ought to behave to its subjects. The point is to vilify the provincial conduct of his opponents. For Livy it is a trope for Roman speakers to use in order to differentiate Roman rule from subjection to the Hellenistic kings. Both authors turn to *patrocinium* in order to communicate idealising visions of empire which emphasise Rome's obligations to its dependants. It is surely the scarcity of comparable projects of persuasion in what survives of Latin discourse that explains why Cicero and Livy account for a disproportionate number of these metaphors. No author other than Cicero gives us access to the rhetoric of the *de repetundis* courts; no other historian provides as many representations of Roman diplomatic rhetoric as does Livy.

From *Roma domina* to *Roma mater*

Lastly a word on a notable absence from the language of Roman imperialism. One might have expected Roman rule over the provinces to be represented in terms of the relations of parents and children, especially where there is a need for an alternative to the paradigm of mastery. The contrast between the figures of father and master is central to debate about the legitimacy of the *princeps*'s authority, as Mathew Roller has shown.[76] Good emperors act like fathers; tyrants like masters. Thus Pliny's *Panegyricus* praises Trajan for comporting himself as a father and not a master, unlike Domitian.[77] Children certainly figure in the iconography of empire. There are, for example, the foreign children on the screen of the Ara Pacis, the Gauls presenting children to Augustus on the Boscoreale

[76] Roller 2001 ch. 3 (focusing on the Julio-Claudian period). [77] See p. 96 n. 68.

cups and the children on the arch of Trajan at Beneventum.[78] But familial language is remarkably rare in textual accounts of Roman rule of empire, when compared to the languages of slavery and even clientage.[79]

A rare exception, illustrating the neglected potential of the metaphor, is to be found in a speech that Livy attributes to a Capuan embassy to Rome in 343 BCE. Beseeching the senate for assistance in their conflict with the Samnites, the ambassadors promise to repay their benefactors:

uobis arabitur ager Campanus, uobis Capua urbs frequentabitur; conditorum, parentium, deorum immortalium numero nobis eritis; nulla colonia uestra erit, quae nos obsequio erga uos fideque superet.

It will be for you that Campanian fields are tilled; for you that the city of Capua is thronged with people. We will count you among our founders, fathers and immortal gods. None of your colonies will surpass us in obedience and loyalty to you. (Livy 7.30.19)

The Capuans promise to reverence the Romans as 'founders, parents and immortal gods'. The paradigm of parenthood is combined with that of city foundation, as often in the discourse of civic praise.[80] Hence the subsequent comparison to *coloniae*. Capua volunteers to *become* a colony – with all the symbolic implications of deference and dependence this entails. The second-century historian Florus employs a similar trope when he represents the Social War as a rising against Italy's 'mother and parent city':

quid calamitosius? cum omne Latium atque Picenum, Etruria omnis atque Campania, postremo Italia contra matrem suam ac parentem urbem consurgeret.

[78] For attempts to elucidate the significance of images of children in the iconography of empire, see p. 6 n. 21. Cf. also Swain 1996 p. 166 on the use of the child as a paradigm for the condition of Greek cities within the Roman empire by Plutarch and Dio Chrysostom.

[79] I set aside the trope of kinship in diplomatic rhetoric. From an early period, Rome participated in a broader Hellenistic practice of cultivating myths of shared descent in its diplomatic relations with other communities in the Mediterranean world (see Battistoni 2009 and Jones 1999 chs. 6–8). For example, the Gallic tribe of the Aedui were granted the title of brothers and kinsmen (*fratres consanguineique*) some time in the second century BCE and continued to be referred to as brothers into the Imperial period (see Caes. *B Gall.* 1.33.2, Cic. *Att.* 1.19.2, Cic. *Fam.* 7.10.4, Tac. *Ann.* 11.25.1). But the trope served to negotiate Rome's relationship to a few privileged communities – not to the empire as a whole.

[80] For cities honouring benefactors as *parentes*, see Nisbet and Rudd 2004 ad Hor. *Carm.* 3.24.27.

What could be more disastrous? All of Latium and Picenum, all Etruria and Campania, and finally all Italy rose against its mother and parent city. (Flor. 2.6.5)

Florus extends the familiar metaphor of the 'mother city' far beyond its traditional colonial context, applying it to Rome's relationship with Italy as a whole.[81] The parental imagery emphasises the beneficent aspect of Rome's power and thus the ingratitude of her rebellious allies. But the metaphor is not extended beyond Italy; Rome's other subjects are her slaves.[82] The distinctive maternal language of this passage serves only to assert the privileged position of Italy within the broader empire.

Another rare example of maternal imagery can be found in a much-cited passage of Pliny the Elder which praises the land of Italy:[83]

nec ignoro ingrati ac segnis animi existimari posse merito, si obiter atque in transcursu ad hunc modum dicatur terra omnium terrarum alumna eadem et parens, numine deum electa quae caelum ipsum clarius faceret, sparsa congregaret imperia ritusque molliret et tot populorum discordes ferasque linguas sermonis commercio contraheret ad conloquia et humanitatem homini daret breuiterque una cunctarum gentium in toto orbe patria fieret.

I know that I might be considered ungrateful and lazy-minded (and rightly so) if I were thus to mention briefly and in passing the land that is simultaneously the nursling and the parent of all other lands – a land which was chosen by divine will to make heaven itself more famous, to herd together scattered dominions, to soften men's manners, to unite so many peoples' dissonant and feral tongues in dialogue in a common tongue, to bring civilisation to man, and – in short – to become the one fatherland of all peoples in the whole world. (Plin. *HN* 3.39)

It has become conventional to see the totalising *Natural History* as a typical product of (and even accomplice in) Roman imperialism.[84] This particular passage is regularly cited as a typical expression of Roman imperial ideology.[85] But too little attention has been given to

[81] For *mater urbs* in the context of colonisation, see the passages cited at *TLL* s.v. *mater* 445.82–446.8.

[82] See pp. 101–4.

[83] See also the conclusion to the *Natural History*, where Italy is described as the 'ruler and second parent of the world' (*rectrix parensque mundi altera*, 37.201) – the first parent being Nature herself (e.g. 37.205). The implicit comparison is part of a broader project of equating the Roman empire with Nature's hegemony. See further Beagon 2007 p. 19, Naas 2002 p. 429 and de Saint-Denis 1972 ad *HN* 37.201.

[84] Murphy 2004, Carey 2003, Naas 2002.

[85] See e.g. Fear 2011, Kousser 2008 p. 90, Kousser 2005 p. 185, Isaac 2004 p. 169 and Braund 1996 p. 162.

the idiosyncrasies of Pliny's vision of the Roman imperial project here. This passage is distinctive in many respects – its identification of Italy not Rome as the imperial power, its focus on the cultural effects of empire,[86] its acceptance of the interdependence of centre and periphery and, not least, its deployment of the affective language of the family. Pliny's text locates itself within a literary tradition of *laudes Italiae*, in which Italy is regularly praised as a mother.[87] Virgil, for example, hailed Italy as the 'Saturnian land, great parent of both crops and men' (*salue magna parens frugum, Saturnia Tellus, magna uirum*, Verg. *G.* 2.173–4). But it is Pliny's innovation to extend the scope of Italy's maternal care from her inhabitants to the empire at large, and to represent Italy not just as a land, but as a political and cultural power that has united empires, civilised all men and become a new focus of political allegiance. Pliny uses the language of the family to express the interdependence of centre and periphery – claiming that Italy is simultaneously the nursling (*alumna*) and parent (*parens*) of all other lands.[88] Pliny here engages with the same issue of dependence on provincial resources that his nephew will in the *Panegyricus*, but in very different terms.[89] This is a distinctive vision of the imperial project, and one to which the paradigm of the family makes an important contribution.

Although it falls beyond the scope of this book, it is worth noting that maternal language plays a much more significant role in late antique representations of the relationship between centre

[86] See p. 15 n. 46.

[87] For the tradition, see Varro, *Rust.* 1.2.3–6, Verg. *G.* 2.136–76, Prop. 3.22, Strabo 6.4.1, Vitr. 6.1.10–11 and Dion. Hal. *Ant. Rom.* 1.36–7. See further Thomas 1998 pp. 179–80.

[88] Kousser 2005 p. 185 notes that *alumna* can mean nurse as well as nursling (cf. *Ciris* 441, with Lyne 1977 pp. 282–3, and Sil. *Pun.* 9.532). But the *eadem* in *alumna eadem et parens* implies that the pairing is meant to be a paradox rather than a pleonasm.

[89] See pp. 168–74. It is worth noting that even Pliny's vision of interdependence leaves room for asymmetry, in so far as *alumna* suggests the relationship of nurse (*nutrix*) and nursling as much as mother and daughter. Since the wet nurse in Roman society was often a slave, the relationship between *nutrix* and *alumnus* was often characterised by affection, but rarely by equality (see further p. 113). In the context of Chapter 2, it is also worth noting that Pliny is willing to represent the condition of the provinces in terms of enslavement elsewhere in the *Natural History.* In a discussion of the provenance of oysters, Pliny writes of a time when 'British coasts were not yet in slavery' (*nondum Britannica seruiebant litora*, Plin. *HN* 9.169). He says of the balsam tree, imported from Judaea, that 'it slaves and pays tribute with its people [i.e. the Jews]' (*seruit nunc haec ac tributa pendit cum sua gente*, Plin. *HN* 12.112) – implying that the Jews, like their flora, are in a state of servile subjection (*seruire*).

and periphery. An anonymous panegyric to Maximian from 289 CE dubs Rome the mother of his empire (*imperii uestri mater*).[90] Many similar examples can be found in the literature of the fourth century. Symmachus calls Rome the parent of all peoples (*populorum omnium parens*).[91] The poet Claudian describes her as nourishing all mankind like a mother, not like a mistress (*matris, non dominae ritu*).[92] ('Mistress' is precisely how Rome is usually described in the period covered by this book.[93]) Rutilius Namatianus calls her the 'mother of the world' (*mundi mater*) and describes the world nourishing its own nourisher (*altricemque suam fertilis orbis alat*) – a paradoxical representation of interdependence reminiscent of the elder Pliny.[94] Later texts reinterpret the iconography of Roma by representing her Amazon's breast as that of a nourishing mother.[95] It is beyond the scope of this work to consider the changed context in which these new maternal ideas of Roma proved productive, though it obviously includes both the extension of the citizenship and the

90 *illa imperii uestri mater Roma* (*Pan. Lat.* 10(2).14.4). Cf. the *Panegyric* honouring Constantine's marriage to Maximian's daughter Fausta (307 CE), which describes Rome as *sancta illa parens* (*Pan. Lat.* 7(6).11.6).

91 Symmachus, *Ep.* 3.11.3.

92 *haec est in gremium uictos quae sola recepit | humanumque genus communi nomine fouit | matris, non dominae ritu, ciuesque uocauit | quos domuit nexuque pio longinqua reuinxit* (Claud. *Cons. Stil.* 3.150–3).

93 On Roma's epithets in Latin poetry see pp. 91–2 with Christ 1938 pp. 83–9 (especially p. 85 on *Roma domina*) and the passages collected by the *TLL* s.v. *domina* 1937.23–34 and 1941.34–9. Even in the fourth century *Roma mater* does not entirely displace *Roma domina*. Cf. *quin etiam rerum dominam Latiique parentem | adpetiit bello, ducibus non freta togatis* (Auson. *Ordo nob. urb.* 53–4, describing Capua and apparently distinguishing between Rome's relationship to Latium and that to the rest of the world) and *per omnes tamen quotquot sunt partes terrarum, ut domina suscipitur et regina* (Amm. Marc. 14.6.6). See also Claud. *Cons. Stil.* 2.224, *Pan. Lat.* 10(2).14.3 and Rut. Namat. 1.194 (and *Italia domina* at Rut. Namat. 2.17 and *Pan. Lat.* 8(5).10.3 and 10(2).2.2).

94 *aeternum tibi Rhenus aret, tibi Nilus inundet,| altricemque suam fertilis orbis alat* (Rut. Namat. 1.145–6). Cf. his comparison of Stilicho and Nero: *hic immortalem, mortalem perculit ille, | hic mundi matrem perculit, ille suam* (ibid. 2.59–60).

95 Note especially Corippus, *Laud. Iust.* 1.289–90 (*exserto et nudam gestantem pectore mammam, | altricem imperii libertatisque parentem*) and Cassiod. *Var.* 2.1.2 (*ut alumnos proprios ad ubera sua Roma recolligat*). The evolution of the iconography of Roma – from Amazon in short tunic through Hadrian's canonical Roma Aeterna in long tunic to its replacement by Maxentius' Dea Roma – has been documented but not yet adequately interpreted. See especially, Mellor 1981 pp. 1011–17, Vermeule 1959, Toynbee 1953 and Toynbee 1947.

withdrawal of the emperor from Rome.[96] What matters for my purposes is that these late antique examples highlight the paucity of similar imagery in the discourse of the earlier period.

It is the language of benefaction and patronage that provides the most important alternative to the language of mastery in conceptualising and representing Roman dominance. The two modes of ruling are sometimes explicitly contrasted. The contrast between patronage and mastery can serve to distinguish Rome from other imperial powers, as for example in Livy's descriptions of Roman diplomacy. But the juxtaposition can also articulate a distinction *among* Rome's dependants, with the privileged represented as clients and the rest as slaves. And the paradigms are not always mutually exclusive. It should by now be evident that many authors use both metaphors at different points in their works, and that they can coexist even in close proximity. The paradigms of mastery and patronage complement each other in Roman discourse, each serving to emphasise different aspects of Roman power. Describing Roman power in terms of benefaction or patronage often serves to affirm Rome's commitment to her dependants or to assert a moral obligation on the part of the provinces, whereas using the language of mastery might emphasise Rome's powers of coercion, the difference between the subject peoples and their Roman rulers or the self-denying service expected from the subjects. There are particular contexts where one paradigm is more appropriate. Thus Cicero's speeches on behalf of the cities of Sicily emphasise the patronal aspect of Roman power (though allusions to mastery can be found even there). The language of slavery, on the other hand, is particularly fitted to the narratives of conquest in the historians. There is no question of a single paradigm defining Roman conceptions of empire. The coexistence of these paradigms embodies the diversity and heterogeneity of this discourse.

[96] See Roberts 2001 on how personifications and metonymic representations of Rome are reworked by Claudian and Rutilius Namatianus to reflect the cultural and religious tensions of the late fourth and early fifth centuries.

6

ADDRESSING THE ALLIES

In a speech delivered during a visit to Rome in the reign of Antoninus Pius, the famous Greek *rhetor* Aelius Aristides praised Rome for surpassing prior empires in every respect.[1] He particularly applauded the Romans for not acting like masters, as had the Persians and other imperial powers:

οὔτε ἐκεῖνοι ἄρχειν ἠπίσταντο οὔτε οἱ ἀρχόμενοι τὸ ἀκόλουθον ἀπεπλήρουν. οὐ γὰρ ἔνεστιν ἄρχεσθαι καλῶς, ὅταν κακῶς οἱ ἄρχοντες ἄρχωσιν. οὔπω γὰρ ἥ τε ἀρχὴ καὶ τὸ δεσπόζειν διῄρητο, ἀλλ᾽ ἦν ἴσον βασιλεὺς καὶ δεσπότης. οὐκοῦν εἰκότως οὐδὲ ἐπὶ μεγάλα προῆλθον· οὐ γὰρ πρόεισιν οἴκου περαιτέρω τοῦτο τὸ ὄνομα, ὅταν δ᾽ εἰς πόλεις τε καὶ ἔθνη ἀφίκηται, ῥᾳδίως παύεται.

They [the Persians] did not know how to rule nor did the subjects fulfil their duty. For it is not possible to be good subjects when the rulers rule badly. Ruling had not yet been distinguished from mastery: king and master were identical. It was thus inevitable that they did not achieve greatness, for this word ['master'] does not travel beyond the house; it is easily stopped whenever it encounters cities and peoples. (Aristid. *Or.* 26.23)

The Romans are later praised for being the first to rule over free peoples (μόνοι γὰρ τῶν πώποτε ἐλευθέρων ἄρχετε, *Or.* 26.36). Aristides is implicitly aligning himself with Aristotle in opposition to Plato's view that all government is a form of a mastery.[2] But he is also making a claim about the rhetoric of empire – insisting that an imperial power must avoid not just the practices but even the *language* (τὸ ὄνομα) of mastery in dealing with its subjects. The third-century senator and historian Cassius Dio makes a similar point in the famous speech of advice that he attributes to Maecenas at the outset of the Augustan principate, a speech which is clearly

[1] See Oliver 1953 pp. 886–7 on the date and occasion of the oration.

[2] See Arist. *Pol.* 1252a and Pl. *Plt.* 258e–259d (with Vlastos 1941 p. 293). Strictly speaking, the claim that statesman, king, master and householder are one and the same thing is not Plato's but that of the 'stranger' in the *Statesman*.

also a manifesto of reform intended for Dio's own time.[3] Among many other measures, Dio's Maecenas recommends the recruitment of worthy provincials into the senatorial and equestrian orders, saying that this will convince the subjects (οἱ ἀρχόμενοι) that they are not being treated like slaves, and so ensure their loyalty:

ὅσῳ γὰρ ἂν πλείους εὐδόκιμοι ἄνδρες συνῶσί σοι, τοσούτῳ ῥᾷον αὐτός ... τοὺς ἀρχομένους πείσεις ὅτι οὔτε ὡς δούλοις σφίσιν οὔθ' ὡς χείροσί πῃ ἡμῶν οὖσι χρῇ, ἀλλὰ τά τε ἄλλα ἀγαθὰ πάντα τὰ ὑπάρχοντα ἡμῖν καὶ τὴν ἡγεμονίαν αὐτοῖς κοινοῖ, ὅπως ὡς οἰκείαν αὐτὴν σπουδάζωσι.

The more well-regarded men who are associated with you, the more easily ... you will persuade the subjects that you are not treating them as slaves or in any way our inferiors, but that you are sharing all our privileges with them, including the empire. In this way they will value it as if it were their own. (Dio 52.19.4–5)

Dio's Maecenas is concerned that the subject peoples might think that they are regarded as *slaves* (δοῦλοι) by their Roman rulers (Maecenas' ἡμεῖς). Read in the context of the imperial rhetoric discussed in the preceding chapters, these Greek texts raise important questions about the representation of Roman power to the provinces. How were Rome's provincial subjects addressed by the officials who governed them? What categories did the centre impose on the population of the periphery? To what extent were they addressed as a class of subject peoples, or even slaves?

One way to answer these questions is to observe how emperors and provincial governors communicated with provincial audiences. Imperial pronouncements take several standard forms: speeches, oral decisions (*decreta*), letters, edicts and *subscriptiones*.[4] Particularly significant for my purposes are the letters that the emperors wrote to the cities of the empire (as well as synods of athletes and performers and some privileged individuals). The vast majority of these letters are responses to municipal

[3] Much of what 'Maecenas' advises would have constituted more or less radical reform in Dio's own time (Reinhold 1988 pp. 180–2 and Millar 1964 pp. 108–18). Exactly which emperor it was written for, and how close Dio was to him, remain controversial questions. Millar argues for a date in the middle of Caracalla's reign, Reinhold for a date under Severus Alexander.

[4] The taxonomy of imperial pronouncements ('constitutions') was established by Wilcken 1920. There are useful overviews in Oliver 1989 pp. 1–24 and Millar 1977 pp. 203–59.

decrees, which were usually conveyed to the emperor by an embassy from the community concerned. Decrees were sent on a wide variety of occasions: to congratulate the emperor on his accession, the birth of a son, the co-option of a colleague or successor, or a victory; to commend the conduct of a governor or local notable; to ask the emperor to intercede in a dispute with other communities; to request the confirmation of privileges; and often for several of these combined.[5] The imperial letters are important both because they devote considerable space to the rhetorical elaboration of the relationship between ruler and ruled and because they survive in relatively large numbers. We have copies, albeit often fragmentary, of some three hundred imperial letters from my period (almost exclusively from the East of the empire – a problem I return to below).[6] Rarer, but still significant, are the imperial edicts. These were used for communication to wider audiences – groups of cities, entire provinces or even the empire as a whole – for which the letter form seems to have been considered inappropriate.[7] Around thirty edicts of emperors from Augustus to Caracalla survive from throughout the empire.[8] We also have a handful of examples of imperial orations to provincial audiences, notably the text of Nero's proclamation of Greek freedom at the

5 Oliver 1989 pp. 11–15 surveys the themes of the surviving letters. For more on the dialogue between the emperor and the cities, see Eck 2009a, Eilers 2009, Millar 1988 and Millar 1977 ch. 7 (esp. pp. 410–34).

6 Oliver 1989 provides the texts of 191 Greek letters of Roman emperors from Augustus to Caracalla. A further 91 are catalogued by Anastasiadis and Souris 2000 pp. 2–12. Subsequent discoveries include *AE* 1999 1523 = *SEG* 49 1149 (Augustus to Samos), *AE* 2006 1403 = *SEG* 56 1359 (three letters of Hadrian to the Dionysiac artists), *AE* 2006 1369 = *SEG* 51 641 (Hadrian to Lokrian Naryka) and *AE* 2004 1423–4 = *SEG* 55 1415–16 (two letters of Hadrian to Hierapolis). For the handful of Latin letters, see n. 53 below.

7 On the use of edicts, see Oliver 1989 pp. 18–21 and Williams 1975 pp. 43–7.

8 Benner 1975 pp. ix–xi and Williams 1975 pp. 44–5 list 26 'edicts' between them (Williams lists only 22, but includes one not in Benner's list of 25) – though not all can be conclusively identified as edicts. One of these, the edict of Severus Alexander on the *aurum coronarium*, is from outside my period. A further 8 texts bring to 33 the number of certain and possible edicts from Augustus to Carcalla: Alföldy 2000 = *AE* 2000 760 (two Augustan edicts from Bierzo), *P Mich.* VII 432 (Domitian on citizenship and *conubium* for veterans of *legio* XXII), Hauken and Malay 2009 (Hadrian on abuse of *vehiculatio* in Asia), *AE* 2005 1348 = *SEG* 55 744 (Hadrian on abuse of *vehiculatio* at Abdera and Maroneia), *P Harr.* II 202 (Pertinax on immunity for veterans), Oliver 254 (Severus and Caracalla on the collection of taxes from sons, fathers, etc.) and Oliver 252 (another fragmentary edict on the same subject).

Isthmian Games in 67 CE.[9] Imperial *subscriptiones* – short replies appended to petitions (*libelli*) from individuals and minor communities – survive in much larger numbers, but their extreme brevity precludes any elaboration on the character of imperial rule.[10] Besides these imperial pronouncements, we have the texts of almost ninety edicts and dozens of letters issued by provincial governors to the communities under their control.[11]

The vast majority of these texts derive from the Greek East and are, with few exceptions, written in Greek.[12] This raises the question of whether the Greek texts we have are original documents written by Roman officials or local translations of documents received in Latin. In the case of the letters, it is almost certain that they were dispatched in Greek. The existence of an imperial secretary for Greek letters (*ab epistulis Graecis*), the consistency of form and language across the surviving letters and the existence of other dossiers in which letters in Greek are inscribed alongside other documents in Latin (usually letters which circulated within the Roman administration) all point in this direction.[13] The situation

[9] Nero: Oliver 296 = Smallwood *GCN* 64. Two damaged papyri purport to record fragments of speeches to the people of Alexandria by Germanicus and Vespasian (?) respectively (Oliver 295 = *P Oxy.* 2435 *recto*; Oliver 297). A fragmentary inscription from Cyrene (Oliver 122) may be a speech by the emperor Hadrian to the Cyrenaeans. Note also *P Oxy.* 2435 *verso* (part of a transcript of Augustus' reception of an embassy from Alexandria) and *SEG* 17 759 (part of a transcript of a hearing by Caracalla in Antioch). There are of course other imperial speeches delivered in Rome or to the armies, but they are not relevant here.

[10] Some 2,500 *subscriptiones* of Hadrianic date or later survive in the Theodosian and Justinian codes. The similar brevity of the handful of *subscriptiones* that survive on papyrus (Turpin 1991 pp. 106–9) and stone (Hauken 1998, Turpin 1991 pp. 109–14, Williams 1986) shows that the lack of preamble is not just a result of compilation.

[11] Surviving praesidial edicts from outside Egypt are catalogued by Meyer-Zwiffelhoffer 2003 pp. 342–3 and Nigdelis and Souris 2005 pp. 119–26 (reproduced in *SEG* 55 2001). For edicts of the Prefect of Egypt, see Katzoff 1980 pp. 810–19, listing 59 edicts from 4 BCE to the end of the fourth century. See also Purpura 1992 (*non vidi*). There is no existing catalogue of praesidial letters. Examples are cited where relevant.

[12] For the few imperial pronouncements in Latin, see pp. 226 n. 53 and 227 n. 60.

[13] Millar 1977 pp. 227–8 concludes that imperial letters were probably sent in Greek. Sherk 1969 pp. 208–9 reaches a similar conclusion about Republican letters. On the *ab epistulis Graecis*, first attested under Nero but with evidence of a similar function under Claudius, see Millar 1977 pp. 86–8 and 226. For letters in Greek inscribed alongside other texts in Latin, see e.g. *CIL* III 7086 (letters of Trajan and a governor to Pergamum in Greek adjoined to a rescript of Trajan to the proconsul and a *senatus consultum* in Latin), *IGRR* IV 571 (a letter of a Hadrianic governor to Aezani in Greek followed by three Latin letters between the emperor, governor and procurator) Oliver 192 (a Greek letter of Marcus

is more complicated for edicts – particularly those issued to the empire at large. The latter were presumably composed originally in Latin (and in two cases we have Latin copies from the East), but they may well have been translated into Greek, either in Rome or on receipt by the governor, for circulation in the East.[14] As for edicts of narrower scope, those addressed to audiences in the East are likely to have been issued in Greek, as letters were.[15]

A second problem concerns dissemination: how did these Roman pronouncements reach the ears (or eyes) of provincials?[16] Imperial letters and edicts were apparently recited publicly upon reception in the cities. A letter of Claudius to the city of Alexandria was published by the Prefect of Egypt because he was concerned that some citizens had been unable to attend the public reading (ἀνάγνωσις) due to the size of the population.[17] An edict of Marcus Aurelius anticipates a similar reading (τὸ ἀναγνωσθ[ῆναι]) at

Aurelius to Miletus in Greek forwarding a copy of an imperial speech in Latin), *CIL* III 13750 (a Greek letter of Commodus (?) to Chersonesus in Greek followed by a Latin letter to officers stationed there) and *ILS* 423 (a letter of a governor to Tyre in Greek following two Latin letters of Severus and Caracalla to Roman officials). If the Greek texts of the imperial and praesidial letters were local translations of documents originally received in Latin, why did the individuals and communities who erected these monuments not translate the other imperial documents as well?

14 So Williams 1975 52–5. The two Latin edicts from the East are Claudius' edict on the *vehiculatio* (Smallwood *GCN* 375 = *ILS* 214) from Tegea (only the beginning of the text survives, so we do not know whether it was followed by a Greek translation) and the edict of Nero (?) on delays in appeals in criminal cases (*FIRA* 91, a papyrus copy from the Arsinoite nome; we do not know the purpose for which the text was copied or the location of the exemplar from which it was copied).

15 So Williams 1975 p. 52 and Eck 2009b pp. 23–4. Of almost 100 imperial edicts of local application and praesidial edicts that survive from the East, all bar three are in Greek. The only monolingual Latin edict of which I am aware, that of L. Antistius Rusticus (93 CE, McCrum–Woodhead 464), was issued to a Roman colony (Pisidian Antioch). However, we do have four praesidial edicts which were inscribed in both Greek and Latin copies: three from Asia – edicts of Paulus Fabius Maximus (*c.* 9 CE, *RDGE* 65), Paullus Fabius Persicus (Claudian, Smallwood *GCN* 380) and T. Aurelius Fulvus Boeonius Antoninus (the future emperor Pius, 134–6 CE, *AE* 1994 1645 b and d) and one from Galatia – that of Sextus Sotidius Strabo Libuscidianus (Tiberian, Mitchell 1976). This shows that at least some governors issued edicts in Greek and Latin simultaneously (or, less likely, in Latin alone). The issuance of edicts in Greek is consistent with the conclusions of Kaimio 1979 pp. 110–29 that most of the Roman administration's dealings with the native population in the Eastern provinces was in Greek.

16 On the publication of these documents, see further Ando 2000 pp. 80–117 and Eck 1998a.

17 Oliver 19 l 2–11.

Athens.[18] Some or all letters may also have been posted as texts, as was the case with that of Claudius to Alexandria. This was certainly the case for edicts, many of which explicitly provide for such publication. The norm seems to have been temporary posting in a conspicuous place on a whitened wooden board (*album* or λεύκωμα) or papyrus.[19] A key point is that there is little evidence of the Roman authorities insisting on a more permanent medium. Most of the letters and edicts that survive do so because they were inscribed on stone (others were copied on to papyrus for private use). It was certainly not the norm for Roman pronouncements to be monumentalised in this way. The surviving texts were inscribed (or copied) on local initiative and for local purposes.[20] A permanent and public copy of the emperor's words might help a city assert its prestige and privileges or an individual to publicise his participation in an embassy or commendation by the emperor. This is a problem I will return to.

This chapter examines the terms in which the inhabitants of the provinces are addressed in this corpus of imperial and praesidial pronouncements. This is certainly not the first study to consider the language of these texts. But most work has focused on formal and stylistic aspects.[21] The most significant exception is Clifford Ando's work on Roman rhetoric in his massive narrative of the process by which provincials came to identify with Rome's imperial

[18] Oliver 184, 37–8. A late third-century Rabbinic midrash describes the ritual of receiving an imperial pronouncement in the provinces: 'They rose to their feet, uncovered their heads and read it in awe, fear, trembling and trepidation' (Lieberman 1944 p. 7). In the fourth century, John Chrysostom exhorts Christians to listen to the Bible with the same formality, silence and awe with which they are accustomed to listen to the emperor's rescripts (*Homilia in genesim* 14.2).

[19] See e.g. Joseph. *AJ* 19. 291 (providing for publication for 30 days) and Oliver 38, 19 (providing for posting ἐν λευκώματι). See Meyer 2004 174 n. 21 on the use of whitened boards for the edicts of the Prefect of Egypt. On the importance of wood as an epigraphic medium, see further Eck 1998b.

[20] See especially Eck 1998a on the motivations that determined the selective monumentalisation – and hence survival – of official documents.

[21] Formal and stylistic aspects are analysed by Oliver 1989 pp. 1–24. Benner 1975 analyses the 'persuasive style' of Roman edicts in general (though her assimilation of edicts addressed to citizens and to provincials obscures some important differences). Williams 1979, Williams 1976 and Alexander 1938 attempt to find idiosyncrasies in the pronouncements of particular emperors. More attention is given to the political significance of these texts by Kokkinia 2004, a brief but suggestive survey of four inscriptions which illustrate the range of different postures adopted by provincial governors in their communications to their subjects.

project – 'the transformation of empire from an *imperium*, a collection of conquered provinces, into a *patria*, a focus for the patriotic loyalty of its subjects', as he describes it (xi). The book as a whole seeks to show that Rome promised, delivered, and was credited with delivering, universal benefits to the empire as a whole.[22] Scattered throughout it are many valuable insights into the rhetoric of official discourse and its ideological implications. Stressing the importance of the ideal of consensus within Roman imperial ideology, Ando argues that from the very beginning of the principate emperors based their claims to legitimacy on the expression of loyalty by all their subjects, including provincial non-citizens (ch. 5). Although Ando chooses to highlight the divisive effect of this 'culture of consensus', arguing that the system of soliciting expressions of consensus from individual communities ensured that the general population was united only in its loyalty to the emperor (135), it must also have worked to promote a vision of the empire as a community of cities, rather than a population divided into rulers and ruled. Ando further suggests that there was a gradual shift in official discourse, by which the idea of the princeps as first citizen was displaced by the image of 'an emperor over many who were equal in their subordination to him' (46). Official discourse, he argues, gradually began to 'interpellate' the inhabitants of the empire as individual subjects of the emperor, encouraging them to think of others (including their governors) as being equally subject (46). ('Interpellation' is borrowed from Althusser.[23] The neologism has the useful function of highlighting the ideological importance of the categories that the state imposes on its subjects.) Ando is vague on the timing of this development, but he suggests elsewhere that Hadrian is the pivotal figure. Where Augustus had sought to maintain a 'great gulf' between citizens and subjects within the empire (299–300, 303, 320), Hadrian 'brought imperial ideology in line with the

[22] Ando 2000. Monumental in scale, Ando's argument is not without its flaws. It is vague on the chronological parameters of the process it describes (the one exception being ch. 8) and pays little attention to legal, social and ethnic divisions within the population of the provinces. But there is no denying that Ando has sketched the outlines of a process which brought about a profound shift in the political loyalties of *at least some* provincials – including non-citizens of relatively low status.

[23] Althusser 1970 uses the term to describe the mechanism by which all ideology constitutes individuals as concrete subjects, obtaining from them 'the recognition that they really do occupy the place it designates for them as theirs in the world' (p. 178).

worldview espoused by provincial intellectuals' (330) and was the first emperor to promote actively an 'ideology of unification' (40–1).

For all its merits, Ando's analysis of official discourse is less than systematic and his claims are sometimes poorly documented (which is perhaps inevitable given the book's extraordinarily broad scope).[24] This chapter will show that his arguments can be both reinforced and nuanced by a more systematic analysis of imperial pronouncements – particularly by looking closely at the categories with which the inhabitants of the provinces are interpellated by their Roman rulers. It will show that these imperial texts do indeed work to obscure any distinctions within the population of the empire. They employ an ecumenical rhetoric that portrays the emperor as the beneficent ruler of the whole human race. But this is not a late development. It is already present in the pronouncements of Augustus and his governors, and has its origins in the Hellenistic discourse that provides the model for the imperial letters. This chapter will also show that this ecumenical style coexists with a more divisive rhetoric. Other imperial texts do insist on the distinction between the Roman people and its allies. And these distinctions persist well beyond the reign of Hadrian and are still to be found in some pronouncements of Severan date. There are more internal contradictions in official discourse in all periods than Ando suggests. These contradictions reflect both the different Roman and Greek traditions that lie behind the imperial pronouncements and a tension between the imperial aspect of Roman identity and the culture of loyalism to the emperor.

The emperor and the cities

One of the earliest surviving imperial letters is that of Augustus to the city of Sardis in Lydia, written in 5 BCE:

[24] For example, Ando repeatedly asserts that the emperors advertised their benefits as universal (e.g. at pp. 47, 51, 65, 79, 176, 337 and 373), but the supporting evidence is essentially limited to the fifth Cyrene edict (pp. 143–5) and pronouncements on the subject of the *aurum coronarium* (pp. 175–90). As I will show, the former is far from representative of the surviving corpus of imperial pronouncements, while the latter date from the third century and later.

αὐτοκράτωρ Καῖσαρ θεοῦ υἱὸ<ς> Σεβα<σ>τὸς ἀρχιερεὺς δημαρχικῆς ἐκξουσίας ιθ', Σαρδιανῶν ἄρχουσι βουλῆι χαίρειν·

οἱ πρέσβεις ὑμῶν Ἰόλλας τε Μητροδώρου καὶ Μηνογένης Ἰσιδώρου τοῦ Μηνογένους συνέτυχον ἐν Ῥώμῃ μοι καὶ τὸ παρ' ὑμῶν ψήφισμα ἀπέδοσαν δι' οὗ τά τε δόξαντα ὑμεῖν περὶ ὑμῶν δηλοῦντες καὶ συνήδεσθε ἐπὶ τῆι τελειώσει τοῦ πρεσβυτέρου μου τῶν παίδων· ἐπαινῶ οὖν ὑμᾶς φιλοτειμουμένους ἀνθ' ὧν εὐεργετῆσθε ὑπ' ἐμοῦ εὐχαρίστους ἀτοὺς εἴς τε ἐμὲ καὶ τοὺς ἐμοὺς πάντας ἐνδείκνυσθαι· ἔρρωσθε.

Imperator Caesar, son of the god, Augustus, *pontifex maximus*, holding *tribunicia potestas* for the 19th time, to the leaders and council of Sardis, greetings.

Your ambassadors Iollas, son of Metrodoros, and Menogenes, son of Isidoros son of Menogenes, met me in Rome and passed on your decree. They used it to show me what you have resolved about your own affairs and to demonstrate that you rejoice with me at the coming of age of the elder of my sons. I therefore commend your eagerness to show yourselves grateful – both to me and to my whole family – for the favours you have received from me. Farewell. (Oliver 7 = *RDGE* 68 = Ehrenberg–Jones 99)

As the letter itself reveals, it was written in response to a decree passed by the city and delivered to the emperor by an embassy. Augustus acknowledges the Sardians' efforts to display (δηλοῦντες, ἐνδείκνυσθαι) their shared pleasure (συνήδεσθαι) at his good fortune and their gratitude for his euergetism. He assures them of his own approval in return (ἐπαινῶ). It is worth noting that the text of the letter survives only because it was subsequently inscribed on a stele which contained a dossier of twelve documents honouring Menogenes, son of Isidoros.[25] The value of this particular text presumably lay in its testimony to his service on an embassy to the emperor.

Two centuries later, Septimius Severus and his son and co-emperor Caracalla sent a letter to the city of Nicopolis ad Istrum in Moesia Inferior (198 CE):

Αὐτοκράτωρ Καῖσαρ . . . Λούκιος Σεπτίμιος Σευῆρος Εὐσεβὴς Περτίναξ Σεβαστὸς Ἀραβικὸς Ἀδιαβηνικὸς Παρθικὸς μέγιστος . . . καὶ Αὐτοκράτωρ Καῖσαρ . . . Μᾶρκος Αὐρήλιος Ἀντωνεῖνος Σεβαστός . . . Νεικοπολειτῶν τῶν πρὸς Ἴστρῳ τοῖς ἄρχουσιν καὶ τῇ βουλῇ καὶ τῷ δήμῳ χαίρ[ει]ν·[26]

[25] See *IGRR* IV 1756 for the full dossier.

[26] I have had the temerity to abbreviate the august emperors' *praescriptio*, which in its full form takes up 20 of the inscription's 37 lines.

φανερωτάτην προθυμίαν ὑμῶν εἴδομεν διὰ τοῦ ψηφίσματος· ὡς γὰρ εὖνοι καὶ εὐσεβεῖς [ἄν]δρες καὶ τὴν ἀμείνω σπουδάζοντες ὑμεῖν ὑπάρχειν παρ᾿ ἡμεῖν κρίσιν οὕτως ἐδηλώσατε τοῖς παροῦσιν συνησθέντες καὶ δημοσίαν ἀγαγόντες ἑορτὴν ἐπὶ τοῖς τῶν ἡμετέρων ἀγαθῶν [εὐ]ανγέλμασι εἰρήνης τε πανδήμου πᾶσιν ἀνθρώποις ὑπαρχούσης τῇ τῶν ἀεὶ θρασυν[ο]μένων περὶ τὴν ἀρχὴν βαρβάρων ἥττῃ καὶ ἡμῶν ἐ[ν] δικαίαι κοινωνίαι συνεζευγμένων, Καίσαρα ἐχόντων οἰκεῖον καὶ γνήσιον. διὸ τὸ ψήφισμα μετὰ τῆς προσεκούσης περὶ ὑμᾶς τειμῆς ἀνέγνωμεν καὶ τὴν συντέλειαν τῶν χρημάτων τὰς ἑβδομήκοντα μυριάδας ὡς παρὰ ἀνδρῶν εὔνων προσηκά[μ]εθα. τὸ ψήφισμα ἔπεμψεν Ὀουίνιος Τέρτυλλος ὁ κράτιστος φίλος ἡμῶν καὶ πρεσβευτής. εὐτυχῶς.

Imperator Caesar Lucius Septimius Severus Pius Pertinax Augustus Arabicus Adiabenicus Parthicus Maximus ... and Imperator Caesar Marcus Aurelius Antoninus Augustus ... to the magistrates, council and people of the Nicopolitans by the Ister, greetings.

We saw your conspicuous zeal in your decree. That you are men of goodwill and piety who are eager for us to have the better opinion of you, you have demonstrated by sharing our joy at present circumstances and celebrating a public festival on account of the announcement of our good fortune, the existence of universal peace for all men through the defeat of the ever insolent barbarians surrounding the empire and our being yoked together in a just partnership by having a Caesar who is of our own house and legitimate. We have therefore read the decree with the proper esteem for you and accepted your money contribution of 700,000 [denarii] as from men of goodwill. The *clarissimus* Ovinius Tertullus, our friend and legate, forwarded the decree.[27] Farewell. (Oliver 217)

Again the emperors write in reply to a city decree and emphasise the city's efforts to display (φανερωτάτη, ἐδηλώσατε) its virtues. The Nicopolitans are commended for sharing the emperor's joy at his successes (συνήδεσθαι again) and for their προθυμία (zeal), εὔνοια (goodwill) and εὐσέβεια (piety). In return the emperors profess their own esteem for (τίμη) and good opinion of (κρίσις) the city. Like the letter to Sardis, this letter survives because it was later inscribed. In this case, however, the broken limestone stele lacks the context that might tell us what purpose it served.

The two letters quoted are somewhat unusual in containing no imperial decision that might be of concrete interest to the cities concerned. Many of the surviving letters communicate a grant or

[27] Whereas the Samian decree had been delivered by an embassy, this decree was forwarded by the governor. The latter practice became common in the late second century (see Oliver 1989 p. 9), though many decrees continued to be delivered by ambassadors from the city.

favour of some kind, if only the confirmation of existing privileges, in addition to the assurances of mutual goodwill. Yet letters such as those to Sardis and Nicopolis highlight the value that both parties placed on the dialogue itself – the ritualistic reaffirmation of the cities' loyalty and the emperor's favour – above and beyond any concrete decisions. Testifying as they do to the production of a civic decree, its conveyance to Rome often by an embassy recruited from the local elite, and its presentation to the emperor; the composition of an imperial response in the appropriate high style, its return journey to the city, publication in some form and in some cases monumentalisation in stone or bronze; the repetition of this process at various points in the reign of each emperor and its multiplication across the cities of the empire – all this represents a massive investment in symbolic production on the part of both the emperors and the cities. As such, these letters are a key source for the symbolic dimension of Roman power.[28]

The juxtaposition of the two letters also highlights the continuity of imperial rhetoric across the two centuries that separate them. Throughout the surviving letters, cities are praised for showing goodwill (εὔνοια), piety (εὐσέβεια) and zeal (προθυμία, σπουδή) and for rejoicing with the emperor.[29] In return, the emperors profess their own goodwill, concern, zeal and affection for the

[28] Ma 2002 ch. 4 is a brilliant analysis of the diverse interests served by an earlier form of this euergetic discourse in Seleucid Asia Minor. Ma argues that the discourse served the Seleucid king by legitimising his authority (through the representation of rule as benefaction and the dissimulation of coercion) and by channelling his subjects' energy into petition rather than resistance. At the same time, the cities endorsed the discourse as a means of manipulating the king and socialising his officials by projecting a norm of reciprocity and euergetism.

[29] εὔνοια: Oliver 1, 3 (Augustus); 13, 8–9 (Tiberius); 19 II, 22 (Claudius); 28, 26 (Claudius); 296 (Nero), Oliver 78 B, 61 (Hadrian); 157, 8 (Marcus Aurelius); 185, 3 (Avidius Cassius); 217, 22 and 35 (Septimius Severus and Caracalla). εὐσέβεια: Oliver 18, 25 (Gaius); 19, 23 and 33; 23, 5; 27, 14; 29, 8–9; 30, 4 (all Claudius); 296, 1–2 (Nero); *SEG* 42 1164, 2 (unknown, *c.* 100 CE); Oliver 217, 22 (Septimius Severus and Caracalla). σπουδή: Oliver 19, 25 and 23, 4–5 (both Claudius). προθυμία: Oliver 217, 21 (Septimius Severus and Caracalla). For the rhetoric of shared joy (συνήδεσθαι, ἥδεσθαι, ἡδονή, χαρά, εὐφραίνεσθαι) see Oliver 7, 25 (Augustus); Oliver 58 B, 11–13 and 64, 8 (Hadrian); Oliver 115, 8 (Antoninus Pius); Oliver 157, 8–9 and 166, 66 (Marcus Aurelius); Oliver 167, 5 (Marcus Aurelius and Lucius Verus); Oliver 212A, 8 and 213, 12 (Septimius Severus); Oliver 217, 5 and 219, 2 (Septimius Severus and Caracalla); Oliver 244, 10 (Caracalla). Here and elsewhere in this section I have included a few edicts and speeches to highlight the continuity in imperial rhetoric through my period.

city concerned and advertise their euergetism.[30] The explanation for this continuity lies in the fact that these letters are following a script that was already well established in the time of Augustus. Like Republican magistrates before him, Augustus was not just writing in Greek but appropriating the forms and idioms of a long tradition of Hellenistic diplomacy.[31] The structure of a dialogue articulated through city decrees and imperial letters, the letter form, and the rhetoric of benevolence and euergetism all follow a pattern that had been established by the Hellenistic kings. The discourse did not remain entirely unchanged in Roman hands. The most striking innovation is the praise of cities for their piety (εὐσέβεια) towards the emperor and his house. While the kings had often mentioned εὐσέβεια, it was always owed to the gods, never to themselves.[32] It is claimed for Roman emperors from the beginning of the principate.[33] Nevertheless, the paradigm of power implicit in this discourse remains distinctly Greek. The emperors speak the long-established language of Greek euergetism – a language that has no place for a rhetoric of mastery.

Even more significant for my purposes is the fact that neither letter makes any mention of the Romans or the Roman people. In this respect they are entirely typical of the surviving imperial letters. Almost without exception, the virtues for which the cities are commended concern their attitude to the emperor and his family. They are praised for showing goodwill, piety and zeal towards the emperor and his house (εἰς/πρός με, ἐμέ, ἐμαυτόν, τὸν ἐμὸν οἶκον). They are expected to share the emperor's joy at his *personal* successes – accession to the throne, the birth of sons, and

[30] Imperial εὔνοια: Oliver 1, 5 (Augustus) and Oliver 34, 25–6 (Nero). πρόνοια: Oliver 19 II, 103 (Claudius), Oliver 297, 6 (Vespasian). σπουδή: Joseph. *AJ* 20.10 (Claudius); Oliver 184 II, 57 (Marcus Aurelius). Vespasian assures the Alexandrians of his exceptional disposition towards them (ἐξαίρετος διάθεσις, Oliver 297, 7–9); Trajan assures them of his special regard (διάθεσις ἰδία, Oliver 46, 10); Caracalla declares his love for Ephesus (φίλτρον, Oliver 244, 13). For the ubiquitous rhetoric of euergetism, see Anastasiadis and Souris 2000 s.v. χάριτες, φιλάνθρωπα and εὐεργεσίαι.

[31] Welles 1934 collects royal letters of the Hellenistic period. The tropes and functions of this discourse are elucidated by Ma 2002 ch. 4 in the context of Seleucid Asia Minor. See also Bertrand 1990 and Welles 1934. Sherk 1969 p. 188–9 discusses Rome's use of the conventions of Hellenistic diplomacy before the Principate.

[32] Welles 9, 7; 26, 14–15; 36, 7; 44, 28; 62, 5; 65, 4; 66, 11; 67, 4 (cf. ibid. 2 and 12).

[33] See Mourgues 1995a pp. 114–15.

the co-option of heirs as well as military victories. Conversely, the emperors profess their own personal goodwill, concern, zeal and affection for the city concerned and describe the privileges and concessions they grant as their own, personal 'favours' (χάριτες, φιλάνθρωπα, εὐεργεσίαι). This focus on the emperor is in striking contrast to documents of the Republican period, when Romans writing to Greek cities had praised them for their goodwill (εὔνοια) and loyalty (πίστις) towards 'the Roman people', 'us' or 'our empire' and for their services to the *res publica* (τὰ δημόσια πράγματα) of the Romans.[34] Such references all but disappear in the Principate. Only four imperial letters (of which three are of Severan date) make any reference to loyalty or services to the Roman people.[35] Indeed, in the almost three hundred imperial letters that survive in whole or in part, there are only ten references of any kind to 'Romans' or 'the Roman people'. Besides the four letters just mentioned, one letter distinguishes between 'Romans' (citizens) and 'Greeks' (non-citizens).[36] Three others refer to Roman citizenship ('the citizenship of the Romans', Oliver 28, 29–30), Roman law ('the law of the Romans', *AE* 2000 1441, 9) and the senate ('a senator of the Roman people', Oliver 256, 7–8). The last two are too fragmentary to say more than that they contained some reference to 'the Roman people' (Oliver 107, 4–5 and Oliver 180). It is worth noting that the letters do, however, regularly

34 πρὸς ἡμᾶς: *RDGE* 14, 51–2; 18, 5 and 11; 34, 25 and 49, B1. πρὸς τὸν δῆμον τὸν Ῥωμαίων: *RDGE* 18, 45. πρὸς τὴν ἡμετέραν ἡγεμονίαν: *RDGE* 18, 4. περὶ τῶν δημοσίων πραγμάτων τοῦ δήμου τοῦ Ῥωμαίων: *RDGE* 18, 8–9 and 58, 16–17.

35 A fragmentary letter of an unidentified first- or second-century emperor to Chersonesus commends the city for its zealous management of matters concerning (the) Romans ([. . . ὅτι τὰ] περὶ Ῥωμαίους προθ[ύμως ἐπεμελήθητε], Solomonik 1964–73 14, 2). The Severans praise Delphi for showing '[zeal and] enthusiasm towards the empire of the Romans' (πρὸς τὴν Ῥωμαίω[ν ἀρχὴν . . .] ἐδείκνυ[εν πᾶσαν σπουδὴν καὶ πρ]οθυμίαν, Oliver 205, 15), Aezani for being a city 'long of service to the empire of the Romans' ([πό]λις ὄντες . . . ἐκ παλαιο[ῦ τῇ τῶν Ῥω]μαίων ἀρχῇ χρήσιμ[ο]ς, Oliver 213, 19–21) and Aphrodisias for 'exceeding all other peoples in attachment to the empire of the Romans' (τῇ Ῥωμαίων ἀρχῇ μᾶλλον ἄλλων προσήκοντας, *A&R* 18 = Oliver 219, 3–5). Similar language can also be found in two imperial edicts cited by Josephus (on which see n. 68 below): an edict of Augustus on the privileges of the Jews praises them for being grateful to the Roman people (εὐχάριστον . . . πρὸς τὸν δῆμον τὸν Ῥωμαίων, Joseph. *AJ* 16.162); Claudius' edict on the privileges of the Jews of the empire similarly commends them for their loyalty and friendship 'to the Romans' διὰ τὴν πρὸς Ῥωμαίους πίστιν καὶ φιλίαν (Joseph. *AJ* 19.289).

36 Oliver 74, 4. This is Hadrian's letter on the question of whether the head of the Epicurean School at Athens had to be a Roman citizen. See further pp. 234–5.

refer to Rome as the place of writing – thus affirming the city's place at the symbolic centre of the empire.[37]

A corollary of the lack of mention of any imperial people (whether 'the Roman people', 'Romans', or a simple 'us') is the total absence of the categories that are the subject of this book – 'the allies' and 'the provinces'. These terms are never used in the surviving letters. Indeed, with the exception of the aforementioned letter distinguishing between 'Romans' and 'Greeks', there is no hint of any dichotomy within the population of the empire. On the contrary, the very structure of this discourse – composed as it is of texts exchanged between the emperor and individual communities – focuses on the particularities of each city's relationship to the emperor. It implies that any hierarchy within the population of the empire reflects a continuum of more and less privileged communities rather than a sharp divide between rulers and subjects.

Whenever the emperors do broaden their focus beyond the particular community to which they are writing, they tend to use universalising categories rather than dichotomies. In their letters to individual cities, the emperors regularly refer to 'the cities' or 'the other cities', thus addressing their subjects as part of a community of cities.[38] Even more striking is the ecumenical style that appears in imperial pronouncements from the very beginning of the principate. Augustus professes his reverence 'for all men' (πρὸς πάντας ἀνθρώπους).[39] Tiberius tells the citizens of Gythium that it is proper both for their city and for 'all men' (πάντας ἀνθρώπους) to give divine honours to the late Augustus on account of his benefactions 'to the whole world' (εἰς ἅπαντα τὸν κόσμον).[40] This language persists through to the end of my period, when Septimius Severus and Caracalla can be found boasting of providing peace to 'all men' (πᾶσιν ἀνθρώποις, in the letter quoted earlier) and establishing peace for the 'whole world' (πᾶσαν τὴν οἰκουμένην).[41]

37 See Anastasiadis and Souris 2000 pp. 214–15 for the regular appearance of ἐν Ῥώμηι or ἀπὸ Ῥώμης at the end of letters.

38 *AE* 1995 1498 = *SEG* 45 1605, 4 (Trajan); Oliver 75 II, 4–5 and Hauken and Malay 2009, 39–40 (both Hadrian); Oliver 149, 7–8; 150, 7; 152, 8; 165, 40 (all Pius); 187, 11–12 (second century); 223 B, 6 (Severus and Caracalla).

39 Joseph. *AJ* 16.165. On the historicity of this and other edicts in Josephus, see n. 68 below.

40 Oliver 15, II 17–19.

41 Oliver 217, 27–8 and *A&R* 18 = Oliver 219, 2–3.

The emperors' ecumenical rhetoric is echoed in the official pronouncements of other Roman officials. Far from representing themselves as members of an imperial people, Roman governors write to the cities as fellow subjects of a divine and beneficent emperor (and, occasionally, as benefactors in their own right).[42] Provincial governors praise the emperor as a benevolent benefactor and commend the cities for their piety towards him.[43] They use the same ecumenical language as the emperor, describing him as the beneficent ruler of all mankind and giving no hint of any divide within the population of the empire. As early as 10 BCE, Paullus Fabius Maximus, governor of Asia, calls Augustus 'the common good fortune of all men'.[44] In a speech to the Alexandrians, Germanicus styles Tiberius 'the true saviour and benefactor of the whole human race'.[45] Paullus' son Paullus Fabius Persicus, himself governor of Asia under Claudius, writes that the emperor 'has taken the whole human race under his particular care'.[46] Nero, says Pomponius Pius (Moesia) 'cares for all men'.[47] Tiberius Julius Alexander (Egypt) declares that Galba 'shines on us for the salvation of the whole human race'.[48] M. Sempronius Liberalis (Egypt) praises Antoninus Pius for his 'care for all men'.[49] The Severans, writes Q. Caecilius Secundus Servilianus (Asia), 'desire their

[42] For the euergetical style in praesidial pronouncements, see e.g. *AE* 1993 1468–70 = *SEG* 43, 765–7, *passim* (three letters of P. Petronius to Ephesus, 29–32 CE) and Smallwood *GCN* 384, 34–5 (Pomponius Pius to Histria, 67–8 CE).

[43] On the emperor's benefactions, see e.g. Paullus Fabius Maximus (governor of Asia) on Augustus' εὐεργετήματα (*RDGE* 65, 17), Lucius Aemilius Rectus (Egypt) on Claudius' εὐεργετικωτάτη ἐπιστολή (Oliver 19, 3–4), Avidius Quietus (Asia) on Hadrian's φιλάνθρωπον (*IGRR* IV 571, 8), Ovinius Tertullus (Moesia Inferior) on the divine munificence (θεία μεγαλοδωρία) of Severus and Caracalla (*ILS* 423, 39–40) and C. Sicinnius Clarus (Thrace) on the divine bounty (θεία δωρεά) of the same (*SIG*^{3} 880, 25–6). Commending provincial εὐσέβεια: Smallwood *GCN* 384, 47–8 (Plautius Aelianus, governor of Moesia under Nero) and *SEG* 27 740, 5–6 (Venuleius Apronianus, Asia under Pius).

[44] τὸ κοινὸν πάντων εὐτύχημα (*RDGE* 65, 8–9).

[45] τῷ σωτῆρι ὄντως καὶ εὐεργέτῃ τοῦ σύμπαντος τῶν ἀνθρώπων γένους (Oliver 17, 34–6).

[46] πᾶν τὸ τῶν ἀνθρώπων γένος εἰς τὴν ἰδίαν ἀνα<δε>δε{ι}γμένος κηδεμονίαν (Smallwood *GCN* 380, 13–14).

[47] πάντων φροντίζοντος (Smallwood *GCN* 384, 33).

[48] ἐπιλάμψαντος ἡμεῖν ἐπὶ σωτηρίᾳ τοῦ παντὸς ἀνθρώπων γένους (Smallwood *GCN* 391, 7). Mourgues 1995b argues convincingly that the edict originally referred to Nero (hence the solar imagery) and was hastily amended after news of his death.

[49] περὶ πάντας ἀνθρώπους κηδεμονία (Abbott–Johnson 175).

whole *oikoumenē* to be strengthened for the better'.[50] This ecumenical language leaves little place for the idea of an internal division within the population of the empire.

There is no difference in the rhetoric of proconsular governors of public provinces and legates and prefects of imperial provinces. All alike represent themselves as grateful subjects of an emperor whose favour extends to the whole human race. Their rhetoric reflects the culture of loyalism that permeated the politics of the empire. Emperors solicited displays of personal allegiance, and cities and even governors competed to demonstrate their loyalty.[51] But it was also in the governors' own interest to associate themselves with a powerful central authority. Highlighting the emperor's supremacy and their connection to him bolstered their influence and prestige in their dealings with the cities of their province.[52]

It is not certain that this ecumenical rhetoric extended to Latin, the language used for communication with the communities of the Western provinces. Indeed it is not even certain that the emperors communicated with Western cities on the same scale as they did with those of the East. In contrast with the three hundred imperial letters from the East, only six have been found in the West.[53] Some scholars have taken this as evidence that imperial letters were a rarity in the West.[54] Yet the surviving texts prove that at least some cities in Italy and the Western provinces did receive imperial letters.

50 πᾶσαν τὴν ἰδίαν αὐτῶν οἰκουμένην αὔξεσθαι πρὸς τὸ κρεῖττον ἐθέλουσιν (*SEG* 32 1149, 32–4).

51 Compare Isaac's perceptive remarks on the use of Latin on milestones in Greek-speaking regions (Isaac 1992 pp. 304–9). He suggests that their purpose was as much to display the loyalty of the governor and his army as it was to foster the allegiance of provincials. In any case, the message was clearly not aimed at the local population. For a broader perspective on the 'culture of loyalism' in the Roman empire, see Rowe 2002.

52 Kokkinia 2009 pp. 49–53 is a suggestive reading of the letter of Avidius Quietus in *IGRR* IV 571 which uses it to argue that 'some governors obviously sought to reinforce their own position by evoking the emperor. They were "borrowing honour" as J. E. Lendon would put it' (52–3).

53 Vespasian to the Vanacini in Corsica (McCrum–Woodhead 460) and Sabora in Baetica (McCrum–Woodhead 461 = *ILS* 6092), Titus to Munigua in Baetica (*AE* 1962 288), Domitian to Falerio in Italy (McCrum–Woodhead 462) and two letters of Antoninus Pius to Obulculo in Baetica (*AE* 1993 1003b; only the *praescripio* to the second survives). The emperors probably also wrote in Latin to some or all Roman colonies in the East, though I am not aware of any surviving example other than the highly fragmentary letter of Caracalla (?) to the colony of Alexandria Troas (*AE* 1973 504).

54 Mourgues 1995a p. 120 thinks the emperors rarely wrote letters to Western cities because there was a different diplomatic tradition in operation in the West. Souris 1984 pp. 64–6

And we know from other sources that they sent embassies to the emperor on the same sorts of occasions that Eastern cities did.[55] The Flavian Municipal Law from Irni (*lex Irnitana*) includes a section regulating service on such embassies.[56] It is unlikely that the emperors neglected to reply. The explanation for the paucity of surviving letters probably lies in differences in civic and epigraphic culture in the West – notably a different approach to service on embassies and the use of bronze tablets rather than stone to monumentalise the emperor's words.[57]

Further uncertainty surrounds the form and content of these Latin letters to the cities of the West. Jean-Louis Mourgues has argued that imperial communications in Latin followed an established Roman diplomatic tradition that remained quite distinct from the Hellenistic tradition adopted in Greek letters and was characterised by an oral rather than written style and by simplicity rather than refinement.[58] It is certainly true that most of the Latin letters that survive are significantly shorter and more functional than the Greek letters with their elaborate professions of mutual εὔνοια.[59] But the sample is so small that it is very dangerous to generalise about the rhetoric of imperial pronouncements in Latin, even when the handful of Latin edicts is included.[60] In

thinks that letters were rare because the Western cities relied more heavily on the mediation of municipal *patroni* and so sent fewer embassies to the emperor. Millar 1977 pp. 418–20 is agnostic.

55 See Eck 2009a p. 198 and Millar 1977 p. 418. Souris 1984 pp. 58–71 compiles epigraphic evidence for 34 embassies from the cities of the West (9 from Africa, 7 from Italy, 5 from the Danubian provinces, 5 from Spain, 3 from Gaul, 4 from Sicily and 1 from Corsica).

56 Gonzalez 1986 tablets VA–VB, §§ F, G, H and I.

57 So Eck 2009a pp. 198–202. Whereas Greek cities inscribed imperial letters on stone, all six of the letters that survive from the West were inscribed on bronze. As Eck observes, the rate of survival for bronze tablets – especially those displayed in public – will have been much lower than for stone, as they were liable to be melted down for other uses (even in antiquity). Eck also argues that service on an embassy was treated as 'a *munus* to be fulfilled, not an *honos* to be gladly undertaken' in the Western provinces, and was therefore less likely to be commemorated by the aristocrats concerned (p. 201).

58 Mourgues 1995a. See especially pp. 106–9 on the differences between the two diplomatic traditions and pp. 121–2 on the Latin letters.

59 Vespasian's letter to the Vanacini covers three matters in as many sentences (McCrum–Woodhead 460). His letter to Sabora shows the same terse efficiency (ibid. 461). Domitian's letter to Falerio and Pius' letter to Obulculo are even more minimalist (ibid. 462 and *AE* 1993 1003b), each consisting of a single sentence drawing their attention to the appended decision.

60 Since my focus is on communication with the communities of the provinces, I exclude the many Latin letters addressed to governors, procurators and other officials and private

any case, even this small corpus offers parallels to the euergetic mode that pervades the Greek letters. A letter of Titus to the town of Munigua in Spain boasts of the emperor's munificence (*indulgentia mea*).[61] An edict of Claudius granting citizenship to an Alpine tribe that was found to have been unlawfully usurping citizen status, insists that this is his personal favour (*beneficio meo, beneficium tribuo*).[62] An edict of Caracalla granting a remission of taxes to some communities in North Africa, the most rhetorically elaborate of the Latin pronouncements, boasts of the emperor's personal generosity (*indulgentia mea, magnifica indulgentia*) and describes the remission of taxes as a personal favour (*beneficium meum, beneficio meo*).[63] The ecumenical language of the Greek texts is echoed in a Hadrianic pronouncement by imperial procurators in Africa which assures the local population that the emperor 'keeps tireless watch for the needs of mankind (*pro humanis utilitatibus*)'.[64] There is thus no evidence that Roman rule was represented very differently in Latin letters than in the Greek letters that survive in much larger numbers.

It should by now be clear that the letters of Roman officials to provincial audiences present a vision of empire that is very different from the idea of a masterly or patronal people that pervades Latin literature. Official discourse privileges the power of the emperor to the almost total exclusion of any imperial people. Provincials and non-citizens are not interpellated as members of a class of subjects within a two-tier empire – still less as slaves. Instead, they are addressed either as citizens of an individual city with its own particular relationship to the emperor or as beneficiaries of the emperor's concern for the whole human race. This is an ecumenical and levelling rhetoric which implies that all are equally

individuals. Besides the six Latin letters, the provinces have also produced seven imperial edicts in Latin: the two Augustan edicts from El Bierzo (Alföldy 2000), Claudius on requisitioned transport (*ILS* 214), Nero (?) on appeals in criminal cases (*FIRA* I 91), Domitian on veterans' privileges (McCrum–Woodhead 404 = *ILS* 9059) and the privileges of veterans of *legio* XXII (*P Mich.* VII 432) and Caracalla on the remission of arrears at Banasa (*AE* 1948 109). We also have a handful of praesidial edicts and letters in Latin (e.g. *RDGE* 61, *RGDE* 65, Mitchell 1976, McCrum–Woodhead 464, Abbott–Johnson 77 and *AE* 1994 1645b).

[61] *AE* 1962 288, 6–7. [62] Smallwood *GCN* 368 = *ILS* 206, 30 and 34.

[63] *AE* 1948 109. See further Williams 1979 and Corbier 1974.

[64] *adsidue pro humanis utilitatibus excubat* (Smallwood *NTH* 464, II 3–5).

subject to the emperor and works to obscure any distinction between an imperial people and its subjects.

Universal pronouncements

Yet some traces of a rhetoric of division can be found even here. Almost contemporaneous with Augustus' letter to Sardis is another text which represents a very different – and distinctly Roman – model for imperial communication. This is the fifth of the so-called Cyrene edicts. When the process for extortion trials was reformed by *senatus consultum* in 4 BCE, Augustus dispatched copies of the new law throughout the empire, prefacing it with a short edict of his own. A copy of the text survives on a marble stele from the agora in Cyrene (where it has been appended to four other edicts that Augustus had issued to the cities of Cyrenaica). This is a famous text, but its distinctiveness within the broader corpus of imperial pronouncements is rarely acknowledged.[65]

αὐτοκράτωρ Καῖσαρ Σεβαστὸς ἀρχιερεὺς μέγιστος δημαρχικῆς ἐξουσίας ιθ' λέγει·

δόγμα συνκλήτου τὸ ἐπὶ Γαίου Καλουισίου καὶ Λευκίου Πασσιήνου ὑπάτων κυρωθὲν ἐμοῦ παρόντος καὶ συνεπιγραφομένου, ἀνῆκον δὲ εἰς τὴν τῶν τοῦ δήμου τοῦ Ῥωμαίων συμμάχων ἀσφάληαν, ἵνα πᾶσιν ᾖ γνωστὸν ὧν κηδόμεθα, πέμπειν εἰς τὰς ἐπαρχήας διέγνων καὶ τῶι ἐμῶι προγράμματι ὑποτάσσειν, ἐξ οὗ δῆλον ἔσται πᾶσιν τοῖς τὰς ἐπαρχήας κατοικοῦσιν ὅσην φροντίδα ποιούμεθα ἐγώ τε καὶ ἡ σύνκλητος τοῦ μηδένα τῶν ἡμῖν ὑποτασ<σ>ομένων παρὰ τὸ προσῆκόν τι πάσχιν ἢ εἰσπράτ<τ>εσθαι.

The emperor Caesar Augustus, *pontifex maximus*, holding *tribunicia potestas* for the 19th time, declares:

A *senatus consultum* was ratified under the consuls Gaius Calvisius and Lucius Passienus with me present and joining in the signature, pertaining to the security of the allies of the Roman people. I have resolved to send it to the provinces so that it will be known to all those under our care and to append it to my edict. This will make clear to all those who inhabit the provinces how concerned I and the senate are that none of those who obey us should suffer or be expropriated unduly. (Oliver 12 = *RDGE* 31 = Ehrenberg–Jones 311 V, 72–82)

[65] For example, Ando 2000 makes much of the edict in his argument that the Roman government founded its claims to legitimacy on the rationality of its rule (see especially pp. 143–5), without ever acknowledging its distinctiveness as a pronouncement to the provinces as a whole.

There follows a copy of the *senatus consultum* itself. This imperial pronouncement differs from the texts discussed thus far in several respects. Instead of the letter form familiar from Hellenistic diplomacy, it takes the distinctively Roman form of an edict – the proclamation of a magistrate with its introductory *dicit* (λέγει in Greek).[66] Its language too is distinctive. The letters and ordinances of the Hellenistic kings and earlier Roman magistrates offer no parallels for the expressions Augustus uses to refer to the provincials: 'those under our care' (ὧν κηδόμεθα), 'our subjects' (οἱ ἡμῖν ὑποτασσόμενοι).[67] Last, and most important, this text was sent not to a particular city, but to the provinces at large. It is in fact the earliest surviving text to address Rome's empire as a whole. Where the imperial letters inscribe Roman rule within the established forms of Hellenistic diplomacy, this innovative text represents it as something new.

Particularly important for my purposes is the fact that the edict eschews the universalism of the letters to locate its recipients within a class of imperial subjects. Whereas the letters address their recipients either as the citizens of an individual city or as members of the human race, this text uses the familiar dichotomies of Roman discourse. The edict specifies that it has been sent to the provinces. Its recipients are interpellated variously as allies (οἱ τῶν τοῦ δήμου τοῦ Ῥωμαίων σύμμαχοι, implicitly contrasted with 'the Roman people' itself) and provincials (αἱ ἐπαρχήαι, πάντες οἱ τὰς ἐπαρχήας κατοικοῦντες, implicitly distinguished from the inhabitants of Italy). The conflation of legal and geographic categories – which blurs the distinction between non-citizens and provincials – is typical of Roman rhetoric (Chapter 1). Both expressions assert the existence of a fundamental dichotomy within the population of the empire.

Similar categories can be found in an edict of Claudius, reproduced by Josephus, which confirms the privileges of Jews throughout

[66] On the edict form, see Oliver 1989 pp. 18–21, Benner 1975, Williams 1975 pp. 43–7 and Reinmuth 1938 pp. 3–10.

[67] The verbs κήδεσθαι and ὑποτάσσειν appear nowhere in the royal pronouncements collected by Ma 2002, Hatzopoulos 1996, Lenger 1980 and Welles 1934 or in the Republican letters in Sherk 1969 (*RDGE*).

the empire.[68] The edict defines its scope as extending to all Jews throughout 'the empire that is subject to the Romans' (ἐν τῇ ὑπὸ Ῥωμαίοις ἡγεμονίᾳ) and 'the world that is subject to us' (ἐν τῷ ὑφ' ἡμᾶς κόσμῳ).[69] The significance of the plural 'us' in the latter expression is clear from the fact that Claudius uses the first person singular elsewhere in the edict. He also commends the Jews for their loyalty and friendship 'to the Romans'.[70] Like Augustus, Claudius leaves most of the population of the empire in no doubt that they are subjects of an imperial people as well as an emperor. The edict ends with a provision for universal publication. It is to be inscribed and displayed by 'the magistrates of the cities, colonies and *municipia*, both in and outside Italy, and the kings and dynasts'.[71] This formula is another example of the rhetoric of division, imposing distinctions on the population of the empire. In this case it asserts the significance of both geography and legal status, simultaneously distinguishing between different civic statuses and between Italy and the provinces.

Another edict of Claudius, found at Tegea, articulates the same distinctions. This is a fragmentary Latin edict aimed at restricting abuses in the requisitioning of transport. Only the preamble

68 The authenticity of the documents cited in the *Jewish Antiquities* is a controversial topic. This particular edict (*AJ* 19.287–91) has variously been judged genuine, selectively edited or an outright forgery (see Pucci Ben Zeev 1998 pp. 333–4 for a useful overview of opinions). The most sceptical see its companion edict on the Jews of Alexandria (Joseph. *AJ* 19.280–5) as a Jewish fabrication based on the most favourable points from Claudius' genuine letter to the Alexandrians, which survives separately in a papyrus copy and contains some material markedly less favourable to the Jews (Oliver 19; see pp. 237–8 below). See most recently Harker 2008 pp. 26–8. But this would have no necessary implications for the edict on the Jews of the empire (as Schwartz 1990 p. 105 acknowledges, concluding that the former is a forgery, but the latter genuine). In any case, the papyrus letter explicitly refers to a previous decision (or decisions) on the privileges of the Jews (ἅπερ καὶ ἐγὼ διακούσας ἀμφοτέρων ἐβεβαίωσα, Oliver 19, 87–8; contrast the present tense of all other pronouncements in the letter). I believe that the Josephan texts are copies – however corrupt or edited – of two genuine edicts which predate the letter. They may well derive from compilations made by and for diaspora communities (so Pucci Ben Zeev 1998 pp. 402–3 on the documents as a whole). As such they will have been subject to repeated scribal errors and perhaps also selective editing. For my purposes, what matters is that the language of Josephus' text can be paralleled in both the fifth Cyrene edict and Claudius' edict on the *cursus publicus*.

69 Joseph. *AJ* 19.288 and 290.

70 διὰ τὴν πρὸς Ῥωμαίους πίστιν καὶ φιλίαν (Joseph. *AJ* 19.289).

71 τοῦτό μου τὸ διάταγμα τοὺς ἄρχοντας τῶν πόλεων καὶ τῶν κολωνιῶν καὶ μουνικιπίων τῶν ἐν τῇ Ἰταλίᾳ καὶ τῶν ἐκτός, βασιλεῖς τε καὶ δυνάστας διὰ τῶν ἰδίων πρεσβευτῶν ἐγγράψασθαι βούλομαι (Joseph. *AJ* 19.291).

survives. In it, the emperor declares his intention to give relief to 'the colonies and *municipia*, not only in Italy but also in the provinces, and the communities of each province'.[72] Again the *municipia* and colonies of Italy are distinguished from their provincial counterparts, and they in turn are marked off from the other provincial communities. The recipients of the emperor's edict are interpellated within this implicit hierarchy of communities.

All three of these texts are edicts. All three are addressed to the empire at large.[73] This is probably not a coincidence. As edicts these texts may well be drawing on an established and distinctive Roman idiom in addition to the tropes of Hellenistic diplomacy. This point should not be overemphasised, as several edicts do share the euergetic and ecumenical mode of the letters.[74] But it may be particularly relevant for universal edicts which were, presumably, composed in Latin and then translated into Greek. Perhaps more significant is the fact that these edicts have to specify their scope. It is characteristic of the edict, unlike the letter, that there is no addressee specified in the *praescriptio*. The emperor or magistrate simply speaks (*dicit*/λέγει). But the text of the edict usually specifies its scope of application, whether local or universal.[75] Proclamations to the empire at large, such as these three texts, have to specify their recipients, and this necessarily involves taking a stance on the presence or absence of significant distinctions within the space and population of the empire. As such, they are inherently more likely than letters (always addressed to a single community) to impose a division on the population of the empire.

[72] *colonias et municipia non solum Ita[lia]e uerum etiam prouinciarum item ciuita[t]es cuiusque prouinciae lebare oneribu[s] ueh[iculor(um)] praebendorum* (Smallwood *GCN* 375 = *ILS* 214, 4–7). Only the beginning of the edict survives. There is no provision for publication, presumably because it would have come at the end of the edict. But publication throughout the provinces can be deduced from the scope of the preamble and the fact that this copy was set up in Tegea.

[73] To be more precise, Augustus' Cyrene edict is addressed to the provinces as a whole, whereas Claudius' edict on the Jews was published throughout Italy, the provinces and in allied kingdoms. The edict on the *vehiculatio* was, to judge from its preamble, published throughout Italy and the provinces.

[74] Among imperial edicts, note the rhetoric of favours in Smallwood *GCN* 368 (Claudius), Oliver 88 (Hadrian) and *AE* 1948 109 (Caracalla), the tropes of *eunoia* and *eusebeia* in Oliver 296 (Nero) and the ecumenical rhetoric of Joseph. *AJ* 16.165 (Augustus).

[75] Williams 1975 pp. 43–4 distinguishes between edicts with a defined, local scope and those of 'universal application'.

These three texts are anomalies within the corpus of surviving imperial pronouncements. Imperial edicts are rare, and edicts addressed to the empire at large rarer still. In comparison to the approximately three hundred imperial letters that survive from the period between Augustus and Caracalla, we have only some thirty edicts; less than half of these were 'universal'.[76] But the paucity of edicts, especially those addressed to the empire at large, is almost certainly misleading. It was local initiative that determined which imperial pronouncements were inscribed on stone (or bronze) for posterity. It follows that the texts most likely to be monumentalised were those that had local value – whether because they affirmed the prestige and privileges of the city or because they redounded to the honour of local notables (most often by commending their service as ambassadors). This means that imperial letters – addressed to a single city, usually in response to an embassy drawn from the local elite – were much more likely to be preserved than edicts which addressed multiple communities or the empire as a whole.[77] Universal pronouncements such as the fifth Cyrene edict were probably more common than they appear from the epigraphic record. They may well have been an important context in which distinctions between Romans and allies and between Italy and the provinces were regularly reaffirmed.[78]

A similar rhetoric of division can be found in the few surviving senatorial decrees that were published throughout the empire. The *senatus consultum Caluisianum* that Augustus forwarded to the provinces under his own edict echoes the emperor in declaring its

[76] See n. 8 above. Williams 1975 pp. 43–4 identifies nine imperial edicts 'of universal application' (but see n. 73 above) and adds four uncertain cases at n. 16. His list of uncertain cases could be expanded to include *FIRA* I 91 and *P Harr.* II 202.

[77] Hauken and Malay 2009 p. 334 reach a similar conclusion that the rarity of edicts in the epigraphic record is misleading.

[78] A fourth edict to address the empire as a whole dates from just outside my period. This is the edict of Severus Alexander remitting the *aurum coronarium* (the 'crown tax') to the cities of the empire (222 CE). The emperor addresses himself to 'all men in all the cities, both of Italy and the other provinces' (ἅπαντες ἐν ταῖς πόλεσιν ἁπάσαις ταῖς τε κατ' Ἰταλίαν καὶ ταῖς ἐν τοῖς ἄλλοις ἔθνεσιν, Oliver 275, II 11). This is strikingly similar to the formula found in Claudius' two edicts. The distinction between types of community has disappeared (unsurprising in the aftermath of Caracalla's citizenship grant), but the distinction between Italy and the provinces survives. The formula may well have been typical of universal edicts.

purpose to be the protection of 'the allies of the Roman people'.[79] Another decree published throughout the provinces was the Tiberian *senatus consultum de Cn. Pisone patre*, reporting the senate's condemnation of Cn. Calpurnius Piso for the murder of Germanicus and attempted revolt. The senate provided for the publication of the edict in the most populous city of each province and in the winter quarters of each legion.[80] The six copies found in Spain alone show that it was actually published even more widely. Its language implies a clear divide between Romans and non-Romans within the empire. Piso is condemned for crucifying not just 'foreigners' (*externi*) – evidently non-citizen auxiliaries in the force that Piso commanded as governor of Syria – but even a centurion who was a Roman citizen.[81] The death of Germanicus is mourned not just by 'the Roman people' but also by 'foreign nations' (*exterae gentes*).[82] When Tiberius takes possession of one of Piso's provincial estates because neighbouring communities had complained of mistreatment, the victims are described as 'allies of the Roman people'.[83] Like the edicts of Augustus and Claudius, these are texts written in a distinctively Roman form and idiom. They too interpellate some of their provincial readers as allies and foreigners.

Lastly, it is worth noting that the subject of citizen status was one context that was always likely to elicit a rhetoric of division. Two of the earlier Cyrene edicts, issued by Augustus to the cities of Cyrenaica in 7–6 BCE, concern relations between citizens and non-citizens in the province. The former are called 'Romans'; the latter 'Greeks'.[84] The same dichotomy is still being used by Hadrian in 121 CE in the context of a concession to the Epicureans at Athens, which relaxed the requirement that the head of their School be a

79 ἐς τὴν τῶν συμμάχων τοῦ δήμου τοῦ Ῥωμαίων ἀσφάλειαν (Oliver 12, 89).

80 Eck, Caballos and Fernandez 1996 lines 165–72.

81 *neq(ue) externos tantummodo, sed etiam centurionem c(iuem) R(omanum) cruci fixsisset* (ibid. lines 49–52). For *externi* used of non-citizens like *peregrini*, see also Plin. *HN* 33.37.

82 [sc. *Germanici*] *interitum non p(opulus) R(omanus) modo, sed exterae quoq(ue) gentes luxserunt* (Eck, Caballos and Fernandez 1996, lines 57–8).

83 *eum saltum placere Ti. Caesari Augusto principi ... reddi ... ne postea iure meritoq(ue) soci p(opuli) R(omani) queri possent* (ibid. lines 85–90).

84 Oliver 8 *passim*; also 11, 64, 67 and 69.

Roman citizen. Both Hadrian and the empress Plotina write to the School on the subject, employing the same distinction between 'Romans' (citizens) and 'Greeks' (non-citizens) that Augustus had used more than a century earlier.[85]

Even in the midst of the levelling rhetoric that appears to dominate the official pronouncements of the Roman state, some evidence can be found of the dichotomies with which the Roman elite articulate their identity as an imperial people. At least some official pronouncements interpellate some of the emperor's subjects as 'allies' rather than Romans and 'provincials' rather than Italians. Indeed this rhetoric of division was probably more prominent than the historical record suggests. Because universal pronouncements such as the fifth Cyrene edict employ a Roman idiom and tend to situate their addressees within the context of the empire as a whole, they were an important medium in which internal dichotomies will have been regularly reaffirmed. Yet, precisely because of their universal remit, they were also much less likely to be monumentalised by communities or individuals than were the imperial letters which concerned them personally. The ecumenical rhetoric of the letters may not have been as dominant as it appears.

Masters and slaves

Although these texts impose divisions on the population of the empire, they do not always imply a relationship of subjection – still less one of enslavement. Structured as it is by a paradigm of euergetism inherited from Hellenistic diplomacy and Greek civic life, official discourse seems to have little place for the language of slavery. But this impression too may be misleading. For starters, there is at least one surviving imperial pronouncement that represents the condition of the provinces in precisely those terms. This is the short speech with which Nero proclaimed 'freedom' for Greece at the Isthmian games of 67 CE, a privileged status which brought immunity from tribute and from the jurisdiction of a Roman

[85] Oliver 73, 20 (Plotina) and 74, 4 (Hadrian). The latter is fragmentary, but can be reconstructed on the basis of Plotina's letter. See also the references to 'Greeks' in a letter of Hadrian to Aphrodisias (Reynolds 2000 I, 6, 7 and 8, with discussion at p. 13).

governor. A copy of the text survives thanks to the decision of a grateful community (Acraephia in Boeotia) to monumentalise the emperor's words. In this speech Nero declares:

πάντες οἱ τὴν Ἀχαΐαν καὶ τὴν ἕως νῦν Πελοπόννησον κατοικοῦντες Ἕλληνες λάβετ' ἐλευθερίαν ἀνισφορίαν, ἣν οὐδ' ἐν τοῖς εὐτυχεστάτοις ὑμῶν πάντες χρόνοις ἔσχετε· ἢ γὰρ ἀλλοτρίοις ἢ ἀλλήλοις ἐδουλεύσατε.

All you Greeks who inhabit Achaea and the land previously [known as] the Peloponnese,[86] accept freedom and immunity – which you never enjoyed universally, even in the time of your greatest good fortune. For you have been slaves either to foreigners or to each other. (Oliver 296 = Smallwood *GCN* 64, 12–15)

The years of Roman domination are presumably included in the sweeping reference to the past slavery from which the Greeks are now to be free. The implication is that their prior condition – and that of most other provincial communities – was indeed one of enslavement.

This is an isolated example. There is no other sign of a rhetoric of provincial slavery in the imperial letters and edicts. But we should again be wary of assuming that the surviving corpus is representative of the full range of imperial pronouncements. The vast majority of the texts that we have were preserved precisely because they were expressions of imperial favour – honouring the cities and their notables and often granting or confirming privileges. It is likely that there were other, less favourable, modes and registers of imperial rhetoric, which have left little or no trace in the epigraphic record because the cities in question would have had no cause to create a permanent memorial to their misfortune. First, there must have been letters in which the emperors denied requests. A rare exception to the monotonous expressions of imperial euergetism is an Augustan rescript denying the Samians their petition for a grant of freedom, on the grounds that it would have devalued the freedom granted to Aphrodisias for its loyalty in the war against Antony (though the emperor still expresses his εὔνοια for Samos). The response survives only because the Aphrodisians valued it as evidence of their own prestige and inscribed a copy on the 'archive wall' in their theatre.[87]

86 On 'the land previously known as the Peloponnese', see p. 99 n. 78.
87 *A&R* 13. Other examples of refusals preserved by interested parties are *A&R* 14 and Oliver 120 and 123. See Reynolds 1982 pp. 105–6.

There must also have been occasions on which emperors or governors found fault with the behaviour of individual cities. According to Fronto, one of the duties of the emperor was 'to curb the faults of the allies with edicts' (*sociorum culpas edictis coercere*, Front. *Ant. de eloquentia* 1.5). A mild example of the rhetoric of rebuke is a letter of Antoninus Pius to Ptolemais-Barca in Cyrenaica, expressing surprise at the city's unprecedented decision to send its own embassy to the Capitoline festival at Rome (whereas in the past it had always been represented by an embassy from Cyrene, the metropolis). Pius warns that this is the sort of innovation (καινοτομεῖν) that causes strife (φιλονεικία) among the cities.[88] The response was inscribed in the rival city of Cyrene as part of a dossier documenting Cyrene's claim to metropolitan status in Cyrenaica.[89] Stronger language is used in the famous letter of Claudius to Alexandria.[90] Claudius assures the Alexandrians that he reciprocates their goodwill and affection, responds to various honours and grants some requests. But there is a change of tone at the end of the letter when the emperor turns to the issue of conflict between Jews and Hellenes within the city, an ongoing problem which had broken out into repeated riots between 38 and 41 CE. Claudius warns the city that he has stored up 'unrelenting wrath' (ὀργὴν ἀμεταμέλητον, 78) against those who renewed the conflict – though he has chosen not to investigate further at this time. If they do not end their hostility, he will be forced to show what a benevolent ruler is like when he turns to 'just wrath' (ὀργὴν δικαίαν, 81). The emperor then gives instructions to the Greeks and Jews of the city separately. The Jews receive an additional warning. If they are found inviting Jews from Syria or Egypt to join them, the emperor will 'punish them exactly as if they were awakening a common

[88] Oliver 124, 83. [89] See Reynolds 1978 for the full dossier.

[90] Oliver 19. The text of the letter survives because it was copied (with numerous errors and possibly even selective editing) for private purposes by Nemesion, a Hellenised Egyptian tax collector at Philadelphia in the Fayum – presumably out of interest in the conflict in Alexandria. See Harker 2008 pp. 25–6, who situates it at the beginning of the tradition of 'Alexandrian stories' – quasi-documentary texts (often worked up and sometimes outright fictions) recording confrontations between Alexandrian Greeks and the Roman authorities – that circulated in Roman Egypt over the following two centuries. He judges that this letter 'belongs to the "documentary" end of the spectrum' (p. 49).

plague for the whole world'.[91] Josephus records an edict of the governor of Syria, P. Petronius, rebuking the citizens of Dora for flouting the emperor's edict and erecting a statue of the emperor in a synagogue. He accuses them of the recklessness of madness (τόλμη ἀπονοίας) and warns them not to seek any further excuse for sedition or disturbance (μηδεμίαν πρόφασιν στάσεως μηδὲ ταραχῆς ζητεῖν).[92] A much later example is Julian's *Misopogon* ('Beard-hater'), a satiric rebuke to the city of Antioch preserved in the literary tradition. As Maud Gleason has shown, this idiosyncratic text stands within a tradition of 'edicts of chastisement' which goes back to the Julio-Claudian period.[93]

Conquest and revolt may well have elicited a harsher rhetoric. After all, these are the contexts in which Roman writers are most likely to use the language of slavery to describe Roman rule (Chapter 2). It is there that we might expect to find the masterly style erupting into the rhetoric of Romans addressing subject communities. Unfortunately, we have no documentary evidence to test this. No such speech survives in the original. But a number of speeches in the historians suggest that conquest and revolt did indeed elicit a rhetoric of mastery. Although most of these texts have already been discussed separately, it is worth reviewing them here. In Florus' account of the conquest of Moesia under Augustus, one of the local chieftains asks the Romans who they are. 'Romans, the *masters* of nations' (*Romani gentium domini*), replies the Roman commander (2.26.14). When Tacitus lays out the abuses that provoked the British revolt under Boudicca, he notes the mistreatment of the local population by the veterans recently settled in the *colonia* at Camulodunum. The veterans evicted many of the natives from their land, he says, calling them captives and *slaves* (*captiuos seruos appellando*, *Ann.* 14.31.3). In both cases, victorious Romans represent themselves as masters to those they have recently conquered.

Also in Tacitus is the speech of a Roman general addressing a community about to rebel against Rome – C. Dillius Vocula's

[91] αὐτοὺς ἐπεξελεύσομαι καθάπερ κοινήν τινα τῆς οἰκουμένης νόσον ἐξεγείροντας (99–100).

[92] Joseph. *AJ* 19.303–11.

[93] Gleason 1986, esp. pp. 116–19.

rebuke to the Treveri and Lingones during the Batavian revolt (*Hist.* 4.57.1–2). The short speech ends with a warning:

nunc hostes, quia molle seruitium; cum spoliati exutique fuerint, amicos fore.

They were enemies now [he said] because their slavery had been an easy one. But once they had been stripped and bared, then they would be friends. (Tac. *Hist.* 4.57.2)

Vocula tells the Gauls that they have rebelled only because their masters have treated them too gently (*quia molle seruitium*). The phrase *spoliati exutique* ('robbed/bared and stripped') also suggests the stripping of a slave for a flogging – the implication being that these Gauls are going to be whipped back into line. The language of slavery gives the lie to the labels *hostes* and *amici* that frame the sentence. The Gauls may think of themselves as being variously Rome's enemies or its friends – but Vocula tells them they will always be slaves. Even more striking is the masterly rhetoric that the Jewish historian Josephus attributes to the future emperor Titus in his account of the Jewish revolt of 66–70 CE. In an appeal to the rebels in Jerusalem to see sense and surrender, Titus wholeheartedly embraces the paradigm of mastery. He rebukes them for the folly of rebelling, when they know that even the Germans are Rome's slaves (ἴστε Γερμανοὺς δουλεύοντας ἡμῖν, 6.331). He ends by comparing the Jews to troublesome slaves and himself to the master of the household:

ῥίψασι δὲ τὰ ὅπλα καὶ παραδοῦσι τὰ σώματα χαρίζομαι τὸ ζῆν, ὥσπερ ἐν οἰκίᾳ πρᾷος δεσπότης τὰ μὲν ἀνήκεστα κολάσας, τὰ δὲ λοιπὰ σώζων ἐμαυτῷ.

Throw down your arms, surrender your bodies, and I will grant you your lives, like a lenient master in a household, punishing the incorrigible but preserving the rest for myself. (Joseph. *BJ* 6.350)

These compositions are far from straightforward evidence for Roman rhetoric in the provinces. They are embedded in works with their own conventions and agendas. As Chapter 3 has shown, the language of slavery has a special thematic importance within Tacitus' accounts of the Batavian and Boudiccan revolts. The complex and often confusing hybrid of Greek, Jewish and Roman cultural codes that is Josephus' *Jewish War* is, if anything, even more problematic. Explanations for the masterly rhetoric ascribed to Titus can be found in the contexts of Greek historiography and Hellenised Jewish writing.[94] Yet it clearly also conforms with the rhetoric used in similar contexts in the Roman historiographical tradition. Whatever their difficulties, these texts are the best evidence we have for the language with which Roman officials confronted provincial revolt. Their collective testimony is some indication that this was indeed a context in which the paradigm of mastery could rise to the surface.

This chapter has shown that some traces of the imperial categories and tropes that characterise the discourse of the Roman elite can also be found in the pronouncements of the Roman state. There were a number of contexts (which may be under-represented in the surviving corpus) in which the voice of Roman power imposed a fundamental dichotomy on the population of the empire, by interpellating some of its inhabitants as 'allies' rather than Romans, or 'provincials' rather than Italians. In moments of conflict, they may even have been addressed as slaves. But the chapter has also demonstrated that this rhetoric of division coexisted with – and may even have been overshadowed by – a very different voice. Many, if not most, imperial and praesidial pronouncements focused on the emperor to the exclusion of the Roman people. They interpellated provincial communities not as subjects of an imperial people, but as subjects of an all-powerful emperor before whom all were equal. The inhabitants of the empire were addressed either as citizens of a particular community with its own personal relationship with the emperor or as members of the human race. This levelling rhetoric reflects the influence of the long tradition of Hellenistic diplomacy, a tradition that the Roman emperors continued in their relations with the cities of the empire. This was a discourse with its own forms (notably the ongoing interchange of civic decrees and imperial letters), its own language and its own paradigms of power. It also reflects the culture of loyalism that permeated the politics of the empire. Emperors solicited displays of

[94] Lavan 2007 explores the significance of Titus' rhetoric for readers who approach the text within these contexts.

personal allegiance, and cities and even governors competed to demonstrate their loyalty.

The ecumenical language of imperial and praesidial pronouncements must have encouraged their provincial recipients to see themselves as part of an empire-wide community. Clifford Ando argues that 'provincials' were from an early period eager to see themselves, and be seen by their rulers, as members of a Roman community that embraced all the inhabitants of the provinces, united by their dependence on an emperor who brought benefits to citizens and non-citizens alike.[95] We may dispute the timing and the extent (both geographic and social) of this development. But it would be hard to deny that an ever-increasing number of provincials – not all of them Roman citizens or local magnates – came to see themselves as 'participants in, rather than subjects of, Roman power' (Ando 2000 p. xii). This development will have been encouraged and reinforced by the levelling rhetoric of official pronouncements.

Lastly it is worth emphasising the continuity of this discourse. This chapter – like much of this book – has deliberately adopted a synchronic rather than diachronic approach. This is because the language of these imperial and praesidial pronouncements does not fit any neat narrative of the progressive expansion of an ecumenical vision in official rhetoric. The ecumenical style is present in Roman pronouncements from the beginning of the principate. Augustus professes his reverence 'for all men' (πρὸς πάντας ἀνθρώπους) in his edict on the privileges of the Jews and is acclaimed as 'the common good fortune of all men' (τὸ κοινὸν πάντων εὐτύχημα) in an edict of Paulus Fabius Maximus, governor of Asia in 10 BCE.[96] Conversely, examples of the rhetoric of division can be found at the very end of my period. Letters of Severus and Caracalla praise Delphi for showing 'zeal and enthusiasm towards the empire of the Romans', Aezani for being a city 'long of service to the empire of

[95] See Ando 2000 ch. 8 (esp. pp. 330–1) and ch. 9 on a growing inclination on the part of provincials to see themselves as members of a Roman community that embraced all the inhabitants of the provinces, and ibid. pp. 385–405 on the appropriation of the emperor as a father figure whose divine beneficence brought benefits to citizens and non-citizens alike.

[96] Joseph. *AJ* 16.165 and *RDGE* 65, 8–9.

the Romans' and Aphrodisias for 'exceeding all other peoples in attachment to the empire of the Romans'.[97] All three letters assert a divide between the 'Romans' and the rest of the empire. Throughout my period, pronouncements of the Roman state employ a wide range of registers, categories and tropes.

[97] Oliver 205, 15 and 213, 19–21; *A&R* 18 = Oliver 219, 3–5. See n. 35 above.

AFTERWORD

This book has sought to offer a new perspective on the culture of Roman imperialism by exploring the language in which Roman writers describe their relationship to the peoples they regard as their subjects. This project is complicated from the outset by the fact that the implicit dichotomy between Roman rulers and provincial subjects is far from self-evident for most of the period covered by this book. Whatever its value in the age of Cicero, a simple dichotomy between Romans and subjects is increasingly inadequate to describe the complex distribution of power and privilege within the empire in the first and second centuries CE. The political disempowerment of the citizen body under the Principate, the intensive settlement of citizens in colonies in the provinces under Caesar and Augustus, the extension of citizenship (only recently granted to Italians) to increasing numbers of provincials, the provincialisation of the legions, the recruitment of wealthy provincials to the equestrian and senatorial orders and ultimately the principate itself, the narrowing cultural divide between Italy and many provincial communities – all these developments worked to complicate the political geography of the empire.

And yet, as this book has shown, Roman writers persist in imposing such a dichotomy on the empire. They regularly distinguish themselves from the majority of the population of the empire by conflating the latter under labels such as *socii* or *prouinciae* and representing them as being their subjects as well as the emperor's. The operative distinction is not always that between citizens and non-citizens. The ruling power with which Roman writers of the first and second centuries CE identify is variously and inconsistently configured as the Roman people, the Romans, Italy, the city of Rome – or simply a vague *nos*, whose extension should not be taken as self-evident. What persists is the sense of an imperial identity: throughout the period covered,

Roman writers regard the conquest and rule of the provinces as a shared project and represent themselves as members of an imperial power elevated above the subject peoples who comprise most of the population of the empire.

The aim of this book has been to better understand this shared imperial project by examining how the condition of the subject population is conceptualised in terms of the paradigmatic forms of dependency in Roman society. The masterly, patronal and parental tropes studied in this book are particularly revealing rhetorical choices. Drawing as they do on modes of domination with which the Roman elite were intimately familiar and whose boundaries they were expected to observe in everyday social practice, these tropes embody very different perspectives on the proper relationship between centre and periphery.

I have insisted throughout that there is no question of slavery, or for that matter patronage, being 'the' Roman paradigm for empire. Roman literature presents us with a range of different visions of empire. This polyphony reflects the coexistence of divergent values and ambitions throughout the period covered by this book. It is also a function of the different agendas pursued by individual texts. Many descriptions of the imperial relationship are embedded within particular projects of persuasion. Cicero's forensic speeches are only the most obvious examples. What this book has aimed to achieve by exploring these paradigms of power is not to delineate some inevitably misleading consensus, but rather to map the shape of a discursive space by tracing some of its most expressive tropes. This survey provides the broad perspective necessary to understand the politics of particular representations of the imperial project – from Caesar's account of the Gauls' struggle to preserve their freedom to the Elder Pliny's praise of Italy as the mother of all other lands.

I have nevertheless chosen to highlight the paradigm of slavery in both the title and the structure of this book. This serves three purposes. First, it reflects the fact that this is the most widely deployed of the paradigms analysed here. It should by now be clear that the language and imagery of chattel slavery are firmly entrenched in the Roman language of empire. From the first century BCE through the third CE, Roman writers boast of the dominance of the 'master people' (*populus dominus*) and describe the condition of some or all of the provincial population in terms of enslavement. The widespread use of the language of slavery is particularly striking given its prominence in the (imagined) rhetoric of Rome's enemies and given the care with which such language is used and more often avoided in the context of relations between the emperor and the Roman elite – both of which illustrate its emotive potential. Second, drawing attention to these assertions of Roman mastery and provincial slavery provides a useful corrective to conventional views about Roman attitudes to the provinces in the Principate. A handful of passages professing a civilising mission are cited again and again as representative of Roman aspirations in this period. Nothing has been said about the more numerous representations of Roman rule as a form of enslavement and the very different perspective on the imperial project they imply. This masterly rhetoric reveals the extent to which Roman writers regarded domination as an end in itself, privileged their own interests and welfare over those of their subjects and acknowledged the coercive basis of Roman rule. Lastly, these metaphors of provincial enslavement are a useful reminder of the presumptive legitimacy of master–slave relations in Roman culture and their capacity to provide a paradigm of legitimate authority. If we find the metaphor of provincial slavery surprising, it is because we have misunderstood not just the character of Roman imperialism, but also the ethical system of a society of masters.

A second and broader theme of this book has been the exclusivism implicit in many Roman accounts of empire. Again, this is intended as a corrective to conventional accounts which credit Romans of the Principate with an integrationist ethos. Throughout the period covered here, Roman writers can be found insisting on the gulf separating them from the peoples they regard as their subjects. This is most obvious in the rhetoric of Roman mastery and provincial slavery. But it is equally present in the superficially very different language of benefaction and patronage: though these embody a more benign vision of the imperial relationship, they are still assertions of Roman superiority. Exclusivism is also inherent in the widespread use of categories such as *socii* and the metonymic *prouinciae* to refer to provincials. These terms implicitly mark off some or all provincials as being a class of imperial subjects. *Prouinciae* and its cognates highlight their geographic displacement from the imperial centre and their subjection to the apparatus of provincial administration. The use of *socii* is even more striking, implicitly excluding them from the Roman state. Some of the strongest expressions of exclusivism arise in the context of revolt, notably in the speeches in Livy, Tacitus and Cassius Dio in which Roman generals seek to mobilise contempt for rebellious provincials.

This sense of distinction bears out recent work on the importance of honour in Roman culture. The seminal work is Ted Lendon's *Empire of Honour*, which illustrates the great value that most members of Roman society placed on their personal honour and demonstrates the central importance of this honour culture for Roman social relations and indeed the functioning of the empire.[1] Susan Mattern's *Rome and the Enemy* draws congruent conclusions about Roman relations with the barbarian peoples beyond the frontier. Mattern shows that Latin literature represents Roman interactions with these peoples as an aggressive competition for honour and status. Great value is placed on displays of deference and subservience by foreign peoples, ranging from giving hostages to granting Rome the right to crown their kings. Conversely, the perceived *superbia* (arrogance) of foreign peoples is regarded as a valid reason for going to war.[2] This is the imperial mission as memorably articulated by Virgil's Anchises: 'Remember, Roman ... to spare the submissive

[1] Lendon 1997.

[2] See Mattern 1999 ch. 5 on competition for status and pp. 175–6 on *superbia* (citing Caes. *B Gall.* 1.33, Verg. *Aen.* 6.851–3, Tac. *Ann.* 1.61 and 6.31 and Plin. *Pan.* 14.1). As early as 168 BCE the senate debated declaring war on Rhodes to punish the Rhodians for their *superbia* in seeking to mediate between the Romans and Perseus during the Third Macedonian War (when they should have sided with Rome). The proposal was rejected, partly through the intervention of Cato the Censor, who responded to the charge of *superbia* by turning the accusation on his own countrymen, asking whether the Romans could reasonably be angry at the Rhodians for being more arrogant than them. His speech is quoted by Gellius: *superbiae quoque crimen, quod tunc praeter cetera in senatu Rhodiensibus obiectum erat, mirifica et prope diuina responsionis figura elusit et eluit. uerba adeo ipsa ponemus Catonis, quoniam Tiro ea praetermisit: 'Rhodiensis superbos esse aiunt id obiectantes, quod mihi et liberis meis minime dici uelim. sint sane superbi. quid id ad nos attinet? idne irascimini, si quis superbior est quam nos?'* (Gell. *NA* 6.3.48–50). On the semantics of *superbia*, see p. 170 n. 37.

and war down the arrogant (*parcere subiectis et debellare superbos*)'.[3] In this context, it is worth revisiting two texts which demonstrate that this sensitivity to *superbia* could extend to the subject population of the provinces as well as foreign peoples beyond the frontier. When Pliny the Younger praises Trajan for his management of the drought in Egypt, it is for having crushed the *superbia* of Egypt by proving that it was Egypt that was dependent on Rome and not the reverse (Plin. *Pan.* 30–2 with pp. 170–1). A similar sensitivity to provincial *superbia* is expressed by the senator Thrasea Paetus in Tacitus' *Annals*, in his speech condemning the practice of allowing provincial councils to pronounce on the merits of provincial governors (*Ann.* 15.20.4 with pp. 60–1). Denouncing provincials who have the temerity to take it upon themselves to judge their betters, he demands action against this new *superbia* of the *prouinciales*.[4] These texts give particularly forceful expression to a wider sentiment that the subject peoples should know their place within the empire and show proper deference to their Roman rulers.

A third theme of this book has been continuity. I have insisted that there is no sign of rupture in the language of Roman imperialism across the three centuries from Cicero to Cassius Dio, despite the transformative processes at work in this period. On the contrary, some of the most exclusivist tropes show a remarkable longevity – notably the label *socii* (still used as a label for the provincial population in the late second century CE) and the rhetoric of Roman mastery and provincial slavery (which is as prominent in Pliny and Tacitus as it was in Cicero and Caesar, and seems to have become more so in the works of Florus and Dio). There are some signs of change, particularly in the parameters of elite identity. The first and second centuries CE see an increasing focus on geography rather than citizen status as the key criterion of distinction. This is evident in the invention and spread of the noun *prouinciales* and the slippage by which *socii* comes to be used of provincial citizens as well as non-citizens. For rupture, however, we must look ahead

3 *tu regere imperio populos, Romane, memento | (hae tibi erunt artes), pacique imponere morem, | parcere subiectis et debellare superbos* (Verg. *Aen.* 6.851–3).

4 *ergo aduersus nouam prouincialium superbiam dignum fide constantiaque Romana capiamus consilium* (Tac. *Ann.* 15.20.4).

to the fourth century CE when dramatic changes are visible: the disappearance of the noun *socii*, a staple of the Roman lexicon of empire for centuries; the use of *prouinciales* as a generic term for all subjects, both Italians and non-Italians; and the proliferation of maternal metaphors for Roman power. Unfortunately the paucity of surviving Latin literature from the late second and third centuries makes it impossible to trace these developments with any confidence, though they are obviously implicated in much wider changes in political culture. Nevertheless, the changed language of the fourth century serves to highlight the discursive continuity through the three centuries covered here.

I have sought to be clear throughout about the limits of our knowledge. It is particularly frustrating that so little survives of the rhetoric of the extortion court. The trials of Roman senators accused of misconduct in provincial office, first in the *quaestio repetundarum* and later in the senate or before the emperor, were evidently a context in which the proper relationship between the imperial elite and their provincial subjects was repeatedly contested. Yet this discourse is almost entirely lost to us. We have only a handful of speeches of Cicero, scattered fragments of other orators and a few allusions in letters and the historians. This is a sobering reminder of the limits of this study.

Some important questions remain. One concerns the distinctiveness of this Roman language of imperialism in its historical context. To what extent is Latin literature exceptional as an imperial literature in its willingness to identify the imperial project with enslavement? The trope of representing subjection to a foreign power as enslavement certainly has precedent in Greek literature. But it is almost entirely limited to the rhetoric of enemies of imperial powers.[5] The surviving corpus offers only a handful of examples of imperial elites describing their own subjects' condition in terms of slavery. In fifth-century Athens, Thucydides is remarkable for his representation of Athenian rule as enslavement. But it is significant that even he employs this language almost exclusively in the rhetoric of Athens' enemies.[6] Moreover, Polly Low has argued that Thucydides' narrative is an

[5] See pp. 108–9. [6] See pp. 109–10.

unreliable guide to the language of Athenian imperialism in the fifth century, which almost certainly incorporated more gestures of inclusion than the historian suggests.[7] In the fourth century, Aristotle is said to have advised Alexander to behave as a leader (ἡγεμονικῶς) to the Greeks but a master (δεσποτικῶς) to the barbarians. He thus embraced slavery as a paradigm for imperial rule – but only for an empire's barbarian subjects.[8] Philip V of Macedon was notorious for having described the three Greek cities which he had garrisoned as the 'fetters' of Greece (τὰς πέδας τῆς Ἑλλάδος) – thus implying that Greece was his slave.[9] But these exceptions are few and far between. The overt avowals of Roman mastery and provincial slavery in Latin literature do seem to mark a break from Greek precedent.

I would not wish, however, to place too much weight on this conclusion. I find it hard to imagine that these and other imperial elites did not represent their dominance in terms of mastery in other contexts, now lost to us. James Scott's model of the 'hidden transcript' is useful here. His influential study of discourse and power argues that dominated groups may express deference and consent 'in public' but invariably create and defend social spaces in which they can contest the terms of their subjection beyond observation by the powerful.[10] These clandestine discourses are what he calls 'hidden transcripts'. This concept has proved useful in recuperating a space for provincial resistance to Roman power.[11] Much less attention has been paid to Scott's insight that the powerful too have a hidden transcript, a guarded discourse articulated in their own private spaces in which they acknowledge aspects of their power

[7] Low 2005. On the language of Athenian imperialism, see further Raaflaub 2004 pp. 166–81 and Strasburger 1958.

[8] Plut. *De Alex. fort.* 329b. The anecdote is consistent with Arist. *Pol.* 1333b–34a. See further p. 118 n. 133.

[9] See Polyb. 18.11.5, Plut. *Flam.* 10.1, App. *Mac.* 8, Livy 32.37.4. The three cities were Acrocorinth, Chalcis and Demetrias. It is not certain when and in what context Philip used the trope (Walbank 1957–79 ad Polyb. 18.11.5). Indeed, according to Pausanias the trope he used was the 'keys' (κλεῖς) of Greece (7.7.6).

[10] Scott 1990.

[11] See e.g. Boyarin 1999 esp. pp. 46–9 on the Torah as a rare survival of a 'hidden transcript' from the Roman provinces. Cf. Mattingly 1997 pp. 13–15. Scott's model has been deployed even more widely in thinking about the public discourse of the Roman elite under the principate. See especially Bartsch 1994 ch. 5.

that they would not openly avow.[12] It is in such contexts – now lost to us – that we might expect fifth-century Athenians, the Greco-Macedonian elites of the Hellenistic kingdoms and other imperial powers to have represented their subjects as slaves. Where Roman culture is distinctive is in the extent to which the trope established itself in the less guarded discourse of literary texts – though it is significant that even in the Roman context it has left no trace in the public pronouncements of the emperor and other imperial officials. The aim of my focus on the paradigm of slavery is not to make a strong case for Roman distinctiveness in this respect, but rather to offer a counterweight to those who would make a very different claim for Roman exceptionalism based on the benevolent and integrationist rhetoric that has been the focus of most scholarship on this subject.

A second important question concerns the relationship between discourse and practice. Does this study of categories and tropes of Latin literature have any implications for the operations of Roman power in the provinces? The analysis has necessarily been limited to the texts that survive, all of which stand at some remove from the practice of empire. The closest are the letters and edicts discussed in Chapter 6, an important medium of communication between centre and periphery, and Cicero's speeches in the extortion court, each a concrete intervention in Roman politics which aimed to convince fellow senators to convict or to exonerate peers accused of misconduct in the provinces. Most of the rest – notably the historiography and verse that figured prominently in Chapters 2 and 3 – emerge from a literary culture that enjoyed some autonomy from social practice. Some pursue complex agendas that have little to do with the administration of the provinces. The most striking example analysed here is Tacitus' careful construction of provincial subjection as an analogue to the condition of the Roman senate under the *princeps*.

Nevertheless, the field of postcolonial studies has given us a significant insight into the political importance of discourse and

[12] 'The powerful, for their part, also develop a hidden transcript representing the practices and claims of their rule that cannot be openly avowed' (xii); 'The powerful have their own compelling reasons for adopting a mask in the presence of subordinates' (10).

representation. Edward Said's *Culture and Imperialism* demonstrated that even the apparently autonomous 'high culture' of the novel, opera and poetry was deeply implicated in the imperial projects of the nineteenth and twentieth centuries, serving to mobilise and renew energies for the continuous enterprise of acquiring and holding distant possessions. Literature is likely to have played a similar role in Roman society. Indeed, Latin literary culture is markedly less autonomous than those studied by Said. Literature was a core element of the aristocratic lifestyle. Many of the texts analysed here were written by men who themselves commanded legions, governed provinces or held other offices in the imperial administration. The senators Caesar, Cicero, the Younger Pliny, Tacitus and Cassius Dio have all figured prominently in this study. Other writers who were not themselves senators or office-holding equestrians moved in similar circles in the city of Rome, depended on the office-holding elite for patronage and could expect a wide readership among them.

The particular discursive operations analysed here are especially significant for practices of power. First, the dichotomies constructed through the use of categories such as *socii*, *prouinciae*, *prouinciales* and *peregrini* will have played an important role in delimiting imagined communities and establishing the limits of solidarity. They must have worked to dissociate imperial officials from their provincial subjects. Second, the metaphors, similes and analogies studied in the core chapters implicitly establish a normative framework for the exercise of Roman power. In so far as the responsibilities of a master to his dependants are very different to those of a patron or parent, these metaphors imply very different visions of the proper ends and means of Roman supremacy. These tropes must have both reflected and shaped the actions of the governing elite in provincial office.

The varied conceptions of the imperial project demonstrated by this book will surely have manifested themselves in a diversity of practice. But we must allow for the masterly style highlighted here to have been realised in the conduct of Roman officials – in the provinces as well as on the frontier. This book suggests that, well into the second century CE, at least some Roman officials will have distanced themselves from their provincial subjects and even regarded them with contempt. They may have seen fit to deploy some of the same practices of authority that they had honed in the management of their slaves in the governance of the provinces. It is particularly significant that the tropes of mastery and slavery are so prominent in the context of conquest and revolt. They legitimate – even demand – the use of the harshest sanctions, normally reserved for slaves, against those who resist Roman rule.

WORKS CITED

Abbott, F. F. and Johnson, A. C. (1926), *Municipal Administration in the Roman Empire*. Princeton.

Accame, S. (1946), *Il dominio romano in Grecia dalla guerra acaica ad Augusto*. Rome.

Achard, G. (1981), *Pratique, rhétorique et idéologie politique dans les discours 'optimates' de Cicéron*. Leiden.

Adams, J. N. (1982), *The Latin Sexual Vocabulary*. Baltimore.

Alexander, P. J. (1938), 'Letters and speeches of the emperor Hadrian', *HSCP* 49: 141–77.

Alföldi, A. (1952), 'The moral barrier on the Rhine and Danube', in A. R. Birley, ed., *Congress of Roman Frontier Studies 1949*, 1–16. Durham.

Alföldy, G. (2000), 'Das neue Edikt des Augustus aus El Bierzo in Hispanien', *ZPE* 131: 177–205.

Allen, J. (2006), *Hostages and Hostage-taking in the Roman Empire*. Cambridge.

Alonso-Nuñez, J. M. (1982), *The Ages of Rome*. Amsterdam.

Althusser, L. (1970), 'Ideology and ideological state apparatuses (notes towards an investigation)', in *Lenin and Philosophy and Other Essays*. New York: 127–86.

Anastasiadis, V. I. and Souris, G. A. (2000), *An Index to Roman Imperial Constitutions from Greek Inscriptions and Papyri: 27 BC to 284 AD*. Berlin.

Ando, C. (2000), *Imperial Ideology and Provincial Loyalty in the Roman Empire*. Berkeley.

Andreau, J. (1993), 'The freedman', in A. Giardina, ed., *The Romans*. Chicago: 175–98.

Arena, V. (2007), 'Invocation to liberty and invective of *dominatus* at the end of the Roman Republic', *BICS* 50: 49–74.

Arnold, W. T. (1889), 'The termination: *ensis*', *CR* 3: 201–2.

Astin, A. E. (1978), *Cato the Censor*. Oxford.

Aubert, J.-J. (2002), 'A double standard in Roman criminal law? The death penalty and social structure in Late Republican and Early Imperial Rome', in J.-J. Aubert and B. Sirks, eds., *Speculum Iuris*. Michigan: 94–133.

Baczko, B. (1984), *Les imaginaires sociaux: mémoires et espoirs collectifs*. Paris.

Badian, E. (1958), *Foreign Clientelae, 264–70 B.C.*. Oxford.

Baillie Reynolds, P. K. (1923), 'The troops quartered in the Castra Peregrinorum', *JRS* 13: 168–89.

Baldwin (1988), 'Four problems with Florus', *Latomus* 47: 134–42.

Balsdon, J. P. V. D. (1979), *Romans and Aliens*. London.

Bannon, C. J. (2009), *Gardens and Neighbors: Private Water Rights in Roman Italy*. Ann Arbor.

Barclay, J. M. G. (1996), *Jews in the Mediterranean Diaspora: From Alexander to Trajan (323 BCE–117 CE)*. Berkeley.

Barnes, T. D. (1984), 'The composition of Cassius Dio's *Roman History*', *Phoenix* 38: 240–55.

(1998), 'Two passages of Justin', *CQ* 48: 589–93.

Barrett, A. (2000), 'The *Laus Caesaris*: its history and its place in Latin literature', *Latomus* 59: 596–606.

Barsby, J. A., ed. (1999), *Terence: Eunuch*. Cambridge.

Bartsch, S. (1994), *Actors in the Audience: Theatricality and Doublespeak from Nero to Hadrian*. Cambridge.

Bastomsky, S. J. (1988), 'Tacitus, *Histories* IV 73–4: a unique view of Roman rule?' *Latomus* 47: 413–16.

Battistoni, F. (2009), 'Rome, kinship and diplomacy', in C. Eilers, ed., *Diplomats and Diplomacy in the Roman World*. Leiden: 73–97.

Beagon, M. (2007), 'Situating nature's wonders in Pliny's *Natural History*', in E. Bispham, G. Rowe and E. Matthews, eds., *Vita Vigilia Est: Papers on Pliny the Elder in Honour of Barbara Levick*. London: 19–40.

Beard, M. (1999), 'The erotics of rape: Livy, Ovid and the Sabine women', in P. Setälä and L. Savunen, eds., *Female Networks and the Public Sphere in Roman Society*. Rome: 1–10.

(2007), *The Roman Triumph*. Cambridge, MA.

Benario, H. W. (1964), 'Tacitus and the principate', *CJ* 60: 97–106.

(1991), 'Tacitus' view of the empire and the Pax Romana', *ANRW* II 33.5: 3332–53.

Bengtson, H. and Werner, R. (1975), *Die Staatsverträge des Altertums. Bd. 2, Die Verträge der griechisch-römischen Welt von 700 bis 338 v. Chr.*, 2nd edn, Munich.

Benner, M. (1975), *The Emperor Says: Studies in the Rhetorical Style in Edicts of the Early Empire*. Gothenburg.

Béranger, J. (1953), *Recherches sur l'aspect idéologique du Principat*. Basel.

(1975), *Principatus: études de notions et d'histoire politiques dans l'antiquité greco-romaine*. Geneva.

Berger, A., ed. (1953), *Encyclopedic Dictionary of Roman Law*. Philadelphia.

Bertrand, J.-M. (1990), 'Formes de discours politiques: décrets des cités grecques et correspondance des rois hellénistiques', in C. Nicolet, ed., *Du pouvoir dans l'antiquité: mots et réalités*. Paris and Geneva: 101–16.

Bessone, L. (1993), 'Floro: un retore storico e poeta', *ANRW* II 34.1: 80–117.

Birley, A. R. (1981), 'The economic effects of Roman frontier policy', in A. King and M. Henig, eds., *The Roman West in the Third Century*. Oxford, 39–53.

(2000), 'The life and death of Cornelius Tacitus', *Historia* 49: 230–47.

Bleicken, J. (1964), 'Review: E. Badian, *Foreign Clientelae*', *Gnomon* 36: 176–87.

Bömer, F. (1969–86), *P. Ovidius Naso. Metamorphosen*, 7 vols. Heidelberg.
Bowditch, P. L. (2001), *Horace and the Gift Economy of Patronage*. Berkeley.
Bowie, E. L. (1970), 'The Greeks and their past in the Second Sophistic', *P&P* 46: 3–41 (reprinted with changes in M. I. Finley, ed., *Studies in Ancient Society*. London, 1974: 166–209).
Bowman, D. A. (1990), 'The *formula sociorum* in the second and first centuries B.C.' *CJ* 85: 330–6.
Boyarin, D. (1999), *Martyrdom and the Making of Christianity and Judaism*. Stanford.
Bradley, K. R. (1984), *Slaves and Masters in the Roman Empire: A Study in Social Control*. Brussels.
(1986), 'Wet-nursing at Rome: a study in social relations', in B. Rawson, ed., *The Family in Ancient Rome: New Perspectives*. London: 201–29.
(1987), 'On the Roman slave supply and slave breeding', in M. I. Finley, ed., *Classical Slavery*. London: 53–81.
(1994a), 'The nurse and child at Rome: duty, affect and socialisation', *Thamyris* 1: 137–56.
(1994b), *Slavery and Society at Rome*. Cambridge.
(2000), 'Animalizing the slave: the truth of fiction', *JRS* 90: 110–25.
(2004), 'On captives under the Principate', *Phoenix* 58: 298–318.
Braund, D. (1982), 'Three Hellenistic personages: Amynander, Prusias II, Daphidas', *CQ* 32: 350–7.
(1996), *Ruling Roman Britain: Kings, Queens, Governors and Emperors from Julius Caesar to Agricola*. London.
Braund, S. M., ed. (2009), *Seneca: De Clementia: Edited with Text, Translation and Commentary*. Oxford.
Brecht, C. H. (1949), 'Patibulum', Pauly-Wissowa, *Real-Encyclopädie der classischen Altertumswissenschaft*, XVIII.4 2167–9.
Breitenbach, A. (2009), *Kommentar zu den Pseudo-Seneca-Epigrammen der Anthologia Latina*. Anthologiarum Latinarum parerga 2. Hildesheim.
Brennan, T. C. (2000), *The Praetorship in the Roman Republic*. 2 vols. Oxford.
Briscoe, J. (1981), *A Commentary on Livy: Books XXXIV–XXXVII*. Oxford.
(2008), *A Commentary on Livy: Books 38–40*. Oxford.
Brock, R. (2007), 'Figurative slavery in Greek thought', in A. Serghidou, ed., *Fear of Slaves – Fear of Enslavement in the Ancient Mediterranean. Peur de l'esclave – Peur de l'esclavage en Méditerranée ancienne (Discours, représentations, pratiques). Actes du XXIXe colloque international du Groupe International de Recherches sur l'Esclavage dans l'Antiquité (GIREA). Rethymnon 4–7 novembre 2004*. Franche-Comté: 209–15.
Brown, R. D. (2003), 'The terms *bellum sociale* and *bellum ciuile* in the late Republic', in C. Deroux, ed., *Studies in Latin Literature and Roman History* XI. Brussels: 94–120.
Brunt, P. A. (1961), 'Charges of provincial maladministration under the early principate', *Historia* 10: 189–227 (= Brunt, 1990: 53–95).

(1966), 'The "fiscus" and its development', *JRS* 56: 75–91 (= Brunt 1990: 134–62).

(1971), *Italian Manpower, 225 B.C.–A.D. 14*. Oxford.

(1974), 'Conscription and volunteering in the Roman imperial army', *SCI* 1: 90–115 (= Brunt 1990: 188–214).

(1976), 'The Romanization of the local ruling classes in the Roman empire', in D. M. Pippidi, ed., *Assimilation et résistance à la culture gréco-romaine dans le monde ancien*. Paris: 161–73 (= Brunt 1990: 267–81).

(1978), '*Laus imperii*', in P. Garnsey and C. R. Whittaker, eds., *Imperialism in the Ancient World*. Cambridge: 159–91 (= Brunt 1990: 288–323).

(1980), 'Evidence given under torture in the principate', *ZRG* 97: 256–65.

(1981), 'The revenues of Rome', *JRS* 71: 161–72 (= Brunt 1990: 324–46).

(1988), *The Fall of the Roman Republic and Related Essays*. Oxford.

(1990), *Roman Imperial Themes*. Oxford.

Büchner, K., ed. (1984), *M. Tullius Cicero: De Re Publica*. Heidelberg.

Buckland, W. W. (1908), *The Roman Law of Slavery: The Condition of the Slave in Private Law from Augustus to Justinian*. Cambridge.

Burbank, J. and F. Cooper (2010), *Empires in World History: Power and the Politics of Difference*. Princeton.

Burton, P. J. (2011), *Friendship and Empire: Roman Diplomacy and Imperialism in the Middle Republic (353–146 BC)*. Cambridge.

Carey, S. (2003), *Pliny's Catalogue of Culture: Art and Empire in the* Natural History. Oxford.

Castoriadis, C. (1987), *The Imaginary Institution of Society*. Cambridge. Trans. of *L'institution imaginaire de la société*. Paris, 1975.

Chastagnol, A. (1992), *Le sénat romain à l'époque imperiale: recherches sur la composition de l'assemblée et le statut de ses membres*. Paris.

Cherry, D. (1998), *Frontier and Society in Roman North Africa*. Oxford.

Christ, F. (1938), *Die römische Weltherrschaft in der antike Dichtung*. Tübinger Beiträge zur Altertumswissenschaft 31. Stuttgart.

Clark, G. (2004), 'Pilgrims and foreigners: Augustine on travelling home', in L. Ellis and F. Kidner, eds., *Travel, Communication and Geography in Late Antiquity*. Aldershot and Burlington, VT: 149–58.

Clarke, K. (2001), 'An island nation: re-reading Tacitus' *Agricola*', *JRS* 91: 94–112.

Claussen, M. A. (1991), '*Peregrinatio* and *peregrini* in Augustine's "City of God"', *Traditio* 46: 33–75.

Clemente, G. (1972), 'Il patronato nei collegia dell' impero Romano', *SCO* 21: 142–229.

Cloud, J. D. (1988), '*Lex Iulia de vi*: part 1', *Athenaeum* 66: 579–95.

(1989), '*Lex Iulia de vi*: part 2', *Athenaeum* 67: 427–65.

Cody, J. M. (2003), 'Conquerors and conquered on Flavian coins', in A. J. Boyle and W. J. Dominik, eds., *Flavian Rome: Culture, Image, Text*. Leiden: 103–24.

Combes, I. A. H. (1998), *The Metaphor of Slavery in the Writings of the Early Church: From the New Testament to the Beginning of the Fifth Century.* Journal for the Study of the Old Testament Supplement 156. Sheffield.

Corbier, M. (1974), 'Le discours du prince d'après une inscription de Banasa', *Ktèma* 2: 211–32 (= *Donner à voir, donner à lire: mémoire et communication dans la Rome ancienne*. Paris, 2006: 197–213).

(1988), 'L'impôt dans l'empire romain: résistances et refus (Ier–IIIe siècles)', in T. Yuge and M. Doi, eds., *Forms of Control and Subordination in Antiquity*. Tokyo: 259–74.

(1991), 'City, territory and taxation', in J. Rich and A. Wallace-Hadrill, eds., *City and Country in the Ancient World*. London: 211–36.

Courtney, E., ed. (1993), *The Fragmentary Latin Poets*. Oxford.

Cova, P. V. (1972), 'Arte allusiva e stilizzazione retorica nelle lettere di Plinio. A proposito di VI, 31, 16–17 ; II, 6 ; VIII, 16 ; VIII, 24 ; VII, 33, 10', *Aevum* 46: 16–36.

Crawford, M. (1996), *Roman Statutes*. 2 vols. London.

Crook, J. A. (1967), *Law and Life of Rome*. London.

Currie, S. (1996), 'The empire of adults: the representation of children on Trajan's arch at Beneventum', in J. Elsner, ed., *Art and Text in Roman Culture*. Cambridge: 153–81.

Dahlheim, W. (1965), *Deditio und societas: Untersuchungen zur Entwicklung der römischen Aussenpolitik in der Blütezeit der Republik*. Bonn.

(1968), *Struktur und Entwicklung des römischen Völkerrechts*. Vestigia 8. Munich.

Damon, C. (1997), *The Mask of the Parasite: A Pathology of Roman Patronage*. Ann Arbor.

Dauge, Y. A. (1981), *Le barbare: recherches sur la conception romaine de la barbarie et de la civilisation*. Collection Latomus 176. Brussels.

David, J.-M. (1992), *Le patronat judiciaire au dernier siècle de la république romaine*. Rome.

Demougin, S. (1988), *L'ordre équestre sous les Julio-Claudiens*. Rome.

Dench, E. (2005), *Romulus' Asylum: Roman Identities from the Age of Alexander to the Age of Hadrian*. Oxford.

Deniaux, É. (1993), *Clientèles et pouvoir à l'époque de Cicéron*. Coll. École Française de Rome 182. Rome.

Devijver, H. (1992), *The Equestrian Officers of the Roman Imperial Army, vol. II*. Mavors: Roman Army Researches 9. Stuttgart.

Dillon, S. (2006), 'Women on the columns of Trajan and Marcus Aurelius and the visual language of Roman victory', in S. Dillon and K. E. Welch, eds., *Representations of War in Ancient Rome*. Cambridge: 244–71.

Dixon, S. (1993), 'The meaning of gift and debt in the Roman elite', *EMC* 37: 451–64.

Dmitriev, S. (2010), *The Greek Slogan of Freedom and Early Roman Politics in Greece*. Oxford.

Domaszewski, A. von (1924), *Bellum Marsicum*. Vienna and Leipzig.
Drummond, A. (1989), 'Early Roman *clientes*', in A. Wallace-Hadrill, ed., *Patronage in Ancient Society*. London: 89–115.
Ducos, M. (1977), 'La liberté chez Tacite: droits de l'individu ou conduite individuelle?' *BAGB* 2: 194–217.
Duff, A. M. (1928), *Freedmen in the Early Roman Empire*. Cambridge.
Dumont, J. C. (1983), 'Conquête et esclavage chez Cicéron: *De Republica* III, 36–37', *Ktèma* 8: 113–28.
Duncan-Jones, R. (1994), *Money and Government in the Roman Empire*. Cambridge.
Durry, M., ed. (1938), *Pline le Jeune: Panégyrique de Trajan*. Paris.
Dyck, A. R. (1996), *A Commentary on Cicero, De Officiis*. Ann Arbor.
Eck, W. (1979), *Die staatliche Organisation Italiens in der hohen Kaiserzeit*. Munich.
(1998a), 'Administrative Dokumente: Publikation und Mittel der Selbstdarstellung', in *Die Verwaltung des römischen Reiches in der hohen Kaiserzeit: ausgewählte und erweiterte Beiträge* III. Basel: 359–82.
(1998b), 'Inschriften auf Holz. Ein unterschätztes Phänomen der epigraphischen Kultur Roms', in P. Kneißl and V. Losemann, eds., *Imperium Romanum. Studien zu Geschichte und Rezeption. Festschrift für Karl Christ zum 75. Geburtstag*. Stuttgart: 203–17.
(2000), 'Provincial administration and finance', in A. K. Bowman, P. Garnsey and D. Rathbone, eds., *Cambridge Ancient History*, vol. XI, 2nd edn. Cambridge: 266–92.
(2009a), 'Diplomacy as part of the administrative process in the Roman empire', in C. Eilers, ed., *Diplomats and Diplomacy in the Roman World*. Leiden,
(2009b), 'The presence, role and significance of Latin in the epigraphy and culture of the Roman Near East', in H. M. Cotton, R. G. Hoyland, J. J. Price and D. J. Wasserstein, eds., *From Hellenism to Islam: Cultural and Linguistic Change in the Roman Near East*. Cambridge: 15–42.
Eck, W., Caballos, A. and Fernandez, F. (1996), *Das senatus consultum de Cn. Pisone patre*. Vestigia 48. Munich.
Eckstein, A. M. (1999), 'Pharos and the question of Roman treaties of alliance in the Greek East in the third century B.C.E.' *CP* 94: 395–418.
Edwards, C. (1993), *The Politics of Immorality in Ancient Rome*. Cambridge.
(2009), 'Free yourself! Slavery, freedom and the self in Seneca's *Letters*', in S. Bartsch and D. Wray, eds., *Seneca and the Self*. Cambridge: 139–59.
Eilers, C. (2002), *Roman Patrons of Greek Cities*. Oxford.
ed. (2009), *Diplomats and Diplomacy in the Roman World*. Leiden.
Erskine, A. (1990), *The Hellenistic Stoa*. London.
(1994), 'The Romans as common benefactors', *Historia* 43: 70–87.
Evans, R. (2003), 'Containment and corruption: the discourse of Flavian empire', in A. J. Boyle and W. J. Dominik, eds., *Flavian Rome: Culture, Image, Text*. Leiden: 255–76.

Fabre, G. (1981), *Libertus. Recherches sur les rapports patron-affranchi à la fin de la République Romaine*. Rome.
Farney, G. D. (2007), *Ethnic Identity and Aristocratic Competition in Republican Rome*. Cambridge.
Fear, A. T. (1996), *Rome and Baetica: Urbanization in Southern Spain c. 50 BC–AD 150*. Oxford.
(1997), 'Review of D. Braund, *Ruling Roman Britain*', *BMCRev* 97.11.18: non pag.
(2011), 'The Roman's burden', in R. Gibson and R. Morello, eds., *Pliny the Elder: Themes and Contexts*. Leiden: 21–34.
Fentress, L., ed. (2000), *Romanization and the City: Creation, Transformations and Failures*. JRA Supplementary Series 38. Portsmouth, RI.
Ferrary, J.-L. (1974), 'Le discours de Laelius dans le troisième livre du De republica de Cicéron', *MEFRA* 86: 747–71.
(1977), 'Le discours de Philus (Cic. *De republica* III, 8, 31) et la philosophie de Carnéade', *REL* 55: 128–56.
(1988), *Philhellénisme et impérialisme: aspects idéologiques de la conquête romaine du monde hellénistique*. Rome.
(1997a), 'De l'évergétisme hellénistique à l'évergétisme romain', in M. Christol and O. Masson, eds., *Actes du Xe Congrès international d'épigraphie grecque et latine, Nîmes, 4–9 octobre 1992*. Paris: 199–225.
(1997b), 'The Hellenistic world and Roman political patronage', in P. A. Cartledge, P. Garnsey and E. S. Gruen, eds., *Hellenistic Constructs: Essays in Culture, History, and Historiography*. Berkeley: 105–19.
Ferris, I. M. (2000), *Enemies of Rome: Barbarians through Roman Eyes*. Stroud.
Finley, M. I. (1980), *Ancient Slavery and Modern Ideology*. London.
Fitzgerald, W. (2000), *Slavery and the Roman Literary Imagination*. Cambridge.
Forni, G. (1953), *Il reclutamento delle legioni da Augusto a Diocleziano*. Rome.
(1974), 'Estrazione etnica e sociale dei soldati delle legioni nei primi tre secoli dell'impero', *ANRW* II 1: 339–91.
Forte, B. (1972), *Rome and the Romans as the Greeks Saw Them*. Rome.
Foucault, M. (1979), 'Governmentality', *Ideology and Consciousness* 6: 5–12 (= G. Burchell, C. Gordon and P. Miller, eds., *The Foucault Effect*. Chicago, 1991: 87–104).
Fraenkel, E. (1916), 'Zur Geschichte des Wortes *fides*', *RhM* 71: 187–99 (= *Kleine Beiträge zur klassischen Philologie*. 2 vols. Rome, 1964: 538–98).
(1957), *Horace*. Oxford.
Frank, T., ed. (1933–40), *Economic Survey of Ancient Rome*. 5 vols. Baltimore.
Frere, S. and Fulford, M. (2002), 'The *collegium peregrinorum* at Silchester', *Britannia* 33: 167–75.
Freyburger, G. (1986), *Fides. Étude sémantique et religieuse depuis les origines jusqu' à l'époque augustéenne*. Paris.
Friedländer, L. (1919–20), *Sittengeschichte Roms*, 9th edn. 3 vols. Leipzig.
Furneaux, H., ed. (1896–1907), *The Annals of Tacitus*, 2nd edn. 2 vols. Oxford.

Galsterer, H. (1996), 'The administration of justice', in A. K. Bowman, E. Champlin and A. Lintott, eds., *Cambridge Ancient History*, vol. x, 2nd edn. Cambridge: 397–413.

Gamauf, R. (2007), '"*Cum aliter nulla domus tuta esse possit…* ": fear of slaves and Roman law', in A. Serghidou, ed., *Fear of Slaves – Fear of Enslavement in the Ancient Mediterranean. Peur de l'esclave – Peur de l'esclavage en Méditerranée ancienne (Discours, représentations, pratiques). Actes du* XXIX*e colloque international du Groupe International de Recherches sur l'Esclavage dans l'Antiquité (GIREA). Rethymnon 4–7 novembre 2004*. Franche-Comté: 145–64.

Gamberini, F. (1983), *Stylistic Theory and Practice in the Younger Pliny*. Hildesheim.

Gardner, J. F. and Wiedemann, T. (1991), *The Roman Household: A Sourcebook*. London.

Garnsey, P. (1966), 'The *lex Iulia* and appeal under the emperor', *JRS* 56: 181–203.

(1970), *Social Status and Legal Privilege in the Roman Empire*. Oxford.

(1996), *Ideas of Slavery from Aristotle to Augustine*. Cambridge.

(2010), 'Roman patronage', in S. McGill, C. Sogno and E. Watts, eds., *From the Tetrarchs to the Theodosians*. Cambridge: 33–54.

Gauthier, P. (1985), *Les cités grecques et leurs bienfaiteurs (*IV*e–*I*er siecles avant J.-C.): contribution a l'histoire des institutions*. Athens and Paris.

Gelzer, M. (1969), *The Roman Nobility*. Oxford. Trans. of *Die Nobilität der römischen Republik*. Leipzig, 1912.

Gerber, A. and Greef, A. (1903), *Lexicon Taciteum*. Leipzig.

Gilmartin, K. (1973), 'Corbulo's campaigns in the East: an analysis of Tacitus' account', *Historia* 22: 583–626.

Ginsburg, J. (1993), '*In maiores certamina*: past and present in the *Annals*', in T. J. Luce and A. J. Woodman, eds., *Tacitus and the Tacitean Tradition*. Princeton: 86–103.

Gleason, M. (1986), 'Festive satire: Julian's *Misopogon* and the New Year at Antioch', *JRS* 1986: 106–19.

Glucker, J. (2001), 'Carneades in Rome: some unsolved problems', in J. G. F. Powell and J. A. North, eds., *Cicero's Republic*. BICS Supplement 76. London.

Gold, B. K. (1987), *Literary Patronage in Greece and Rome*. Chapel Hill.

Goldbeck, F. (2010), *Salutationes. Die Morgenbegrüßungen in Rom in der Republik und der frühen Kaiserzeit*. Klio Beiheift 16. Berlin.

Goldhill, S., ed. (2001), *Being Greek under Rome*. Cambridge.

Gomme, A. W. (1962), 'The concept of freedom', in *More Essays in Greek History and Literature*. Oxford: 139–55.

Gonzalez, J. (1986), 'The *lex Irnitana*: a new copy of the Flavian municipal law', *JRS* 76: 147–243.

Goodyear, F. R. D. (1972–81), *The Annals of Tacitus*. 2 vols. Cambridge.

Gotter, U. (2008), 'Cultural differences and cross-cultural contact: Greek and Roman concepts of power.' *HSCP* 104: 179–230.

Griffin, M. T. (2003), '*De beneficiis* and Roman society', *JRS* 93: 92–11.
Gruen, E. S. (1982), 'Greek *pistis* and Roman *fides*', *Athenaeum* 60: 50–68.
(1984), *The Hellenistic World and the Coming of Rome*. 2 vols. Berkeley.
Grünewald, T. (2004), *Bandits in the Roman Empire: Myth and Reality*. London. Trans. of *Räuber, Rebellen, Rivalen, Räucher*. Mainz, 1999.
Guillemin, A. M. (1929), *Pline et la vie littéraire de son temps*. Paris.
Habinek, T. N. (1998), *The Politics of Latin Literature: Writing, Identity and Empire in Ancient Rome*. Princeton.
Hall, C., ed. (2000), *Cultures of Empire: Colonizers in Britain and the Empire in the Nineteenth and Twentieth Centuries*. Manchester.
Hammond, M. (1957), 'Composition of the senate, A.D. 68 to A.D. 235', *JRS* 47: 74–81.
(1963), '*Res olim dissociabiles: principatus ac libertas*. Liberty under the early Roman empire', *HSCP* 67: 93–113.
Harker, A. (2008), *Loyalty and Dissidence in Roman Egypt: The Case of the Acta Alexandrinorum*. Cambridge.
Harmand, L. (1957), *Un aspect social et politique du monde romain: le patronat sur les collectivités publiques des origines au Bas empire*. Paris.
Harper, K. (2011), *Slavery in the Roman World, AD 275–425*. Cambridge.
Harries, J. (forthcoming), 'The senatus consultum Silanianum: court decisions and judicial severity in the early Roman empire', in P. J. Du Plessis, ed., *New Frontiers: Law and Society in the Roman World*. Edinburgh.
Harris, W. V. (1979), *War and Imperialism in Republican Rome, 327–70 BC*. Oxford.
Hatzfeld, J. (1919), *Les trafiquants italiens dans l'Orient hellénique*. Paris.
Hatzopoulos, M. B. (1996), *Macedonian Institutions under the Kings*. 2 vols. Athens.
Hauken, T. (1998), *Petition and Response: An Epigraphic Study of Petitions to Roman Emperors*. Monographs from the Norwegian Institute at Athens 2. Bergen.
Hauken, T. and Malay, H. (2009), 'A new edict of Hadrian from the province of Asia setting regulations for requisitioned transport', in R. Haensch, ed., *Selbstdarstellung und Kommunikation: Die Veröffentlichung staatlicher Urkunden auf Stein und Bronze in der römischen Welt*. Munich: 327–48.
Haynes, H. (2003), *The History of Make-Believe: Tacitus on Imperial Rome*. Berkeley.
(2004), 'Tacitus's dangerous word', *ClAnt* 23: 33–61.
(2006), 'Survival and memory in the *Agricola*', *Arethusa* 39: 149–70.
Hellegouarc'h, J. (1963), *Le vocabulaire Latin des relations et des partis politiques sous la république*. Paris.
Helzle, M. (1989), *Publii Ovidii Nasonis Epistularum ex Ponto liber IV: A Commentary on Poems 1–7 and 16*. Hildesheim.
Hemelrijk, E. A. (1999), *Matrona docta: Educated Women in the Roman Elite from Cornelia to Julia Domna*. London.

Henderson, J. (1989), 'Tacitus/The world in pieces', *Ramus* 18: 167–210 (= *Fighting for Rome*. Oxford: 257–300).

Hengel, M. (1978), *Crucifixion in the Ancient World and the Folly of the Message of the Cross*. Philadelphia.

Heubner, H. (1963–82), *P. Cornelius Tacitus: Die Historien*. 5 vols. Heidelberg.

(1984), *Kommentar zum Agricola des Tacitus*. Göttingen.

Heuss, A. (1933), *Die völkerrechtlichen Grundlagen der römischen Aussenpolitik in republikanischer Zeit*. Klio Beiheift 31. Leipzig.

Heyworth, S. J. (1993), 'Deceitful Crete: *Aeneid* 3.84. and the Hymns of Callimachus', *CQ* 43: 255–7.

Hingley, R. (2005), *Globalizing Roman Culture: Unity, Diversity and Empire*. London and New York.

Hitzig, H. (1901), 'Crux', Pauly-Wissowa, *Real-Encyclopädie der classischen Altertumswissenschaft*, IV 1728–9.

Hopkins, K. (1980), 'Taxes and trade in the Roman empire (200 B.C.–A.D. 400)', *JRS* 70: 101–25.

(1993), 'Novel evidence for Roman slavery', *P&P* 138: 3–27.

Horn, H. (1930), *Foederati*. Frankfurt.

Hose, M. (1998), '*Libertas an pax*. Eine Beobachtung zu Tacitus' Darstellung des Bataveraufstandes', *Hermes* 126: 297–309.

Hughes, J. (2009), 'Personifications and the ancient viewer: the case of the Hadrianeum "nations"', *Art History* 32: 1–20.

Hunter, V. (1973/4), 'Athens *tyrannis*', *CJ* 69: 120–6.

Hurlet, F., ed. (2008), *Les Empires: antiquité et moyen âge. Analyse comparée*. Rennes.

Isaac, B. (1992), *The Limits of Empire: The Roman Imperial Army in the East*. 2nd edn. Oxford.

(2004), *The Invention of Racism in Classical Antiquity*. Princeton.

Jacques, F. (1984), *Le privilège de liberté. Politique impériale et autonomie municipale dans les cités de l' Occident romain (161–244)*. Rome.

Jacques, F. and Scheid, J. (1990), *Rome et l'intégration de l'empire (44 av. J.-C.–260 ap. J.-C.). Tome 1, Les structures de l'empire romain*. Paris.

Jal, P., ed. (1967), *Florus: Œuvres*. Paris.

(1987), 'A propos des Histoires Philippiques: quelques remarques', *REL* 65: 194–209.

Jens, W. (1956), '*Libertas* bei Tacitus', *Hermes* 84: 331–52.

Jones, A. H. M. (1940), *The Greek City from Alexander to Justinian*. Oxford.

(1974), 'Taxation in antiquity', in *The Roman Economy: Studies in Ancient Economic and Administrative History*. Oxford: 151–85.

Jones, C. P. (1999), *Kinship Diplomacy in the Ancient World*. Cambridge, MA.

Joshel, S. R. (1992), 'The body female and the body politic: Livy's Lucretia and Verginia', in A. Richlin, ed., *Pornography and Representation in Greece and Rome*. Oxford: 112–30 (= L. K. McClure, ed., *Sexuality and Gender in the Classical World*. London, 2002: 163–87).

Joshel, S. R. and Murnaghan, S. (1998), *Women and Slaves in Greco-Roman Culture: Differential Equations*. London.

Kaimio, J. (1979), *The Romans and the Greek Language*. Helsinki.

Kajanto, I. (1969), 'Tacitus on the slaves: an interpretation of the *Annals* XIV, 42–5', *Arctos* NS 6: 43–60.

Kallet-Marx, R. M. (1996), *Hegemony to Empire: The Development of the Roman Imperium in the East from 148 to 62 B.C.* Berkeley.

Kaster, R. A. (2002), 'The taxonomy of patience, or when is *patientia* not a virtue?' *CP* 97: 133–44.

Katzoff, R. (1980), 'Sources of law in Roman Egypt: the role of the Prefect', *ANRW* II 13: 807–44.

Keay, S. and Terrenato, N., eds. (2001), *Italy and the West: Comparative Studies in Romanization*. Oxford.

Keitel, E. (1978), 'The role of Parthia and Armenia in Tacitus *Annals* 11 and 12', *AJP* 99: 462–73.

(1993), 'Speech and narrative in *Histories* 4', in T. J. Luce and A. J. Woodman, eds., *Tacitus and the Tacitean Tradition*. Princeton: 39–58.

Kenney, E. J. (1979), '*Iudicium transferendi*: Virgil, *Aeneid* 2.469–505 and its antecedents', in D. West and A. J. Woodman, eds., *Creative Imitation and Latin Literature*. Cambridge. 103–20.

Kienast, D. (1982), '*Corpus imperii*: Überlegung zum Reichsdanken der Römer', in G. Wirth, ed., *Romanitas-Christianitas: Untersuchungen zur Geschichte und Literatur der römischen Kaiserzeit, Johannes Straub zum 70. Geburtstag*. Berlin: 1–17.

Kissel, T. K. (1997), '*Sub iugum mittere*: zur kollektiven Bestrafung unterworfener Kriegsgefangener im republikanichen Rom', *AW* 28: 501–7.

Kleiner, D. E. E. and Buxton, B. (2008), 'Pledges of empire: the Ara Pacis and the donations of Rome', *AJA* 112: 57–89.

Koestermann, E., ed. (1963–8), *Cornelius Tacitus: Annalen*. 4 vols. Heidelberg.

Kokkinia, C. (2004), 'Ruling, inducing, arguing: how to govern (and survive) a Greek province', in L. De Ligt, E. A. Hemelrijk and H. W. Singor, eds., *Roman Rule and Civic Life: Local and Regional Perspectives. Proceedings of the Fourth Workshop of the International Network Impact of Empire (Roman Empire, c. 200 B.C.–A.D. 476)*. Amsterdam: 39–58.

(2009), 'The role of individuals in inscribing Roman state documents: governors' letters and edicts', in R. Haensch, ed., *Selbstdarstellung und Kommunikation: Die Veröffentlichung staatlicher Urkunden auf Stein und Bronze in der römischen Welt*. Munich: 191–206.

Kolb, A. (2001), 'Transport and communication in the Roman state', in C. Adams and R. Laurence, eds., *Travel and Geography in the Roman Empire*. London: 95–105.

Kolendo, J. (1981), 'L'esclavage et la vie sexuelle des hommes libres à Rome', *Quaderni Camerti di Studi Romanistici* 10: 288–97.

Kornemann, M. (1900), '*Colonia*', Pauly-Wissowa, *Real-Encyclopädie der classischen Altertumswissenschaft*, IV 511–88.

Kotula, T. (1982), *Les principales d'Afrique*. Warsaw.

Kousser, R. (2005), 'From conquest to civilization: the rhetoric of imperialism in the Early Principate', in J.-J. Aubert and Z. Várhelyi, eds., *A Tall Order: Writing the Social History of the Ancient World: Essays in Honor of William V. Harris*. Munich: 185–202.

(2008), *Hellenistic and Roman Ideal Sculpture: The Allure of the Classical*. Cambridge.

Kubitschek, W. (1894), 'Alimenta', Pauly-Wissowa, *Real-Encyclopädie der classischen Altertumswissenschaft*, I 1484–9.

Kübler, B. (1937), 'Peregrinus', Pauly-Wissowa, *Real-Encyclopädie der classischen Altertumswissenschaft*, XIX.1 639–55.

Kuhn, H.-W. (1982), 'Die Kreuzesstrafe während der frühen Kaiserzeit. Ihre Wirklichkeit und Wertung in der Umwelt des Urchristentums', *ANRW* II 25.1: 648–793.

Kuttner, A. L. (1995), *Dynasty and Empire in the Age of Augustus: The Case of the Boscoreale Cups*. Berkeley.

Lakoff, G. and Turner, M. (1980), *Metaphors We Live By*. Chicago.

Langlands, R. (2006), *Sexual Morality in Ancient Rome*. Cambridge.

Lauffer, S., ed. (1971), *Diokletians Preisedikt*. Berlin.

Lavan, M. (2007), 'Slaves to Rome: the rhetoric of mastery in Titus' speech to the Jews (*Bellum Judaicum* 6.328–50)', *Ramus* 36: 25–38.

(2011), 'Slavishness in Britain and Rome in Tacitus' *Agricola*', *CQ* 61: 294–305.

(2013), 'Florus and Dio on Rome's rise to mastery', *CCJ* 59.

Leeman, A. D. (1973), 'Structure and meaning in the prologues of Tacitus', *YClS* 23: 169–208.

Lendon, J. E. (1997), *Empire of Honour: The Art of Government in the Roman World*. Cambridge.

Lenger, M.-T. (1980), *Corpus des 'Ordonnances' des Ptolémées*, 2nd edn. Brussels.

Lieberman, S. (1944), 'Roman legal institutions in early rabbinics and in the *Acta Martyrum*', *Jewish Quarterly Review* 35: 1–57.

Liebeschuetz, J. H. W. G. (1966), 'The theme of liberty in the *Agricola* of Tacitus', *CQ* 16: 126–39. (reprinted with revisions in R. Ash, ed., *Oxford Readings in Tacitus*. Oxford, 2012: 73–94)

(1979), *Continuity and Change in Roman Religion*. Oxford.

Lintott, A. (1981a), 'The *leges de repetundis* and associated measures under the republic', *ZRG* 98: 162–212.

(1981b), 'What was the "*Imperium Romanum*"?' *G&R* 28: 53–67.

(1992), *Judicial Reform and Land Reform in the Roman Republic: A New Edition with Translation and Commentary of the Laws from Urbino*. Cambridge.

(1993), *Imperium Romanum*. London.

(2008), *Cicero as Evidence: A Historian's Companion*. Oxford.

Long, A. A. (1995), 'Cicero's politics in *De officiis*', in A. Laks and M. Schofield, eds., *Justice and Generosity: Studies in Hellenistic Social and Political*

Philosophy. Proceedings of the Sixth Symposium Hellenisticum. Cambridge: 213–40.

Low, P. (2005), 'Looking for the language of Athenian imperialism', *JHS* 125: 93–111.

Lyne, R. O. A. M., ed. (1977), *Ciris: A Poem Attributed to Vergil*. Cambridge.

Ma, J. (2002), *Antiochos III and the Cities of Western Asia Minor*. Oxford.

MacMullen, R. (1986), 'Judicial savagery in the Roman empire', *Chiron* 16: 147–66 (= *Changes in the Roman Empire: Essays in the Ordinary*. Princeton. 1990: 204–17).

(1988), *Corruption and the Decline of Rome*. New Haven.

(2000), *Romanization in the Age of Augustus*. New Haven.

Mann, J. C. (1983), *Legionary Recruitment and Veteran Settlement during the Principate*. Institute of Archaeology Publications 7. London.

(1988), 'The castra peregrina and the "peregrini"', *ZPE* 74: 148.

Manuwald, G., ed. (2007), *Cicero, Philippics 3–9*. Berlin.

Marquardt, J. (1881–5), *Römische Staatsverwaltung*. 3 vols. Leipzig.

Marshall, A. J. (1968), 'Friends of the Roman people', *AJP* 89: 39–55.

Martin, D. B. (1990), *Slavery and Salvation*. New Haven.

Mathisen, R. W. (2006), '*Peregrini, barbari,* and *cives Romani*: concepts of citizenship and the legal identity of barbarians in the Later Roman Empire', *AHR* 111: 1011–40.

(2009), '*Provinciales, gentiles,* and marriages between Romans and barbarians in the late Roman empire', *JRS* 99: 140–55.

Mattern, S. P. (1999), *Rome and the Enemy: Imperial Strategy in the Principate*. Berkeley.

Matthaei, L. E. (1907), 'On the classification of the Roman allies', *CQ* 1: 182–204.

Mattingly, D. J. (1997), 'Dialogues of power and experience in the Roman Empire', in id., ed., *Dialogues in Roman Imperialism: Power and Discrepant Experience in the Roman Empire*. Portsmouth, RI.

Mayer, R., ed. (2001), *Tacitus: Dialogus de Oratoribus*. Cambridge.

Maza, S. C. (2003), *The Myth of the French Bourgeoisie: An Essay on the Social Imaginary, 1750–1850*. Cambridge, MA.

McCarthy, K. (2000), *Slaves, Masters, and the Art of Authority in Plautine Comedy*. Princeton.

McGing, B. (1982), 'Syncrisis in Tacitus' *Agricola*', *Hermathena* 133: 15–25.

Mellor, R. (1975), *ΘΕΑ ΡΩΜΗ: The Goddess Roma in the Greek World*. Göttingen.

(1981), 'The goddess Roma', *ANRW* II 17.2: 950–1030.

Meritt, B. D., Wade-Gery, H. T. and McGregor, M. F. (1939–53), *The Athenian Tribute Lists*. 4 vols. Cambridge, MA.

Méthy, N. (1992), 'La représentation des provinces dans le monnayage de l'époque imperiale', *NAC* 21: 267–95.

Meyer, E. A. (2004), *Legitimacy and Law in the Roman World: Tabulae in Roman Belief and Practice*. Cambridge and New York.

Meyer-Zwiffelhoffer, E. (2003), *Πολιτικῶς ἄρχειν: Zum Regierungsstil der senatorischen Statthalter in den kaiserzeitlichen griechischen Provinzen*. Historia Einzelschrift 165. Stuttgart.
Michel, J.-H. (1962), *Gratuité en droit romain*. Brussels.
Millar, F. (1964), *A Study of Cassius Dio*. Oxford.
(1977), *The Emperor in the Roman World (31 BC–AD 337)*. Ithaca, NY.
(1986), 'Italy and the Roman empire: Augustus to Constantine', *Phoenix* 40: 295–318 (= Millar 2004: 372–98).
(1988), 'Government and diplomacy in the Roman empire during the first three centuries', *International History Review* 10: 345–77 (= Millar 2004: 195–228).
(2004), *Rome, the Greek World and the East. Volume 2: Government, Society and Culture in the Roman Empire*. Chapel Hill.
Mitchell, S. (1976), 'Requisitioned transport in the Roman Empire: A new inscription from Pisidia', *JRS* 66: 106–131.
(1983), 'The Balkans, Anatolia and Roman armies across Asia Minor', in id., ed., *Armies and Frontiers in Roman and Byzantine Anatolia*. Oxford: 131–50.
Momigliano, A. (1942), 'Camillus and Concord', *CQ* 36: 111–20.
Mommsen, T. (1864–79), *Römische Forschungen*. 2 vols. Berlin.
(1887–8), *Römisches Staatsrecht*, 3rd edn. 3 vols. Leipzig.
(1899), *Römisches Strafrecht*. Leipzig.
Mommsen, T. and Meyer, P. M., eds. (1905), *Theodosiani libri XVI cum constitutionibus Sirmondianis et leges novellae ad Theodosianum pertinentes*. Berlin.
Moore, T. J. (1993), 'Morality, history, and Livy's wronged women', *Eranos* 91: 38–46.
Morford, M. (1991), 'How Tacitus defined liberty', *ANRW* II 33.5: 3420–50.
Morris, I. and Scheidel, W. (2009), *The Dynamics of Ancient Empires: State Power from Assyria to Byzantium*. Oxford.
Mourgues, J.-L. (1995a), 'Écrire en deux langues: bilinguisme et pratique de chancellerie sous le Haut-Empire romain', *DHA* 21: 105–29.
(1995b), 'Le préambule de l'édit de Tiberius Julius Alexander, témoin des étapes de son élaboration', *BCH* 119: 415–35.
Mouritsen, H. (1998), *Italian Unification: A Study in Ancient and Modern Historiography*. BICS Supplement 70. London.
(2011), *The Freedman in the Roman World*. Cambridge.
Moussy, C. (1966), *Gratia et sa famille*. Paris.
Murgatroyd, P., ed. (1980), *Tibullus I*. Pietermaritzburg.
Murphy, T. (2004), *Pliny the Elder's Natural History*. Oxford.
Mutschler, F.-H. and Mittag, A., eds. (2008), *Conceiving the Empire: China and Rome Compared*. Oxford.
Naas, V. (2002), *Le projet encyclopédique de Pline l'Ancien*. Coll. École Française de Rome 50. Rome.
(2011), 'Imperialism, *mirabilia* and knowledge: some paradoxes in the *Naturalis Historia*', in R. Gibson and R. Morello, eds., *Pliny the Elder: Themes and Contexts*. Leiden: 57–70.

Nauta, R. (2001), *Poetry for Patrons: Literary Communication in the Age of Domitian*. Mnemosyne Supplement 206. Leiden.
Neesen, L. (1980), *Untersuchungen zu den direkten Staatsabgaben der römischen Kaiserzeit (27 v. Chr.–184 n. Chr.)*. Bonn.
Neuhauser, W. (1958), *'Patronus' und 'Orator': eine Geschichte der Begriffe von ihren Anfängen bis in die augusteische Zeit*. Innsbruck.
Nicolet, C. (1991), *Geography, Space and Politics in the Early Roman Empire*. Ann Arbor. Trans. of *L'inventaire du monde: géographie et politique aux origines de l'empire Romain*. Paris, 1988.
Nicols, J. (1979), 'Zur Verleihung öffentlicher Ehrungen in der römischen Welt', *Chiron* 9: 243–60.
(1980a), 'Pliny and the patronage of communities', *Hermes* 108: 365–85.
(1980b), '*Tabulae patronatus*: a study of the agreement between patron and client community 50 BC–AD 250', *ANRW* II 13: 535–61.
(1988), 'Prefects, patronage and the administration of justice', *ZPE* 72: 201–17.
(1990), 'Patrons of Greek cities in the early principate', *ZPE* 80: 81–100.
Nigdelis, P. M. and Souris, G. A. (2005), *Ανθύπατος λέγει. ένα διάταγμα των αυτοκρατορικών χρόνων για το γυμνάσιο της Βέροιας*. Thessaloniki.
Nipperdey, K. and Andresen, G., eds. (1915), *P. Cornelius Tacitus Annalen*, 11th edn. 2 vols. Berlin.
Nisbet, R. G. M. and Hubbard, M. (1970), *A Commentary on Horace: Odes Book 1*. Oxford.
(1978), *A Commentary on Horace: Odes Book 2*. Oxford.
Nisbet, R. G. M. and Rudd, N. (2004), *A Commentary on Horace: Odes Book III*. Oxford.
Nörr, D. (1989), *Aspekte des römischen Völkerrechts: die Bronzetafel von Alcántara*. Munich.
Noy, D. (2000), *Foreigners at Rome*. London.
Nutton, V. (1978), 'The beneficial ideology', in P. Garnsey and C. R. Whittaker, eds., *Imperialism in the Ancient World*. Cambridge: 209–22.
O'Gorman, E. (1993), 'No place like Rome: identity and difference in the *Germania* of Tacitus', *Ramus* 22: 135–54.
(1995), 'Shifting ground: Lucan, Tacitus and the landscape of civil war', *Hermathena* 158: 117–31.
Oakley, S. P. (1997–2005), *A Commentary on Livy Books VI–X*. 4 vols. Oxford.
Ogilvie, R. M. (1965), *A Commentary on Livy Books 1–5*. Oxford.
Ogilvie, R. M. and Richmond, I. A. (1967), *Tacitus: Agricola*. Oxford.
Oliver, J. H. (1953), *The Ruling Power: A Study of the Roman Empire in the Second Century after Christ through the Roman Oration of Aelius Aristides*. Philadelphia.
(1989), *Greek Constitutions of Early Roman Emperors from Inscriptions and Papyri*. Philadelphia.
Östenberg, I. (2009), *Staging the World: Spoils, Captives, and Representations in the Roman Triumphal Procession*. Oxford.

Pagden, A. (1995), *Lords of All the World: Ideologies of Empire in Spain, Britain and France c. 1500–c. 1800*. New Haven.

Panciera, S. (1982), *Epigrafia e ordine senatorio: Atti del Colloquio internazionale AIEGL Roma, 14–20 maggio 1981*. 2 vols. Rome.

Parente, F. (1979), '*Patibulum, crux, furca*: alcune osservazioni a proposito di un libro recente', *RFIC* 107: 369–78.

Parisi Presicce, C. (1999), 'Le rappresentazioni allegoriche di popoli e province nell'arte romana imperiale', in M. Sapelli, ed., *Provinciae fideles*. Milan: 83–105.

Patterson, J. R. (2002), 'The emperor and the cities of Italy', in T. Cornell and K. Lomas, eds., *Bread and Circuses: Euergetism and Municipal Patronage in Roman Italy*. London: 89–104.

Paul, G. M. (1984), *A Historical Commentary on Sallust's Bellum Jugurthinum*. Liverpool.

Percival, J. (1980), 'Tacitus and the Principate', *G&R* 27: 119–33.

Peter, H. (1901), *Der Brief in der römischen Literatur*. Leipzig.

Philippides, S. N. (1983), 'Narrative strategies and ideology in Livy's "Rape of Lucretia"', *Helios* 10: 113–19.

Pomeroy, A. J. (2003), 'Centre and periphery in Tacitus' *Histories*', *Arethusa* 36: 361–74.

(2005), 'Tacitus' *Histories*', *CR* 55: 147–9.

Premerstein, A. von (1900), 'Clientes', Pauly-Wissowa, *Real-Encyclopädie der classischen Altertumswissenschaft*, IV.1 23–55.

Pucci Ben Zeev, M. (1998), *Jewish Rights in the Roman World: The Greek and Roman Documents Quoted by Josephus Flavius*. Tübingen.

Purcell, N. (1986), 'The arts of government', in J. Boardman, J. Griffin and O. Murray, eds., *The Oxford History of the Classical World*. Oxford: 560–91.

(2000), 'Rome and Italy', in A. K. Bowman, P. Garnsey and D. Rathbone, eds., *Cambridge Ancient History*, vol. XI, 2nd edn. Cambridge: 405–43.

(2006), 'Romans in the Roman world', in K. Galinsky, ed., *Cambridge Companion to the Age of Augustus*. Cambridge: 85–105.

Purpura, G. (1992), 'Gli editti dei prefetti d'Egitto. I sec. a.C. – I sec. d.C.' *ASGP* 42: 485–71.

Raaflaub, K. (1979), '*Polis tyrannos*: Zur Enstehung einer politischen Metapher', in G. W. Bowersock, W. Burkert and M. C. J. Putnam, eds., *Arktouros: Hellenic Studies Presented to Bernard M. W. Knox*. Berlin, 237–52.

(2003), 'Stick and glue: the function of tyranny in fifth-century Athenian democracy', in K. A. Morgan, ed., *Popular Tyranny: Sovereignty and Its Discontents in Ancient Greece*. Austin: 59–93.

(2004), *The Discovery of Freedom*. Chicago. Trans. of *Die Entdeckung der Freiheit: Zur historischen Semantik und Gesellschaftsgeschichte eines politischen Grundbegriffes der Griechen*. Munich, 1985.

Ramsby, T. R. and Severy-Hoven, B. (2007), 'Gender, sex and the domestication of the empire in art of the Augustan age', *Arethusa* 40: 43–71.

Rathbone, D. (1996), 'The imperial finances', in A. K. Bowman, E. Champlin and A. Lintott, eds., *Cambridge Ancient History*, vol. x, 2nd edn. Cambridge: 309–23.

Reinhold, M. (1988), *From Republic to Principate: An Historical Commentary on Cassius Dio's Roman History, Books 49–52 (36–29 BC)*. Atlanta.

Reinmuth, O. W. (1938), 'The praefectural edict. I. The *praescriptio*', *Aegyptus* 16: 3–28.

Reynolds, J. (1978), 'Hadrian, Antoninus Pius and the Cyrenaican Cities', *JRS* 68: 111–21.

(1982), *Aphrodisias and Rome: Documents from the Excavation of the Theatre at Aphrodisias Conducted by Professor Kenan T. Erim, Together with Some Related Texts*. London.

(2000), 'New letters from Hadrian to Aphrodisias: trials, taxes, gladiators and an aqueduct', *JRA* 13: 5–20.

Rich, J. (1989), 'Patronage and international relations in the Roman republic', in A. Wallace-Hadrill, ed., *Patronage in Ancient Society*. London: 117–35.

(2008), 'Treaties, allies and the Roman conquest of Italy', in P. de Souza and J. France, eds., *War and Peace in Ancient and Medieval History*. Cambridge: 51–75.

Richardson, J. (1986), *Hispaniae: Spain and the Development of Roman Imperialism, 218–82 BC*. Cambridge.

(1991), '*Imperium Romanum*: empire and the language of power', *JRS* 81: 1–9.

(2003), '*Imperium Romanum* between empire and republic', in L. De Blois, P. Erdkamp, O. Hekster, G. De Kleijn and S. Mols, eds., *The Representation and Perception of Roman Imperial Power. Proceedings of the Third Workshop of the International Network Impact of Empire (Roman Empire, c. 200 B.C.–A.D. 476), Netherlands Institute in Rome, March 20–23, 2002*. Amsterdam: 137–47.

(2008), *The Language of Empire: Rome and the Idea of Empire from the Third Century BC to the Second Century AD*. Cambridge.

Ricoeur, P. (1986), *Lectures on Ideology and Utopia*. New York.

Riggsby, A. (1999), *Crime and Community in Ciceronian Rome*. Austin.

(2006), *Caesar in Gaul and Rome: War in Words*. Austin.

Robert, L. (1969), 'Théophane de Mytilène à Constantinople', *CRAI* 113.1: 42–64 (= *Choix d'écrits*. Paris, 2007: 604–21).

Roberts, M. (1988), 'The revolt of Boudicca (Tacitus, *Annals* 14.29–39) and the assertion of *libertas* in Neronian Rome', *AJP* 109: 118–32.

(2001), 'Rome personified, Rome epitomized: representations of Rome in the poetry of the early fifth century', *AJP* 122: 533–65.

Rodgers, R. (2003), 'Female representations in Roman art: feminising the provincial "other"', in S. Scott and J. Webster, eds., *Roman Imperialism and Provincial Art*. Cambridge: 69–93.

Roller, M. B. (2001), *Constructing Autocracy: Aristocrats and Emperors in Julio-Claudian Rome*. Princeton.

Romilly, J. de (1963), *Thucydides and Athenian Imperialism*. Oxford. Trans. of *Thucydides et l'impérialisme athénien: la pensée de l'historien et la genèse de l'oeuvre*. Paris, 1947.

Rood, T. (1998), *Thucydides: Narrative and Explanation*. Oxford.

Rose, C. B. (1990), 'Princes and barbarians on the Ara Pacis', *AJA* 94: 453–67.

Rose, P. W. (1995), 'Cicero and the rhetoric of imperialism: putting the politics back into political rhetoric', *Rhetorica* 13: 359–99.

Rosenberger, V. (1992), *Bella et expeditiones. Die antike Terminologie der Kriege Roms*. Stuttgart.

Rouland, N. (1979), *Pouvoir politique et dépendance personelle dans l'antiquité romaine. Genèse et rôle des rapports de clientèle*. Collection Latomus 166. Brussels.

Rowe, G. (2002), *Princes and Political Cultures: The New Tiberian Senatorial Decrees*. Ann Arbor.

Roymans, N. (2004), *Ethnic Identity and Imperial Power: The Batavians in the Early Roman Empire*. Amsterdam Archaeological Studies 10. Amsterdam.

Rutledge, S. (2000), 'Tacitus in tartan: textual colonization and expansionist discourse in the *Agricola*', *Helios* 27: 75–95.

Sachers, E. (1948), 'Tutela [1–3]', Pauly-Wissowa, *Real-Encyclopädie der classischen Altertumswissenschaft*, 2.7.2: 1497–599.

Saddington, D. B. (1970), 'The Roman auxilia in Tacitus, Josephus and other early imperial writers', *AClass* 13: 89–124.

Said, E. (1978), *Orientalism: Western Conceptions of the Orient*. New York.

(1993), *Culture and Imperialism*. London.

Sailor, D. (2004), 'Becoming Tacitus: significance and inconsequentiality in the prologue of the *Agricola*', *ClAnt* 23: 139–177.

(2008), *Writing and Empire in Tacitus*, Cambridge.

Saint-Denis, E. de (1972), *Pline l'Ancien: Histoire Naturelle livre XXXVII*, Paris.

Saller, R. P. (1982), *Personal Patronage under the Early Empire*. Cambridge.

(1983), 'Martial on patronage and literature', *CQ* 33: 246–57.

(1989), 'Patronage and friendship in early imperial Rome: drawing the distinction', in A. Wallace-Hadrill, ed., *Patronage in Ancient Society*. London: 49–62.

(1991), 'Corporal punishment, authority and obedience in the Roman household', in B. Rawson, ed., *Marriage, Divorce and Children in Ancient Rome*. Oxford: 144–65.

(1994), *Patriarchy, Property and Death in the Roman Family*. Cambridge.

(2000), 'Status and patronage', in A. K. Bowman, P. Garnsey and D. Rathbone, eds., *Cambridge Ancient History*, vol. XI, 2nd edn. Cambridge: 817–54.

Salmon, E. T. (1969), *Roman Colonization under the Republic*. London.

Sapelli, M., ed. (1999), *Provinciae fideles*. Milan.

Sblendorio Cugusi, M. T., ed. (1982), *M. Porci Catonis: Orationum reliquiae*. Turin.

Scheidel, W., ed. (2009a), *Rome and China. Perspectives on Ancient World Empires*. Oxford.

(2009b), 'Sex and empire: a Darwinian perspective', in I. Morris and W. Scheidel, eds., *The Dynamics of Ancient Empires: State Power from Assyria to Byzantium*. Oxford: 255–324.

Schmitt, H. H., ed. (1969), *Die Staatsverträge des Altertums. Bd. 3, Die Verträge der griechisch-römischen Welt von 338 bis 200 v.Chr.* Munich.

Schneider, R. (1986), *Bunte Barbaren: Orientalenstatuen aus farbigem Marmor in der römischen Repräsentationskunst*. Worms.

Schrickx, J. G. (2006), 'Provincialis', *Thesaurus Linguae Latinae*, vol. X.2, fasc. XV: 2342–5.

Schuller, W. (1978), *Die Stadt als Tyrann: Athens Herrschaft über seine Bundesgenossen*. Konstanz.

Schwartz, D. R. (1990), *Agrippa I: The Last King of Judaea*. Tübingen.

Schwind, J. (1995), 'Peregrinus', *Thesaurus Linguae Latinae*, vol. X.1, fasc. IX: 1307–16.

Scott, J. C. (1990), *Domination and the Arts of Resistance: Hidden Transcripts*. New Haven.

Seager, R. and Tuplin, C. (1980), 'The freedom of the Greeks of Asia: on the origins of a concept and the creation of a slogan', *JHS* 100: 141–54.

Shackleton Bailey, D. R. (1979), 'On Cicero's speeches', *HSCP* 83: 238–85.

Shaw, B. D. (1981), 'The Elder Pliny's African geography', *Historia* 30: 424–71.

(2000), 'Rebels and outsiders', in A. K. Bowman, P. Garnsey and D. Rathbone, eds., *Cambridge Ancient History*, vol. XI, 2nd edn. Cambridge: 361–403.

Sherk, R. K. (1969), *Roman Documents from the Greek East*. Baltimore.

Sherwin-White, A. N. (1966), *The Letters of Pliny: A Historical and Social Commentary*. Oxford.

(1973), *The Roman Citizenship*, 2nd edn. Oxford.

(1982), 'The *lex repetundarum* and the political ideas of Gaius Gracchus', *JRS* 72: 18–31.

(1984), *Roman Foreign Policy in the East, 168 B.C. to A.D. 1*. Oxford.

Shumate, N. (2006). *Nation, Empire, Decline: Studies in Rhetorical Continuity from the Romans to the Modern Era*. Classical Interfaces 5. London.

Smallwood, E. M. (1976), *The Jews under Roman Rule: From Pompey to Diocletian*. Leiden.

Smith, R. R. R. (1988), '*Simulacra gentium*: the *ethne* from the Sebasteion at Aphrodisias', *JRS* 78: 50–77.

Solomonik, E. I., ed. (1964–73), *Novye epigraficheskie pamiatniki Khersonesa I–II*. Kiev.

Souris, G. A. (1984), 'Studies in provincial diplomacy under the principate', unpub. diss. Cambridge University. Cambridge.

Souza, P. de (2011), 'War, slavery and empire in Roman imperial iconography', *BICS* 54: 31–62.

Spurr, D. (1993), *The Rhetoric of Empire: Colonial Discourse in Journalism, Travel Writing and Imperial Administration*. Durham, NC.

Ste Croix, G. E. M. de (1972), *The Origins of the Peloponnesian War*. London.

(1981), *The Class Struggle in the Ancient Greek World: From the Archaic Age to the Arab Conquests*. London.

Steel, C. E. W. (2001), *Cicero, Rhetoric and Empire*. Oxford.

Strasburger, H. (1958), 'Thukydides und die politische Selbstdarstellung der Athener', *Hermes* 86: 17–40 (= *Studien zur älten Geschichte*. 3 vols. Hildesheim, 1982–90: II.676–708).

Strocchio, R. (1992), *I significati del silenzio nell'opera di Tacito*. Turin.

Swain, S. (1996), *Hellenism and Empire: Language, Classicism, and Power in the Greek World, AD 50–250*. Oxford.

Syme, R. (1937), 'Who was Decidius Saxa?' *JRS* 27: 127–37 (= *Roman Papers*, I 31–41).

(1938), 'Caesar, the senate and Italy', *PBSR* 14: 1–31 (= *Roman Papers*, I 88–119).

(1939), *The Roman Revolution*. Oxford.

(1955), 'Missing senators', *Historia* 4: 52–71 (= *Roman papers*, I 271–91).

(1958), *Tacitus*. 2 vols. Oxford.

(1988), 'The date of Justin and the discovery of Trogus', *Historia* 37: 358–71.

(1999), *The Provincial at Rome*. Exeter.

Tamiolaki, H.-M. (2010), *Liberté et esclavage chez les historiens grecs classiques. Le discours historique et politique d'Hérodote, Thucydide et Xénophon*. Paris.

Täubler, E. (1913), *Imperium Romanum: Studien zur Entwicklungsgeschichte des römischen Reichs*. Leipzig.

Ternes, C.-M. (1990), 'Le discours de Cerialis aux Trévires et aux Lingons (Tac. *Hist*. 4. 73 sqq). Une "charte de la Romanisation"?' *REL* 68: 112–22.

Teutsch, L. (1962), *Das Städtewesen in Nordafrika in der Zeit von C. Gracchus bis zum Tode des Kaisers Augustus*. Berlin.

Thomas, R. F. (1998), *Virgil: Georgics I–II*. Cambridge.

Touloumakos, J. (1988), 'Zum römischen Gemeindepatronat im griechischen Osten', *Hermes* 116: 304–24.

Toynbee, J. M. C. (1934), *The Hadrianic School*. Cambridge.

(1947), 'Roma and Constantinopolis in late-antique art from 312 to 365', *JRS* 37: 135–44.

(1953), 'Roma and Constantinopolis in late-antique art from 365 to Justin II', in G. E. Mylonas and D. Raymond, eds., *Studies Presented to David Moore Robinson on his Seventieth Birthday*. 2 vols. St. Louis: II 261–77.

Tränkle, H. (1977), *Livius und Polybios*. Basel.

Treggiari, S. (1969), *Roman Freedmen during the Late Republic*. Oxford.

Tuplin, C. (1985), 'Imperial tyranny: some reflections on a Classical Greek political metaphor', in P. A. Cartledge and F. D. Harvey, eds., *Crux: Essays in Greek History Presented to G.E.M. de Ste. Croix on his 75th Birthday*. London: 348–75.

Turpin, W. (1991), 'Imperial subscriptions and the administration of justice', *JRS* 81: 101–18.

Uzzi, J. D. (2005), *Children in the Visual Arts of Rome*. New York.

van den Hout, M. P. J. (1999), *A Commentary on the Letters of M. Cornelius Fronto*. Leiden.

van Nijf, O. M. (1997), *The Civic World of Professional Associations in the Roman East*. Amsterdam.

Vasaly, A. (1993), *Representations: Images of the World in Ciceronian Oratory*. Berkeley.

(2002), 'Cicero's early speeches', in J. M. May, ed., *Brill's Companion to Cicero's Speeches*. Leiden: 71–111.

Venturini, C. (1979), *Studi sul crimen repetundarum nell'età repubblicana*. Milan.

Verboven, K. (2002), *The Economy of Friends: Economic Aspects of Amicitia and Patronage in the Late Republic*. Brussels.

(2003), 'Review of Claude Eilers, *Roman Patrons of Greek Cities*, Oxford: Oxford University Press, 2002', *BMCRev* 2003.06.19: non pag.

Vermeule, C. (1959), *The Goddess Roma in the Art of the Roman Empire*. Cambridge, MA.

Versnel, H. S. (1970), *Triumphus: An Inquiry into the Origin, Development and Meaning of the Roman Triumph*. Leiden.

Veyne, P. (1993), '*Humanitas*: Romans and non-Romans', in A. Giardina, ed., *The Romans*. Chicago: 342–69.

Vielberg, M. (1987), *Pflichten, Werte, Ideale: eine Untersuchung zu den Wertvorstellungen des Tacitus*. Hermes Einzelschriften 52. Stuttgart.

Vittinghoff, F. (1952), *Römische Kolonisation und Bürgerrechtspolitik unter Caesar und Augustus*. Wiesbaden.

Vlastos, G. (1941), 'Slavery in Plato's thought', *PhR* 50: 289–304.

Vogt, J. (1974), *Ancient Slavery and the Ideal of Man*. Oxford. Trans. of *Sklaverei und Humanität. Studien zur antiken Sklaverei und ihrer Erforschung*, 2nd edn. Wiesbaden, 1972.

Volkmann, H. (1990), *Die Massenversklavungen der Einwohner eroberter Städte in der hellenistisch-römischen Zeit*, 2nd edn. Stuttgart.

Vout, C. (2003), 'Embracing Egypt', in C. Edwards and G. Woolf, eds., *Rome the Cosmopolis*. Cambridge: 177–202.

Wagenvoort, H. (1947), *Roman Dynamism: Studies in Ancient Roman Thought, Language and Custom*. Oxford.

Walbank, F. W. (1957–79), *A Historical Commentary on Polybius*. 3 vols. Oxford.

Wallace, S. L. (1938), *Taxation in Egypt from Augustus to Diocletian*. Princeton.

Wallace-Hadrill, A. (1983), *Suetonius*. London.

(1989a), 'Introduction', in Wallace-Hadrill 1989c: 1–13.

(1989b), 'Patronage in Roman society: from republic to empire', in Wallace-Hadrill 1989c: 63–87.

ed. (1989c), *Patronage in Ancient Society*. London.

Walsh, J. J. (1996), 'Flamininus and the propaganda of liberation', *Historia* 45: 344–63.

Waltzing, J.-P. (1895–1900), *Les corporations professionelles chez les Romains*. 4 vols. Brussels and Louvain.

Ward Perkins, J.B. (1970), 'From republic to empire: reflections on the early imperial provincial architecture of the Roman west', *JRS* 60: 1–19.
Warde Fowler, W. (1913), 'Passing under the yoke', *CR* 27: 48–51.
Watson, A. (1975), *Rome of the XII Tables*. Princeton.
Webster, G. (1978), *Boudicca: The British Revolt against Rome AD 60*. London.
(1998), *The Roman Imperial Army of the First and Second Centuries AD*, 3rd edn. Norman.
Wegner, M. (1969), *Untersuchung zu den lateinischen Begriffen socius and societas*. Hypomnemata 21. Göttingen.
Welles, C. B. (1934), *Royal Correspondence in the Hellenistic Period: A Study in Greek Epigraphy*. New Haven.
(1965), 'Greek liberty', *JJP* 15: 29–47.
White, P. (1978), '*Amicitia* and the profession of poetry in early imperial Rome', *JRS* 68: 74–92.
(1993), *Promised Verse: Poets in the Society of Augustan Rome*. Cambridge, MA.
Whitmarsh, T. (2001), *Greek Literature and the Roman Empire*. Oxford.
(2006), '"This in-between book": language, politics and genre in the *Agricola*', in B. McGing and J. Mossman, eds., *The Limits of Ancient Biography*. Swansea: 305–33.
Whittaker, C.R. (1997), 'Imperialism and culture: the Roman initiative', in D.J. Mattingly, ed., *Dialogues in Roman Imperialism: Power, Discourse and Discrepant Experience in the Roman Empire*. Portsmouth, RI: 147–63.
Whitton, C. L. (2010), 'Pliny, *Epistles* 8.14: senate, slavery and the *Agricola*', *JRS* 100: 118–39.
Wilcken, U. (1920), 'Zu den Kaiserreskripten', *Hermes* 55: 1–42.
Williams, C. A. (1999), *Roman Homosexuality: Ideologies of Masculinity in Classical Antiquity*, 2nd edn. Oxford.
Williams, W. (1975), 'Formal and historical aspects of two new documents of Marcus Aurelius', *ZPE* 17: 37–78.
(1976), 'Individuality in the imperial constitutions: Hadrian and the Antonines', *JRS* 66: 67–83.
(1979), 'Caracalla and the authorship of imperial edicts and epistles', *Latomus* 38: 67–89.
(1986), 'Epigraphic texts of imperial subscripts: a survey', *ZPE* 66: 181–207.
Wilson, A. J. N. (1966), *Emigration from Italy in the Republican Age*. Manchester.
Winterling, A. (1999), *Aula Caesaris. Studien zur Institutionalisierung des römischen Kaiserhofes in der Zeit von Augustus bis Commodus (31 v. Chr.–192 n. Chr.)*. Munich.
(2008), 'Freundschaft und Klientel im kaiserzeitlichen Rom', *Historia* 56: 298–316.
Wirszubski, C. (1950), *Libertas*. Cambridge.
Wiseman, T. P. (1971), *New Men in the Roman Senate, 139 B.C.–A.D. 14*. London.
(1985), *Catullus and his World: A Reappraisal*. Cambridge.

Woodman, A. J. (2006), 'Mutiny and madness: Tacitus *Annals* 1.16–49', *Arethusa* 39: 303–30.
Woolf, G. (1990), 'Food, poverty and patronage: the significance of the epigraphy of the Roman alimentary schemes in imperial Italy', *PBSR* 58: 197–228.
(1993a), 'Becoming Roman, staying Greek: culture, identity and the civilising process in the Roman East', *PCPS* 40: 116–43.
(1993b), 'Roman peace', in J. Rich and G. Shipley, eds., *War and Society in the Roman World*. London: 171–94.
(1995), 'The formation of Roman provincial cultures', in J. Metzler, M. Millett, N. Roymans and J. Sloistra, eds., *Integration in the Early Roman West: The Role of Culture and Ideology*. Luxembourg: 9–18.
(1998), *Becoming Roman: The Origins of Provincial Civilization in Gaul*. Cambridge.
Wortman, R. S. (1995–2000), *Scenarios of Power: Myth and Ceremony in Russian Monarchy*. 2 vols. Princeton.
Yardley, J. C. (2000), 'Justin on tribunates and generalships, Caesares, and Augusti', *CQ* 50: 632–4.
(2003), *Justin and Pompeius Trogus: A Study of the Language of Justin's Epitome of Trogus*. Phoenix Supplement 41. Toronto.
Yardley, J. C. and R. Develin (1994), *Justin, Epitome of the Philippic History of Pompeius Trogus*. Atlanta.
Yardley, J. C. and Heckel, W., eds. (1997), *Epitome of the Philippic History of Pompeius Trogus. Volume 1. Books 11–12: Alexander the Great*. Oxford.
Yarrow, L. M. (2006), *Historiography at the End of the Republic: Provincial Perspectives on Roman Rule*. Oxford.
Zetzel, J. E. G. (1995), *Cicero, De Re Publica: Selections*. Cambridge.
Zucker, F. (1928), 'Plinius *epist.* VIII 24 – ein Denkmal antiker Humanität', *Philologus* 84: 209–32.

INDEX OF PASSAGES DISCUSSED

This index includes only passages which are quoted or discussed with reference to their language. Mere citations are excluded. Epigraphic and papyrological texts are listed separately.

Literary texts

Epigraphic and papyrological texts

GENERAL INDEX